T0383879

Indigenous People and Economic Development

Indigenous peoples are an intrinsic part of countries like Australia, New Zealand, Canada, Finland, the USA, India, Russia and almost all parts of South America and Africa. A considerable amount of research has been done during the twentieth century, mainly by anthropologists, sociologists and linguists in order to describe and document their traditional lifestyle for the protection and safeguarding of their established knowledge, skills, languages and beliefs. These communities are engaging and adapting rapidly to the changing circumstances partly caused by post modernisation and the process of globalization. These have led them to aspire to better living standards, as well as preserving their uniqueness, approaches to the environment, and close proximity to social structures and communities. For at least the last two decades, patterns of increased economic activity by indigenous peoples in many countries have been viewed to be significantly on the rise.

Indigenous People and Economic Development reveals some of the characteristics of this economic activity, 'coloured' by the unique regard and philosophy of life that indigenous people around the world have. The successes, difficulties and obstacles to economic development, their solutions and innovative practices in business – all of these elements, based on research findings, are discussed in this book and offer an inside view of the dynamics of the indigenous societies which are evolving in a globalised and highly interconnected contemporary world.

Katia Iankova is a Senior Lecturer in Tourism at the University of Greenwich. She has a PhD in Urban Studies from the University of Quebec, Canada. Katia is a specialist in Indigenous studies and is a frequent contributor to books and journal articles on tourism and indigenous peoples.

Azizul Hassan is a member of the Tourism Consultants Network of the UK Tourism Society, and is currently working towards a PhD at Cardiff Metropolitan University. His main areas of research are focused on ethnography and tourism.

Rachel L'Abbé has a PhD in Sociology from the University of Quebec, Canada. She is the founding President of the Sustainable Destinations Consultancy, a firm dealing with the sustainable development of tourist destinations in Latin American countries.

Indigenous People and Economic Development

An International Perspective

Edited by
KATIA IANKOVA, AZIZUL HASSAN AND RACHEL L'ABBÉ

Routledge
Taylor & Francis Group
LONDON AND NEW YORK

First published 2016 by Routledge

2 Park Square, Milton Park, Abingdon, Oxfordshire OX14 4RN
52 Vanderbilt Avenue, New York, NY 10017

Routledge is an imprint of the Taylor & Francis Group, an informa business

First issued in paperback 2019

British Library Cataloguing in Publication Data
A catalogue record for this book is available from the British Library

Library of Congress Cataloging-in-Publication Data
Iankova, Katia.
   Indigenous people and economic development : an international perspective / by Katia Iankova, Azizul Hassan and Rachel L'Abbee.
      pages cm
   Includes bibliographical references and index.
   ISBN 978-1-4724-3485-2 (hardback : alk. paper) — ISBN 978-1-3155-8834-6 (ebook) — ISBN 978-1-3171-1730-8 (epub)   1. Indigenous peoples–Economic conditions.   2. Economic development.   3. Community development.   I. Hassan, Azizul.   II. L'Abbee, Rachel.   III. Title.
   GN380.I26 2015
   305.8—dc23
   2015018106

ISBN: 978-1-4724-3485-2 (hbk)
ISBN: 978-0-367-87957-0 (pbk)

Typeset in Myriad Pro
by Apex CoVantage, LLC

Contents

List of Figures

List of Tables

List of Contributors

Oyewo Adetola (e-mail: ollytola@yahoo.com) is a PhD candidate in Teacher Development Studies at the University of KwaZulu-Natal, Durban, South Africa. She is a member of the Tourism Research Information Network; the European Association for International Education; Nigeria Union of Teachers (NUT), and the Historical Society of Nigeria. Her areas of research focus on excursion tourism, higher education, educational tourism, social educational justice, gender education, educational policies, and leisure tourism.

Dr. Norliza Aminudin (e-mail: norlizaaminudin@yahoo.co.uk) is head of the Tourism Management Studies Centre at the University of Technology MARA in Malaysia. She received her PhD in Consumer Behaviour and an MBA from the same university, where she currently teaches. She also has a BA in International Relations from Keele University, UK. Her research centres on tourism destination analysis, particularly cross-border second home, homestay, and community-based and Indigenous tourism. She has also been a guest speaker on various courses conducted by government agencies.

Dr. Beau J. Austin (email: beau.austin@cdu.edu.au) is a Postdoctoral Research Fellow on an ARC-funded project entitled *Integrating Measures of Indigenous Land and Sea Management Effectiveness.* Before joining Charles Darwin University's Research Institute for the Environment and Livelihoods (RIEL) he worked in community development and government. He has bachelor's degrees in politics and international business, and wrote his PhD thesis on success factors for Indigenous wildlife-based enterprise in northern Australia.

Dr. Marie-Pierre Bousquet (e-mail: marie-pierre.bousquet@umontreal.ca) has been an associate professor in the Department of Anthropology of the University of Montreal since 2002. She specialises in questions related to the Natives of Quebec, particularly the Anishinabek (Algonquin), with whom she has conducted fieldwork since 1996. Passionate about everything concerning Canada's Natives, she loves to diversify. Since becoming a professor at Montreal, Marie-Pierre has been part of very different teams, working not only with ethnologists but also with social workers, criminologists, and specialists in religious studies.

Dr. Jeremy Buultjens (e-mail: jeremy.buultjens@scu.edu.au) is an associate professor in the Business School at Southern Cross University, and managing editor of the *Journal of Economic and Social Policy*. He has taught a number of subjects, ranging from economics and industrial relations through to tourism planning and Indigenous tourism. His research interests include Indigenous entrepreneurship, regional development and tourism, tourism in protected areas, and employment relations. His work has appeared in *Tourism Management, Journal of Industrial Relations, International Journal of Employment Studies, International Journal of Contemporary Hospitality Management, Labour and Industry*, and the *Australasian Journal of Business and Social Enquiry*. He has also presented widely at national and international conferences and has conducted numerous consultancies. His clients have included the NSW National Parks and Wildlife Service; the NSW Crown Solicitor's Office; WA Department of Conservation and Land Management; and the Northern Rivers Area Consultative Committee.

Dr. Jin Hooi Chan (e-mail: jinhooi@cantab.net) is a multidisciplinary researcher with 20 years' experience in academia and industry. He was trained as an engineer and holds Chartered Engineer and Chartered Environmentalist titles awarded by royal institutions in the UK. His experience extends across Europe, Africa, China, and South East Asia. Dr. Chan received his PhD in Management Studies from Judge Business School, and MPhil in Sustainable Development at University of Cambridge. He is a Shell Centenary Chevening and Dorothy Hodgkin scholar. His research focuses on industrial organisation, industrial policy, entrepreneurship, and innovation (with specialisation in sustainability, environment, and cleantech industry), and is based at the Energy Policy Research Group at Cambridge. He has delivered guest lectures and taught at various universities worldwide, including Cambridge, Greenwich, Coventry, and Minzu in China.

Dr. Ibrahima Diallo (e-mail: pibdiallo@gmail.com) holds a PhD in regional development from the University of Quebec at Chicoutimi (UQAC), Canada. He is a research assistant at the Research Centre of Regional Development. He is also lecturer at UQAC and an international consultant.

Professor Dr. Stephen T. Garnett (email: stephen.garnett@cdu.edu.au) is an environmental scientist with an interest in the knowledge needed to live sustainably in the tropics. Educated at the Australian National University (ANU) and James Cook University (JCU), he has spent the last 30 years in the Australian tropics, primarily in private enterprise and government. He joined Charles Darwin University (CDU) as Professor of Tropical Knowledge in 2004, and is former director of the School for Environmental Research. Apart from threatened species conservation and management, he is also involved in a range of studies on the knowledge economy in tropical Australia.

Professor Rolf Gerritsen (e-mail: rolf.gerritsen@cdu.edu.au) is an experienced researcher who has produced over 120 consultancy reports and academic publications. He is a political economist and has taught at postgraduate level (public policy at the Australian National University) as well as supervising many successful PhD students. Professor Gerritsen has published in about 10 fields of public policy, including natural resource management, Indigenous policy, economic policy, intergovernmental relations, regional development policy, and local government. His consultancy work has been for Australian federal, state and local government agencies.

Azizul Hassan (e-mail: M.Hassan15@outlook.cardiffmet.ac.uk) is a member of the Tourism Consultants Network of the UK Tourism Society, and is currently working towards a PhD at Cardiff Metropolitan University. His main areas of research are: technology-supported marketing in tourism; innovative marketing dynamics; destination branding in tourism; cultural heritage tourism; heritage interpretation; and sustainable management/marketing alternatives for cultural heritage industries. He is a regular reviewer of the *International Journal of Human Resource Management* and the *International Journal of Ecotourism*.

Dr. Katia Iankova (e-mail: ik08@gre.ac.uk) is a senior lecturer at the business school of the University of Greenwich, UK. She holds a doctorate in urban studies from the University of Quebec in Montreal, where she specialised in the economic development of the Indigenous people of Canada. Her current research interests are oriented towards the sustainability and social enterprises networking of young entrepreneurs; technological innovations in the accommodation sector; and innovative strategies of start-up businesses of minorities in the UK.

Jayson Ibanez (email: riel@cdu.edu.au) joined Charles Darwin University's Research Institute for the Environment and Livelihoods (RIEL) in 2010 as a PhD student, studying the integration of Indigenous knowledge and western science in Indigenous planning in the Philippines. He holds a

BSc and MSc in Biology and has worked with an environmental NGO since 1996. Besides research on endangered species, he has also supervised community-based projects with Indigenous peoples since 2003.

Mashrur Imtiaz (e-mail: mashrur.imtiaz@du.ac.bd) is a lecturer in the Department of Linguistics, University of Dhaka, Bangladesh, from where he holds a master's in Linguistics on Trace Deletion Hypothesis (TDH) in the Bengali language. He has also researched phonetic variation among social classes in Bangladesh. Imtiaz has written a number of online articles covering different aspects of language, including phonetics, syntax, applied linguistics, language, culture and ethnicity, language technology, and clinical linguistics.

Dr. Rachel L'Abee (email: rachel@destinationequitable.com) earned her PhD in Sociology from the University of Quebec, Canada. She is the founding president of the Sustainable Destinations Consultancy, a firm dealing with the sustainable development of tourist destination in Latin American countries.

Dr. Tom McDonald (e-mail: tom.mcdonald@ucl.ac.uk) is a research associate at the Department of Anthropology, University College London (UCL). His research focuses on how consumption is changing the lives of ordinary people in China, and he has published on a range of topics related to modern China – including hospitality, clothing, the home, and the internet. He is currently also conducting research on how social media is transforming rural China as part of a large European Research Council funded cross-cultural comparative study.

Dr. Char-lee McLennan (e-mail: c.mclennan@uq.edu.au) is a Research Fellow with the Centre for Tourism, Sport and Services Research at Griffith University, Queensland. Char-lee has previously worked in research positions for organisations such as Gold Coast City Council, Tourism Research Australia, and Tourism Queensland. She obtained her PhD in 2012 from the University of Queensland. Her research has focused on change, transformation and strategic policy, and planning practices in the tourism industry, and is published in leading journals such as *Annals of Tourism Research*, *Journal of Sustainable Tourism*, *Tourism Analysis*, and the *Journal of Hospitality and Tourism Research*. Char-lee is currently working on projects relating to the co-existence of tourism and mining; Indigenous tourism; tourism and water; tourism PhD dissertations; and transforming Australian tourism towards sustainable pathways, amongst others.

Jason Paul Mika (email: J.P.Mika@massey.ac.nz) is a supernumerary lecturer in the School of Management at Massey University's Palmerston North campus. Jason is a descendant of the Tūhoe, Ngāti Awa, Whakatōhea, and Ngāti Kahungunu tribes of Aotearoa/New Zealand. Jason is currently preparing to submit his PhD thesis on the role of enterprise assistance in Māori entrepreneurship. His interests are Indigenous management and entrepreneurship research, teaching, and practice. He has written on related topics, including a book on the history of Tūhoe fisheries, and co-authored an article on Māori management and conference papers on the role of culture in Māori international business, trade, and entrepreneurial activity. Jason is an associate member of the Australian and New Zealand Academy of Management (ANZAM), an editorial review board member for the *Journal of Small Business Management*, and a member of ANZAM's Indigenous Issues Special Interest Group. Previously he was a self-employed management consultant and a government policy analyst.

Dr. Naomi Moswete (e-mail: moatshen@mopipi.ub.bw) is a lecturer in the Department of Environmental Science at the University of Botswana. She is also an executive member of the International Tourism Research Centre and a member of the Community-Based National Resource

Management (CBNRM) National Forum and Kavango-Zambezi Conservation Area National Steering Committee. Her research interests include tourism as a strategy for rural development, community-based ecotourism, cultural heritage management, and gender-based empowerment through arts-based tourism. She has conducted empirical research and published on issues related to trans-boundary conservation areas in Southern Africa.

Dr. Nor'Ain Othman (e-mail: norain568@salam.utim.edu.my) is Associate Professor in the Faculty of Hotel and Tourism Management, Universiti Teknologi MARA (UiTM), Shah Alam, Selangor, Malaysia. She has more than 10 years' experience as an Assistant Director in the Malaysia Tourism Promotion Board and joined UiTM in 1993. She received an MSc in Tourism and Marketing Management from the University of Bournemouth, UK and a PhD in Tourism from the University of Queensland. Her research interests focus on tourism partnership and collaboration, sustainable tourism, tourism marketing, event management, heritage tourism, and Islamic tourism. She has published widely in international journals and books, and presented papers at local and international conferences. She is the vanguard researcher for the university under the Centre of Research Excellence: Humanity and Quality of Life. She was former chair of the Tourism Task Force, Joint Business Council (JBC) and Indonesia, Malaysia, Thailand Growth Triangle (IMTGT); and former Deputy Dean (Research and Industry Linkages). She was also appointed as director of Universal Crescent Standard Center (UCSC), Malaysia.

Dr. Marc-Urbain Proulx (e-mail: Marc-Urbain_Proulx@uqac.ca) holds a PhD in regional economics, specialising in small communities development in the Canadian periphery. He is a professor at the University of Quebec at Chicoutimi and director of the Centre de recherche sur le développement territorial. He publishes books and scientific papers on a regular basis, and in 2012 was appointed vice-minister with the government of Quebec.

Dr. (Vincent) Xiaoguang Qi (e-mail: Xiaoguang.Qi@xjtlu.edu.cn) is an associate professor at Xi'an Jiaotong-Liverpool University; holds an Honorary Professorship at the University of Liverpool; is Visiting Research Professor in Peking University; and is a Visiting Fellow of Wolfson College, University of Cambridge. He received his PhD through a joint programme between University College London (with a UCL Research Award) and Minzu University of China (with a scholarship awarded by the China Scholarship Council), and earned an MBA (Executive programme) from the University of Cambridge. His research interests are economic anthropology and business anthropology, global logistics and the shipping industry, and cross-cultural management.

Dr. Lisa Ruhanen (e-mail: l.ruhanen@uq.edu.au) is a senior lecturer and the postgraduate coursework programme director for the School of Tourism, University of Queensland. She has been involved in almost 30 academic and consultancy research projects in Australia and internationally in the areas of Indigenous tourism, sustainable tourism and climate change, destination policy and planning and knowledge management and governance. Her research areas include Indigenous tourism, sustainable tourism destination policy and planning, and climate change. Lisa has worked extensively as a consultant, external collaborator, and executive committee member with a variety of divisions of the United Nations World Tourism Organization. In 2010 she was awarded a fellowship under the Oxford Brookes University International Visiting Fellow Scheme in the United Kingdom.

Peter Shepherd (email: busines@bigpond.net.au) is a business and management consultant specialising in strategic planning in the not-for-profit sector, having worked extensively with art centres and other similar community businesses across Australia. Peter has had 30 years providing assistance to people in establishing businesses of all types, and works extensively with Indigenous people aiming to enter the mainstream economy as individuals or in groups.

Dr. Amanda Shoebridge (e-mail: amanda.shoebridge@scu.edu.au) is a project manager at Southern Cross University (SCU) and assistant editor of the *Journal of Economic and Social Policy*. Prior to this she was project manager at SCU's Regional Futures Institute, network manager of the Australian Regional Tourism Network, and researcher at the Australian Regional Tourism Research Centre. Amanda has an honours degree in Tourism Management and her research interests include Indigenous entrepreneurship, employment and tourism.

Dr. Teresa C. H. Tao (e-mail: c2tao73@gmail.com) was Assistant Professor of Geography at the University of Hong Kong. She received her master's and doctoral degrees at the University of Waterloo, Canada, and was awarded the George Leslie Mackey Thesis Award from the Canadian Association of Taiwan Studies in 2008. Dr. Tao is well known for her research in the areas of sustainable livelihoods, Indigenous knowledge, cultural sustainability, sustainable tourism in the parks of East Asia, recreation resource administration and development, ecotourism and cultural tourism, and interpretive services. She has been involved in several international projects on sustainable tourism for such agencies as the International Union for Conservation of Nature (IUCN), Parks Canada, and the Pacific Cultural Foundation in Taiwan. Dr. Tao has published a book and several papers to elucidate tourism-related issues and is a co-author of *Guidelines for Tourism in Parks and Protected Areas of East Asia* (2001), which was translated into several languages. For her contributions to the understanding of tourism and recreation, Dr. Tao is a member of the International Society of Ethnobiology; the Association for Society and Natural Resources; the Best Education Network of Sustainable Tourism, Education and Training; the Council for Australasian University Tourism and Hospitality Education; and the Canadian Asian Studies Association.

Dr. Brijesh Thapa (e-mail: bthapa@hhp.ufl.edu) is a professor in the Department of Tourism, Recreation, and Sport Management at the University of Florida. He is also director of the Eric Friedheim Tourism Institute and an Affiliate Faculty in multiple academic units. Overall, his research encompasses tourism, conservation, and sustainability. He has been involved in numerous projects in over 30 countries. Dr. Thapa is currently focused on capacity building and institutional development projects through curriculum development, research, and training in tourism, nature and cultural heritage conservation, and natural resources management. As a principal investigator (PI) and Co-PI, he is involved in several long-term funded projects in Armenia, Turkey, Russia, Nepal, and the Southern Africa region.

Dr. Elena Yegorovna Totonova (email: elena.totonova@mail.ru) is an associate professor at the State University of Yakutsk, Russia. She obtained a master's from the Geography Faculty of Moscow State University and her PhD from the Economic Research Institute, Russian Academy of Sciences (Khabarovsk). Her research interests encompass the problems/prospects of tourism development and government economic regulations of the northern part of Russia. She also has interest in studying the roles of small and medium enterprises (SMEs) for the development of Indigenous peoples.

Umoh Samuel Uwem (e-mail: samumo800@gmail.com) is a PhD candidate in International Studies at the University of KwaZulu-Natal, Durban, South Africa, where he also tutors in the Department of Culture and Heritage Tourism. Prior to taking up full-time doctoral study, he was a teaching assistant in the Department of History and Strategic Studies, University of Lagos, Nigeria. He is a member of the Tourism Research Information Network and Historical Society of Nigeria. His main areas of research are cultural heritage, tourism management, spiritual tourism, educational tourism, conflict management, democratic institutions, peace studies, and political elites.

Dr. Ram Vemuri (e-mail: ram.vemuri@cdu.edu.au) is Honorary Associate Fellow of the Northern Institute, Charles Darwin University (CDU), Australia. Since 1976, Ram has worked in various academic institutions, including the University of Birmingham (UK), the Indian Institute of Technology in Bombay, Yarmouk University (Jordan), and the University of Papua New Guinea. His expertise covers interdisciplinary environmental management; health care planning; macroeconomic management; economic impact assessment and sustainable development; the role of Indigenous knowledge systems in decision making; and natural resource management including waste management.

Dr. Geoffrey Wall (e-mail: gwall@uwaterloo.ca) is Professor of Geography and Environmental Management at the University of Waterloo, Canada. He is interested in the implications of tourism of different types for destination areas with different characteristics, and the planning and management implications of such information. Much of his research has been conducted in Asia, especially China, but also including Taiwan and Indonesia. He has written a number of books on tourism, most recently *Planning for Indigenous Tourism* (Ashgate, 2006). In 2011 he received the Award for Scholarly Distinction in Geography from the Canadian Association of Geographers. He is an Honorary Professor of Nanjing University and Dalian University of Technology, and holds Friendship Awards from Hainan, Xinjiang Uygur Autonomous Region, and the People's Republic of China. He is a founder member and past president of the International Academy for the Study of Tourism.

Dr. Michelle Whitford (e-mail: m.whitford@uq.edu.au) is a senior lecturer and higher research degree coordinator at Griffith University's Department of Tourism, Sport, and Hotel Management. Michelle has co-coordinated several projects in the area of Indigenous tourism and events with a focus on capacity development, entrepreneurship, authenticity, and commodification. She has also co-coordinated research projects for various organisations, including the Sustainable Tourism Cooperative Research Centre; the Australian Institute of Aboriginal and Torres Strait Island Studies; and Indigenous Business Australia. She is the recipient of several awards, including Outstanding Paper BESTEN Think Tank, Vienna (2010); the UTAS Faculty of Business Award for Best Paper in Sport and Event Tourism (2010); Best Paper (Special Mention) 2005, Council for Australasian Tourism and Hospitality Education (CAUTHE) – Charles Darwin University; and Best Paper at the Las Vegas International Hospitality and Convention Summit (2004).

Dr. Kerstin K. Zander (e-mail: Kerstin.zander@cdu.edu.au) is a natural resource economist and demographer working on Indigenous population mobility, particularly in the area of natural resource management; the willingness of Indigenous people to provide ecosystem services; and the willingness of the Australian people to pay for them. She has previously worked with Indigenous peoples in Africa, Asia, and South America.

Dr. Benxiang Zeng (e-mail: benxiang.zeng@cdu.edu.au) is a Senior Research Fellow at Charles Darwin University. Since 1989, he has been involved in research and/or research management in the fields of economics, tourism management, community participation, natural resources management, and environmental management. He has a strong research focus on and interest in socio-cultural and economic impacts of industries such as tourism and services on local communities. Dr. Zeng has engaged in a number of projects that have resulted in the publication of over 50 client-focused reports and scholarly works.

Dr. Ying Zhang (e-mail: zhangyingmuc@163.com) is a professor at the School of Management and the deputy director of the Office of International Relations at Minzu University of China. She received her PhD from Peking University, and was a professor at Cesar Ritz in Switzerland in 2007–2008 and a visiting scholar of University of California, Berkeley (2008–2009). Her research interests are cultural heritage management, sustainable development of tourism, and marketing of cultural and heritage tourism. She has managed several national-level research projects, either as principal or key investigator.

Introduction

The present book contains material related to the theme of the economic development of indigenous people, these minority populations that often remain on the outskirts of society demographically, politically, and socially; yet they are so significant for the imagery, cultural significance, and historical memory of the whole of humanity. Often subjects of admiration, curiosity, and sympathy, they provoke nostalgic feelings in the heart of the western man, lamenting the disappearance of a utopia lost; a better, simpler, more equal world. Of course this belief is somewhat exaggerated and warped. Many indigenous populations had in their history bloody wars and fights for dominance; experienced the rise and fall of their empires; and developed their own survival techniques and interpretations of reality, thus forming unique civilisations and cultures. Some of them are lost; others amalgamated with other indigenous and non-indigenous cultures, while some conserved their original lifestyle and still live in remote geographical locations. In any of these cases their uniqueness gives them a chance to adopt their own linguistic, cultural, and economic paradigms alongside the dominant westernised societal streams.

The economy, material expressions, and wellbeing are, in human development, the platform for healthy societies. Thus for this reason the editors of this book wanted to create a volume which discusses the issues and current tendencies within the economic development of indigenous populations, as we believe this is one of the most important conditions for cultural, linguistic, and identity protection for any minority population. Surprisingly, the attention of researchers in the last few decades has not focussed on this topic, but rather has followed the major research streams related to land rights, political structure, cultural expression, language disappearance, and health problems of indigenous people.

With this book, our humble wish is to contribute to the understanding of mechanisms of economic prosperity and the specific tools for wellbeing and wealth relating to native peoples; and potentially to be of use to them and to all researchers studying these populations around the world.

To realise this project, we invited colleagues from the international circle of indigenous studies specialists. As only a few specialists at the moment are working on this concrete topic, to complete the book we launched an additional call for contributions to international networks in Arctic studies: CIÉRA, DIALOG, TRINET. Thus, we collected 18 chapters related to the targeted themes.

When we designed the project, two criteria were most important. First, we only accepted contributions based on concrete research results or an overview of decades of accumulated academic knowledge of the researchers. Second, our ambition was to embrace cases from all five continents where indigenous people still live today. Unfortunately, we could not obtain a study from Latin America due to unforeseen circumstances which meant that some authors could not contribute as expected and, time pressing, we decided to publish the book as it in its current state.

Conceptual papers were rejected, as well as those too far from the mainstream of economic development topics. The initial idea was to collect texts dealing exclusively with economic growth and entrepreneurship. Later we widened these limits to include chapters about management of business companies, sustainable development and traditional indigenous economic activities, and national policies related to the native economies.

Initially, our idea was to arrange the chapters by geographical criteria: continent by continent. Later, at the final stage of collating the contributions, we realised that there were several main themes emerging from the content of the chapters and that it would be more logical to group them by theme rather than by geographical location. Thus, we structured the book into five topics: macro-economical tendencies of indigenous societies; sustainable management of the resources of indigenous populations; know-how and strategies of indigenous governance; challenges and issues of indigenous tourism development; and entrepreneurship within indigenous societies.

Colleagues working in different countries – specialising in disciplines such as anthropology, geography, economy, management, and tourism – provided analyses of different facets of indigenous economies and the challenges, successes, and obstacles blocking their further development. Practical recommendations and solutions are provided in the majority of the chapters, which we hope will be helpful for all indigenous practitioners and managers and non-indigenous researchers or business partners working with indigenous communities.

As indigenous populations live not in isolation but in synergy or competition – more or less in conflict with the non-indigenous economic and cultural context of their countries – written texts shedding light on these issues proved extremely valuable for our work.

Ibrahima Diallo and Marc-Urbain Proulx's study uses statistical methods evaluating the state of economic development for the whole of the Canadian province of Quebec: its indigenous communities; the role of partnerships in local economic development for indigenous communities; the specificities of their economic structure; and an interesting reflection about the nature of the traditional collectivist spirit translated within more socialist economies. Marie Pierre Bousquet, another Canadian author, presents the dynamic nature of the economic world of native Canadian communities in a post-colonialist context and new social relations formed nowadays. These authors provide valuable insights into the particular Canadian context of economic development giving these indigenous communities extensive land rights and opportunities for growth compared to other countries.

Australia is the other continent where the native communities are presented in this collection with rich and interesting material. Based on a lifetime career experience, Ram Vemuri's chapter summarises observations about adapted indigenous managers' business management, reflecting on specific indigenous business culture. This research is fundamental for indigenous business managerial philosophies and a sustainable approach towards land and natural resources, and contributes to the strength and variety of this collection.

Benxiang Zeng and Rolf Gerritsen analyse the role of 'culture' in indigenous tourism management. Successful cases of businesses from Central Australia suggest that typical indigenous values are important determinants on the supply side of Aboriginal tourism business management and its degree of compatibility with western cultures.

Amanda Shoebridge and Jeremy Buultjens discuss the effectiveness of government assistance programmes facilitating indigenous business development in New South Wales, Australia, and the problems associated with them – such as inappropriate funding and duplication of programmes, lack of consistency, and lack of ownership of the outcomes from some programmes. The authors propose some concrete solutions for more efficient management of these programmes.

A group of five chapters dealing with tourism is central to the book. Tourism is often perceived as a panacea for economic problems in the context of declining traditional economic activities, and many of the indigenous communities around the world aspire to economic gain through tourism. The chapter by Elena Totonova proposes an overview of the general socio-economical context in the northern territories of Russia, areas with the highest concentration of native communities and their participation in their respective economies. Tourism appears as one suitable way towards a better life, and some obstacles and points for improvement are presented by the author. This Russian case study is valuable because despite the long historic tradition of research, we can very rarely read translated results from Russia about such specific topics.

In the same line of research is the chapter by Jayson Ibanez, Beau Austin, and Stephen T. Garnett on indigenous communities from Mindanao Island, Philippines. Similar to the Australian communities, the results reveal that the indigenous knowledge and worldview – with a special approach to both the living and spiritual world – need to be more closely incorporated into their business, being compatible and not incompatible with business logic.

Discussing indigenous tourism in the context of business sustainability, Lisa Ruhanen, Charlee McLennan, and Michelle Whitford present the perceptions of 41 indigenous operators in Australia, highlighting the issues, opportunities and challenges associated with running a tourism business. The authors propose recommendations and strategies for sustainability.

Stephen T. Garnett, Beau Austin, Peter Shepherd, and Kerstin K. Zander make a comparative analysis of the economic opportunities for culture-based versus natural resources based industries in Australian aboriginal communities in the Northern Territory. They examine economic growth, obstacles, and the role of the government for new and well-established culture-based enterprises.

Jason Mika's chapter stands out with a topic rarely investigated by researchers – namely, the role of elders in the formation and stability of Māori enterprises in New Zealand. In contrast with the role of elders for indigenous businesses, Katia Iankova discusses the factors in the success of young entrepreneurs, adding a different facet to this recently emerged stream of research related to indigenous entrepreneurship.

In his chapter, Azizul Hassan evaluates the livelihood activities and comparative advantages for various industries in the specific political and socio-cultural context of three countries in South Asia: Bangladesh, Myanmar, and Nepal. The same author, in collaboration with Bangladeshi colleague Mashrur Imtiaz, critically evaluates how the provision of Bengali and English (the main languages spoken in Bangladesh) affects the integration of Garo indigenous communities into the workforce. These case studies include indigenous communities from areas where poverty exacerbates their problems – the recommendations for poverty reduction join those of other authors working on this geographical region for an integrated approach towards indigenous communities there.

Two chapters present different industries related to indigenous people in Botswana and Nigeria which highlight the challenges to these communities on the African continent. The chapter on the problematic nature of community-based tourism in the Kalahari region, written by Naomi Moswete and Brijesh Thapa, joins the other tourism-related studies in this book about the benefits and challenges of this type of activity for African native communities. The chapter on the palm oil industry by Umoh Samuel and Oyewo Adetola includes interesting illustrative material and provides an overview of the constraints and points for improvement in terms of management and technologies in order to optimise the benefits for the native communities studied in Nigeria.

The theme of sustainability is the backbone for the majority of the chapters in this book, and the one by Teresa C.H. Tao and Geoffrey Wall is no exception. It considers the viability of a 'sustainable livelihood' approach and the importance of institutional arrangements for its successful implementation in Taiwan, presenting case studies of the Cou community in Chashan.

Nor'Ain Othman and Norliza Aminudin's chapter joins the group of studies on government policy programmes in different countries to combat poverty. In this case they reassess the integrated programme of the Tenth Malaysia Plan, 2011–2015, involving land development and ownership projects targeting indigenous communities living on and below the poverty threshold and helping them to become landowners and active farmers. The authors present the challenges and issues in implementing an integrated programme and its sustainability in improving the economy of the native communities in Malaysia.

We are fortunate to have chapters from the five largest countries in the world (by territory). The final case study is from China, written by Jin Hooi Chan, Ying Zhang, Tom McDonald, and Xiaoguang Qi. They join the stream of researchers seeking solutions for sustainable and integrated regional management in a territory occupied by three indigenous communities in the south-east of the country, where there is land use conflict between the traditional rice plantations on UNESCO-protected terraces and the newly established international tourism industry. Some suggestions and recommendations point out more sustainable and mutually beneficial management strategies of the economic activities for the whole fragile ecosystem of the rice terraces in China.

The predominance of case studies comprising this collection gives the reader the opportunity to compare and potentially deduce some new concepts related to indigenous economies throughout the world. Despite the geographical differences, political systems, and cultural connotations, we can reveal some threats intrinsic to all indigenous communities – such as desire for control of resources, intellectual property rights, and the 'indigenisation' of approaches to business and management.

A central discussion in this book relates to the fine line between external help (governmental, NGO, or voluntary groups) and the capacity for self-empowerment of the native groups for successful and sustainable economic development. While not being the focus, the idea of the role of championship and leadership in entrepreneurial start-up businesses is apparent in many of the case studies throughout this book. Another major theme discussed here is the power of the collective acceptance or rejection of some methods of economic development based on traditional cultural and belief systems unique to the indigenous communities, and the importance of respect for and specific integration of these in any economic model they might adopt. The level of integration of the western capitalist model into their socio-economic fabric and the emergence of new integrated 'indigenised' models converging to the more 'collectivistic' worldview of the indigenous communities need to be well balanced in order to optimise the effectiveness of their initiatives. The discussion engendered in this book around the efficiency and the appropriateness of a purely capitalistic free market approach versus the collectivistic and socially suitable to the indigenous tradition model is one, I believe, that will persist as a predominant stream of future research in order to estimate the just model for each community incorporating its traditional values.

It is important not only to see globalisation as an opportunity for economic growth but also to understand its dangers in jeopardising the survival of traditional structures and economies in this rapidly changing economic environment.

Banking on their preserved, vibrant, rich cultural capital, many indigenous communities join successfully today in the postmodern stream of creative industries such as cultural events, arts, crafts, design, architecture, music, fashion, alternative medicines, film, and all forms of digital industries. Indigenous people with their originality have a real chance to use this new (intangible by nature) industrialisation and turn it in their favour to achieve financial stability and economic growth.

Now that this book is a reality after many months of collection and communication with all authors, I would like to thank them for their trust and patience. I leave the present book in the hands of the readers to discover new and exciting realities of the world's indigenous peoples as well as new concepts and new ideas for future research.

I hope it will be useful for all colleagues working on questions related to the indigenous peoples, especially for the young researchers and those indigenous managers, chiefs, agents of economic development, and well- and newly established businessmen and businesswomen who believe in the economic prosperity and bright future of their people.

Dr. Katia Iankova
Editor

PART I
SOCIO-ECONOMIC DEVELOPMENT AND INSTITUTIONAL PLANNING

1

Socioeconomic Dynamics of Aboriginal Communities in Quebec

Ibrahima Diallo and Marc-Urbain Proulx

Chapter Synopsis

There are about 50 Aboriginal communities distributed among 11 nations throughout Quebec, Canada. The analysis in this chapter showed a persistent lag compared with the non-Aboriginal communities in general, but also an interesting positive dynamic between the two survey periods covered (2001 and 2006). This is confirmed empirically by the average and median levels of socioeconomic indicators, which increased overall. Despite the low levels observed in indicators of socioeconomic development, the study showed that communities could diversify in areas of training, profession, and industrial development with a more important stress on secondary sectors with manufacturing and tertiary services. Numerous observations emerged from our analysis. They can be found in the form of factors of success or weakness. Pertaining to success factors, we discuss population growth generating human capital as a source of wealth; the ability of these communities to meet labour demands; the broad range of training offered; diversification in occupations throughout, with diversification indices often close to unity; strong diversification in areas of industrial activity; and the fact that proximity of urban centres encourages openness, and therefore a high level of diversification. However, areas of weakness are rated as low levels of schooling in the community as a whole, and low graduation rates – more than half the population has no diploma, degree, or certificate; the problem of securing an Aboriginal workforce available, increasingly, to meet companies' staffing needs; and lack of openness for some communities is a source of weakness in linguistic diversity and also in the level of income and activity.

Introduction

There are about 50 Aboriginal communities distributed among 11 nations in Quebec. In logical comparison to non-Aboriginal communities, the observation whereby socioeconomic characteristics are generally less attractive is a reality. This is the case with income, education, diversity of activities, diversity of training and industry, and degree of openness. This is however not sufficient for a more detailed insight into situations and movements of these communities and for their own dynamic economic development. The problem of development in Aboriginal communities evolving between tradition and modernism raises several questions. How do Aboriginal communities evolve in Quebec? In recent years, what changes have communities experienced in regard to socioeconomic indicators? In an approach that integrates all the above aspects, have the communities evolved uniformly or have they followed different socioeconomic directions?

Principles of Socioeconomic Development of Communities

For the present study we include in factors of socioeconomic development any that may increase the independence of Aboriginal communities, both economically and socially. For instance, this is the case of diversity reducing dependence on the outside due to reallocating risk as opposed to a strong specialisation which creates dependence on market fluctuations of small numbers of activities.

The evolutionary models of economic development are in line with the same dynamic internalisation process of socioeconomic development. In fact, like the theories that highlight the stages of development – promoted mainly by Modigliani (1963), Vernon (1990), and Rostow (1960) – socioeconomic development is a step in a process that occurs beyond a certain threshold (see Figure 1.1). This view of the concept presupposes a community as part of a progress dynamic which implies supporting the management of wealth accumulation factors as well as shifting populations towards change. Observation of the characteristics of Aboriginal peoples reveals a certain variation with these models partly due to their attachment to the past, to their culture, and to the prominent position held by adults in decision making etc.

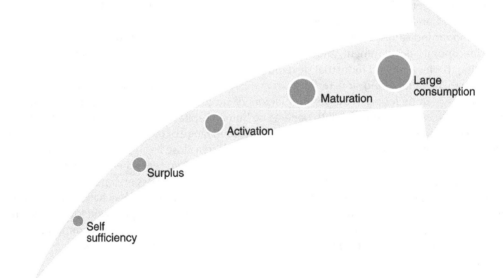

Figure 1.1   Rostow's stage growth model (1960)

Source: Author's conception.

An automatic regional equilibrium model reflects a variation of the neoclassical theory at territory level. Indeed, as the name implies, differences in income or socioeconomic development between territories may be a source of inter-jurisdictional mobility of populations, who will tend to migrate to the most profitable areas. Adjustments in wages will then mark an automatic adjustment and, accordingly, a state of equilibrium or socioeconomic development as previously defined. This neoclassical approach may be described as dynamic and horizontal next to procedural approaches present in the economic field rather than vertical.

Relations with the outside world, with the interregional adjustment model, benefit the community and are likely to provide them with a surplus, allowing accumulation of income and eradication of disparities between Aboriginal communities and the rest of Quebec. This trend, however, is not observed in the evolution over the period of two analyses of median incomes and levels of employment and unemployment in Aboriginal communities.

From a different angle, this idea comes from theories on the exporting base (Aydalot, 1985) which implies competitiveness at local level (the base) outwards. This allows the territory to record positive benefits because of the multiplier effect of gains from the marketing of local products to outside markets. Thus, beyond the dynamic nature of this model, openness to outside markets appears to occupy a prominent place. In regard to Aboriginal communities, revenues are different at this level and depend on multiple factors – such as distance from the central markets and proximity to the Montreal/Toronto axis. These reasons are physical alongside others that we considered institutional, namely the lack of acknowledgement of certain communities due to the remoteness of their reserves.

Admittedly, in the analyses above models tend towards equilibrium, a fact made possible only with external interaction. In addition, the concept of socioeconomic development cannot be dissociated from the ability to manage through mechanisms intended for the relevant communities and work in the long term. This dimension of understanding of the concept is widely supported by the theory of endogenous development. It places at the centre of its reasoning endowments of communities remaining favourable to their own undertaking through their development.

Conventional economic analysis models of the propensity for Aboriginal communities to become involved in capitalist areas is often difficult since there are significant differences between traditional Aboriginal cultures and Western culture on how to manage business and understand wealth. They manifest themselves in collectivism, community property, division of property, consensus, the social, the traditional, etc.

Aboriginal communities are unique in regard to cultural and organisational levels and also in composition, not only because of their heterogeneity but also because of their differences in economic management. Moreover, they are not evenly distributed across reserves and show increasingly differentiated dynamics of development (see Table 1.1).

Table 1.1   Differences between Native and non-Native culture

Non-Native Culture	Native Culture
Capitalism	Collectivism
Individuality	Community
Separation of property	Division of property
Prioritising innovation and change	Entrenched traditional values
Decisions by majority	Consensus
Gender centred	Matriarchal
Close to power	Far from power
Sedentary lifestyle	Recently settled population
Involvement of elders in the decision-making process	Age is not a determining factor
Traditional economy	Social economy
Modernisation	Traditional activities (hunting, fishing, trapping)

The fact that these communities value cooperation between members, focus on family obligations, and consider the community as unity of action, the importance of the above-mentioned values, leads to a more suitable conceptual field through which Aboriginal communities situate themselves – namely, social economy. Hence, the importance of their desire to enter the economy with the appropriate tools and to integrate, as best as possible, these differences. Such a situation highlighting the hybrid or associative character of the economic dynamics of Aboriginal communities is evident at two levels.

Firstly, it concerns an entry framework as part of a capitalist and individualistic logic (Anderson et al. 2004). Following this logic, the active accommodation requirements of the capitalist economy is one of the attitudes observed in the communities. They emphasise that Aboriginal communities have opted to act from within through struggles for land and other rights in order to contribute to the economy. Our analysis of socioeconomic development incorporates this attitude through key indicators of the level of entrepreneurship, and for which verification is possible from available sources of harmonised data. Essentially, it is about activity levels and median income.

Secondly, taking into account the multi-faceted nature of economics leads to exceeding the market logic and integrating other requirements of a domestic or distributive nature (Polanyi, 1944), or of combinations of the above-mentioned approaches (Laville, 1995). This leads us into a social economy that, in its reasoning, gives priority to three basic dimensions taking us a step closer to the model of Aboriginal communities: redistribution, reciprocity, and the market.

The literature on organisational dynamics applied to Aboriginal communities underpins the argument of specialisation or dispersion as characteristics of economic development. In fact, based on Fayol's (1916) study on the structural plan of a community, socioeconomic development may be observed from its structure. At the elementary level, the so-called sun or basic structure reflects a society in which specialisation is the exception and the rule is dispersion. Depending on the development, management bodies deal with an increasing number of specific tasks. This reasoning is consistent at community levels with the diversification of activities as a relevant index for assessing socioeconomic development.

Sustainability, which is a fundamental feature of socioeconomic development, is difficult to observe in a context where communities are struggling to follow the cyclical fluctuations in the levels of production fields and management methods as well as socioeconomic and demographic changes. The fluidity of inter- and intra-community migration as well as flows with the outside, the multiplicity of courses of study, levels of activity of the population are all factors facilitating flexibility as well as adaptability of communities (see Table 1.2).

Its numerous other features may be guessed from its definition. All the above evidence certifies it is true, of a prolix field of understanding of the concept, but will not be included in the models of this study. However, based on these elements, some key indicators of socioeconomic development will be selected depending on our empirical contingencies: essentially openness to the outside world; specialisation or measurable diversification through dispersion indices; training; levels of activity and income; and diversification in professional, educational, and industrial domains. These factors provide as much information on socioeconomic attributes as on level of socioeconomic development.

More information emerged from socioeconomic data or criteria of socioeconomic development of Aboriginal communities, some of which we attempt to present succinctly here (see Figure 1.2). For some communities, openness and diversification run along the same lines. At one extreme is the case of the Innu Pakuashipi community, with a diversity index of zero for training. This reflects an extreme concentration of their population in regard to education. Thus, they recorded the lowest coefficient for degree of openness. Population growth is often greater in the more remote Aboriginal communities and more closed if one relies on the openness ratio. This is the case of the Inuit, with rates of 10–66% outside communities such as the Puvirnituq,

Table 1.2   Adaptation and flexibility factors of Aboriginal communities in Quebec

Adaptation factors and sources	Rigidities and sources
• The settlement of Aboriginal people for the last 60 years marks their entry into the modern world. • Communities located near major centres are integrated into urban and regional life. • The fact that they settled permanently in an area led them to develop new relationships with Quebec society and to increase their participation in community projects. • Although some remote communities have retained their traditional way of life, they are not, however, completely isolated; technology and transportation have greatly facilitated their communication with the rest of Quebec. • The level of economic development varies between communities, depending on three factors: proximity to markets, road links to their villages, and schooling • For most of the Nations, English or French is a first language: 3 out of 11 Nations speak French more than their local language (Abénaquis, Malécites, Huron-Wendats).	• Rooted in ancestral culture (hunting, fishing, trapping, etc.). • With the exception of the Mohawk who have English as their first language, an important number of communities – following the example of the Inuit, Innu, and Cree – prefer their local languages.

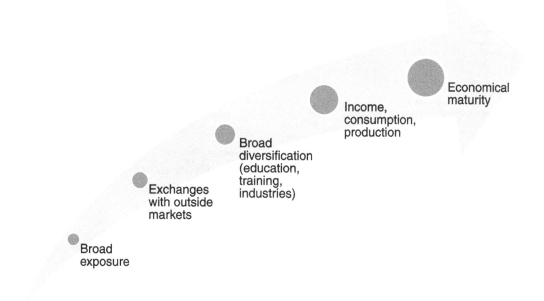

Figure 1.2   Factors of socioeconomic development in Aboriginal communities in Quebec

Source: Author's conception.

Kuujjarapik, and Kangiqsujuaq. Diversification of Malécites is more than respectable and is 0.86 compared to 0.85 for the entire province. The community is very open and evolves to 100% off-reserve. Wôlinak, near urban centres, is very open and shows a high level of diversification.

This pattern, however, is not observed everywhere and the data provides some exceptions among. Population growth itself is generally more important for all Aboriginal communities in relation to Quebec (4.3%). Territories that have greater natural resources (e.g. Kuujjuaq, Kangirsuk, Kangiqsualujjuaq, Whapmagoostui) are those that generally have the majority of high median income – often higher than the Quebec average of $24,000 – a low rate of training with low income. This is the case of Lac-Simon, La Romaine, Matimekosh, and of Innus as a whole.

Activities and Work: Surmountable Obstacles

From the observations made on income, the level of employment among Natives is lower than that of non-Natives, varying between 42% for the Manawan and 90% for the Aupaluk. In the latter, the rate is significantly higher than the provincial rate, and for this group the median income gap between men and women is very important. With the exception of Native Indians of the reserve of Lac-Simon, of Winneway, who record significantly lower levels of 31.2% and 48%, the rate is acceptable for the Algonquin, in comparison to the rest of Quebec and Canada as a whole, where they are 60.4% and 62.4% respectively (see Figure 1.3).

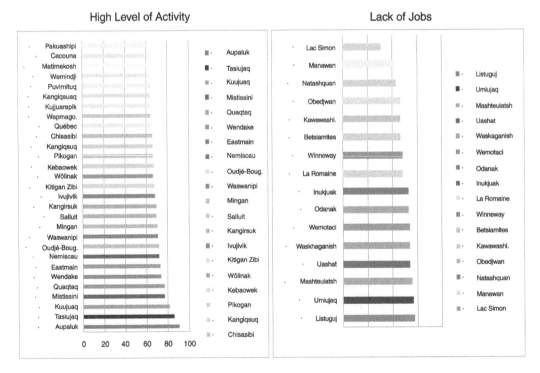

Figure 1.3   **Levels of activity in communities and lack of jobs**

Source: Statistics Canada, EAPA, 2006.

In contrast, observation of the evolution of unemployment in Aboriginal communities precludes establishing a rule for various nations. However, for the Inuit, Innu, and Cree peoples, the majority of their constituent communities showed increased levels of unemployment (see Figure 1.4).

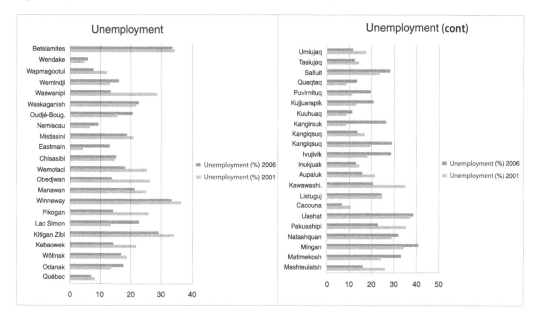

Figure 1.4   Evolution of unemployment in communities

Source: Statistics Canada, EAPA, 2001.

Over the two survey periods, the rates of change of Aboriginal peoples were quite heterogeneous holistically. Adaptability, flexibility, and responsiveness are, as shown for training, indices of socioeconomic development. This is why it would be interesting to see the patterns of unemployment rate according to changes of attitude pertaining to population growth (Figure 1.5 and 1.6).

Analysis of changes in population growth on the one hand and increase in unemployment on the other demonstrated that over all 45 communities studies as many communities record developments in the same direction of these two variables as the opposite. This confirms the theory that, on the whole, demographic pressures have not been determinative in reducing unemployment; or, conversely, that unemployment levels have not led communities to waver in their progression.

Underestimation of the Virtues of Training

Despite the significant relationship between levels of education and activity as shown by empirical data, the desire for training seems less noticeable. Indeed, the 2006 study shows quite disturbing findings in the field of education for Aboriginal communities in Quebec. Nearly 66% of the population did not exceed secondary level, and 47% of the Odanak population has no

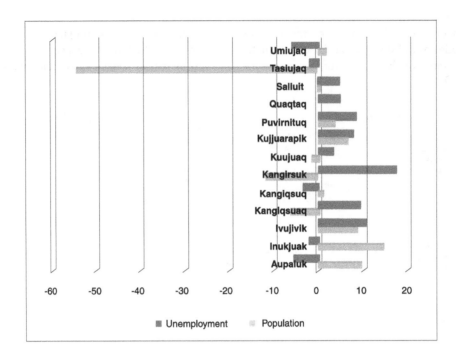

Figure 1.5   Comparison of changes in population growth rate and unemployment among the Innu Nation

Source: Statistics Canada, EAPA, 2006.

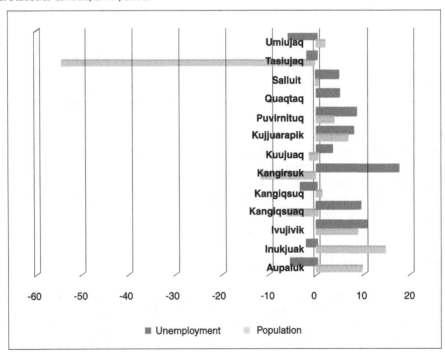

Figure 1. 6   Comparison of changes in population growth rate and unemployment among the Inuit Nation

Source: Statistics Canada, EAPA, 2006.

certificate, diploma, or degree. Thus, although dispersion is good in the field of education, there is a problem of mass or popular registration because enrolment in and duration of studies are well below provincial and federal levels (see Figure 1.7).

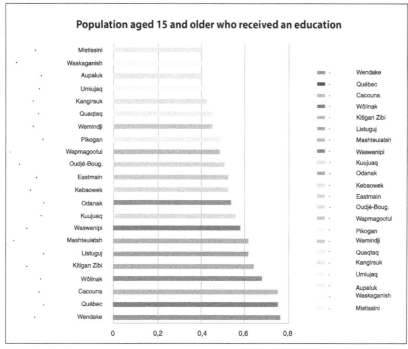

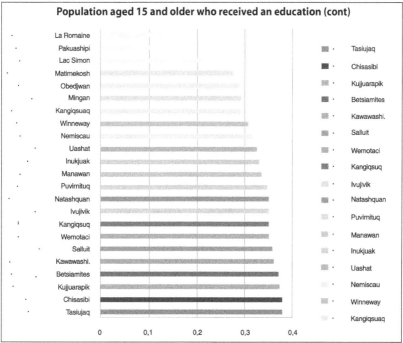

Figure 1.7   Educated population aged 15 and older in Aboriginal communities in Quebec

Source: Statistics Canada, EAPA, 2006.

These figures illustrate the strong link between education and access to major centres. Indeed, most of the communities found at the top are near the Quebec–Montreal axis: basically, communities such as Wendake, Cacouna, Wôlinak, Kitigan Zibi, Listuguj, Mashteuiatsh, and Waswanipi. On the northeastern side are communities such as Pakuashipi, La Romaine, Mingan, and Uashat; and the Inuit communities in the far north – Puvirnituq, Ivujivik, Inukjuak, Salluit, Kangiqsujuaq, Kangiqsualujjuaq (among others) – steal the show in regard to low levels of education (see Figure 1.8).

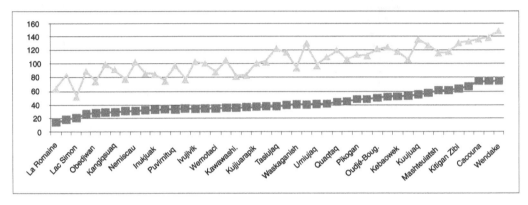

Figure 1.8   Comparative growth in levels of activity and training among Aboriginal communities in Quebec

Source: Statistics Canada, EAPA, 2006.

Although the correlation coefficient of 0.34 observed between these two variables was barely significant, the previous scatter plot shows that the rate of activity in Aboriginal communities is not insensitive to the level of training. Compared to the province of Quebec, which shows high values that position it on the far right along with communities relatively near urban centres – such as Wôlinak, Cacouna, and Wendake – we find at the other end communities that record the lowest levels of education and employability. Reading the results of the data, we see clearly that activity levels are highly dependent on levels of training of Native people. Levels of education are, in turn, dependent on the distances from major centres in Quebec.

Proximity to Urban Centres (Markets)

Overall, communities closest to markets are more open in terms of communication with the outside. Observation of openness depending on the diversity of languages and the primacy of classical languages (French or English) over traditional languages shows an interesting relationship between the variables (see Figure 1.9). In this study, calculation of proximity is done by taking the Quebec–Montreal axis as the centre. Consolidation was made between communities 20 km, 40 km, 60 km, etc. distant or communities located in areas from which access to the centre is by air or areas more than 900 km from the centre.

As shown in this bivariate analysis, an attempt to visualise the relationship between proximity to centres and linguistic diversity, the range of languages spoken by communities increases according to the reconciliation of communities with markets. The vacuum observed in the lower-left quadrant, proximity to markets, is a key factor in diversification and openness in terms of language. Even though for the Malécites the position seems obvious due to the fact that they

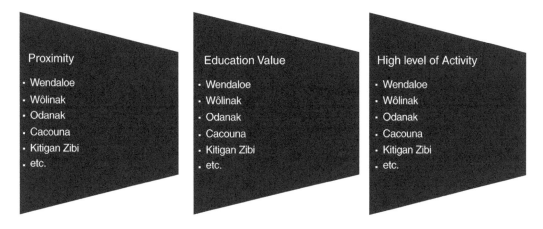

Figure 1.9   Improvement process of levels of activity

Source: Statistics Canada, EAPA, 2006.

operate almost completely off-reserve, we find one of the most important in terms of numbers, namely the Mohawk communities. Distance to market for a sizeable portion of the communities – including the Innu, Cree, Atikamekw, Algonquin, and Inuit – should be stressed (see Figure 1.10).

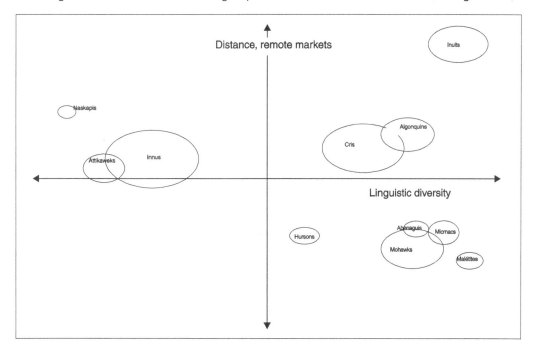

Figure 1.10   Aboriginal nations and linguistic diversity

Source: Statistics Canada, EAPA, 2006.

Table 1.3 presented shows the overall relatively weak position in all Aboriginal communities compared to the rest of Quebec. Indeed, the low enrolment rates observed in both short-term training and in the educational system, as well as low levels of activity and median incomes,

Table 1.3   SWOT analysis of socioeconomic situation of communities

Strengths	Weaknesses
• An improvement in the Aboriginal populations which recorded significantly higher growth rates than observed in non-Native populations • Ability in entrepreneurship • Willingness to take part in the economy • Natives' belief in their ability to integrate into mainstream economy without sacrificing their core values collectivism, environmental protection, traditional activities, etc.).	• Lack of time for general training • Low levels of schooling for some communities; e.g., 66% of the population have not passed secondary education; 47% of Odanak have no certificate, diploma, or degree • Low enrolment in the educational system • Low levels of income for the vast majority of communities • Low levels of employment and activity • In a context of high prevalence of single-parent families, negative relationship between population and available housing • Elusive Native assets within the reserves; they cannot be used as loan guarantees to finance enterprises • The problem of linking the available and ever-expanding Aboriginal workforce to rising staff needs of enterprises
Opportunities	Threats
• Positive effects of activity rates on training levels; although the correlation is of 0.34 participation rate, it is positive. Of the 45 assessed communities, the table shows a marked sensitivity • Diversified training • Diversification in occupations throughout all indices often close to unity • Strong diversification of industrial activities • Strong demand for labour	• Strong population growth is unfortunately accompanied by increased unemployment • Situations engendering surge in criminality • Lack of openness of certain communities is a source of weakness in linguistic diversity and in income levels and activity • Over half the population has no diploma, degree, or certificate

explain this fully. However, it should be noted that high diversity in professional, industrial, and training activities inspires hope for future possibilities of a reversal of trends.

Based on the above analysis, we find that both the decline and revival of Aboriginal communities are measured in part by the indicators examined in this section. Some empirical results allow us to see this inertia in socioeconomic level. Firstly, the low levels of socioeconomic development compared with the rest of Quebec persisted over the two survey periods even if, in the vast majority of cases, the average levels showed a positive trend. Then, strong population growth is accompanied less by improvements in activity, socioeconomic development and a rise in unemployment. Finally, it is notable for many communities that land availability is synonymous with higher median income. This demonstrates that, in certain ways, progress is not completely dependent on a strong commitment to significant improvement in socioeconomic conditions.

However, the situation is not entirely bleak since, following this study, some factors showed that Aboriginal communities are showing encouraging signs in the observed progressions as much as in the relationship between certain variables involving effort to achieve. First, it is clear that the activity rate among Aboriginal people overall is not insensitive to the level of training. Again, proximity to centres promotes linguistic diversity of Native communities. Second, proximity to major centres is an explanatory factor for high or low levels of education. Finally, differences in general and socioeconomic development have increased between the two survey periods.

Although relevant to understanding the socioeconomic situation of Native communities, the situation recounted in this section, in addition to static tables, primarily focused on two criteria or variables of socioeconomic development. The inclusion of other factors such as those outlined earlier – for instance, industrial diversity and education as in professional levels – will deal more accurately in the second part with evaluation of socioeconomic development of Aboriginal communities, and the follow-up over the two periods covered by the surveys.

Evolutionary Dynamics and Dispersions

PROGRESS OF COMMUNITIES IN TERMS OF ACTIVITY AND INCOME

Assessment of the standards of living of Native communities was accompanied by an increase in disparities between them, as shown by the comparative figures from the two survey periods. Indeed, using bivariate analysis charts, the economic situation is dealt with in a limited perspective through visualisation of the movements over the two survey periods, quality of life (median income) based on the economic dynamics (activity) (see Figure 1.11 and 1.12).

The evolution of the two periods of activity levels and incomes of Aboriginal communities shows a clear variation of the differences between them. Indeed, from an agglomeration that indicates a degree of uniformity of standard of living, they pass to a situation where differences in income are more pronounced, although, overall, there has been a marked improvement in average levels of the two variables (income and activity).

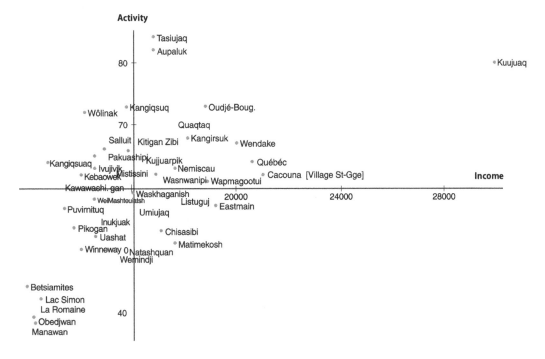

Figure 1.11   Activity levels and income in communities, 2001

Source: Statistics Canada, EAPA, 2001.

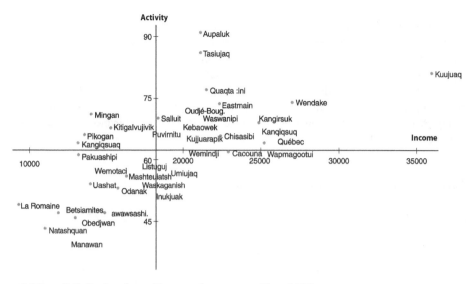

Figure 1.12   Activity levels and income in communities, 2006

Source: Statistics Canada, EAPA 2006.

DEMOGRAPHIC CHANGES IN COMMUNITIES IN TERMS OF ACTIVITY AND INCOME

In the following sections, we will use factor analysis and, more specifically, principal component analysis with data that allow us to observe socioeconomic status (income, occupation) according to demographic changes; comparisons will also be made over the two survey periods.

By choosing as criteria changes in population, income, and activity levels, not only are evaluation methods between the two periods not significantly different, but they will also make possible comparisons in respect of the changing socioeconomic development of communities throughout the periods (see Figures 1.13–1.15).

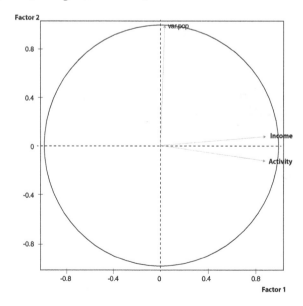

Figure 1.13   Criteria of socioeconomic development

Source: Statistic Canada, EAPA, 2001.

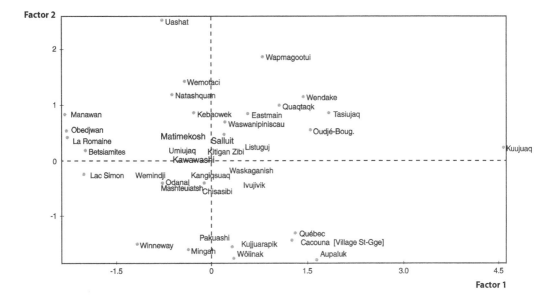

Figure 1.14   Socioeconomic positioning, 2001

Source: Statistic Canada, EAPA, 2001.

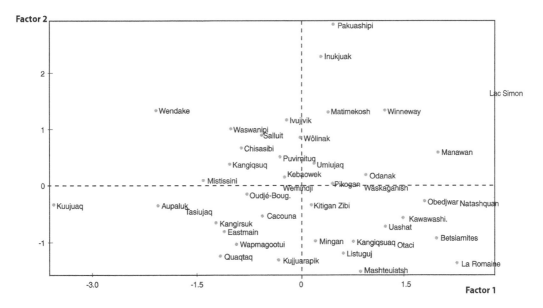

Figure 1.15   Socioeconomic positioning, 2006

Source: Statistic Canada, EAPA, 2006.

The principal component analysis (PCA) table clearly shows a strong correlation between employment and income in Aboriginal communities. Many movements are noted as a result of a comparison of the different Aboriginal communities depending on their socioeconomic situation with regard to income and activity levels on the one hand, and population growth on the other. Although these movements are observed overall, variations are more pronounced among communities in relatively precarious situations that have changed their behaviour in terms of lower population growth. However, rates are generally higher than the provincial level.

Table 1.4   Classification and trends of Aboriginal communities in Quebec based on demographic and socioeconomic status, 2001 and 2006

High population growth and low economic situation	High population growth and significant socioeconomic levels
• Uashat (↓)	• Whapmagoostui (↓)
• Wemotaci (↓)	• Eastmain (↓)
• Natashquan (↓)	• Quaqtaq
• Keboawek (↓)	• Tasiujaq (↓)
• Manawan (.)	• Oujé-Bougoumou (↙)
• Obedjiwan (↓)	• Waswanipi (.)
• La Romaine (↓)	• Listuguj (↙)
• Betsiamites (↓)	• Nemiscau (.)
• Umiujaq (↓)	

Low population growth levels and socioeconomic indicators	High levels of socioeconomic indicators and low population growth
• Lac Simon	• Québec (.)
• Wemindji	• Kujjuaq (.)
• Kawawachikamach (.)	• Cacouna (←)
• Kangiqsualujjuaq	• Aupaluk (.)
• Puvirnituq (.)	• Kujjuarapik (←)
• Chisasibi (↗)	• Wôlinak (↖)
• Winneway (↑)	• Ivujivik (↖)
• Mashteuiatsh (.)	• Kangiqsuq (↑)
• Mingan	
• Pakuashipi (↑)	
• Odanak (.)	
• Kitigan Zibi (.)	
• Salluit (↗)	
• Mistissini	
• Waskaganish (.)	

Note: The direction of the arrows indicates the quadrant in which the community is found in the second survey period; the point indicates a status quo.

Strengthening of lower quadrants reinforces the idea that population growth was not necessarily accompanied by an improvement in living standards (see Table 1.4).

Observation of the two tables from 2001 and 2006 shows in both situations a high concentration in areas of lower socioeconomic development. However, it is evident that the concentration is less important in 2006 than in 2001, with a greater dispersion of demographic and socioeconomic levels of Aboriginal communities.

Conclusion

The uniqueness of the Aboriginal communities in their habits, combined with their strong development compared with the rest of Quebec, describes a table raising, in the field of economics, questions about their future in the province. The answer to these questions requires, first, a good knowledge of their economic situation and especially its evolution, which contains just as much or even more relevant information on their development dynamic. Thus this chapter's analysis pertaining to these communities focused on socioeconomic and demographic factors. Basically, the results showed not only persistent lag compared with non-Aboriginal communities in general, but also an interesting positive dynamic between the two survey periods (2001 and 2006). This is confirmed empirically by the average and median levels of socioeconomic indicators, which increased overall. Despite the low values observed in indicators of socioeconomic development, the study showed that communities could diversify in areas of training, profession, and industrial development with emphasis on secondary sectors with manufacturing and tertiary services.

Numerous observations emerged from our analysis in the form of factors of success or weakness. Success factors included:

- population growth generating human capital as a source of wealth;
- the ability of these communities to meet the demand for labour;
- a broad range of training offered;
- diversification in occupations throughout, with diversification indices often close to unity;
- strong diversification in areas of industrial activity;
- the fact that proximity to urban centres encourages openness and, therefore, a high level of diversification.

However, factors of weakness are rated as:

- low educational levels of communities as a whole, including low graduation rates – more than half the population has no diploma, degree, or certificate;
- the problem of securing an Aboriginal workforce available to meet companies' rising staffing needs;
- lack of openness for some communities being a source of weakness in linguistic diversity; and
- levels of income and activity.

Ultimately, the degree of heterogeneity or homogeneity of the positions occupied on the perceptual map is dependent upon the criteria used for their preparation. Thus, the PCA table, which shows a strong inertia in the explanatory variables of socioeconomic development to the two quadrants on the left, seems clear enough to divide Aboriginal communities into four groups:

1. communities with somewhat significant socioeconomic development;
2. those communities that tend to show relative socioeconomic development;

3. the overwhelming majority of Inuit communities, except for a few such as the Kuujjuaq, which are at an average level of socioeconomic development compared to all Aboriginal communities.

4. most of the communities of Quebec's Lower North Coast, which have relatively lower socioeconomic development in view of the criteria in the proposed models.

However, this study is far from exhaustive and could have been improved significantly by the inclusion of other criteria that better reflect entrepreneurship such start-ups observed in different communities. It would be interesting to see the evolution of the socioeconomic development of communities with surveys in 2011 incorporating all the variables that are included in the analyses drawn from the 2006 data. Indeed, they will enable appreciation of the socioeconomic development in Aboriginal communities in Quebec on a wider basis than possible during the 1996–2001 period. Future extension of this work could be considered at three levels that seem interesting. The first is to assess the depth of partnership mechanisms, which is reported in several situations, as a significant hindrance to access to decision-making communities. The second is to monitor the extent of evolution of the observed differences on the development of Aboriginal peoples at both intra- and extra-community level. The last is to explore partnerships maintained by some Aboriginal communities with immigrants.

References

Anderson, R., Nkongolo-Bakenda, J.-M., and Giberson, R. (2004). Entrepreneuriat et développement économique en milieu autochtone: approche régulationniste de la Bande Indienne du Lac La Ronge (Entrepreneurship and economic development in Aboriginal Communities: a regulationist approach in the Indian band of La Ronge Lake). *21st Canadian Council for Small Business and Entrepreneurship (CCSBE) Annual Conference*. Regina, Saskatchewan, 11–13 November.

Aydalot, P. (1985). Économie régionale et urbaine. Paris: Économica. (In French).

Fayol, H. (1917). *Administration industrielle et générale*. Paris: Dunod. (In French).

Laville, J. L. (1995). Économie solidaire, économie sociale et état social, dans Lévesque, B. Repenser l'économie du Québec. Quebec: Presses Universitaires du Québec. (In French).

Modigliano, F. (1963). The life cycle hypothesis of savings. *American Economic Review*, 53(3), pp. 433–443.

Polanyi, K. (1944). *The Great Transformation*. Boston: Beacon.

Rostow, W. (1960). *The Stages of Economic Growth: A Non-Communist Manifesto*. Cambridge: Cambridge University Press.

Statistics Canada (2001/2006). *Enquêtes auprès des peuples autochtones/Aboriginal Peoples Survey* (EAPA/APS).

Vernon, R. (1990). A Schumpeterian model of the product life cycle. *American Economic Review*, 80(5), pp. 1077–1091.

2

Contrasting Indigenous and Non-Indigenous Ways of Thinking about Capacity Building for Achieving Sustainable Development

Ram Vemuri

Chapter Synopsis

This chapter examines the way values shape management of development. It is based on my understanding and observations, as a non-Indigenous participant, of Indigenous and non-Indigenous interactions attempting to manage environments while pursuing sustainable development goals. Over 20 years of experience in observing and taking part in interactions between Indigenous and non-Indigenous participants in projects from the Northern Territory of Australia provided me with the opportunity to learn from these experiences. Two cases in this chapter illustrate these interactions. The dynamics of engaging in projects underpinning the cases has led me to believe that Indigenous values exhibit a development ethic of either working with what people have, or not working at all because they have very little to work with. They do not strategically position themselves and their societies to pursue what they do not have. In contrast, the non-Indigenous use their skills to extend their reach and work towards what they do not have. This is fundamentally because Indigenous values stem from an ethos of managing scarcity, while the mainstream is overly concerned with identifying the best strategy for achieving management goals. The chapter constructs a view that, in the new era of environmental scarcity, management education should include capacity building based on Indigenous approaches to sustainable development.

Introduction

This chapter draws on reflections of my experiences over the last 20 years working on different projects involving Indigenous people on their lands in the Northern Territory (NT) of Australia. I have witnessed many changes, in the last two decades, in interactions between Indigenous and non-Indigenous peoples. In this chapter non-Indigenous also refers to being Western. It seems in a general sense the more things change, the more they remain the same. Management of development has steadily changed over the years, but the underlying approach to what managers do – and are being trained to do – has remained by and large the same. Until recently, encounters and interactions between Indigenous and Western systems of management focused mainly on adopting an analytical approach. However, work cited by Muller (2000: 184) and others challenges this model:

> *Recent work by postcolonial scholars that exposes biases and assumptions of Western scholarship (Guerrero, 1997; Jaimes, 1992; Mohanty, 1994) can help management scholars to question dominant culture assumptions of pedagogy and research in which critical historical legacies are omitted.*

If we are to make any headway in relation to educating managers, it is necessary to approach interpretations of encounters between managers and those being managed through an open lens and select an approach. This involves the empirical investigation of a particular contemporary phenomenon within its real-life context, using multiple sources of evidence (Saunders et al., 2007).

The first part of this chapter explores how the distinctive features of the Northern Territory provide a useful case study for sustainable development through capacity building. It discusses why the NT's remoteness and isolation, small but highly diverse, multi-cultural population, and large public sector provide an exceptional opportunity to understand the underlying complexities. The second part of the chapter highlights and analyses complex issues that provide learning opportunities for policy makers and developers. In particular, encounters with Indigenous Australians allow for a stylised analysis of the interactions between Indigenous and non-Indigenous peoples. The third part of the chapter examines a framework for working in conditions of scarcity, while the final part discusses implementation of this framework as a way forward.

Significance of Territory Features

The Territory features of geography, isolation, and diverse government policy mixes aimed at promoting development and cross-cultural interactions between the Indigenous and non-Indigenous populations all contribute to an understanding of how sustainable development may be approached.

GEOGRAPHICAL FEATURES

The NT is geographically isolated from all other major population centres and is situated in the Central and Northern Regions of Australia. For some, its isolation comes at a price. It is considered the 'outback' of the Australian continent. Many have commented on the 'tyranny of distance'. However, its isolation is also a salient feature for learning because there is a mix between pristine environments (where managerial practices are not marred by influences of modernisation) and state-of-the-art management speak and thought. Parts of the NT are so isolated that 'didactic methodologies of traditional teachings' continue to interact, and even sometimes compete, with Western models of learning. Most interactions between people in the NT reveal interplay of several dimensions of learning strategies. These dimensions alternate between formal/informal learning, guided/self-directed learning, teacher-centred/learner-centred/experiential learning, active/passive/interactive learning, and preference for the use of sensory channels for learning, place and time dependent or independent learning. In short, one school of thought or specific pedagogy does not dominate management in the NT.

LAND FEATURES

The NT covers approximately 17.5 per cent of the land mass of Australia, which translates to about 1,346,200 square kilometres. Land plays a significant role in shaping management behaviour. Christa Walck (2003: 205) suggests the importance of land in grounding the teaching of management:

> The natural environment is the space in which all managers operate. Everything managers use comes at some point from nature. Managerial decisions about production, marketing, and distribution all affect that natural environment and, in the short and long run, our collective quality of life.

Climate variations are a growing concern for modern managers, and dealing with extreme weather events is increasingly becoming a challenge. The issues surrounding these events largely stem from uncertainties, and managers are required to develop strategies to address them. Globally, most decision makers are expected to consider adapting to uncertainty as a crucial strategy. In the territory, earnest searches are underway to build a pool of management excellence to deal with these changes. Because of the small professional base, NT managerial experience invariably involves developing multi-disciplinary teams. The NT experience can therefore inform effective management with a range of options for dealing with similar variations.

DEMOGRAPHIC FEATURES

The population density of the NT is in the vicinity of 0.1 people per square kilometre, and there are over 700 small communities ranging from 50 to 250 inhabitants. Low population density and the existence of small communities mean higher overhead costs that pose managerial challenges. There are concerted attempts being made to mobilise people into more economically viable population density structures. The creation of shires and their evolving governance structures are having significant impacts on managers. Restructuring the organisational landscape and challenges in promoting market-based activities is increasingly becoming a concern in the NT. The Northern Territory also has a culturally diverse population: 'The Indigenous population constitutes 31.6 per cent of the territory's total population' (Northern Territory Government, 2008: 25).

Two stylised organisational skins, Indigenous and non-Indigenous, have emerged in the economic landscape as a result of the past 200 years of interactions. Each has sustained their operations by developing routines and rituals. However, what one sees in today's world are managerial practices that stem from their differences. It is these differences that influence interactions between participants in any group interaction. It is therefore important to understand the implications of differences in these business approaches to management education.

The NT has all the complexities that management education is attempting to come to terms with. Learning can be enhanced by case studies from this region because the:

> Key issue in management education is identifying the appropriate strategy and this is assisted if, firstly, the methodologies are viewed as viable options rather than mutually exclusive sets. Secondly, the elements of the content and the learner can be examined to give some indication of the appropriate strategy for a particular situation. (Delahaye, 1992: 10)

Management educators facing these features recognise several challenges, very similar to those identified by Napier et al. (2008). Several findings have emerged on challenges when 'Western-style' management education enters developing countries:

> (a) the difficulty for local managers to change mind-sets as the economy shifts (Soulsby, 2001);
> (b) how infrastructure challenges such as lack of power, water, or classroom equipment can affect education (Napier et al., 1997);
> (c) how hard it is for foreigners and locals to connect when they lack shared language or conceptual models (Michailova and Husted, 2003; Napier, 2006; Puffer, 1996; Von Kopp, 1992; Vu and Napier, 2000);
> (d) difficulty in building equal relationships between local and foreign partners (Napier et al., 2002); and
> (e) the impact of culture and technology on communication and the communication infrastructure (Barrett, 2002).

SIGNIFICANCE OF MANAGEMENT EDUCATION FOR SUSTAINABLE DEVELOPMENT

Sustainable development is the epitome of development. Some would even suggest that the concept 'seems innocuous enough. After all, who would favour "unsustainable development"?' (Taylor, 2002: 1).

The question of what constitutes sustainable development has not been universally agreed. While, most are aware of what needs to be done, the challenge is in prescribing realistic alternatives to existing policies and developing management calibre to pursue them. Such awareness has put tremendous demand on our capacity to manage sustainable development, highlighting one of the core challenges of management education. Variables of management education (subject, content, and process) that 'would appear to have a reasonably straight-forward relationship' (Delahaye, 1992: 10) are increasingly coming under scrutiny. There are many reasons for this.

First and foremost, it is implicitly accepted in the field of management education that the 'current Western system of free markets, property rights, and the rule of the law is in fact the best hope for environmentally sustainable development' (Taylor, 2002: 1). Second, there is a genuine acknowledgement and recognition of the knowledge of Indigenous peoples. Principle 22 of the Rio Declaration accorded Indigenous people a high status with regard to environmental management:

> *Indigenous people and their communities, and other local communities, have a vital role in environmental management and development because of their knowledge and traditional practices. States should recognise and duly support their identity, culture and interests and enable their effective participation in the achievement of sustainable development. (UN, 1992)*

Finally, there was an overwhelming agreement that the bio-physical realities under which economic performance continues to operate and perform must choose 'societies planning for an orderly transition, or letting the physical limits and environmental change dictate the timing and course of transition' (Goodland et al., 1991: 2).

Building on the above premises, a conviction has emerged to embrace an interdisciplinary approach to management education in order to provide a holistic world view to address the needs of sustainable development. The aim is to enable managers with an organic and holistic world view, where things may be incommensurate and values hierarchical and often conflicting:

It is premised on endogenous, interdependent 'preferences' of individuals and groups, socially defined and limited private ownership, a variety of evolving entitlements, and a political economy where political and economic power mix with market forces in a process that serves both private interest and social need (although it may do neither well). (Swaney, 1987: 8–10)

There is a call for management education to promote development that will generate a truly multi-dimensional and multi-time perspective. Such a task is not an easy one, especially in the absence of known 'boundaries of time, space and activities' (Norgaard, 1994: 9). There have been several attempts at creating a framework based on sustainable development for the management education curriculum. Some argue for extending the models based on business cycles to incorporate cradle-to-grave transformations. Ecological economists in particular suggest the use of dynamic and computable models to address the complexities of sustainable development. Still others suggest the need to focus on the process rather than the target approach. In spite of all these attempts, a trans-disciplinary theory that will generate a truly multi-dimensional perspective is still not readily available. Countries throughout the world have resorted to providing management education training to work with second best solutions.

A disaggregated approach to holism has once again been adopted. Management education focuses on building management competency in a hierarchical series of tasks: (1) economic, (2) social, (3) cultural, (4) human, (5) political, (6) ecological, and (7) spiritual development. Management education once again focused on building the capacity of Indigenous people to deal with economic aspects of sustainable development, rather than incorporating Indigenous knowledge in an interdisciplinary approach.

Capacity building is concerned with many matters including the activities or strategies to address perceived 'gaps' in skills and knowledge, and the knowledge base it is addressing. It was originally embedded within the individual, organisation, and society as an aspect of everyday holistic lives. Today, capacity building is seen as a complex transformational tool in a rapidly changing world. The issue is, what is it that we are attempting to transform? For the majority it is 'understood to mean a combination of training, institutional strengthening and networking' (Goodland and Mercier, 1999: 13). Although there is a desire to go beyond a one-size-fits-all approach to a position that brings new learning and knowledge from within the local context and cultures, and engages with aspects of modern economic thought for survival, there is lack of management calibre to do this.

In capacity building for sustainable development, management education needs to address issues such as context, connection, continuity, and cooperation. It must place operational environments in the context of 'real-world' interactions. Currently, development activities are still pursued in the context of competitive markets. In designing a management education curriculum it is important to recognise that the purpose is not to pursue competition for its own sake, but to connect business operations to enhance productivity and improve efficiency in a pluralistic world. As a result, any attempts at building capacities must address the competencies and capabilities of both the learner and the teacher, within the context of existing governance arrangements. The two projects briefly described below highlight the challenges of finding a suitable approach to capacity building.

Case Study Projects

Preparing a Business Plan for Establishing a New Business Venture for Environmental Management Project
The Environmental Impact Statement (EIS) for an NT mining operation stated that they would provide local employment and training, and establish a business venture for environmental

rejuvenation after mining excavation. The objective was to build capacity for members of the Indigenous community to prepare a business plan and operate a business based on seed collection. The demographic and social aspects of the community are as follows:

- The 2003 Census counted 2,454 people, of which the majority (over 99 per cent) were Indigenous.
- The unemployment rate is very high as the majority have not completed schooling past Year 10.
- Existing business enterprises include aquaculture, barge operations, and arts and crafts.
- Like many Indigenous communities, this is considered a 'welfare economy' as welfare payments accrue mostly to organisations and the business sector.
- Health status is poor.

Over the course of community consultations, it was very clear that most of the participants focused on capacity building to conduct feasibility analysis and prioritise activities. An ability to carry out these tasks was considered critical to the ongoing development of the community. Each aspect of the proposed enterprise was examined, including the existing skills base, and the extent and cost of infrastructure required for implementation. A comparison was made between what currently exists and what needs to exist in relation to employment and income projections for the enterprise and markets.

As the community consultations progressed the priorities of the potential members of the enterprise shifted once there was a clear understanding of the management tasks and the level of commitment and training that would be required for establishing a *successful* business. It was suggested that an external consultant be engaged to prepare a feasibility report. The feasibility of the establishing a business enterprise in line with notions of sustainable development was reduced to the commercial/economic dimension of business.

Lack of capacity to carry out business in a sustainable manner was stated explicitly as a concern by all parties. A need for building capacities was identified. It was felt that further capacity building is needed to implement plans once approved. Capacities were also needed to determine a training plan. A 'business as usual' approach prevailed.

For sustainable development to be achieved capacity building must be approached in a different way. There are ramifications for preparing business plans for sustainable development with Indigenous resources. Business plans have to be prepared that take into consideration more than conventional features such as the financial aspects of a business. In short, there is a need to consider business plans in a holistic manner. This involves changing the way people think about business plans. Business plans need to be based on context, content, connection, capability, continuity, and cooperation. Context here refers to spatial, geographical, historical, and socio-cultural aspects. Content relates to the way organisational architecture is formed. Business plans need to have sense of connectivity with the members of the community in which these businesses are being established. Sustainable businesses need to be built on the fundamental principle of continuous improvement; hence the capabilities of community members must be understood as a baseline measure. Finally, business plans need to allow for evolving business practices and operational procedures that will promote sustainable institutions.

CAPACITY BUILDING FOR PREPARING A COMMUNITY ENGAGEMENT STRATEGY PROJECT

The EIS for a mine expansion provided for an engagement strategy involving the local Indigenous community to achieve better outcomes in employment, training, education, and health. The methodology adopted covered a number of aspects. First, it built on existing work, including reports. Second, it involved the environmental staff of the organisation. Third, it was based on extensive consultations to ensure that people were at the forefront. It was capacity building where people mattered. The process commenced with the formation of a project team comprising academic and administrative staff from outside the area as well as staff working on the ground. The project team also included a staff member working with the organisation who was also a member of the clan and a native language speaker. Establishing a series of focus group meetings was considered the most appropriate methodology to seek input from stakeholders.

An analytical framework was developed for identifying Indigenous peoples' belief about the mine and its impact with staff, particularly the project officers, and members of the project team. The involvement of staff of the organisation was significant in the implementation of this framework for two reasons: a) to have the on-the-ground contacts and logistics, and provide the necessary context for previous work; and b) for staff to be involved in the facilitation process to not only hear directly from the stakeholders but also to provide clarification and interpretation when necessary. The interactions between Indigenous and non-Indigenous people were also incorporated into further work in the area of sustainable development in management education. The framework enabled the specification of indicators through several perspectives and imagery. Provision was also made for classification of these indicators according to people's perception of importance of primary, secondary, and tertiary indicators. Finally, the framework had built-in potential for enabling continuity of involvement for monitoring, evaluating, and managing impacts through indicator assessments.

The project team considered the indicator approach to be the most appropriate for a number of reasons. The indicator approach does not involve the establishment of a causal nexus and therefore avoids the 'blame-game'. This does not necessarily imply abdication of responsibility by any one segment of the community; it simply acknowledges that reality is complex. An indicator approach summarises the 'wash-out' effect of several interdependent factors. It enables values to be subsumed to such an extent that alternative ways for managing impacts can be explored. Such a framework does not lock people or discussions into a corner. In the words of one of the focus group participants, it 'allows people to talk openly about issues'.

In this case, the success of developing indicators based on discussions of focus groups by and large depended upon three factors: a) the formation of the focus group participants; b) the conduct of discussion in focus groups; and c) the ability to comprehend the discussion. The project methodology explicitly addressed three issues: representation, participation, and information dissemination. While, this process identified the capacity needed by all parties (project proponents and affected parties) to improve outcomes and promote sustainable development, most were hesitant to shift their world views. What eventually resulted in this case was very similar to what Rosile (2008: 790) noted: 'With the best of intentions and the best of designs, there is the ever-present danger of co-optation', with management education as the potential to expand beyond 'an appearance of wealth that is realised only for a small minority'. This will not be achieved with an approach that examines everything through a business lens.

Implications for Training

In an Indigenous context, businesses are not based on a 'try and try again' philosophy:

> Very frequently there would be no second, third or subsequent chances. Resources were simply scarce to permit much in the way of 'practice', and time was often too short to dictate it to anything but real production. (Ross, 1992: 35)

Only business practices that continue through generations are considered effective. However, based on non-Indigenous experience, we know that experimentation is essential to the establishment of new business models, especially sustainable businesses. Non-Indigenous businesses operate in market environments. While there are several explanations of organisational theories emerging in the literature (Simon, 1991; Loasby, 1990; Williamson, 1975), it is sufficient, in the context of this chapter, to recognise that modern-day non-Indigenous businesses have evolved 'by combining Adam Smith's doctrine of the division of labour with Darwin theory'(Loasby, 1990: 110). The fundamental tenets of modern-day businesses are embodied in the connecting principle of Marshall (1959: 241), who stated that: 'the development of the organism … involves an increasing subdivision of functions between its separate parts on the one hand and, on the other a more intimate connection between them'.

Modern-day businesses use their rituals and routines to not only explore the ways in which interconnectedness takes place between individual components but also to examine 'alternative patterns of subdivisions and integration' (Loasby, 1990: 110). This is essential for experimentation to occur. It is also necessary to recognise that despite these fundamental differences in emphasis both Indigenous and non-Indigenous businesses continue to share a common economic landscape. Each has a deep ancestry and each continues to operate in the presence of the other. There is a sense of cohabitation that sometimes takes on a symbiotic relationship of 'the flea and the elephant' (Handy, 2002).

Non-Indigenous Business

Non-Indigenous businesses employ a 'device for organising the knowledge of all who work in it and for using that organised knowledge as a basis for new initiatives' (Loasby, 1990: 114). As knowledge in reality is complex, most non-Indigenous businesses break these complex tasks of organising knowledge and workers into manageable components. They have a business plan that clearly states a long-term vision. They form teams. They evolve strategies based on market analysis of the past, present, and the future, and examine problems and opportunities by comparing their competencies against their competitors'. Finally, resource requirements are analysed along with risk and reward calculations and financial plans are prepared for the conduct of their business operations. Non-Indigenous businesses also operate for 'overcoming the gaps in knowledge that exist throughout society and of transcending the little scarcity problems that confront each one of us' (Kirzner, 1984: 6).

Holism is conceptualised as a sum of the parts. The distinguishing feature of non-Indigenous businesses is that, where economically feasible, it is possible to achieve integration among the individual parts, irrespective of whether they are individual parts within or outside organisations. Integration is achieved either horizontally or vertically depending on the surplus value created. Organisations can perform well in some areas and not others. It is not surprising to find that non-Indigenous businesses do well in the area of financial reporting: 'Several reports have expressed concern with an overemphasis on financial measures of corporations' (Kaplan and Norton, 1996: 38).

Social and environmental aspects are by and large of secondary concern to most non-Indigenous businesses. Therefore, it is not surprising that these businesses are reacting in a well-rehearsed manner to public concerns about environmental issues that have steadily been on the rise since the sixties. Many environmental groups have emerged in the political arena in the form of environmental/green parties as well as in the organisational arena through the rise of non-governmental organisations (NGOs). Increasing demands by citizens and citizen groups has led to unprecedented levels of consumer advocacy, social activism, legislative changes for adopting stricter controls, and requirements to address issues such as greenhouse gas emissions.

The audience for business and, in particular, company performance reports has expanded from the financial stakeholders like shareholders and financiers to include not only regulators, employees, customers, and suppliers but also environmental organisations and the community at large (Vallentine, 2001). Businesses respond to this demand for information in several different ways. The common premises from which businesses make decisions have remained by and large intact. While strategically accommodating calls for better environmental and social outcomes, managers continue to make business decisions based on factors such as whether potential investors and customers will be influenced and attracted to businesses; what the affect on share price might be; and what is the likelihood impact of reducing costs for meeting mandatory requirements. The net effect of all these responses has been to simply extend the 'non-financial aspects of reporting to incorporate environmental and social performance aspects' (Vallentine, 2001: 98).

Management education continues to focus on skills acquisition for preparing business plans, building and working in teams, and conducting market analysis and risk assessments. If we go down this path only the future is rather bleak. We need to recognise the contribution of Indigenous knowledge to a number of factors, including management philosophy and leadership styles, which contribute to decision-making structures and processes.

Understanding the Ethos of Indigenous Businesses

Indigenous businesses are subsets of the economic landscape, which are 'composed of and serve the interests of Indigenous people' (Uphoff, 1996: viii). The concept of holism, and recognition that the sum of the parts is not equal to the whole, is an underlying feature of most Indigenous businesses. Holism is more than an aggregation issue. It relates to the reference point or the benchmarks used: 'Not only was that whole greater than the sum of its parts; none of the parts could be fully understood without reference to the whole' (Ross, 1992: xxvi).

This approach to business has far-reaching implications for management education. By their very existence, Indigenous businesses exhibit interconnectedness with all dimensions; there is no separateness between dimensions and institutions. There is little sense of specialisation because 'it is the interconnectedness of every part which makes a complete description of any one part in isolation an impossible task' (Ross, 1992: xxvi). Another aspect of Indigenous business is an alternate world view based on a premise that people see 'themselves as a part of nature rather than its antagonists, cooperating with their environment rather than attempting to subdue it' (Coombs, 1978: 26).

This is reflected in a business ethos of working with nature. In the modern-day context it is seen as either working with what one has or not working at all, because one has very little to work with, rather than aspiring to what one does not have. It is based on a notion that the environment – be it economic, financial, environmental, social, or cultural – both *provides* and *takes*. It is simultaneously a 'sink' and a 'source'. It is important to recognise that the reference point is neither the individual nor groups of individuals, but the environment itself. It is also why the word 'business' in the Indigenous context is much broader than what is normally understood in the 'mainstream' society. Indigenous business refers to all human activity in relation to the environment. Thus it encompasses all aspects of human involvement in cultural, social, environmental, and economic pursuits. This raises the question of the role of the individual and the implications for developing business strategies. Ross (1992: 39) writes:

> *It was clear that individual success counted for very little, even in the individual's own mind. It was overall success in the enterprise (which had both spiritual and physical dimensions) that was important, for that was what mattered for the group. None of this involved, I suspect, fear*

of failure as a personal embarrassment. People saw their own importance only in terms of the group, including the group's relation with the spiritual world. In fact, they were required to deny themselves the luxury of indulging individual egos. What resulted was a kind of mandatory egalitarianism, supported by all, not only in terms of possessions but in all other respects as well, including criticism, praise, advice-giving, censure and the indulgence of anger, grief or other emotional turmoil.

Various studies have attempted an understanding of rules governing Indigenous conservation techniques. Some of the techniques cited in the literature are seasonal exploitation (Tindale, 1959), limited exploitation (Berndt and Berndt, 1964), and 'protection of over-exploitation of resources by developing systems of taboo, enforcing restrictions of diet on certain social groups and on certain age grades' (Tindale, 1959: 40). The focus of management education therefore is to 'come to terms with their environment, and by a complex of social and economic means they successfully established a balance on which harmony depended' (Coombs, 1978: 28).

The essence of management education in an Indigenous domain is the collapsing of all features of business into one. If one aspect of a business is not functioning adequately, there is an imminent prospect of the collapse of the business itself. Thus the focus of management education is not to perfect and improve an individual component of business, but to address an aggregated picture of the total:

Successful activity, then, required waiting until all of the physical variables promised optimum opportunity, all the preparatory thought promised optimum performance and, just as importantly, all the preparatory spiritual dedication promised optimal cooperation from the spirit world. Only then could it be said that the time was right for acting with the greatest chance of success. (Ross, 1992: 39)

To embrace the lessons of Indigenous business management, management education must focus on adapting to holism without disaggregating individual business components. A strategic framework should be developed from the base of the cultural framework, which addresses the likely and actual impacts of any development affecting land, water, and/or air. The basis of the strategic framework must be deeply rooted in the multi-cultural paradigm, which takes into account economic, social, cultural, and spiritual well-being. As 'financial objectives represent the long-term goal of the organisation' (Kaplan and Norton, 1996: 61), there is a need for closer scrutiny of how to achieve these in the context of Indigenous businesses. A detailed examination of how financial objectives can be incorporated, if at all, into the cultural framework must be a key component of management education.

Cultural Paradigm–Cultural Framework–Strategic Framework

According to this process, strategic planning works from a foundation of core cultural values and a cultural framework, thereby creating and maintaining a durable, sustainable system of planning and assessment (Gray and Tankersley, 2000). While many recognise the importance of land issues in management education, most consider a unidirectional relationship between economic wants, education, and management. Management education is broadly concerned with a version of economic history that is narrated from a perspective of land belonging to people. It builds on:

a story of the way man has worked to satisfy his material wants, in an environment provided by nature but capable of improvement, in an organisation made up of his relations with his fellows, and in a political unit whose head enjoys far-reaching power to aid, control, and appropriate. (Heaton, 1936: 7)

But what are the implications to management education if non-Indigenous people had an Indigenous perspective on issues related to ownership of land? Instead of land belonging to people, what if people considered that they belong to land? They are not the owners but custodians.

This requires us to shift our way of thinking about management education. The management education curriculum needs to incorporate the '10 themes' identified by Christa Walck (2003: 208):

> *As long as there is life, there will be land (transcendence). We can understand land best when we view it in a specific place (locality) and recognise it as a system of interdependencies and networks (community). Although land is resilient, there are limits to what we can do to it and maintain land health (limits). We need to honour those limits and take responsibility for land (morality). We will be more likely to take responsibility for land if we have an emotional connection to it (emotion). If we can see the land's beauty (beauty), we are more likely to connect to it and protect it. We express our emotion and describe the beauty through language (stories). Land is still the source of our livelihoods (work), but the way our social, political, and economic systems function often reduces land health (culture).*

The ownership of land and responsibility for climate change are challenging problems, past and present. For businesses to operate in a sustainable manner they need to be able to react successfully to external demands. Strategic management evolved as a field of inquiry in its own right that was concerned with business development. Mintzberg (1981: 103–4) states that 'configuration' and a 'fit' – that is, the appropriate combination of structural elements and situation – are key to organisational success. The characteristics of organisations fall into natural clusters, or configurations. When these characteristics are mismatched – wrong ones are put together – the organisation does not achieve natural harmony. If managers are to design effective organisations, they need to pay attention to the fit. In designing a better fit, four internal aspects of business – managerial philosophies, management practices, leadership styles, and decision structures – need to be examined.

Managerial Philosophies

Managerial philosophies about interactions between business and the environment are quite distinct in Indigenous and non-Indigenous businesses. Both evolved their managerial philosophies based on learning from direct observation and experiences of interaction with nature. In each case, different world views, systems of knowledge, and approaches to things and experiences can either create or stifle opportunity. By operating predominantly in a cultural framework, Indigenous businesses developed a managerial philosophy of not distinguishing between the environment and the business. Businesses are very much contained in the environment in which they operate. For example, Nugget Coombs (1994: 7) noted that:

> *the model used by Aborigines is a metaphor using the structure of their own family-based society; a metaphor which is extended to comprehend all living creatures and indeed the physical universe itself which to them is also imbued with life, consciousness and a capacity to communicate.*

Their managerial philosophy has largely been one of exercising the precautionary principle and engaging in risk only in non-spiritual activities such as financial matters related with businesses, which sit outside the purview of their strategic framework.

Modern non-Indigenous businesses view themselves as a system that 'not only responds to opportunities but creates them' (Loasby, 1990: 119). Therefore managerial philosophies reflect the underlying nature of risk assessments in all spheres of economic activity and are predominately concerned with possible ways for managing risk.

Non-Indigenous businesses seek to examine their most basic components, quantify and qualify their contributions, and discern patterns of interrelationships among them. As organisational success can only be realised by achieving a proper 'fit' between internal structural elements and external scenarios, different philosophies have emerged to address the manner by which the fit can be created:

> It can adapt continuously to the environment at the expense of internal consistency – that is, steadily redesign its structure to maintain external fit. Or it can maintain internal consistency at the expense of a gradually worsening fit with its environment, at least until the fit becomes so bad that it must undergo sudden structural redesign to achieve a new internally consistent configuration. (Mintzberg, 1981: 115)

The underlying managerial philosophy is to experiment and examine alternate forms of fit and search for a best-fit model through experimentation, learning, and providing compensations for mistakes.

Managerial Practices

Management philosophies manifest themselves in managerial practice. This is most evident in businesses wherein managerial practices based on a philosophy of risk avoidance differ from those that are based on risk taking or those that are risk neutral. Managerial practices dealing with uncertainties need to be examined and incorporated into management training. Indigenous managerial practices:

> tend to emphasise the need to negotiate the content of knowledge in particular environmental and social contexts and see negotiation as a continuing process, never finally finished, but to be activated as required. (Coombs, 1994: 11)

Negotiation is seen as a continuous process in non-Indigenous contexts as well. However, the basic difference between the two is what is being negotiated. Non-Indigenous businesses tend to negotiate rules for appropriating knowledge in contexts and environments, whereas Indigenous businesses tend to negotiate the content of knowledge. As rules may not necessarily be the same in all contexts and environments, and as there is room for renegotiation and experimentation, managerial practices tend to focus attention on rules for negotiation and rules for compliance and retribution once the negotiations are completed for that context and environment.

Interpretations given to the inadequacies of managers in performing their tasks are a case in point. Adopting a non-Indigenous perspective, inadequate compliance is construed as a result of businesses being environmentally 'unfriendly' or 'bad'; and, following on from that, managerial practice would advocate the use of punitive and other retributive measures to 'punish' the wrongdoers. The emphasis is on the doer rather than on what went wrong. An Indigenous perspective on inadequate compliance, on the other hand, elicits a managerial practice of suggesting the need for further 'teaching' and 'training' as well as for 'treating an illness that requires healing'. The emphasis of managerial practice is on attempting to build capacity to rectify what went wrong rather than who should pay how much for the wrong outcomes.

Leadership Styles

Philip Selznick (1957) identified a number of key tasks of an organisational leader. They are:

(1) clear vision and purpose
(2) ability to inspire other members
(3) protect against attacks on the core values and distinct identities
(4) address internal conflicts
(5) manage internal and external relations
(6) recruit 'dependable' staff that will carry out 'rituals' appropriately; and
(7) manage change.

While there are a number of different types of leadership in both Indigenous and non-Indigenous businesses, there are fundamental aspects of leadership that emanate as contrasts based on different management philosophies.

The characteristics of leaders in the Indigenous business context are by and large those of being a transitional leader, called upon to exercise their skills in a specific context. It is therefore neither permanent nor constant to be a leader. Prowess and proven track record in one area does not automatically transfer to other areas. It is about 'exercising leadership skills as the occasion demands, rather than having authority over others given to you for a set of period of time' (Ross, 1996: 58). Moreover, leadership 'is exercised in a way that does not involve chains of hierarchical command and obedience' (Ross, 1996: 58).

The emphasis of leadership is on the tasks to be performed rather than on leading people. Thus leaders are held socially accountable for the tasks they need to perform, and have a fiduciary obligation to those who accorded them temporary and contextual leadership status. The reward for leadership is for individuals and groups to continue to perform similar leadership roles constrained to similar tasks within the same context.

In the non-Indigenous business context, leadership is considered to be a trait that involves having the capacity to lead others using many ways of persuasion. Two important characteristics have been identified that characterise leadership qualities in a non-Indigenous context; 'First, the leader must help the organisation choose the right path-vision, goal, or plan. Second, the leader must help motivate people to follow it' (Brickley et al., 2001: 498). The emphasis is on being a leader among people. It is important to recognise the importance of the tasks leaders are expected to perform: 'The two tasks at the heart of the popular notion of leadership are goal setting and motivating' (Gardner, 1990: 11).

As leadership is not seen as an exclusive domain of a few, the selection is based on proof and proven track record of being able to lead people successfully. Thus leaders are held individually accountable for their actions. They have a legal and moral obligation to perform the tasks of leadership, and the rewards are both of monetary and non-monetary nature. The proven track record of leadership can be transferred from one context to another. There is some suggestion that transformational and transactional leadership styles may help build better Indigenous businesses; however, this would once again emphasise changing the way Indigenous people operate. It would reinforce an approach that favours negotiation and project outcomes over holistic sustainable outcomes. A deeper understanding of holistic Indigenous leadership styles would better serve our purpose.

Leadership qualities are needed that promote better environmental, social, cultural, and financial accountability. Education must take into account this challenge in producing business leaders. We must get away from the structural divide that continues to exist in modern-day discussions wherein Indigenous people are savvier about social, cultural, and environmental aspects of leadership and non-Indigenous are more successful in leadership of the economic aspects. There is a need to incorporate into management education a more holistic approach to managing organisational competencies. We must take heed of Coombs' observation and build a new way of approaching managing leadership education for sustainable development: 'what might be called accountable autonomy [where] societies show structural divisions into complementary pairs, based upon different criteria by which the power to act and responsibility are divided' (Coombs, 1994: 222).

Decision Structures

Decision making seeks to engage individuals and groups of individuals in discussing the underlying conditions for getting involved, with the appropriateness of adopting a particular framework the focal point in decision-making deliberations. Transactions and exchanges are articulated in terms of rights and obligations of people involved in the discussions. For example, Indigenous involvement in employment in the modern economy context is when a decision needs to be made by an individual:

> Employment or other involvement in the Australian economy involves a trade-off between the potential to earn cash and a range of such other Aboriginal activities. In some instances the strength of obligations dictated by Aboriginal custom, for example attendance at ceremonies, are in principle absolute, in many powerful and in almost all at least persuasive. (Coombs et al., 1989: 85–8)

Time, Money, and Risk

In Australia, two distinct types of business have evolved in the contemporary economic landscape of today: Indigenous and non-Indigenous. Management education still focuses on non-Indigenous business practice. Interactions between Indigenous and non-Indigenous business ethos devolve into discussions around time, money, and risk.

Individuals and organisations allocate time and money in pursuing goals – be they economic, environmental, social, or cultural. As businesses make decisions based on past experience (present expectations that will be realised in the future) they are also subject to some form of risk assessment. Therefore time, money, and risk factors are all intertwined to constitute the basic psyche of business. In particular, time is a significant factor in business decisions. Time and timing has both:

> Become a major competitive weapon in today's competition. Being able to respond rapidly and reliably to a customer's request is often the critical skill for obtaining and retaining valuable customers' business. (Kaplan and Norton, 1996: 86)

No matter what type of business one is involved with, it takes time to produce a product:

> A typical product development process ... could have two years of product development followed by five years of sales. So the first success indicator of a product's development process may not appear for three years (the first year after the initial year of sales). (Kaplan and Norton, 1996: 110)

There is a need to recognise that business activities, especially of a financial nature, will predominantly be affected by an inherent characteristic of 'cash now for claims to cash flows in the future' (Bishop et al., 1988: 1). In some instances, linear time is not a critical factor:

> It involves not only taking time to walk through possible courses of action in advance but also preparing one's self emotionally and spiritually for the course chosen. It also requires not acting until there is a conviction that the task can be performed successfully. (Ross, 1992: 38–9).

Time is also interconnected with risk: 'In general, risk management is an overlay, an additional objective that should complement whatever expected return strategy the business unit has chosen' (Kaplan and Norton, 1996: 51). Businesses take decisions based on risk assessment. As a result most businesses 'incorporate explicit risk management objectives into their financial perspective' (Kaplan and Norton, 1996: 60) and regard risk as one of the many variables for businesses to consider in decision making.

For some, risk is not a variable in decision making. Addressing risk *is* the decision. Risk is not an additional objective for a business to consider. It is the objective on which decisions are made. The decision-making process focuses on whether to take the risk, avoid the risk, or be risk neutral and do nothing. Most contemporary businesses make decisions to avoid taking a social, cultural, and environmental risk, but are prone to taking a financial risk for short-term gains – hence the need for shifting the educational paradigm for sustainable development.

Conclusion

Interactions between Indigenous and non-Indigenous managers in the Northern Territory provide clear distinctions between non-Indigenous businesses that operate from an economic framework and Indigenous businesses that have better competencies for adopting a cultural/environmental framework. Geographic isolation, diverse climates and environments, and low population of the NT has meant that Indigenous management practices have 'found a place at the table' regarding local sustainable development projects. Non-Indigenous management techniques do not dominate. The case studies in this chapter illustrate how non-Indigenous management techniques complement and, in some cases, undermine Indigenous project objectives. These and other examples present an excellent learning opportunity. By examining different management philosophies, management practice, leadership styles, and decision-making processes in light of project outcomes we can clearly see where additional competencies are needed. This augurs well for stronger and more successful economic development for the Indigenous businesses and emerging enterprises. Based on lessons from the NT, the opportunity now exists to improve sustainable development through a more holistic approach. With the increasingly fragile state of the environment, it is time that management education focused on building capacity of managers to deliver socially, culturally, environmentally, and economically sustainable outcomes.

References

Barrett, C. (2002). *Intel's Barrett: 'Best is ahead'*. Retrieved from: http://bit.ly/1wDcsVh.

Berndt, R. M. and Berndt, C. H. (1964). *The world of the first Australians*. Sydney: Ure Smith.

Bishop, S. R., Crapp, H. R., and Twite, G. J. (1988). *Corporate finance*. Sydney: Holt, Rinehart and Winston.

Brickley, J. A., Smith Jr. C., and W. and Zimmerman, J. L. (2001). *Managerial economics and organizational architecture*. Boston: McGraw-Hill.

Coombs, H.C., McCann, H., Ross, H., and Williams, N.M. (eds) (1989). *Land of promises: Aborigines and development in the East Kimberley*. Canberra: Australian National University Press.

Coombs, N. (1978). *Kulinma: Listening to Aboriginal Australians*. Canberra: Australian National University Press.

——— (1994). *Aboriginal autonomy: Issues and strategies*. Melbourne: Cambridge University Press.

Delahaye, B. (1992). A theoretical context of management development and education. In B. Smith (ed.), *Management development in Australia*. Sydney: Harcourt Brace Jovanovich, pp. 1–18.

Gardener, J. (1990). *On leadership*. New York: Free Press.

Goodland, R. and Mercier, J.-R. (1999). The evolution of environmental assessment in the World Bank: From 'approval' to results. *Environment Working Paper No. 67*. Washington: World Bank.

———, Daly, H., and El Serafy, S. (1991). Environmentally sustainable economic development: Building on Bruntland. *Environment Working Paper No. 46*. Washington: World Bank.

Gray, R. M. M. and Tankersley, M. L. M. (2000). The cultural paradigm for impact assessment: Te ahua tikak-a mo te papatak-a whakamatauria. *Proceedings of the Indigenous Peoples Section of the International Association for Impact Assessment's 2000 Annual Conference, Indigenous Peoples, Industry and SIA: Moving Towards the Development of Guidelines*. Quebec: 20–23 June.

Handy, C. B. (2002). *The elephant and the flea: Reflections of a reluctant capitalist*. Boston: Harvard Business School Press.

Heaton, H. (1936). *Economic history of Europe*. New York: Harper.

Kaplan, R. S. and Norton, D. P. (1996). *The balanced scorecard*. Boston: Harvard Business School Press.

Kirzner, I. M. (1984). *The role of the entrepreneur in the economic system*. St Leonards, NSW: Centre for Independent Studies.

Loasby, B. J. (1990). Firms, markets and the principle of continuity. In J. K. Whitaker (ed.), *Contemporary essays on Alfred Marshall*. New York: Cambridge University Press, pp. 108–126.

Marshall, A. (1959). *Principles of Economics*. London: Macmillan.

Michailova, S. and Husted K., (2003). Knowledge sharing hostility in Russian firms. *California Management Review*, 45(3), pp. 59–77.

Mintzberg, H. (1981). Organization design: Fashion or fit. *Harvard Business Review*, January–February, pp. 103–116

Muller, H. J. (2000). It takes a community to create an American Indian business and management course. *Journal of Management Education*, 24, pp. 183–212.

Napier, N. K. (2006). Cross-cultural learning and the role of reverse knowledge flows in Vietnam. *International Journal of Cross Cultural Management*, 6(1), pp. 47–64.

———, Harvey, M. and Usui, K. (2008). Management education in emerging economies: The impossible dream? *Journal of Management Education*, 32(6), pp. 792–819.

———, Ngo, M. H., Nguyen, M. T. T., Nguyen, V. T., and Vu, T. V. (2002). Bi-cultural team teaching: experiences from an emerging business school. *Journal of Management Education*, 26(4), pp. 429–448.

———, Vu, D. A., Ngo, M. H., Nguyen, V. T., and Vu T. V. (1997). Reflections on building a business school in Vietnam: Falling into an opportunity for 'making a difference'. *Journal of Management Inquiry*, 6(4), pp. 340–354.

Norgaard, R. B. (1994). *Development betrayed: The end of progress and a co-evolutionary revisioning of the future*. London: Routledge.

Northern Territory Government (NTG). (2008). *Northern Territory Economy Budget Papers 2008–09*. Darwin: Northern Territory Government Press.

Puffer, S. M. (1996). The booming business of business management education. In S.M. Puffer and Associates (eds), *Business and management in Russia*. Cheltenham: Edward Elgar, pp. 96–106.

Rosile, G. A. (2008). Commentary on management education and the base of the pyramid. *Journal of Management Education*, 32(6), pp. 782–791.

Ross, R. (1992). *Dancing with a ghost: Exploring Indian reality*. Markham, ON: Octopus.

——— (1996). *Returning to the teachings: Exploring Aboriginal justice*. Toronto: Penguin.

Saunders, M., Lewis, P., and Thornhill, A. (2007). *Research methods for business students*. London: Prentice Hall.

Selznick, P. (1957). *Leadership in administration*. Evanston: Row, Peterson.

Simon, H. (1991). Organizations and markets. *Journal of Economic Perspectives*, 5(2), pp. 25–44.

Soulsby, A. (2001). The construction of Czech managers' careers. *International Studies of Management and Organization*, 31(2), pp. 48-64.

Swaney, J. A. (1987). Elements of a neo-institutional environmental economics. *Journal of Economic Issues*, 21(4), pp. 1739–1779.

Taylor, J. (2002). Sustainable development: A dubious solution in search of a problem. *Policy Analysis*, 449, pp. 1–49.

Tindale, N. B. (1959). Ecology of primitive man in Australia. In A. Keast, R. L. Crocker, and C. S. Christian (eds), *Biogeography and ecology in Australia*. The Hague: Junk, pp. 36–51.

United Nations (UN). (1992). *Principle 22 of the Rio Declaration: Report of the United Nations Conference on Environment and Development*. Retrieved from: http://bit.ly/1sDJT95.

Uphoff, N. (1996). Preface. In P. Blunt and D.M. Warren (eds), *Indigenous organizations and development*. London: Intermediate Technology.

Vallentine, J. M. B. (2001). *Triple bottom line reporting: A new challenge for accounting education*. Darwin: Northern Territory University.

Von Kopp, B. (1992). The Eastern Europe revolution and education in Czechoslovakia. *Comparative Education Review*, 36(1), pp. 101–113.

Vu, T. V. and Napier, N. K. (2000). Paradoxes in Vietnam and the United States: 'Lessons earned' – part II. *Human Resource Planning*, 23(1), pp. 9–10.

Walck, C. (2003). Using the concept of land to ground the teaching of management and the natural environment. *Journal of Management Education*, 27(2), pp. 205–219.

Williamson, O. E. (1975). *The economic institutions of capitalism*. New York: Free Press.

3

Planning Sustainable Development within Ancestral Domains: Indigenous People's Perceptions in the Philippines

Jayson Ibanez, Beau Austin, and Stephen T. Garnett

Chapter Synopsis

In the Philippines, planning for development of Indigenous lands, including for economic development, is encapsulated in Ancestral Domain Sustainable Development and Protection Plans. The current framework for such plans is based on a template produced by the National Commission on Indigenous Peoples. We asked Indigenous peoples from 10 communities on Mindanao Island what they thought constituted a good planning system for sustainable development within ancestral domains. We asked specifically about the resources and processes that they considered important and what the content of the plan should be. Informants valued participatory and inclusive processes, but also appreciated external financial and technical support. While economic upliftment is strongly desired, there was also a general feeling that, more Indigenous knowledge should be incorporated into the plans, and that means to revitalise Indigenous culture and ways of knowing should form part of plan strategies. Results also reflected a conception of a world that is shared with mystical beings, with the land itself being sacred and at the core of people's lives. A communal ethic of equity, reciprocity and sharing was also considered important. The national planning framework, however, seemed ill-equipped to protect the integrity and sacredness of ancestral domains against mainstream development.

Introduction

With the global recognition of Indigenous peoples' rights to direct their own development, there has been considerable attention given to planning as a platform to exercise Indigenous self-determination (Jojola, 2008, Hibbard et al., 2008, Lane et al., 1997). As Lane (2006: 305) has remarked, 'planning is crucial to fashioning sustainable futures for Indigenous communities'.

Strategically, it can activate the process of empowerment at both individual and community levels (Sadan, 2004), and can help build self-reliant and autonomous communities (Friedmann, 1987). Such theorisation on the strategic value of planning puts emphasis on decentralisation, participation and control of processes and use of knowledge the 'right way'. Equally, while planning is about rights, it is also about the material benefits that would flow once those rights are recognised (Porter, 2004).

In the Philippines, the Indigenous Peoples' Rights Act (IPRA) respects, protects and promotes the Indigenous way of life, including rights to own ancestral domains and priority in the use of the resources they contain. In a country where Indigenous peoples are largely a marginalised 'cultural minority' (Scott, 1982; Rovillos and Morales, 2002; Erni, 2008), the law was seen to 'accelerate the emancipation of our Indigenous peoples from the bondage of inequity' (Bennagen, 2007).

he law also encourages Indigenous people to exercise their rights to create Indigenous plans for natural and human resources development within ancestral domains. As prescribed by s. 2.2. of the *Indigenous Peoples' Rights Act of 1997* (Philippines), the Ancestral Domain Sustainable Development and Protection Plan (ADSDPP) would be the planning framework that will describe (i) the manner by which the domain will be protected; (ii) development programmes in relation to livelihoods, education, self-governance, environment and others; (iii) community policies on how the development programs will be implemented; and (iv) the management system, including how benefits and responsibilities are shared.

As of 2011, at least 156 Certificates of Ancestral Domain Titles (CADT) have been awarded, but only 95 of these had completed plans (IWGIA, 2012). Much of the planning was facilitated by the National Commission on Indigenous Peoples (NCIP). However, the planning process has not satisfied some groups. According to a manifesto sent to Philippine President Aquino in 2010 by Indigenous rights advocates:

> the ADSDPP process itself is defective and is being implemented for compliance sake, instead of coming up with meaningful plans that are identified by Indigenous peoples themselves.

Experts from the International Work Group on Indigenous Affairs also observed that, in practice, the planning system 'puts a heavy emphasis on investment generation at the expense of the protection of rights and culturally appropriate processes' (IWGIA, 2012).

One element lacking from the process appears to have been any consultation with Indigenous peoples themselves about what they consider to be a sound planning process. That is, despite the range of possibilities that planning can achieve and the perceived shortcomings in the government framework, no attempt has yet been made to ask the Indigenous peoples directly, and to understand from their perspective, what constitutes the '*right way*' to plan. It is in this context that the research described here was undertaken to gain an understanding of desired standards for planning from an Indigenous perspective.

Study Area and Research Participants

Mindanao, the second largest island in the Philippine archipelago, is home to at least 30 Indigenous groups (Padilla, 2008). Together they are estimated to comprise 61 per cent of the country's Indigenous population (Cariño, 2010). Eleven of these Indigenous groups gave their voluntary consent to participate in the project. Ten of these groups, representing ethno-linguistic groups in eastern, northern and central Mindanao, joined focus groups and completed questionnaire-based surveys, with the eleventh acting as a pilot group (Figure 3.1 and Table 3.1). Each group had its own ancestral domain and constituted a legally registered Indigenous peoples' organisation (IPO).

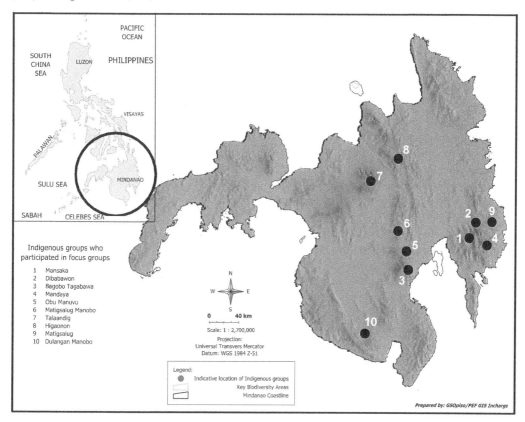

Figure 3.1   **Location of 10 Indigenous ethno-linguistic groups on Mindanao Island who joined the focus groups and questionnaire-based surveys**

Table 3.1   **Indigenous ethno-linguistic groups in Mindanao who participated in the focus groups and questionnaire-based survey**

Indigenous group	Location
Mandaya	Brgy Taocanga, Manay, Davao Oriental
Dibabawon	Montevista, Compostela Valley Province
Obu Manuvu	Brgy Carmen, Baguio District, Davao City
Higaonon	Malaybalay City, Bukidnon
Talaandig	Pangantucan, Bukidnon
Bagobo-Tagabawa	Brgy Sibulan, Toril, Davao City
Manobo-Matigsalug	Brgy Sumalili, Arakan, North Cotabato
Mandaya-Mansaka	Compostela, Compostela Valley Province
Matigsalug	Brgy Salaysay, Marilog District, Davao City
Manobo-Dulangan	Senator Ninoy Aquino, Sultan Kudarat

Our access to the community was through the IPO, which provided the consent on behalf of the community and signed an agreement with the primary researcher. With the exception of one group (Obu Manuvu), all had completed an ancestral domain management plan created using the government's framework.

Methods

Analysis of the planning process followed three steps. First, we identified criteria that defined standards in an Indigenous planning system. Based on a desktop review of theoretical and empirical papers we identified 65 factors considered important for sustainable planning. Those relating to the planning framework we grouped into three broad categories: (i) planning processes, (ii) planning resources, and (iii) plan characteristics (Table 3.2).

Those relating to planning content were classified, for conceptual convenience, using categories derived from the classes of capital identified in the Sustainable Livelihoods Framework – i.e. human, natural, physical/financial, social and cultural (following Chambers and Conway, 1992; Bebbington, 1999).

Second, focus group discussions were held with each of the 10 Indigenous groups to understand, from their perspective, what a good Indigenous planning framework would look like. We first asked participants to discuss, then write down, which planning processes and resources they thought were the most important and what vital community activities, projects or programmes should be in the plan. In this part of the workshop we did not raise the best practice criteria listed in Part 1, to enable them to volunteer top-of-mind concerns about the planning process without being unduly influenced by theoretical considerations.

In Part 3, however, the participants in the focus group discussions were asked to complete a questionnaire that specifically asked them to rank the criteria generated from the literature in Part 1. This was to ensure that the participants had access to the full range of options when considering a plan, bearing in mind what they had discussed collectively earlier the same day. The questionnaire was pre-tested with one Indigenous group and modified before delivery to the other 10 groups. Each focus group discussion participant was asked to choose their top five criteria listed under each of the eight categories in the questionnaire (three for the planning framework, five for the plan content). Each rank was then scored; with five points given to the highest rank and one for the lowest. Items that were not ranked were given a score of zero. Summaries were then derived by taking the total scores for each criterion and averaging across the number of respondents. The average scores for all 10 Indigenous groups were then used to identify which among the literature criteria were thought of as very important.

Results

FOCUS GROUP DISCUSSION PARTICIPANTS

A total of 170 people (average 19 per group) participated in the survey. They were either officers (64 per cent) or members (36 per cent) of the Indigenous organisation. Most of them (85 per cent) had taken part in planning for their ancestral domain. There were more male participants (74 per cent) than females. Many were farmers (76 per cent), while the rest were engaged in a variety of trades. The estimated monthly cash income among 149 participants ranged from $19 to $130 (21 did not declare their monthly income).

Table 3.2   Attributes that define sound Indigenous planning systems

Attributes	Details	References
Important Planning Processes		
Need for planning to be understood and recognised	Participants understand and agree on why a plan is being prepared and why it is important	Umemoto, 2001; Walsh and Mitchell, 2002; Hill, 2011
Local leaders involved	Planning involves Indigenous community leaders	Baum, 1999; Esquimaux and Calliou, 2010; Hill, 2011
Strong cooperation	The people collectively creating the plan and cooperating well	Baum, 1999; Beard, 2003; Hill, 2011
Inclusive planning	Many members of the community are participating, including women, elders and young people	Friedmann, 1987; Lane et al., 1997; Lane and Hibbard, 2005; Sobrevila, 2008; United Nations, 2008; Hill, 2011
Planners are culturally sensitive	Non-Indigenous planners understand and respect the local culture	Lertzman, 1999; Umemoto, 2001; Lertzman and Vredenburg, 2005; Porter, 2004; Hill, 2011
Community-based mapping	Community is helping with identifying and mapping out the resources within the ancestral domain	Letrzman, 1999; Kwaku Kyem, 2000; Chapin et al., 2005; Sobrevila, 2008
Oral traditions valued	Indigenous narratives and stories valued as important sources of planning information	Kliger and Cosgrove, 1999; Lertzman, 1999; Sandercock, 2003; Esquimaux and Calliou, 2010
Sound monitoring and feedback procedures	There is regular feedback on how plan implementation is progressing	Esquimaux and Calliou, 2010; Lertzman, 1999
Important Planning Resources		
Indigenous facilitators	Planning facilitated by Indigenous individuals or organisations from within the community	Umemoto, 2001; Walsh and Mitchell, 2002; Hill, 2011
Non-Indigenous planners	Planning facilitated and plan put together by experienced and culturally sensitive non-Indigenous planners	Friedmann, 1989; Sadan, 2004; Walsh and Mitchell, 2002; Moran, 2004; Lane, 2006; Matunga, 2006; Porter, 2004; Hill, 2011
Adequate financial resources	Community has access to sufficient money to support the planning process	Agrawal and Gibson, 1999; Walsh and Mitchell, 2002; Esquimaux and Calliou, 2010
Planning database	A database of the community's resources created and stored on a computer	Lane et al., 1997; Lane, 2006
External sources of planning information	Participants having enough information from outside (e.g. demographic, socio-economic and biological information) for planning	Walsh and Mitchell, 2002; Hill, 2011
Adequate time	Participants have enough time to devote to planning	Walsh and Mitchell, 2002; Zaferatos, 2004; Sobrevila, 2008
Adequate technical assistance	Technical assistance from outside the community (e.g. GIS-based mapping, resource inventories, planning facilitation)	Agrawal and Gibson, 1999; Walsh and Mitchell, 2002; Hill, 2011

Table 3.2   Attributes that define sound Indigenous planning systems (*concluded*)

Attributes	Details	References
Government planning system or framework	Clear planning system or guides in the legislation	Porter, 2004; Lane, 2002; Lane, 2006
Government support	Support from government agency concerned with Indigenous affairs	Zaferatos, 2004; Berke et al., 2002; Lane, 2002; Hill, 2011; Lane and Hibbard, 2005
Local governments	Support from local governments	Agrawal and Gibson, 1999; Zaferatos, 2004; Berke et al., 2002; Erni, 2005
Indigenous communities	Support from neighbouring Indigenous communities	Mason and Beard 2008; Hill, 2011
NGOs	Assistance from non-governmental organisations	Agrawal and Gibson, 1999; Emery, 2000; Lane, 2002; Erni, 2005; Hill, 2011
Local leaders	Support from non-Indigenous, local political leaders	Agrawal and Gibson, 1999; Zaferatos, 2004; Erni, 2005
Non-Indigenous stakeholders	Support from non-Indigenous stakeholders	Karjala et al., 2003; Hill, 2011
Important Plan Characteristics		
Clear vision	An overall vision of what the plan will try to achieve	Jojola, 2008; Esquimaux and Calliou, 2010; Hill et al., 2011
Indigenous aspirations (goals) articulated	Plan clearly describes aspirations that are still bound by the national laws to which Indigenous laws are subservient	Lane et al., 1997; Lane, 2006; Hibbard et al., 2008
Clear objectives	Objectives are clear and measurable	Lane et al., 1997; Walsh and Mitchell, 2002; Matunga, 2006; Hill, 2011
Clear actions	The specific steps to meet the objectives are clearly described	Walsh and Mitchell, 2002; Matunga, 2006; Hill, 2011;
Priority actions	Actions prioritised by the participants and to be implemented by them identified in the plan	Walsh and Mitchell, 2002; Natcher and Hickey, 2002; Hill, 2011
Factual basis	Clear what data were used as foundations of the plan	Karjala et al., 2003; Karjala and Dewhurst, 2003
Monitoring indicators	Culturally appropriate indicators of how well plan implementation is doing identified and described	Karjala and Dewhurst, 2003; Karjala et al., 2003, Sobrevila, 2008; Hill et al., 2011
Performance monitoring procedures	The procedures to know whether the plan is meeting its objectives are clearly described	Lane, 2002; Esquimaux and Calliou, 2010; Hill et al., 2011
Plan updating procedures	Clear steps for modifying the plan if conditions change	Karjala et al., 2003; Sherry et al., 2005

PLANNING ATTRIBUTES

Iterative analysis of planning literature identified 29 elements of a planning framework that were thought to be important for sound Indigenous planning, including 8 planning processes, 12 categories of planning resource and 9 plan characteristics (see Table 3.2). Each of these could be justified by literature, and thus be the basis for ranking by focus group discussion participants in terms of what they considered important for their planning.

Elements identified from the literature as being important facets of plan content were then categorised into five of the categories characterised as capitals under the Sustainable Livelihoods Framework (Scoones, 1998; Bebbington, 1999; see Table 3.3). Of these, eight were categorised as developing human capital; six as retaining natural capital; six as improving economic/financial capital;[1] five as enhancing social capital; and nine as reinforcing cultural capital (considered here as separate from social capital).

Table 3.3   Attributes that define the contents of sound Indigenous plans

Attributes	Details	References
Human		
Eradicate hunger and deprivation	Actions to eliminate hunger and deprivation	Bebbington, 1999; McNeish and Eversole, 2005; Tebtebba, 2008; Mason and Beard, 2008; Asadi et al., 2008
Strengthening capacity for environmental management	A strategy for enhancing capacity for land and resource management	Lertzman, 1999; O'Faircheallaigh and Corbett, 2005; Suchet-Pearson and Howitt, 2010
Child health	Actions to reduce child mortality	Stephens et al., 2006; Tebtebba, 2008; United Nations, 2008; United Nations Declaration on the Rights of Indigenous Peoples, 2008
Maternal health	Actions to improve maternal health	Stephens et al., 2006; Gracey and King, 2009; Tebtebba, 2008; United Nations, 2008
Human population	A strategy to regulate human population	De Sherbinin et al., 2008; *Bremner et al., 2010*
Formal education	A strategy to improve access to formal education	Rovillos and Morales, 2002; Tebtebba, 2008; United Nations, 2008; Friedmann, 2011
Adult literacy	A strategy to improve adult literacy	Rao and Robinson-Pant, 2006; Tebtebba, 2008
Gender concerns	Actions that promote gender equality and women's empowerment	Tebtebba, 2008; Krook and True, 2012
Natural		
Local tenure map	A map of who has current use rights (titled or usufructory) over which piece of land	Alcorn, 2000; Roth, 2009; Sletto, 2009
Land use map	A map of land-cover types and its uses	Alcorn, 2000; Walsh and Mitchell, 2002; Chapin et al., 2005; Roth, 2009

---

1   Other authors identified 'physical capital' or the infrastructures and tools and technology that support rural livelihood as a separate category of livelihood asset (Carney, 1998, 2003). In this work, we followed Scoones (1998) who treated physical capital as being part of economic/financial capital.

Table 3.3   Attributes that define the contents of sound Indigenous plans

Attributes	Details	References
Forest restoration	Strategies and actions that restore forest health within Indigenous territories	Lertzman, 1999; Sunderlin et al., 2005
Biodiversity conservation	Biodiversity conservation is part of the plan	Sanderson and Redford, 2003; Adams et al., 2004; Tebtebba, 2008; Pretty et al., 2009; Rands et al., 2010
Monitoring species and management indicators	A system in place to monitor indicators of species and their management	Lertzman, 1999; Natcher and Hickey, 2002; Adam and Kneeshaw, 2011
Sustainable water system	A programme to ensure sustainable access to safe drinking water	Rovillos and Morales, 2002; Tebtebba, 2008; Friedmann, 2011
Financial/Economic		
Farming support	Financial and technological support to farming	Scoones, 1998; Weinberger and Lumpkin, 2007
Off-farm livelihood support	Financial and technological support to off-farm livelihood (paid work or self-employment)	Scoones, 1998; De Janvry and Sadoulet, 2001; Altman, 2007; Jonasson and Helfand, 2010
Employment	Wages from regular employment	Scoones, 1998; De Janvry and Sadoulet, 2001; Jonasson and Helfand, 2010
Co-managed corporate ventures	Plan describes the terms of co-managed corporate ventures	Lertzman, 1999; Lertzman and Vredenburg, 2005; Gibson and O'Faircheallaigh, 2010
Joint ventures following the plan	Plan policy that joint ventures incorporate plan actions into their own operations	Gibson and O'Faircheallaigh, 2010
Rules for benefit-sharing	Rules for distributing benefits from commercial ventures on the ancestral estate	Botes and van Rensburg, 2000; Gibson and O'Faircheallaigh, 2010; O'Faircheallaigh, 2011; Hill, 2011; Hill et al., 2011
Social Capital		
Clear who makes decisions about what	Clear process of decision-making: authorities identified and their roles and responsibilities defined	Sadan, 1997; Agrawal and Gibson, 1999; Colchester, 2000; Zaferatos, 2004b; Hill, 2011
Community institutions that enforce plan actions	Local institutions such as customary laws and governance units are identified and invoked throughout the plan	Agrawal and Gibson, 1999; Moran, 2004; Berkes, 2008; Lertzman and Vredenburg, 2005; Jojola, 2008; Sobrevila, 2008; Esquimaux and Calliou, 2010
Policies against corruption	There is a clear description of policies to prevent malpractice and corruption by decision-makers and leaders	Robbins, 2000; Corbridge and Kumar, 2002; Esquimaux and Calliou, 2010
Activities that build unity	Community activities that foster community cohesion	Toomey, 2011; Walsh and Mitchell, 2002; Hill, 2011
Strategies that enhance networks and partnerships	Ways to build meaningful partnerships with both Indigenous and non-Indigenous entities	Esquimaux and Calliou, 2010; Hill, 2011

Table 3.3   Attributes that define the contents of sound Indigenous plans (*concluded*)

Attributes	Details	References
Cultural Capital		
Indigenous worldview described	Belief about the relationship between people, land, resources and the cosmos	Eketone, 2006; Jojola, 2008; Hibbard et al., 2008; Ross et al., 2011
The plan reflects Indigenous worldview and vision	Plan goals and actions are consistent with the Indigenous worldview and vision for the future	Jojola, 2008; Hibbard et al., 2008; Ross et al., 2011; Hill, 2011
Indigenous issues prioritised	Plan addresses cultural issues of particular importance to Indigenous people	Zaferatos, 2004; Lertzman and Vredenburg, 2005; Eketone, 2006; Esquimaux and Calliou, 2010; Ross et al., 2011
Indigenous ecological knowledge described	Empirical Indigenous knowledge of the land and how to manage it is described in the plan	Berkes, 2008; Ross et al., 2011
Plan engages IEK	Empirical Indigenous knowledge of the land and how to manage it being reflected in plan actions	Lertzman, 1999; Corburn, 2003; Campbell and Vainio-Matilla, 2003; Berkes, 2008; Sherry et al., 2005
Indigenous knowledge systems and practices used	Indigenous knowledge systems and practices reflected in the plan	Hibbard et al., 2008; Sandercock, 2003; Porter, 2006; Jojola, 2008; Ross et al., 2011
Ways of passing on Indigenous culture	Ways of passing on traditional culture and knowledge being built into the plan	Walsh and Mitchell, 2002; Tebtebba, 2008; Ross et al., 2011
Sites of cultural values accounted for	Mapping and description of important cultural sites (including why important) and how they should be managed	Lertzman, 1999; Stephenson, 2008
Land tenure traditions described	Traditions on how land is inherited	Jojola, 2008; Matunga, 2006

FOCUS GROUP PLANNING PRIORITIES

The views of the Indigenous groups on planning processes expressed in the focus group discussions are summarised in Figure 3.2a. Of the 18 processes listed by participants, 8 out of 10 Indigenous groups valued (i) 'adequate community consultation'. Other processes valued were (ii) that the 'final plan approval should be based on a consensus by Indigenous leaders or elders', and (iii) there is enough representation from social groups such as youth, women and elders. Religious rituals (iv) during important plan phases were also seen as important; and, finally, (v) that members of the community are united during planning, including being patient and respectful of other people's views.

Out of eight possible important planning resources, all except two groups listed money as important. Six groups believed that assistance from outside is necessary and that a group or organisation based in the community should lead the planning. A quarter of the Indigenous groups thought that skilled Indigenous facilitators are also important.

Out of the 22 categories used to characterise plans, livelihood programmes such as sustainable agriculture and agro-forestry top the list. This was followed by activities/projects that restored

Planning process

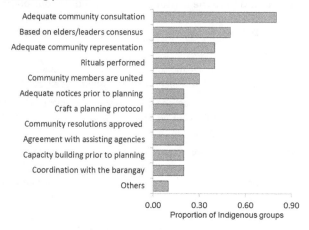

Plan characteristics

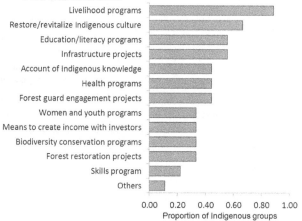

Planning resources

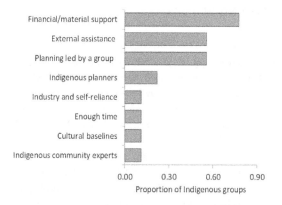

Figure 3.2   Proportion of Indigenous groups in Mindanao, Philippines, listing planning framework elements (processes, resources, and characteristics) as important for their own Indigenous planning (n=10)

Note: A barangay is the smallest administrative division in the Philippines, comprising territorial enclaves called sitios.

Indigenous culture. Education for both young and adults and infrastructure projects such as roads, tribal halls and mini hydro-electric facilities followed. Some groups wanted accounts of Indigenous culture and knowledge in the plan as well as health programmes and the engagement of forest guards.

RANKING OF STANDARDS FOR 'BEST PRACTICE'

The results for ranking generally corroborated the results of the focus group discussions (see Figure 3.3). In ranking planning processes for example, three of the four factors that received the highest mean scores – (i) the involvement of leaders (#2, based on elders and leaders consensus); (ii) cooperation among participants (#5, participants are united); and (iii) many are participating (#3, adequate representation) – are the same factors that were listed by most groups in the focus group discussions. The second most important process from the literature, 'participants understand plan purpose and value', was not listed during focus group discussions but is actually a most likely outcome of 'adequate community consultations' which topped the focus group discussion list.

The focus group discussions and ranking results for planning resources were also similar. Money or financial resources topped both exercises. The focus group discussions listed external assistance as the second most important resource, which in the ranking appeared to be the National Commission on Indigenous Peoples (NCIP). There was one important process listed in the focus group discussions that was absent in the literature list: that planning should be led by a group from within the Indigenous community.

With respect to the characteristics of a plan, the articulation of a vision, clear objectives and clear steps to meet objectives were ranked the highest. A description of the database or what is normally referred to as situationer/context was also ranked as an important section of the plan.

Of the factors aimed at strengthening human capital, programmes that reduce poverty and hunger were ranked highest, followed closely by education on how to manage land and resources. Formal education and maternal health were also highly ranked.

Of the seven important natural capitals that should be in a plan, biodiversity conservation and ecosystem restoration were ranked the highest, followed by a map of individual estates and systems for monitoring species and management.

The three most important features of a plan with respect to economic growth were livelihood diversification, agricultural intensification and off-farm employment.[2] Not surprisingly, livelihoods also topped the list of important plan content during the focus group discussions. The other three highly ranked elements for economic capital related to attracting but governing joint ventures.

When considering the contributions a plan might make to improving social capital, it was considered important to respondents that the plan make explicit mention of who makes decisions about what. The high ranking for strategies in the plan for reducing corruption may reflect fund mismanagement in the past. Also important was the role for community institutions such as traditional community leaders and organisations in plan implementation.

The articulation of Indigenous worldviews in the plans was considered the most important element in a plan for cultural capital. The use of Indigenous ecological knowledge was valued more than specific traditions such as how land is inherited and how traditional sites are managed (see Figure 3.4).

---

2   None of the best practice planning features identified from the literature could be categorised as physical capital.

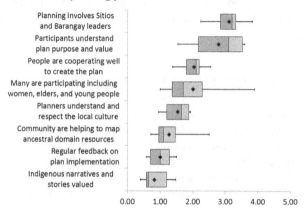

Ranks of planning processes

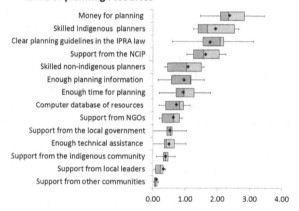

Ranks of planning resources

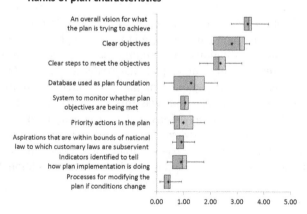

Ranks of plan characteristics

Figure 3.3   Ranking of the importance of planning framework attributes (processes, resources, characteristics) by respondents from 10 Indigenous groups in Mindanao, Philippines (n=170; ranks 1–5; mean, SE, range, and median)

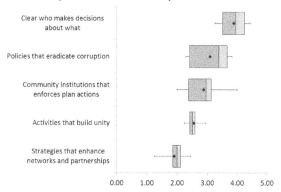

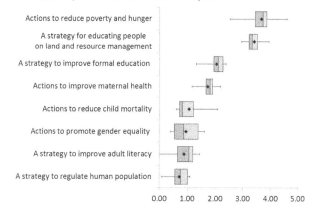

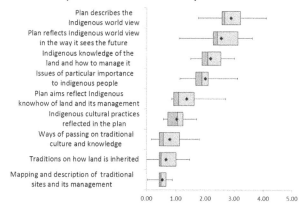

Figure 3.4   **Ranking of the importance of planning content elements by participants from 10 Indigenous groups in Mindanao, Philippines (n=170; ranks 1–5; mean, SE, range, and median) classified by categories of the Sustainable Livelihoods Framework**

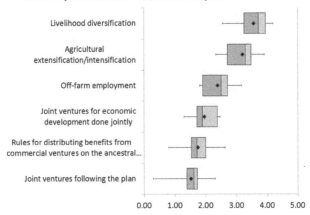

Ranks of plan contents – Economic Capital

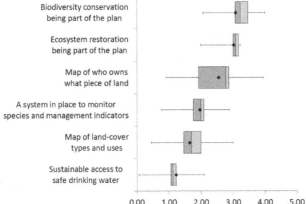

Ranks of plan contents – Natural Capital

Figure 3.4   **Ranking of the importance of planning content elements by participants from 10 Indigenous groups in Mindanao, Philippines (n=170; ranks 1–5; mean, SE, range, and median) classified by categories of the Sustainable Livelihoods Framework (*concluded*)**

Combined Results

Combining the results from the focus group discussions and ranking, eight planning processes were most valued (see Table 3. 4).

Nearly all groups listed 'adequate community consultation' as an important planning process, while a 'need for planning understood and recognised' topped the ranking. In both processes, reaching community consensus appeared to be a prime indicator. Focus groups also valued 'adequate preparation', which covered a range of activities such as carefully looking at planning needs and making sure they are available, identifying who is going to do what, and organising planning baselines. Focus groups and ranking results agreed that the 'role of leaders and/or elders' as sources of planning wisdom and decisions is vital and should be acknowledged. Participation by all social groups in the community (inclusive participation) was in the top three in the ranking.

Table 3.4 Desired attributes of a good Indigenous planning process based on focus group discussions and participant ranking and scoring of best practice standards derived from the literature

Attributes	Description
Adequate community consultation	Enough meetings and discussions until a consensus is reached. Also include enough community assemblies, adequate discussion of important issues, and clan-based consultations
Need for planning understood and recognised	Participants understand and agree on why a plan was being prepared and why it is important
Adequate preparation	Adequate preparation prior to planning, including evaluating needs, tasking and an inventory of ancestral domain resources
Role of elders and/or leaders respected	Indigenous leaders and elders are involved and their important role during planning is acknowledged and respected
Inclusive planning	Many members of the community are participating, including women, elders and young people
Participants united and cooperating	Planning partners are united and are patient and respectful of other people's views, including those of the women and the youth
Indigenous rituals	Holding of Indigenous rituals during important phases of planning
Planners being culturally sensitive	Non-Indigenous planners understanding and respecting the local culture

Both procedures also showed that values of 'unity and cooperation' amongst participants as well as with non-Indigenous facilitators are considered key to planning success. 'Indigenous rituals' to secure spiritual consent and guidance during important phases of planning and 'non-Indigenous planners being culturally sensitive' completed the top five for focus groups and ranking, respectively.

Out of eight important planning resources, money was number one in both group and ranking procedures (see Table 3.5). Both also showed that 'Indigenous facilitators' or 'community planners' are desired. The national government (through its agencies) was ranked as an important external resource, and the focus groups added NGOs and local government. There is an apparent preference for a government-endorsed planning framework as it scored third highest in the ranking. Outsider-generated information about the community and the ancestral domain as planning baselines ranked fifth. Focus groups added the knowledge and expertise of traditional leaders and elders as well as the unique skills held by members as another vital resource. Assistance from non-Indigenous planners was also appreciated. Lastly, adequate time allotted for planning came out as an important factor in both procedures.

With respect to the general (strategic) content of an Indigenous plan, the articulation of a vision, clear objectives and clear steps to meet objectives were ranked the highest. A description of the database, or what is normally referred to in strategic plan templates as 'situationer' or 'context', was also ranked as an important section of the plan. Monitoring procedures to be used to see if plan implementation is achieving its intended targets were also desired.

Table 3.5   **Desired planning resources based on focus group discussions and participant ranking and scoring of best practice standards derived from the literature**

Attributes	Description
Financial resources	Community has access to sufficient money to support planning
Indigenous facilitators	Planning facilitated by Indigenous individuals, groups or organisations from within the community
External partners	Support from external partners such as NGOs, government agencies and local government
Government planning system or framework	Clear planning system or guides in the legislation
External sources of planning information	Participants having enough information from outside (e.g. demographic, socio-economic and biological) for planning
Indigenous experts	Elders, chiefs and technical persons from the village who can articulate the philosophy, history, culture and resources of the community
Adequate time	Participants are given enough time to devote to planning
Non-Indigenous planners	Experienced and culturally sensitive non-Indigenous planners helping out with facilitation and putting together the plan

A total of 20 themes for plan content were summarised from focus groups, and those common in many groups were combined with high-ranking literature criteria to obtain a shorter list of very important plan contents (see Figure 3.5).

For actions that build human capital, means to eradicate hunger topped the ranking. They also wanted projects that enhance Indigenous skills to manage natural resources, and also education assistance (both formal and non-formal), to benefit the youth and unschooled adults, respectively. Projects that relate to reproductive health and those that reduce child malnutrition and mortality were also desired. Finally, gender-related concerns such as female-directed projects that improve their well-being were prioritised, including freedom from violence and exploitation.

With respect to enhancing the natural resource stock (natural capital), efforts to conserve biodiversity and restore forests were prioritised. Mapping of who owns what land within the ancestral domain (local tenure) was also desired. Although this appears to contradict the idea of communal tenure espoused by IPRA, ancestral domains in reality are indeed parcelled, with each piece of land having definite owners (individual, family or clan) whose tenure rights are recognised and respected. A system to monitor success indicators of species and their management was also valued, as was the 'engagement of Indigenous guards' who would do forest patrols and monitoring.

Actions that 'strengthen Indigenous culture and identity' (cultural capital) were very much valued by 6 out of 10 Indigenous groups. Based on rankings, respondents wanted a collective conception of their relationship with their environment (worldview) written into plans. Next, they wanted plan goals and actions that are consistent with their Indigenous worldview and vision for the future. They also wanted the plan to address cultural issues that are of particular significance to them. A description of their own (Indigenous) ecological knowledge (or IEK) pertinent to ancestral domain management was desired, and they wanted the documented IEK to be incorporated into plan implementation.

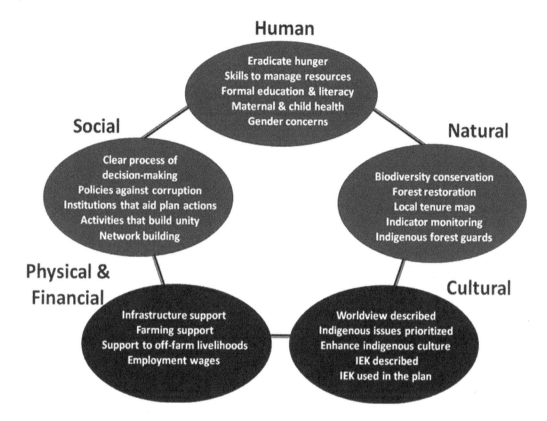

Figure 3.5   **Important elements of Indigenous plans based on focus group discussions and ranking of literature criteria. Elements are grouped according to the five Sustainable Livelihood Frameworks capitals**

Sources: Chambers and Conway, 1992; Bebbington, 1999.

As for physical and financial capital, the focus groups listed projects that fell under 'infrastructure support': farm-to-market roads, village halls, rural electrification projects, day care and health centres and a few more. The most desired financial asset-building items on the plan were financial and technological support for farming and off-farm enterprises. Full-time or part-time employment that adds to household wages was also valued.

Out of five literature criteria for augmenting community 'social capital', ranking showed that a 'clear process of decision-making' was perceived as a very important part of the plan. In particular, the plan must mention who makes decisions about what, and how decisions are to be made. Outlining policies that prevent decision-makers from being corrupt was second, apparently to guard against what Colchester (1994) called 'Lairdism' – the cooptation, corruption and undemocratic tendency of some Indigenous leaders (Li, 2002). They also valued an account of local institutions (i.e. customary laws, traditional governance structure) in the plan which would be invoked when carrying out plan actions. In addition, focus groups valued activities that foster village unity and those that build external networks: assets that O'Brien et al. (2005) have referred to as 'bridging' and 'bonding' social capital, respectively.

Discussion

PARTICIPATORY PLANNING

There is a strong yearning for a nuanced form of participatory planning with/by Indigenous peoples. Many of the desired attributes of a planning process – such as adequate community consultations, need for planning to be adequately understood and recognised, inclusive planning, adequate time for planning and participants united and cooperating – are all essential elements of participatory or collaborative planning. But what is participatory planning? With roots in the theory of participatory democracy (Freire, 1970; Chambers and Conway, 1992), participatory planning, according to Blahna and Shepard, is when a 'broad range of interests is represented and participants are integrally involved throughout the planning processes, from initiation through decision implementation, and monitoring' (as cited by Moote et al., 1997). In the context of rural development, planning is said to be participatory when all local community members participate and decide in meetings and workshops and that particular attention is paid to include marginalised and disadvantaged groups (Chambers, 1997). Opportunity therefore is given to all and individuals participate as citizens, not representatives (Allmendiger, 2009), allowing all voices to be heard (Irazabal, 2009).

It is clear in the NCIP guidelines for ADSDPP formulation that participatory planning is one of the principles underpinning the process (NCIP, 2004). However, just as Bennagen (2007) said of the IPRA law in general, the process has been amended in practice, more often in the breach. Contrary to direct participation that is the goal of a theoretical conception of planning that uses a participatory democracy lens, a close inspection of contemporary ADSDPP samples shows that planning participation appears to be only for a privileged few.

Based on a recent analysis of a sample of plans (Ibanez, 2014), the typical approach to ADSDPP formulation for ancestral domains has been to invite just a few people from each of the many villages to participate and plan on behalf of the community at centralised meetings. Although this may sound efficient in terms of time and resources, it risks potential disadvantages. First, chosen representatives may not necessarily represent community interests, especially if no village-level planning has occurred. Second, representative-based planning can be biased towards the interests of more confident Indigenous elites rather than the politically vulnerable, shy and less confident sectors or villages. Lastly, it is prone to political patronage where only government and/ or federation allies are allowed to participate. In short, centralised and unified planning can further obscure the voices of the already disenfranchised Indigenous sectors.

The representative-based planning approach seems to arise from an assumption that Indigenous communities represent a monolithic, homogenous group (Gatmaytan and Dagondon, 2004). However, although Indigenous communities may appear culturally and ethnically homogenous and share the same language, they represent multiple interests split along social divides (Gatmaytan and Dagondon, 2004; Agrawal and Gibson, 1999; Natcher and Hickey, 2002; Li 2002). Between communities, some may prefer cultural isolation while others assimilation; some may desire corporate investment while others prefer localised production and self-sufficiency. Such disparate views on which particular development path is desirable can also be true for individuals of the same villages who tend to espouse divergent perspectives and interests (Li, 2002; Theriault, 2011). Agrawal and Gibson (1999) called this the politics of the local, and results in the voices of sub-groups being excluded in representative-based centralised planning, running the risk of further marginalising those who could already be internally disenfranchised.

The above discussion about the centrality of participatory approaches also illustrates the level with which Indigenous planning can be undertaken in the Philippines. Given a requirement for direct and inclusive participation, village-level planning appears to be optimal. It also seems consistent with descriptions of traditional governance systems for ancestral domains: based on available Philippine ethnographies, the locus of political functions among Indigenous peoples seems always to have been the village level. Among the nineteenth-century Manuvus (Davao City/ North Cotabato Manobo) for example, Manuel (1973) wrote that 'there is no group ever conceived larger than the village organization'.[3] He also added that villages in the Manobo landscape are politically independent units, with political unification being more of an (infrequent) exception rather than the rule. Scott (1982: 40) similarly observed that Indigenous villages of Luzon during the early periods of colonisation were: 'not politically unified. They were all composed of autonomous communities whose relations with each other, whether of the same language or different, varied from isolation to cooperation or conflict according to circumstances.' Bennagen (2007: 185) also commented on this functional autonomy when he said that 'the Indigenous communities in what later became as the Philippines were independent, self-determining communities with minimum social interactions with other groups'.

PLANNING AND EXTERNAL SUPPORT

Another theme that emerged both in focus groups and the ranking exercise was a desire for support from government and other external partners. Unlike Indigenous movements of the north that often had a secessionist undertone (Engle, 2010), respondent perceptions in Mindanao about the role of government appears consistent with an internal self-determination policy (self-determination within the framework of the state constitution) for Indigenous peoples in the Philippines. These perceptions, however, may change in the light of actual performance by government. A planning guide has been provided by the state through NCIP Administrative Order No. 1 of 2004, which emphasises that:

> The formulation of the ADSDPP shall primarily be guided by the principle of self-determination, participatory planning and cultural integrity with the main objective of ensuring the sustainable development and protection of ancestral domain resources and the enforcement of the rights of ICCs/IPs to their ancestral domain as well as their rights as a people and as citizens. (NCIP 2004: 6)

However, such principles appear not to have been followed in many cases, including by the International Child Development Programme (ICDP) (Bennagen, 2007; Sanz, 2007; Gatmaytan, 2007).

The state ideally has much to offer with respect to addressing the desired planning resources such as *financial assistance*, *planning information*, and *non-Indigenous planners*, among others. As the Philippines is a welfare state, the government remains nominally accountable for providing basic services to its Indigenous citizens, including providing adequate support and incentives to the statutory ADSDPP process. But there are many risks in pinning hopes on a budget-deprived government agency with a very limited pool of competent staff (IWGIA, 2012).[4] Parochialism (if

---

3   Manuel (1973) describes a Manobo village as comprising at most 50 families organised under a multiple authority system of chiefs (*Datus*), assistants (*Panadsang*), warriors (*Baganis*), judges (*Ta:usay*), arbiters (*Melaw*), and shaman/priests (*Walian*), all of whom wield the same powers and authority. Each village also has corporate ownership of a distinct territory bounded from its neighbours by natural landmarks (rivers or mountain ridges). Resource use within a territory is exclusive to village members, and they need not seek consent from village authorities.

4   As an example of how limited NCIP funding is, the Director of the Ancestral Domains Office was quoted in a conference proceeding by the Asian Indigenous and Tribal People's Network (2008) as saying that there were 'no funds to be used by Legal Officers/Regional Hearing Officers' for cases related to ancestral domain rights of indigenous peoples.

not total indifference) among the ranks of some regional NCIP offices has also been a problem. For example, NGOs have been providing planning resources and assistance to many Indigenous communities, but some of these NGO-assisted plans have not been officially recognised because they were supported by NGOs critical of the NCIP (IWGIA, 2012).

Indeed, many NGOs have filled the gap left by government in providing many social services (David, 1998; Clarke, 1998), including, as mentioned earlier, help with ancestral domain planning. This might have resulted from an increasing adoption of neo-liberal approaches to social development whereby the government has selectively withdrawn from forms of social service provision through policy shifts that encourage 'self-regulation' where individuals and communities 'assume responsibility for their own actions – and failures' (Bryant, 2002). But NGO interventions in Indigenous affairs are not necessarily unproblematic. According to Bryant (2002), for instance, NGO contributions to social change may be 'more ambiguous than is often thought' as they 'appear to serve a fundamentally proactive role in the assertion of political mechanisms of control and surveillance (by the government), sometimes in spite of deeply held individual and organizational beliefs to the contrary in the NGO sector'. In the same vein, Hirtz (2003) observes that rather than an 'understanding of themselves in their differences in norms, lifestyles, and practices (is) appropriately distinguished and (administrativelyand legally) secured', NGOs that mirror a 'phenomenon of the western world' force Indigenous groups to express and portray themselves 'in direct contradiction to the social norms of Indigenous peoples'. Nevertheless, despite these criticisms of NGO interventions, NGOs have played a central role in international, national and local recognition of and action towards alleviating the plight of the Indigenous poor. Both government and NGOs, however, need to recognise the centrality of Indigenous ownership of the planning process to which they are providing assistance.

PLANNING AND INDIGENOUS KNOWLEDGE SYSTEMS

Respondent recognition of the critical role of Indigenous knowledge holders/stewards during planning was not unexpected. Elders, chiefs and religious leaders are the holders of Indigenous knowledge which, until the advent of formal education and knowledge codification, was transmitted across generations though oral communication and actual performance. Documentation of contemporary Indigenous governance systems shows that elders and cultural leaders continue to perform leadership functions in rural Indigenous villages, such as in settling land and civil disputes and petty crimes using customary laws, and in administering community feasts and religious ceremonies or rituals (Buendia et al., 2006).

However, in contrast to these locally respected village leaders, some politically connected Indigenous elites appear to have found the group rights (Indigenous self-determination) policy of the state beneficial to securing their personal, sometimes at the expense of collective, interests. Small and remote Indigenous communities that are mostly poor by mainstream standards and with little opportunity for formal education – the *minorities within the minorities* – are particularly vulnerable to these self-interested elites. Post-IPRA arrangements of unified, federated and representative-based governance of ancestral domains show evidence of these undemocratic tendencies among some politically powerful chieftains and their advantage over internal minorities. With ample access to the political and economic (and in some cases, military) machineries of the state, these *'supreme'* chiefs tend to exercise political power arbitrarily and broker projects out of self-interest to maintain power and accumulate material wealth (Gatmaytan, 2007; Sanz, 2007). The seemingly growing incidence of coercive power and corruption among powerful chiefs gave rise to the pejorative term 'tribal dealers' (Bennagen, 2007), a satirical anagram of 'tribal leaders'.

Indeed, it seems that the cooption of contemporary Indigenous governance systems by some Indigenous power elites mirrors the kind of predatory politics that characterises the country's version of representative democracy (Putzel, 1999; Quimpo, 2009). This seems antithetical to the kind of traditional governance systems described by ethnographies where leadership based on custom law is generally marked by virtues of personal valour, fortitude and charisma (Yengoyan, 1996) and bravery and wisdom (Scott, 1979): with the village leaders being generally friendly and personable (Fox, 1982); helpful, merciful, and intelligibly alert to the conditions and problems of the people (Manuel, 1973); and, more importantly, adept at juridical negotiation and arbitration (Frake, 1955; Manuel, 1973; Yengoyan, 1996; Scott, 1979). Many of these qualities were alluded to by most respondents during focus groups when they identified traditional village leaders as important sources of planning wisdom and authority.

The engagement and codification of Indigenous knowledge during planning arose as another theme. Largely absent in conventional, mainstream planning processes, spiritual blessing of important phases of the plan through religious rituals is a unique aspect of Indigenous planning methods. It resonates with emergent research methods whereby Indigenous ceremonies and rituals are emphasised as having an important place in knowledge generation with and by Indigenous peoples (Kovach, 2010; Smith, 1999). This is largely reflective of the universal Indigenous cosmology of sharing the physical world with mystical or spiritual beings who either own natural resources, have power to influence positive (and conversely inflict negative) outcomes, or both. Such a worldview was strongly expressed during focus groups. One participant from the *Manobo Dulangan* described why it is important to hold rituals:

> One must ask consent from each water body and other element referred to as being 'of the forest'. Because we believe that there are people we can't see ... one evidence is when in a sacred place, one person who entered their territory will get sick, that person wondering what happened as just moments ago he/she was well ... that person trespassed without seeking permission. And that's one reason why there is a need for rituals; rituals of appeasement; rituals for those you can't see; rituals as one's respect for the dwellers of the forests. That's what they [non-Indigenous peoples] do not understand ... But one must respect traditions. Put yourself in this situation. You entered this area without permission from the owner. Who will reprimand you? The owner, who would then ask why you entered without consent. That's the belief ... That's why various forms of respect are shown through rituals.[5]

Another dimension of Indigenous planning that is often taken for granted in the largely dehumanised (detached, neutral, and value-free) models of mainstream rational planning was the emphasis of the respondents on the value of unity, cooperation and respect during planning. This is not surprising as many Indigenous communities, especially those influenced strongly by kinship relations, value an egalitarian ethic (Duhaylungsod, 2001). Such desire for the relational elements of planning squarely resonates with emerging transformative theories of *transactive* planning (Friedman, 2011), *deliberative* planning (Forester, 1999), *communicative* planning (Innes, 1998) and *collaborative* planning (Healey, 1999). An emerging feminist conception of planning as inevitably affective (loving attachment, Porter et al., 2012) also appears consistent with Indigenous perceptions of planning as both emotional and relational.

---

5   Translation of a quote from a Bisayan transcript of a focus group meeting held on 4 September 2011 with members of the ManoboDulangan Indigenous group from the municipality of Senator Ninoy Aquino, Sultan Kudarat.

PLANNING AND POVERTY

Focus groups wanted Indigenous plans to include development centred on economic empowerment. Such results corroborate pan-Indigenous recognition of improving the material (economic) well-being of Indigenous communities in the expression of collective self-determination as indicated by global meetings among Indigenous peoples to identify their own indicators of well-being (Tebtebba, 2008). It is also consistent with observations that the global pursuit of Indigenous rights and entitlements over the past four decades is principally motivated by a quest for economic justice (Engle, 2010). Eradicating poverty and hunger, which is the first of the global Millennium Developmental Goals (UN, 2008), also tops the list of desired actions in the plan content (see Figure 3.3). These and the material dispossession generally characterise the world's Indigenous populations.

Results suggest that agricultural intensification/extensification, both capital-led (supported by external capital) and labour-led (based on own resources), is the preferred livelihood strategy among the 10 groups involved. This is consistent with the background of the Indigenous groups to which our respondents belong – traditional horticulturist societies that have combined subsistence farming, gathering and hunting as the main means of living in the past (Duhaylungsod, 2001). In contemporary times, farming (both for the market and for subsistence) remains the chief means of livelihood (Rovillos and Morales, 2002). Based on this apparent cultural predilection, it is quite understandable that respondents prefer a farm-based livelihood over employment in corporate investments such as mining and logging, both of which the government has been very keen to allow within public lands.

The *Mandaya* ancestral domain owners of Manay are particularly against corporate logging and mining. In defence of the ecological, economic, and socio-cultural value of ancestral lands to its Indigenous members, the tribal chieftain said the following:

> It is true that there are others, particularly outsiders [and] capitalists who want to do logging or mining [within our ancestral domains] but I refused and really said no ... to declaring [a portion of ancestral domain as] a mineral reservation because we saw that only the millionaires will benefit. Once they earn the money, they will leave. The ancestral domain ... is gone, destroyed. And the abandoned natives are left to die from landslides. The same is true for logging. They will buy one tree for Php 1,000 [Aus $25] but profit between Php 80,000–150,000 [Aus $2,000–3,750], while again, the ancestral domain owners stay poor and destitute ... Once it is exploited, once big capitalists are in, they will be the ones who will gain as they are rich and powerful. The tribe will get none.

Given this, one wonders whether the inclusion of engagements with corporate investors for resource extraction within ancestral domains in some contemporary Indigenous plans is an artefact of centralised planning schemes inordinately influenced by Indigenous political elites operating at the behest of government and corporations (Ibanez, 2014). Mineral extraction has been leading the new millennium development strategy for the Philippines, with the government 'aggressively touting its mineralization to the global mining industry' (Bravante and Holden, 2009). Ancestral domains are not spared by earnest mine prospectors. Invoking the doctrine of imminent domain, supreme court magistrates Puno and Kapunan, who evaluated the constitutionality of the IPRA law, have reiterated the concept of *juris regalia* and the state's ownership of all natural and mineral resources within ancestral domains, with Indigenous peoples having only the entitlement of *priority* rights to their development and exploitation, subject to state decision (*Cruz and Europa v. DENR and BM, and NCIP*, 2000). Clearly invoking such notions, the government in many cases railroaded mining within ancestral domains in complicity with dubious Indigenous leaders at the expense of the rights and livelihoods of communities (Sanz, 2007; Whitmore, 2012). The devastating effects of corporate mining on Indigenous well-being – particularly through the erosion of social relations and longer-term Indigenous food security and traditional agricultural practices – has been well documented in the Philippines and elsewhere (Whitmore, 2012). This has happened despite the fact that a major state goal of recognising Indigenous peoples' rights over their ancestral domains is to foster sustainable development to benefit both present and future Indigenous generations.

Conclusion

Findings from this study on Indigenous planning in the Philippines have important implications for both policy and practice. Many facets of planning thought desirable by those involved in the current research were strongly embedded in traditional Indigenous culture but appear to be little practised by those helping Indigenous people plan their estates.

This may be partly through ignorance. Those assisting in Indigenous planning may not realise the importance to Indigenous people of the need for their plans to express their worldview; to hold ceremonies and perform rituals to ensure their plans are blessed by the spiritual owners of their ancestral lands; and to reflect the unified desires of all elements in the community. Other external planners may have been more closely aligned with the representatives of the Indigenous communities rather than the fully democratic principles that underpinned the original planning laws and guidelines.

The research described in this chapter spells out what should be in Indigenous plans, and could form the basis of new guidelines for Indigenous planning to be undertaken at the village level that fully represents the planning processes that Indigenous people feel are important, the support that they feel leads to the best outcomes and the characteristics of a well-formed plan. The results also point to the human, financial, physical, natural, social and cultural elements that should be considered when making plans.

What this research also did was to illustrate that not all Indigenous groups are the same and have the same perceptions of what should and should not be in their plans, or even the way in which planning should be conducted. Given the importance of process to all Indigenous planning, one aspect of any future planning process among Indigenous people in the Philippines may be to undertake an exercise such as was carried out here as part of our research at the start of the planning process. Ask directly which aspects of planning an Indigenous group feels are important, ensuring that they are fully informed of options and approaches taken elsewhere, and build the plan on that basis rather than applying a one-size-fits-all plan based on some average. Such an approach would recognise the diversity among Indigenous groups, although care must be taken in every case to ensure that the planning reflects the views of those who are usually rendered voiceless.

Finally, Indigenous ownership of planning and the processes that underpin it from start to finish is essential if economic development is to benefit all Indigenous people equitably in a manner that increases not only wealth but also well-being. Planning alone is insufficient, especially if controlled by elites who benefit at the expense of less-powerful members of the Indigenous community.

References

Adam, M. and Kneeshaw, D. (2011). Expert opinion on the criteria and indicator process and Aboriginal communities: Are objectives being met? *Forestry Chronicle*, 87(3), pp. 358–366.

Adams, W. M., Aveling, R., Brockington, D., Dickson, B., Elliott, J., Hutton, J. Roe, D., Vira, B. and Wolmer, W. (2004). Biodiversity conservation and the eradication of poverty. *Science*. 306(5699), pp. 1146–1149.

Agrawal, A. and Gibson, C. (1999). Enchantment and disenchantment: The role of community in natural resource conservation. *World Development*, 27, pp. 629–649.

Asian Indigenous and Tribal Peoples Network (AITPN). (2008). *National institutions on Indigenous peoples: The experience of the Philippines*. Retrieved from: http://www.aitpn.org/IRQ/Vol-III/issues_2–3/story06.html (accessed: 21 December).

Alcorn, J. (2000). Borders, rules and governance: Mapping to catalyse changes in policy and management. *Paper no. 91*. London: International Institute for Environment and Development.

Allmendinger, P. (2009). *Planning theory*. Basingstoke: Palgrave Macmillan.

Altman, J. (2007). Alleviating poverty in remote Indigenous Australia: The role of the hybrid economy. *Development Bulletin*, 72, pp. 47–51.

Asadi, A., Akbari, M., Fami, H., Iravani, H., Rostami, F. and Sadati, A. (2008). Poverty alleviation and sustainable development: The role of social capital. *Journal of Social Sciences*, 4(3), pp. 202–215.

Baum, H. (1999). Community organizations recruiting community participation: Predicaments in planning. *Journal of Planning Education and Research*, 18, pp. 187–199.

Beard, V. (2003). Learning radical planning: The power of collective action. *Planning Theory*, 2(1), pp. 13–35.

Bebbington, A. (1999). Capitals and capabilities: A framework for analyzing peasant viability, rural livelihoods and poverty. *World Development*, 27(12), pp. 2021–2044.

Bennagen, P. (2007). Amending IPRA, negotiating autonomy, upholding the right to self determination. In A. Gatmaytan (ed.), *Negotiating autonomy: Case studies on Philippine Indigenous peoples' land rights*. Copenhagen: IWGIA.

Berke, P., Ericksen, N., Crawford, J. and Dixon, J. (2002). Planning and Indigenous people: Human rights and environmental protection in New Zealand. *Journal of Planning Education and Research*, 22, pp. 115–134.

Berkes, F. (2008). *Sacred Ecology*. New York: Routledge.

Botes, L., and Van Rensburg, D. (2000). Community participation in development: nine plagues and twelve commandments. *Community Development Journal*, 35(1), pp. 41–58.

Bravante, M., and Holden, W. (2009). Going through the motions: The environmental impact assessment of nonferrous metals mining projects in the Philippines. *Pacific Review*, 22(4), pp. 523–547.

Bremner, J., Lopez-Carr, D., Suter, L. and Davis, J. (2010). Population, poverty, environment, and climate dynamics in the developing world. *Interdisciplinary Environmental Review*, 11(2), pp. 112–126.

Bryant, L. (2002). Non-governmental organizations and governmentality: 'Consuming' biodiversity and Indigenous people in the Philippines. *Political Studies*, 50, pp. 268–292.

Buendia, R. G., Brilliantes, A. B. and Mendoza, L. C. (2006). *Mapping and analysis of Indigenous governance practices in the Philippines and proposal for establishing an indicative framework for Indigenous people's governance: Towards a broader and inclusive process of governance in the Philippines*. Bangkok: United Nations Development Programme.

Campbell, L. M., and Vainio-Mattila, A. (2003). Participatory development and community-based conservation: Opportunities missed for lessons learned? *Human Ecology*, 31, pp. 417–436.

Cariño, J. (2010). *Country technical notes on Indigenous peoples' issues: Republic of the Philippines*. Manila: AIFAD/AIPP.

Carney, D. (1998). Implementing the sustainable rural livelihoods approach. Paper presented to *the Department for International Development Natural Resource Advisers' Conference*. London: 10–14 July.

——— (2003). *Sustainable livelihoods approaches: Progress and possibilities for change*. London: Department for International Development.

Chambers, R. (1997). *Whose reality counts? Putting the first last*. London: Earthscan.

——— and Conway, G. (1992). Sustainable rural livelihoods: Practical concepts for the 21st century. *Discussion Paper 296*. Brighton: Institute of Development Studies.

Chapin, M., Lamb, Z. and Threlkeld, B. (2005). Mapping Indigenous lands. *Annual Review of Anthropology*, 34, pp. 619–638.

Clarke, G. (1998). *The politics of NGOs in South-East Asia: Participation and protest in the Philippines.* London: Routledge.

Colchester, M. (1994). Salvaging nature: Indigenous people, protected areas and biodiversity conservation. *Discussion Paper No. 55*. Geneva: UNRISD.

Colchester, M. (2000). Self-determination or environmental determinism for Indigenous peoples in tropical forest conservation. *Conservation Biology*, 14, pp. 1365–1367.

Corbridge, S. and Kumar, S. (2002). Community, corruption, landscape: Tales from the tree trade. *Political Geography*, 21(6), pp. 765–788.

Corburn, J. (2003). Bringing local knowledge into environmental decision making improving urban planning for communities at risk. *Journal of Planning Education and Research*, 22(4), pp. 420–433.

Environmenal Law Alliance Worldwide (2000). *Cruz and Europa v. Secretary of Environment and Natural Resources, Secretary of Budget and Management, and the Chair and Commissioners of the National Commission on Indigenous Peoples*. G.R. No. 135385, 347 SCRA 128, Philippines-2000. Retrieved from: http://www.elaw.org/node/1335 (accessed: 1 December 2013).

David, K. (1998). From present looking back: A history of Philippine NGOs. In G. S. Silliman and L. G. Noble (eds), *Organizing for democracy: NGOs, civil society, and the Philippine state*. Honolulu: University of Hawaii Press, pp. 26–49.

De Janvry, A. and Sadoulet, E. (2001). Investing in rural development is good business. In R. Echeverria (ed.), *Development of rural economies in Latin America and the Caribbean*. Washington: Inter-American Development Bank, pp. 1–36.

de Sherbinin, A., VanWey, L., McSweeney, K., Aggarwal, R., Barbieri, A., Henry, S. and Walker, R. (2008). Rural household demographics, livelihoods and the environment. *Global Environmental Change*, 18(1), pp. 38–53.

Duhaylungsod, L. (2001). Rethinking sustainable development: Indigenous peoples and resource use relations in the Philippines. In: Bijdragen tot de Taal-, Land- en Volkenkunde, *The Philippines Historical and Social Studies*, 57(3), pp. 609–628.

Eketone, A. (2006). Tapuwae: A vehicle for community change. *Community Development Journal*, 41, pp. 467–480.

Emery, A. (2000). *Guidelines: Integrating Indigenous knowledge in project planning and implementation*. Washington DC: World Bank.

Engle, K. (2010). *The elusive promise of indigenous development: Rights, culture, strategy*. Durham, NC: Duke University Press.

Erni, C. (2005). Indigenous people's self-determination and local government: Exploring the options. *In Indigenous Peoples and Local Government: Experiences from Malaysia and the Philippines*. Philippines: Cordillera Peoples Alliance, pp. 5–12.

———. Non-violence in a frontier: The strategy of avoidance and the struggle for Indigenous control over land resources on Mindoro Island. In D. Geiger (ed.), *Frontier encounters: Indigenous communities and settlers in Asia and Latin America*. Copenhagen: IWGIA.

Esquimaux, C. and Calliou, B. (2010). *Best practices in Aboriginal community development: A literature review and wise practices approach*. Banff: Banff Centre.

Forester, J. (1999). *The deliberative practitioner: Encouraging participatory planning processes*. Cambridge, MA: MIT Press.

Fox, R. (1982). Religion and society among the Tagbanua of Palawan Island, Philippines. *Monograph No. 9*. Manila: Philippine National Museum.

Frake, C. (1955). Social organization and shifting cultivation among the Sindangan Subanun. *Unpublished PhD thesis*. Yale University.

Freire, P. (1970). *Pedagogy of the oppressed*. New York: Continuum.

Friedmann, J. (1987). *Planning in the public domain: From knowledge to action*. Princeton: Princeton University Press.

——— (1989). Planning in the public domain: Discourse and praxis. *Journal of Planning Education and Research*, 8(2), pp. 128–130.

——— (2011). *Insurgencies: Essays in Planning Theory*. Abingdon: Routledge.

Gatmaytan, A. (2007). Philippine Indigenous peoples and the quest for autonomy: Negotiated or compromised? In A. Gatmaytan (ed.), *Negotiating autonomy: Case studies on Philippine Indigenous peoples' land rights*. Copenhagen: IWGIA.

——— and Dagondon, G. (2004). *Sustainability and survival: Four case studies from Indigenous communities in Northern Mindanao*. Bogor, Indonesia: ICRAF.

Gibson, G. and O'Faircheallaigh, C. (2010). *IBA community toolkit: Negotiation and implementation of impact and benefit agreements*. Ottawa: Walter and Duncan Gordon Foundation.

Gracey, M. and King, M. (2009). Indigenous health part 1: Determinants and disease patterns. *Lancet*, 374(9683), pp. 65–75.

Healey, P. (1999). Institutional analysis, communicative planning, and shaping places. *Journal of Planning Education and Research*, 19, pp. 111–21.

Hibbard, M., Lane, M. and Rasmussen. K. (2008). The split personality of planning: Indigenous peoples and planning for land and resource management. *Journal of Planning Literature*, 23(2), pp. 136–151.

Hill, R. (2011). Towards equity in Indigenous co-management of protected areas: Cultural planning by Miriuwung-Gajerrong people in the Kimberley, Western Australia. *Geographical Research*, 49(1), pp. 72–85.

Hill, R., Walsh, F., Davies, J. and Sandford, M. (2011). *Our country our way: Guidelines for Australian Indigenous Protected Area Management Plans*. Cairns: CSIRO.

Hirtz, F. (2003). It takes modern means to be traditional: On recognizing Indigenous cultural communities in the Philippines. *Development and Change*, 34(5), pp. 887–914.

Ibanez, J. (2014). Knowledge integration and Indigenous planning in the Philippines. *Unpublished manuscript*. Darwin: Charles Darwin University.

Indigenous Peoples Rights Act (1997). s. 2.2. (Phils). Retrieved from http://www.opapp.gov.ph/resources/indigenous-peoples%E2%80%99-rights-act-1997 (accessed: 3 December 2013).

Innes, J. (1996). Planning through consensus-building. *Journal of the American Planning Association*, 96(62), pp. 460–473.

——— (1998). Information in communication planning. *Journal of the American Planning Association*, 64(1), pp. 52–63.

International Work Group for Indigenous Affairs (IWGIA). (2012). *The Indigenous World 2012: Philippines*. Copenhagen: IWGIA.

Irazabal, C. (2009). Realizing planning's emancipatory promise: Learning from regime theory. *Planning Theory*, 8(2), pp. 115–139.

Jojola, T. (2008). Indigenous planning, an emerging Context. *Canadian Journal of Urban Research*, 17(1), pp. 37–47.

Jonasson, E. and Helfand, S. (2010). How important are locational characteristics for rural non-agricultural employment? Lessons from brazil. *World Development*, 38(5), pp. 727–741.

Karjala, M., Sherry, E. and Dewhurst, S. (2003). *The Aboriginal forest planning process: A guidebook for identifying community-level criteria and indicators*. Vancouver: University of Northern British Columbia.

Karjala, M. and Dewhurst, S. (2003). Including aboriginal issues in forest planning: A case study in central interior British Columbia, Canada. *Landscape and Urban Planning*, 64, pp. 1–17.

Kliger, B. and Cosgrove, L. (1999). Local cross-cultural planning and decision-making with indigenous people in Broome, Western Australia. *Cultural Geographies*, 6(1), pp. 51–71.

Kovach, M. E. (2010). *Indigenous methodologies: Characteristics, conversations, and contexts*. Toronto: University of Toronto Press.

Krook, M. and True, J. (2012). Rethinking the life cycles of international norms: The United Nations and the global promotion of gender equality. *European Journal of International Relations*, 18(1), pp. 103–127.

Kwaku Kyem, P. (2000). Embedding GIS applications into resource management and planning activities of local and Indigenous communities: A desirable innovation or a destabilizing enterprise? *Journal of Planning Education and Research*, 20(2), pp. 176–186.

Lane, M. (2002). Buying back and caring for country: Institutional arrangements and possibilities for Indigenous lands management in Australia. *Society and Natural Resources*, 15, pp. 827–46.

——— (2006). The role of planning in achieving indigenous land justice and community goals. *Land Use Policy*, 23, pp. 385–394.

——— and Hibbard, M. (2005). Doing it for themselves: Transformative planning by Indigenous peoples. *Journal of Planning Education and Research*, 25, pp. 172–184.

———, Brown, A. and Chase, A. (1997). Land and resource planning under Native title: Towards an initial model. *Environmental and Planning Law Journal*, 14(4), pp. 249–258.

Lertzman, D. (1999). Planning between cultural paradigms: Traditional knowledge and the transition to ecological sustainability. *Unpublished doctoral dissertation*. Vancouver: University of British Columbia.

——— and Vredenburg, H. (2005). Indigenous peoples, resource extraction and sustainable development: An ethical approach. *Journal of Business Ethics*, 56, pp. 239–254.

Li, T. M. (2002). Engaging simplifications: Community-based resource management, market processes and state agendas in upland Southeast Asia. *World Development*, 30(2), pp. 265–283.

Manuel, E. A. (1973). *Manuvu social organization*. Quezon City: Community Development Research Council.

Mason, D. and Beard, V. (2008). Community-based planning and poverty alleviation in Oaxaca, Mexico. *Journal of Planning Education and Research*, 27, pp. 245– 260.

McNeish, J.-A., and Eversole, R. (2005). Introduction: Indigenous peoples and poverty. In R. Eversole, J.-A. McNeish and A. D. Cimadamore (eds), *Indigenous peoples and poverty: An international perspective*. London: Zed.

Matunga, H. (2006). The concept of Indigenous planning as a framework for social inclusion. *Planning Quarterly*, 161, pp. 24–8.

Moote, M., McClaran, M. and Chickering, D. (1997). Theory in practice: Applying participatory democracy theory to public land planning. *Environmental Management*, 21(6), pp. 877–889.

Moran, M. (2004). The practice of participatory planning at Mapoon Aboriginal settlement: Towards community control, ownership and autonomy. *Australian Geographical Studies*, 42(3), pp. 339–355.

Natcher, D. and Hickey, C. (2002). Putting the community back into community-based resource management: A criteria and indicators approach to sustainability. *Human Organization*, 61(4), pp. 350–363.

National Commission on Indigenous Peoples (NCIP) (2004). *Guidelines on the formulation of the Ancestral Domain Sustainable Development and Protection Plan (ADSDPP)*. NCIP Administrative Order No. 1.

O'Brien, D., Phillips, J. and Patsiorkovsky, V. (2005). Linking indigenous bonding and bridging social capital. *Regional Studies*, 39(8), pp. 1041–1051.

O'Faircheallaigh, C. and Corbett, T. (2005). Indigenous participation in environmental management of mining projects: The role of negotiated agreements. *Environmental Politics*, 14(5), pp. 629–647.

Padilla, A. (2008). Indigenous peoples, settlers and the Philippine Ancestral Domain Land Titling Program. In D. Geiger (ed.), *Frontier encounters: Indigenous communities and settlers in Asia and Latin America*. Copenhagen: IWGIA.

Porter, E. (2004). Unlearning one's privilege: reflections on cross-cultural research and practice in southeast Australia. *Planning Theory and Practice*, 5(1), pp. 104–109.

Porter, L. (2006). Planning in (post)colonial settings: Challenges for theory and practice. *Planning Theory and Practice*, 7(4), pp. 383–396.

———, Sandercock, L., Umemoto, K., Bates, L., Zapata, M., Kondo, M., Zitcer, A., Lake, R., Fonza, A., Sletto, B. and Erfan, A. (2012). What's love got to do with it? Illuminations on loving attachment in planning, *Planning Theory and Practice*, 13(4), pp. 593–627.

Pretty, J., Adams, B., Berkes, F., de Athayde, S., Dudley, N., Hunn, E., and Pilgrim, S. (2009). The intersections of biological diversity and cultural diversity: Towards integration. *Conservation and Society*, 7(2), pp. 100–112.

Putzel, J. (1999). Survival of an imperfect democracy in the Philippines. *Democratization*, 6(1), pp. 198–223.

Quimpo, N. (2009). The Philippines: Predatory regime, growing authoritarian features. *Pacific Review*. 22(3), pp. 335–353.

Rands, M., Adams, W., Bennun, L., Butchart, S., Clements, A., Coomes, D. and Vira, B. (2010). Biodiversity conservation: Challenges beyond 2010. *Science*, 329(5997), pp. 1298–1303.

Rao, N. and Robinson-Pant, A. (2006). Adult education and indigenous people: Addressing gender in policy and practice. *International Journal of Educational Development*, 26(2), pp. 209–223.

Robbins, P. (2000). The rotten institution: corruption in natural resource management. *Political Geography*, 19(4), pp. 423–443.

Ross, A., Pickering, S., Snodgrass, J., Delcore, H. and Sherman, R. (2011). *Indigenous peoples and the collaborative stewardship of nature: Knowledge binds and institutional conflicts*. Walnut Creek: Left Coast.

Roth, R. (2009). The challenges of mapping complex indigenous spatiality: From abstract space to dwelling space. *Cultural Geographies*, 16(2), pp. 207–227.

Rovillos, R. and Morales, D. (2002). *Indigenous peoples/ethnic minorities and poverty reduction: Philippines*. Manila: Asian Development Bank.

Sadan, E. (2004). *Empowerment and community planning: Theory and practice of people-focused social solutions*. Tel Aviv: Hakibbutz Hameuchad.

Sandercock, L. (2003). Out of the closet: The importance of stories and storytelling in planning practice. *Planning Theory and Practice*, 4(1), pp. 11–28.

Sanderson, S. E. and Redford, K. H. (2003). Contested relationships between biodiversity conservation and poverty alleviation. *Oryx*, 37(04), pp. 389–390.

Sanz, P. (2007). The politics of consent: The state, multinational capital and the Subanon of Canatuan. In A. Gatmaytan (ed.), *Negotiating autonomy: Case studies on Philippine Indigenous peoples' land rights*. Copenhagen: IWGIA.

Scoones, I. (1998). Sustainable rural livelihoods: A framework for analysis. *IDS Working Paper No 72*. Brighton: Institute of Development Studies.

Scott, W. (1979). Class structure in the unhispanized Philippines. *Philippine Studies*, 27(2), pp. 137–159.

——— (1982). *Cracks in the parchment curtain*. Quezon City: New Day.

Sherry, E., Dewhurst, M. and Karjala, M. (2005). Aboriginal forest planning: Lessons from three community pilot projects. *Canadian Journal of Native Studies*, 25(1), pp. 51–91.

Sletto, B. (2009). Indigenous people don't have boundaries: Reborderings, fire management, and productions of authenticities in indigenous landscapes. *Cultural geographies*, 16(2), pp. 253–277.

Smith, L. (1999). *Decolonizing methodologies: Research and Indigenous Peoples*. Dunedin: University of Otago Press.

Sobrevila, C. (2008). *The role of Indigenous peoples in biodiversity conservation: The natural but often forgotten partners*. Manila: World Bank.

Stephens, C., Porter, J., Nettleton, C. and Willis, R. (2006). Disappearing, displaced, and undervalued: A call to action for Indigenous health worldwide. *Lancet*, 367(9527), pp. 2019–2028.

Stephenson, J. (2008). The cultural values model: An integrated approach to values in landscapes. *Landscape and Urban Planning*, 84(2), pp. 127–139.

Suchet-Pearson, S. and Howitt, R. (2006). On teaching and learning resource and environmental management: Reframing capacity building in multicultural settings. *Australian Geographer*, 37(1), pp. 117–128.

Sunderlin, W. D., Angelsen, A., Belcher, B., Burgers, P., Nasi, R., Santoso, L. and Wunder, S. (2005). Livelihoods, forests, and conservation in developing countries: An overview. *World Development*, 33(9), pp. 1383–1402.

Tebtebba. (2008). *Indicators relevant for Indigenous peoples: A resource book*. Baguio City: Tebtebba Foundation.

Theriault, N. (2011). The micropolitics of Indigenous environmental movements in the Philippines. *Development and Change*, 42, pp. 1417–1440.

Toomey, A. 2011. Empowerment and disempowerment in community development practice: Eight roles practitioners play. *Community Development Journal*, 46(2), pp. 181–195.

Umemoto, K. (2001). Walking in another's shoes: Epistemological challenges in participatory planning. *Journal of Planning Education and Research*, 21, pp. 17–31.

United Nations (UN). (2008). *Resource kit on Indigenous peoples' issues*. New York: United Nations Permanent Forum on Indigenous Peoples.

United Nations Declaration on the Rights of Indigenous Peoples (UNDRIP) (2008). Retrieved from: http://www.unesco.org/new/en/indigenous-peoples/related-info/undrip/ (accessed: 1 December 2013).

Walsh, F. and Mitchell, P. (eds) (2002). *Planning for country: Cross-cultural approaches to decision-making on Aboriginal lands*. Alice Springs: Jukurrpa Books.

Weinberger, K. and T. A. Lumpkin (2007). Diversification into horticulture and poverty reduction: A research agenda. *World Development*, 35(8), pp. 1464–1480.

Whitmore, A. (2012). *Pitfalls and pipelines: Indigenous peoples and extractive industries*. Manila: Tebtebba Foundation and IWGIA.

Yengoyan, A. (1996). Origin, hierarchy and egalitarianism among the Mandaya of southeast Mindanao, Philippines. In J. Fox. and C. Sather (eds), *Origins, ancestry and alliance: Explorations in Austronesian Ethnography*. Canberra: ANU Press.

Zaferatos, N. (2004a). Tribal nations, local governments, and regional pluralism in Washington State. *Journal of the American Planning Association*, 70(1), pp. 81–96.

———— (2004b). Developing an effective approach to strategic planning for Native American Indian reservations. *Space and Polity*, 8(1), pp, 87–104.

4

Government Programmes and Indigenous Business in the Bundjalung Nation, Australia

Amanda Shoebridge and Jeremy Buultjens

Chapter Synopsis

Aboriginal and Torres Strait Islander Australians have been encouraged to become entrepreneurs in order to counter their entrenched economic and social disadvantage. However, entering the mainstream Australian economy, especially for regional and rural Indigenous business, is a significant challenge. In an attempt to address some of the challenges governments provide a number of assistance programmes. This chapter presents findings from a study that examined, in part, the perceived effectiveness of government business assistance programmes. The qualitative study took place in a regional setting within the Bundjalung Nation in northeast New South Wales (NSW), Australia. The study participants had an interest in Indigenous economic and business development, such as Indigenous Economic Development Officers, Business Mentors and Consultants, and representatives from government agencies and non-profit organisations as well as small business owners. Government assistance programmes were perceived as playing an important role in facilitating business development; however participants also highlighted a series of problems including inappropriate funding; a duplication of programmes; a lack of consistency, and a lack of ownership of the outcomes from some programmes. It is hoped by highlighting both the negative and positive aspects of programmes that future programmes may be developed to provide the best possible outcomes.

Introduction

Indigenous Australians suffer considerable social and economic disadvantage in comparison to the rest of the population. For example, despite improvements in employment rates over the past 20 years (Gray et al., 2013), the unemployment rate for Aboriginal and Torres Strait Islanders is more than three times that of their non-Indigenous counterparts – 17.09% in comparison to 5.63% as at the 2011 Census (Australian Bureau of Statistics (ABS), 2011a, b). A number of solutions have been proposed in order to address this disadvantage, with one solution – the promotion of Indigenous enterprise, being increasingly advocated (Peredo et al., 2004; Fuller et al., 2003). Indigenous enterprise development has the potential to reconcile inequitable financial and social situations in a way which empowers and instils pride in people and, with proper management, can resonate with and complement Indigenous cultural values (Fuller et al., 2005). This is particularly important for Indigenous peoples living in regional areas for two reasons. Firstly, in Australia, Indigenous people have traditionally been employed in the public sector; however in regional areas there are limited public sector employment opportunities. Most employment opportunities in regional areas exist predominantly in the private sector rather than the public sector (Malezer, 2008). Secondly, in regional areas there is a predominance of small businesses in the private sector, and there is a perception that small business employers are less likely to employ Indigenous people than their larger counterparts. Furthermore, it is believed that Indigenous sector organisations are major employers of Aboriginal and Torres Strait Islander people, increasing the necessity to further develop Indigenous enterprise (Sullivan, 2010).

The importance of creating Indigenous enterprise has encouraged governments at both the federal and state level to provide a number of assistance programmes aimed at facilitating its development (Buultjens et al., 2005; Whitford et al., 2001). However, despite government attempts to encourage such development, the number of Indigenous businesses in Australia remains relatively low, especially in regional areas (Steering Committee for the Review of Government Service Provision, 2011). The lack of programme success has, in part, resulted in a number of government inquiries into Indigenous entrepreneurship and the factors that facilitate or hinder its development. In addition there have been an increasing number of academic studies in this area, however very little research has been undertaken on the relationship between regional location and enterprise development.

The research reported in this chapter examines the perceived efficacy of government Indigenous development programmes in a regional setting. The qualitative study was undertaken in the Bundjalung Nation, which is located in northeast NSW and southeast Queensland. The chapter begins by providing an overview of Indigenous Australia, followed by a review of literature on Indigenous enterprise and government programmes offered in this area. The next section includes an overview of the methodology used in the study. The results concerning the perceived effectiveness of government programmes are then discussed, and the chapter concludes by providing some suggestions for improving the government assistance offered for Indigenous enterprise development in Australia.

Indigenous Australians

According to the national Census there were 548,370 Indigenous Australians in 2011 comprising 2.6% of Australia's population (ABS, 2011a), representing an increase of 20.5% since the 2006 Census (ABS, 2006). The majority of Indigenous people (43%) live in regional areas, 32.9% live in greater capital city areas, and 25% in remote areas. More than half (59.9%) of Aboriginal and Torres Strait Islanders live in the eastern states of Queensland and New South Wales. Despite living in one of the world's wealthiest nations, a large proportion of Indigenous Australians continue to experience endemic poverty and subsequently suffer from poor health rates, low literacy and numeracy levels, and unacceptably poor standards of living (Nguyen, 2013; Hunter, 1997; Stark, 2013).

The social determinants of health – such as housing, employment, and adequate income – are ultimately responsible for the health inequalities faced by Aboriginal and Torres Strait Islander

Australians, and these are shaped by the distribution of power, wealth, and resources at both local and national levels (Douglas, 2012). Within the Northern NSW local health district more than 55% of Aboriginal households are overcrowded, compared to 38% of Aboriginal households elsewhere in Australia; one-third of young Aboriginal men and women (15–24 years) are unemployed – twice the unemployment rate of non-Aboriginal youth; and incarceration rates are approximately 25 times that of non-Aboriginal and Torres Strait Islander Australians (Douglas, 2012). There is a strong correlation between standards of living and the prevalence of risk behaviours such as drinking alcohol, illicit drug taking, and smoking.

The poor socio-economic indicators outlined above often result in poor employment outcomes which further exacerbate Indigenous poverty. According to the Department of Families, Housing, Community Services and Indigenous Affairs (2013), the employment rate for Indigenous Australians in 2011 was 46.2%, which represented a decrease in employment from 48.0% in 2006. In comparison, the employment rate for non-Indigenous Australians rose over the same period from 71.7% to 72.2%. There has been some debate over whether the inclusion or not of the Community Development Employment Projects (CDEP) programme in employment figures reveals the most accurate picture of Indigenous employment.[1] If the CDEP programme were excluded from these figures the results reveal a 2.3% increase in employment rates from 2006 to 2011 for Indigenous Australians.

In 2011, an estimated 207,600 Indigenous people were in the labour force (that is, either employed or unemployed), representing a 57.7% labour force participation rate for Indigenous people (aged 15 years and over) in comparison to a non-Indigenous labour force participation rate of 77.3% (ABS, 2012). Accurate data which reflects the size, diversity, location, and growth of the Indigenous private sector is limited. The Commonwealth Government Report on Overcoming Indigenous Disadvantage (SCRGSP, 2011) reported that in non-remote areas, and for the age bracket of 18–64 years, 6.7% of Indigenous Australians were self-employed in comparison to 10.9% of non-Indigenous Australians.

There have been a number of solutions suggested for overcoming the entrenched poverty and disadvantage faced by Aboriginal and Torres Strait Islander Australians, although not all are universally accepted (Dockery, 2010). One solution that has been increasingly advocated is the development of Indigenous businesses and entrepreneurship (Peredo et al., 2004; Lindsay, 2013; Anderson et al., 2004; Fuller et al., 2005; Wood and Davidson, 2011; Pearson and Kostakidis-Lianos, 2004). Successful enterprise development can assist in improving health and livelihood outcomes, and enables Indigenous Australians and their families to move away from passive welfare (Pearson, 2000) as well as enter the workforce more successfully. Other benefits experienced as a consequence of Indigenous business ownership or employment within Indigenous-owned and operated businesses include high levels of self-esteem, pride, enthusiasm and social well-being (Pearson and Helms, 2010; Dockery and Milsom, 2007; Royal Commission into Aboriginal Deaths in Custody, 1991), and increased cultural understanding (Sofield and Birtles, 1996).

Indigenous Entrepreneurship

Despite Indigenous Australians having a long history of entrepreneurial behaviour that existed well before the establishment of European settlement in 1788 (Trudgen, 2000; Mitchell, 1995; Tinedale, 1974), in contemporary times there have been relatively low levels of Indigenous entrepreneurial behaviour and very little increase in self-employment rates over the past

---

1   The CDEP programme had two primary aims: to preserve Aboriginal culture and empower the people; and to help Aboriginal people find meaningful, permanent employment to finally break the cycle of welfare and poverty.

decade (Steering Committee for the Review of Government Service Provision, 2011). In order to facilitate greater levels of entrepreneurial behaviour among Indigenous Australians there is a need for greater understanding of the issues surrounding its development; however the field is still relatively under-researched (Pearson and Helms, 2010), especially in regard to the impact of geographical location. The lack of research is a problem since, in order to promote Indigenous entrepreneurship, policy-makers need to have a good understanding of the factors that promote or hinder its development.

Government assistance programmes which provide business planning, mentoring, advice, and access to capital, are seen as a critical factor in Indigenous enterprise development (Bennett, 2005; Foley, 2004; Fuller et al., 2005; Finlayson, 2007). Slowing economic growth since the Global Financial Crisis (GFC), with a consequential reduction in jobs, has placed greater importance on active labour market programmes and government policies designed to reduce Indigenous Australian labour inequality (Gray et al., 2012). In order to be effective government assistance programmes must be of adequate duration, accessible, well targeted, practical and, most importantly, culturally compatible (Buultjens et al., 2005). It is also recognised that government programmes need to be developed in close consultation with Indigenous business owners/managers and/or communities (Fuller et al., 2005; Australian Indigenous Chamber of Commerce, 2008).

Governments can also provide other types of Indigenous entrepreneurship development assistance. For example, the American and Canadian governments provide Indigenous businesses with specific or additional tax exemptions or reductions. The Australian Indigenous Chamber of Commerce (AICC) in a submission to Parliament in 2008 recommended several taxation measures that would encourage Indigenous businesses in Australia. The measures suggested by the AICC included: tax-deductible deposit accounts; tax incentives for companies using Aboriginal sub-contractors; and tax exemptions for Aboriginal Venture Capital Funds to encourage investment in Indigenous entrepreneurship (AICC, 2008). Governments could also provide incentives for both government organisations and private enterprises to partner with, as well as utilise, the products and services of Indigenous enterprises as a means of supporting Indigenous business. This may be achieved, for example, by establishing target levels for government procurement from Indigenous businesses. Many academics, industry bodies, and associations support the provision of financial incentives or tax deductions to encourage partnerships between Indigenous and private enterprise (AICC, 2008; House of Representatives Standing Committee on Aboriginal and Torres Strait Islander Affairs, 2008; Fuller et al., 2005).

Clearly the impact of government programmes can be substantial; however a number of difficulties associated with their design and implementation have been identified. Many of these programmes are confusing, unwieldy, poorly coordinated, and difficult for Indigenous people to access (Buultjens et al., 2005; Whitford et al., 2001; Shoebridge, 2009). In addition, the application process is often complicated. The access to programmes in remote areas is limited and is often insufficient to meet demand (Ivory, 2003). In addition, Dockery and Milsom (2007) suggest that the evaluation of government programmes continues to focus on current political philosophies and policy rather than the less easily quantifiable measures of self-determination, Indigenous choice, and well-being. Some believe the effectiveness of government employment policies and programmes are flawed by a 'whiteness' view and epistemology (Abdulah-Wendt, 2008; Moreton-Robinson, 2006).

Another criticism of government programmes is that they have been too focused on the entrepreneurial environment including Indigenous factor endowments – land, human capital (education and training), and capital – rather than on the entrepreneur themselves (Altman, 1998). It is argued that more attention needs to be placed upon empowering and building individual capacity rather than influencing external environments.

Government programmes are also criticised because they appear to stifle innovation and creativity – a necessary characteristic of entrepreneurial success (Legge and Hindle, 2004). It is argued that grant funding is likely to be made only to those businesses that were seen to be conservative and 'a safe bet'. There is a reluctance to approve risk-taking (Bennett, 2005). It appears that there needs to be a point of compromise between providing effective supporting mechanisms and burdening grant recipients with overly bureaucratic procedures and requirements. An additional problem is that it appears that cultural values and practices are not considered when developing, delivering, and marketing government programmes. This makes it difficult to adapt programmes to different cultural environments (Lindsay, 2005; Dana, 2000, 2001).

A further obstacle for Indigenous entrepreneurs is their lack of access to capital funding. Indigenous people generally have low savings due to their economic circumstances. Personal savings are the predominant source of funding for the establishment of non-Indigenous small businesses (Fuller et al., 2003). The lack of access to finance is exacerbated by the fact that, although many Indigenous communities own land through Native Title, an individual will find it hard to borrow money against this asset due to the reluctance of mainstream lending organisations to use this asset as security (Ivory, 2003).

The isolation of many Indigenous communities is also a problem since the facilities required to equip Indigenous people with the necessary commercial, trade, or technical skills – important skills for small business owners/managers – are not located within close proximity. Similarly, there are very few opportunities for Indigenous people from remote communities to receive on-the-job training or to concurrently undertake formal training away from work to enhance their skills set (Fuller et al., 2003).

These limited prospects have led to the urbanisation of many Indigenous Australians in search of improved labour market prospects. The withdrawal of the CDEP government assistance programme from regional areas with established economies is likely to further heighten migration numbers. However research by Biddle (2010), which models the labour market impacts of Indigenous migration to urban areas, found that those people who did relocate to urban areas suffered worse employment prospects than those who stayed. Therefore, although there are financial advantages to governments for greater urbanisation of Indigenous Australians, such as cheaper service provision, many who do move struggle to compete in the urban labour market. This suggests that programmes must be designed to better manage the process of urbanisation if this is to be considered a viable strategy. The importance of 'country' to Indigenous Australians' culture and health must also be acknowledged and given weight in this debate.

The Bundjalung Nation

The Bundjalung Nation (highlighted in Figure 4.1) covers the region known as the Northern Rivers as well as some parts of southeast Queensland and includes the Aboriginal language groups of the Widjabal, Arakwal, Minjungbal, Yaegal, Githabal, and Kalibal peoples (Sharpe, 1985).[2]

---

2   The Bundjalung Nation stretches from the Richmond Range in the south to the Logan River at Coolangatta in the north and out west to the foothills of the Great Dividing Range. The statistical region that best fits with the Bundjalung Region is called the Northern Rivers Region; however different government departments use different 'regions' that are somewhat comparable to the Bundjalung Nation. For example, there is the Richmond-Tweed Statistical Division, the Northern Rivers, and Northern NSW. A compilation of data from the ABS Statistical Divisions of Richmond-Tweed and Clarence Valley and the Local Government Areas (LGAs) of Lismore, Ballina, Byron, Tweed, and Kyogle provides the best ABS data for the area most comparable to the Bundjalung Nation. For the purpose of this chapter, data which was compiled from these sources will be referred to as the Northern Rivers Region.

Figure 4.1   The Bundjalung Nation

Source: Kwamikagami, 2013.

According to McBryde (1974) evidence exists of Aboriginal settlement within the Bundjalung Nation from the mid fifth millennium BC. Tindale (1974) estimated the Bundjalung population at the turn of the century to be between 300 and 600 people. According to Lloyd and Norrie (2004), the Bundjalung people have successfully preserved and maintained their story, language, and songs; assisted by the presence of an active Bundjalung Elders committee. The Bundjalung language is one of the best-preserved examples of Aboriginal Australian dialect, and has reportedly been adopted by other Aboriginal Australian peoples whose language has been lost.

Currently many Aboriginal and Torres Strait Islander people live in the towns and villages scattered throughout the Northern Rivers and southeast Queensland, while many also live in one of the 13 Aboriginal communities of the Bundjalung Nation. These communities are located in: Baryulgil; Malabugilmah; Yamba; Coraki; Casino; Grafton; Kyogle; Ballina; Tabulam; Woodenbong; Lismore; Tweed Heads, and Maclean. The Northern Rivers Region (the statistical region closest to that of the Bundjalung Nation, see footnote 2) had a population of 277,286 in 2011 and a higher than average population of Indigenous Australians – 4.3% identified as Indigenous Australian compared to 3% nationally (ABS, 2013d).

Research Methods

The research process used for this project was guided by a consultative advisory group. The advisory group was made up of members from the Northern Rivers Aboriginal Economic Development Team known as the 'E Team'. The E Team, with a view to increasing Indigenous business development and employment within the Bundjalung Nation, has members from key organisations with a vested interest in promoting and enhancing Indigenous business and employment. The following organisations are represented: Indigenous Business Australia (IBA); NSW Department of Industry and Investment; Indigenous Community Volunteers (ICV); Many Rivers Opportunities; Department of Education and Communities – State Training Services; Aboriginal Economic Development Officer Program (AEDO); Southern Cross University (SCU); NSW Department of Aboriginal Affairs (DAA); NSW State Aboriginal Lands Council (NSW ALC); the Department of Employment, Education and Workplace Relations (DEEWR); Alstonville Ballina Community College; Northern Rivers Chamber of Commerce; Salvation Army Employment; Local Employment Coordinator (DEEWR); First Sun Employment; and the Enterprise Training Company (ETC).

The advisory group provided advice on the scope of the project, the nature of the interview process, and wording of guiding questions (including the cultural suitability of content) as well as assisting the researchers to identify potential interview participants. The group also assisted the researchers in determining appropriate strategies to overcome the barriers and hindrances identified during the interview process.

This study was conducted using a mixed methods research design to obtain a more comprehensive understanding of the problem than would be possible using just a single method (Mertens, 2005; Tashakkori and Teddlie, 2003). Firstly a literature review was undertaken to gain an overview of the issues involved in Indigenous enterprise development. As part of the literature review, there was an audit of existing Indigenous businesses within the Northern Rivers Region of NSW. The researchers used internet searches, directory searches, emails, and phone calls to investigate and list details of current Indigenous enterprise operating within the study area. Existing studies and sources of information such as Australian Bureau of Statistics (ABS) Community Profiles; Job Services Australia and Labour Market Economics Office; Department Workplace and Education and Employment Relations; Labour Market Information Portal (LMIP); Department of Community Services (DOCS); Northern Rivers Health; Regional Development Australia Northern Rivers (RDA), etc. were consulted and information compiled. On completion of the literature review the findings were validated by the members of the team.

On completion of the literature review, a series of in-depth interviews were conducted with various relevant stakeholders over a period of six months from mid/late 2012. These interviews usually occurred at a place of convenience for the interviewee. By the end of the interview period 25 stakeholders had been interviewed. The in-depth interviews were conducted to determine the views of industry professionals, Indigenous business people, and key stakeholders regarding the current position of Indigenous industry and future possibilities for Indigenous industry within the Bundjalung Nation. Face-to-face, semi-structured interviews were considered the most appropriate method for a number of reasons. Firstly, they allow time and opportunity for in-depth, rich data to emerge, and also time to develop a rapport with participants (Gilham, 2000). As such this method can provide greater insight into a participant's experiences (Berglund, 2001; Ward and Holman, 2001). Interviews can be casually structured and not dissimilar to a 'yarning' session, which can help make participants more comfortable and create an environment of trust. As such, in-depth interviews are considered an appropriate tool to collect information from vulnerable and/or marginalised people (Hesse-Biber and Leavy, 2005; Liamputtong, 2007).

Participants for this study were purposely selected (Patton, 1990) as researchers aimed to interview people who were involved in the Indigenous industries in the Northern Rivers Region either as an Indigenous employer or business owner, or as a representative of a government or training organisation with a mandate to assist Indigenous enterprise growth. Prompting questions were asked to develop discussion and ensure the interviews covered the range of subject areas intended; however, for the most part, the interviewers allowed participants to bring up concerns or topics without prompting to enable examination of the themes that arose naturally. The interviewers aimed to create a relaxed and informal environment for their interviews to encourage discussion (Kingsley et al., 2010). Each interview lasted between one and two hours. The interviews were based around the following themes:

- future possibilities for Indigenous business development in the region;
- barriers to Indigenous business development;
- measures/assistance needed to help to facilitate Indigenous business development;
- the value of government assistance programmes; and
- the impact of regional location on business development.

The interviews were recorded and transcribed and the transcripts checked for errors and accuracy by interviewees before coding through the use of thematic analysis. Data analysis involved coding interview data, then extracting and grouping common themes (Strauss and Corbin, 2004). All results were tabled in an analysis grid to enable lucid interpretation of results. The results, once completed, were then sent to the respondents for comment, and emendations as necessary. This part of the process was important not only to provide validation to the results but also because, in the past, Indigenous voices have often been marginalised by the way traditional research outcomes have been presented (Rigney, 1999).

Findings

AVAILABLE GOVERNMENT ASSISTANCE PROGRAMMES

There are a number of federal and state programmes aimed at assisting Indigenous business development, such as the Business Development Assistance Program, which is administered by IBA and provides business support services and finance, and the Indigenous Capital Assistance Scheme, which offers Indigenous businesses access to commercial finance ($20,000–$500,000) and professional support services. There are also not-for-profit organisations such as Many Rivers that support aspiring business owners through microfinance. These various programmes offer a range of assistance, including: the provision of entrepreneurship and business facilitation training and workshops; the identification of possible business opportunities, including undertaking feasibility studies; clarifying business opportunities and developing business plans and proposals; and the provision of advice or support services to small business owner/operators in developing their skills, markets, and networks.

The programme which received the most comments throughout the interviews was the NSW State Aboriginal Enterprise Development Officer (AEDO) Program. This program enables local Aboriginal organisations to employ and train people who can then act as mentors and provide support for Aboriginal people wishing to establish a business. AEDOs are Aboriginal or Torres Strait Islander Australians who have had experience in establishing and managing a small business and who understand the unique needs of Indigenous business people (NSW Department of Education and Communities, 2013). AEDOs can provide mentoring, support, and business advice; can arrange accredited training and financial management advice; and can also provide assistance on government funding programmes. Other organisations offering small business support that are active in the region include IBA and Many Rivers.

PERCEIVED EFFECTIVENESS OF GOVERNMENT ASSISTANCE PROGRAMMES

It was noted by most participants that government programmes had a very important role to play in improving Indigenous business outcomes through the provision of training, funding, and mentoring. The AEDO Program was seen as being successful due to its flexibility and the ability of its officers to form relationships with business owners or those wishing to establish a business:

> *The Aboriginal Enterprise Development Officer, that's pretty good. For someone who has no business experience, it's good to put them onto them – they can give them a bit of a run down. I guess it's a little bit like going through our workshops, they then make a decision whether they want to go ahead with it or not, and if they do then they take on initial training. (Personal Comments, Participant 16)*

The availability of programmes which provide capital financing, including those offered by IBA, was considered adequate by one participant; however the delivery of assistance programmes was thought to need further improvement:

> *I think there are enough programmes in place for [capital financing], but I think the delivery could be improved. IBA could do with improvement. I think the red tape there is incredible. (Personal Comments, Participant 6)*

PERCEIVED ISSUES WITH GOVERNMENT ASSISTANCE PROGRAMMES

Despite the perceived success of some programmes the participants suggested that some of the government programmes were not successful in achieving their aims. There were a number of reasons as outlined below that prevented assistance programmes from being fully effective. All these problems have been identified in previous studies, as outlined in the literature review.

LACK OF APPROPRIATE FUNDING IN PROGRAMMES

Clearly, considering the lack of savings among Indigenous people, the provision of funding is a very important consideration. However, participants noted that the funding offered in some programmes needed to be improved. For example, assistance is often available for micro-loans of up to $5,000 and for larger loans of $10,000 or more. However, there is a dearth of funding between $5,000 and $10,000 available for business expansion:

> *That's overwhelming [having between $5,000 and $10,000] for a little owner who's probably just struggling to reach that big stage of going for out and out marketing, getting manufacturers etc. (Personal Comments, Participant 12)*

Some participants believed that government funding for Indigenous programmes is poorly managed and/or misused:

> *Extraordinary. Honest to God, the incompetence and waste of taxpayers' money is frightening, it's just frightening. (Personal Comments, Participant 7)*

In some cases organisations, despite their previous poor performance, continued to receive funding:

> But the problem of the people, all the organisations that they're giving funding to, one – don't have a proven track record; two – aren't delivering a good service, but they're continuing to get new contracts and they're continuing to give them to these [organisations]. (Personal Comments, Participant 17)

The conditions tied to some funding programmes, including the milestones required in the programme, were often unrealistic and therefore resulted in failure. In addition, programmes were often underfunded or not funded for long enough periods, resulting in failed outcomes.

DUPLICATION OF PROGRAMMES

The variety of programmes provided by various government departments, both federal and state, was found to confuse the small business owner. In addition, duplication also occurred as a result of a lack of coordination between the programmes. For example, some businesses received advice from two or more mentors. This was considered a poor use of resources:

> Yeah, there's a lot of money out there at the moment for Indigenous employment and training ... But it's fragmented with all the government departments involved. Everybody's got an Indigenous officer to look after their role in that particular department, and that's always been an issue of mine. (Personal Comments, Participant 8)

LACK OF CONSISTENCY IN PROGRAMMES

The interview participants noted that there was a lack of consistency/continuity with Indigenous business programmes. It was not uncommon for the priorities of government funding to change or to completely stop due to a change in policy direction or a change in minister and/or government. The continual changes became deflating for both the participants and on-the-ground deliverers of the programmes. The continual changes also resulted in a mistrust of government:

> And governments are at fault at times, too. But how often does, havin a government department say 'we're sendin off [name of person], we'll come and do this with you, we're gunna work with you', startin to get it to happen: next you know, we get a change of government ... they cut that programme! 'We're gunna have to [cut the programme], look, sorry mate ... (Personal Comments, Participant 1)

> They [the community] don't understand the politics behind it. All they know is, oh, f_ _k: you come in and promise me this, and now ... you're not doing anything. You know? And you wonder why they're sceptical of governments and ... bureaucracy. (Personal Comments, Participant 1)

AN UNDERVALUING OF INDIGENOUS PROGRAMMES BY GOVERNMENT

Some participants felt that government support of Indigenous programmes was insincere and lacked real conviction and/or action. Participants felt that other policy areas were given greater credence since Indigenous affairs was not considered a priority:

> I get cynical. You see some of these highway upgrades; they get finished quick and under budget, under time. Whether they pay lip service or whether the department says, look: just make it happen,

the Aboriginal employment stuff just gets pushed to the back. That's not based on anything: it's my feelings on it all. (Personal Comments, Participant 1)

SCALE OF DISADVANTAGE VERSUS AVAILABLE ASSISTANCE

Some participants involved with delivering government assistance programmes believe the scale of the problem outweighs the assistance provided through government programmes. Frustration was expressed over the expectation to transform people with poor literacy and numeracy skills and with little or no employment experience into successful business operators without adequate time or resources:

How could you make a person who has been unemployed for nearly 10 years to become an overnight businessman? (Personal Comments, Participant 18)

Interviewees detailed the frustration and disappointment that occurs on behalf of both the jobseeker and those providing assistance as a result of support agencies' lack of capacity to provide the kind of in-depth assistance which is often required:

Because [of our] KPI – we only work according to our criteria and according to the process. But we cannot really make a person that is unemployed for 10 years to become business-savvy, business-ready. (Personal Comments, Participant 18)

A LACK OF TOLERANCE FOR RISK

Another criticism of government assistance was that it was unlikely to be provided for what were considered 'risky' projects, despite the necessity of some degree of risk-taking for business success. Small business in particular needs to innovate, embrace change, and take risks in order to excel in a competitive and fast-moving economic environment. It was also noted that small businesses suffer a high failure rate, and many are not successful upon first attempt. This needs to be reflected within funding guidelines and allowances made for future business opportunities:

See that's the question though, how much failure can you tolerate. You know, a business is about putting your creative [sic], you're creating money from your risk, you know, so maybe the funding bodies that are supporting these businesses aren't willing to tolerate that risk, you know, but they've got this unrealistic perception that we're going to fund a business plan, then we're going to give you a loan and then your business is going to run okay, It's like you know, it's going to go to the f_ _ n wall at least two times before ... (Personal Comments, Participant 6)

OVERWORKED AND UNDERFUNDED CONSULTANTS AND MENTORS

Many of the interview respondents believed that the consultants and mentors working within government programmes and assisting Indigenous business owners were both underfunded and overworked. It was seen as commonplace for these people to work substantial additional unpaid hours and spend extensive amounts of time travelling to the businesses they were assisting. This extra commitment was required in order for consultants and mentors to achieve their goals:

Okay you've got this guy who hasn't done tourism before, or worked in tourism, so you want him to understand the business plan, and the business plan be written, and the research done ... but you don't have enough funding to see it through … so the consultants would put in three times the amount of hours they got paid for, to be nice to the client, and usually they would be highly engaged. (Personal Comments, Participant 6)

LACK OF OWNERSHIP OF BUSINESS PLANS

A number of programmes funded the development of a business plan. However participants noted that in many cases the business plans were often written by consultants or programme managers with little or no involvement of the Indigenous business owner. It was suggested that the while some consultants or programme managers were keen to ensure businesses had an effective plan, some were more interested in reaching key milestones than meeting the needs of the recipient. A lack of involvement of the businesses owner in the development of the plan was seen as resulting in their having a lack of understanding of the planning process and the requirements of the plan. As a result it was difficult, if not impossible, for the Indigenous person to implement the business plans, therefore gaining little or no benefit:

The mentors were going in, writing up a, a business plan, and the, the community or the locals had no idea what [laughs] … what to do with it! Put the business plan on the shelf … Tick! Tick! (Personal Comments, Participant 1)

Participants also felt that the benefits offered within many business start-up programmes were inadequate and that further skills are required in order for them to be successful. Training and skills development in areas such as strategic management, due diligence, and risk management were thought to be lacking from many programmes. It was also noted that the confidence required to be successful in business cannot be acquired through an assistance programme.

[T]heir skills are limited too, you know; they'll set them up with a business plan and this and that. The big issue is that, if you want to do business with other companies, they do a lot of due diligence, risk management and confidence. So, no one does any work on the pre-requisites of tendering, you know, for large companies. (Personal Comments, Participant 2)

NEPOTISM AND INEFFECTIVE LEADERSHIP IN GOVERNMENT ORGANISATIONS

There was a strong feeling amongst some participants that nepotism was prevalent within some government organisations tasked with providing Indigenous support. It was felt that some of the people employed in government positions lacked the capacity and/or experience to undertake their roles effectively:

You know, there are Indigenous people in Indigenous roles in Indigenous programmes who shouldn't be there because they don't have the capacity … they have fantastic links to the community … you know … so that's all good from that kind of supply side but they simply don't have the capacity and they'll lock anybody out who does … If people are there way above their level, and therefore it's really difficult to get anything done, and they feel threatened. (Personal Comments, Participant 7)

RED TAPE

Red tape was problematic for many interviewees who related instances of difficulties dealing with government departments and/or accessing funding through different programmes:

> So what you get in the Indigenous context, you get the red tape and the bullshit, and the fees and the registration and all that but then when you get staff that don't come from an educated background and themselves aren't helpful and aren't trained properly, it's just a double whammy. Because they can't work through it together you know, and the Indigenous person quite rightly, takes it personally. Yeah so, I think that is a big problem for small business generally. (Personal Comments, Participant 6)

> [T]here's a layer upon layers of regulations, at any single point, and I think that's what a lot of the Indigenous business services help with. (Personal Comments, Participant 6)

> They need to work harder at getting rid of red tape, making those models that businesses have to comply to like work cover. Making those models more effective, more efficient. (Personal Comments, Participant 20)

LACK OF AWARENESS OF EXISTING SERVICES

The problems associated with the duplication of programmes and the difficulty associated with accessing them were exacerbated by lack of awareness of what support services were currently available and the types of assistance they provide. Respondents suggested that it was difficult for government representatives to be aware of all the programmes, let alone individuals seeking help:

> What I've come across as a barrier is just not knowing who's out there [offering assistance]. (Personal Comments, Participant 19)

The Impact of Regional Location and Government Assistance Programmes

One problem identified as an issue arising from being located in a regional setting is the amount of travel required for mentors to adequately mentor their clients. Some participants felt that travel time was often not considered in the provision of funding because programmes were designed by bureaucrats and politicians in capital cities. It was also noted that remoteness and lack of access to transport made it important for assistance providers to travel out to communities. Again, it was felt there was no appreciation of the fact that in regional and remote areas it was important for programmes to be delivered in situ.

Another issue, noted by the participants, with Indigenous entrepreneurship development in the Bundjalung Nation was that there were very limited opportunities due to the small scale and limited economy of many of the towns located in the region. It was noted that even in some of the larger towns in the region there were limited opportunities for business development. A further problem associated with remoteness was the lack of a market and lack of business networks for many perspective Indigenous entrepreneurs:

> [W]ith the locality being up near [a regional rainforest waterfall] it was actually somewhere that could be made great, but just the logistics of it, it was very hard to run. And then the missus really

needed to have more of a social thing, having a young child, so we moved down into the [coastal, more populated] area and we found we had greater access to people and that really helped us develop the business more. So isolation was a big thing up there and then trying to work in with the bus ventures that were already established. (Personal Comments, Participant 9)

Finally, it is increasingly being acknowledged that effective Indigenous programmes as well as effective regional development policies need to adopt a 'bottom-up' approach rather than a 'top-down' one. However it is clear that this approach has yet to be embraced in Australia, and therefore it was not surprising that participants felt that government needed to listen more to people at a local level. There was a feeling that government programmes would benefit from local input. The feeling of disengagement from the political and bureaucratic decision-making processes was exacerbated by the fact that the Northern Rivers Region is such a long way from Sydney, the capital of NSW.

Conclusion

It is a common feature of research examining Indigenous business and employment programmes to focus largely on aspects of the programmes which do not work. This came through strongly in this research also. Whilst, not wanting the positive aspects of assistance programmes to be overshadowed by the negative, it is important to understand and review the obstacles to success in order to escape the perpetual cycle of doing the same things and expecting different outcomes. Drawing out the difficulties and hindrances associated with assistance programmes provides the opportunity to redesign and resolve past issues and to prevent future obstacles. It is also important to identify what impact regional location can have on the effectiveness of programmes.

The successful elements of the programmes studied were found to be the flexibility to tailor and adapt funding and assistance to individual requirements, and the opportunity for Indigenous business people to have contact with and be mentored by other Indigenous Australians who have had experience operating a business. Some of the difficulties encountered centred on inadequacies of funding and overstretched resources; duplication and inconsistency of programmes; a lack of tolerance for risk, nepotism; and ineffective leadership, red tape, and a lack of awareness of assistance programmes and initiatives.

The complexities of designing, developing, and delivering assistance programmes to a non-homogenous group of people – whose culture, geographic location, educational background, business knowledge, and general situation in life can vary to great extremes – is by no means a simple task. The task is also made even harder due to geographical differences. Indeed it is likely to take many long years of learning, adjusting, assessing, and readjusting to develop a programme with any strong likelihood of success. Sadly, given the pressure for political parties to differentiate themselves from their political opponents, a change of government often leads to a change of policy, and years of work can be lost (Altman et al., 2008).

This research highlights the importance of continually learning, monitoring, and adapting programmes to suit changing conditions and clientele whilst also preserving knowledge of what works and what does not, and maintaining a core continuity of support. The research also highlights the fact that there are many Indigenous people in the Bundjalung Nation who are very enthusiastic about establishing a network of Indigenous businesses. It should be noted that whilst government assistance programmes play an important role in helping to develop and facilitate Indigenous business, they are by no means a panacea for all the problems faced by Aboriginal and Torres Strait Islander Australians. A holistic approach which addresses the health, housing, social, economic, and education inequalities faced by Indigenous Australians is required if they are to escape disadvantage through business development and entrepreneurship.

References

Abdullah-Wendt, R. (2008). Indigenous governance: Does it improve indigenous employment outcomes? and if so how? In K. A. Brown, M. Mandell, C. W. Furneaux, and S. Beach (eds), *Contemporary issues in public management: The 12th Annual Conference of the International Research Society for Public Management*. Brisbane: Queensland University of Technology, 26–28 March.

Altman, J. C. (1998). Indigenous communities and business: Three perspectives, 1998–2000. *CAEPR Working Paper No. 9/2001*. Canberra: Australian National University.

Altman, J. C., Biddle, N., and Hunter, B. H. (2008). How realistic are the prospects for 'closing the gaps' in socioeconomic outcomes for Indigenous Australians? *CAEPR Discussion Paper No. 2ki np-0./':{ =87/2008*. Canberra: Australian National University.

Anderson, R. B., Hindle, K., Giberson, R. J., and Kayseas, R. (2004). Understanding success in Indigenous entrepreneurship: An exploratory investigation. In G. L. Murray, J. Butler, E. Douglas, K. Hindle, F. L. Pira, N. Lindsay, D. Shepherd, J. Yencken and S. Zara (eds), *Regional frontiers of entrepreneurship research 2004: Proceedings of the first annual regional entrepreneurship research exchange*. Melbourne: Babson College and Brisbane Graduate School of Business, pp. 83–100.

Australian Bureau of Statistics (ABS) (2006). *Census community profile series – 2006*. Retrieved from: http://www.censusdata.abs.gov.au/ABSNavigation/prenav/ViewData?&action=404&documentproductno=0&documenttype=Details&tabname=Details&areacode=0&issue=2006&producttype=Community%20Profiles&&producttype=Community (accessed: 28 June 2013).

——— (2009). *National Aboriginal and Torres Strait Islander social survey – 2008*. Retrieved from: http://www.abs.gov.au/ausstats/abs@.nsf/mf/4714.0/ (accessed: 26 July 2013).

——— (2011a). *Census of population and housing: Aboriginal and Torres Strait Islander Australian (Indigenous) profile*. Retrieved from: http://wwa.censusdata.abs.gov.au/census_services/getproduct/census/2011/communityprofile/0?opendocument&navpos=230 (accessed: 28 June 2013).

——— (2011b). *Census of population and housing: Basic community profile*. Retrieved from: http://www.censusdata.abs.gov.au/census_services/getproduct/census/2011/communityprofile/0?opendocument&navpos=230 (accessed: 28 June 2013).

——— (2012). *Labour force characteristics of Aboriginal and Torres Strait Islander Australians: Estimates from the labour force survey, 2011*. Retrieved from: http://www.abs.gov.au/AUSSTATS/abs@.nsf/DetailsPage/6287.02011?OpenDocument (accessed: 26 July 2013).

Australian Indigenous Chamber of Commerce (AICC) (2008). *Submission from the Australian Indigenous Chamber of Commerce to the House of Representatives Inquiry into Indigenous Business Development*. Retrieved from: http://www.aph.gov.au/house/committee/atsia/indigenousenterrpsies/subs/sub050.pdf (accessed: 26 July 2013).

Bennett, J. (2005). Indigenous entrepreneurship, social capital, and tourism enterprise development: Lessons from Cape York. *Unpublished PhD thesis*. Victoria: La Trobe University.

Berglund, C. A. (2001). *Health research*. Oxford: Oxford University Press.

Biddle, N. (2010). Indigenous migration and the labour market: A cautionary tale. *Australian Journal of Labour Economics*, 13(3), pp. 313–330.

Buultjens, J., Waller, I., Graham, S., and Carson, D. (2005). Public sector initiatives for Aboriginal small business development in tourism. In C. Ryan and M. Aicken (eds), *Indigenous tourism: The commodification and management of culture*. Oxford: Elsevier, pp. 127–147.

Dana, L. P. (2000). Change and circumstance in Kyrgyz markets. *Qualitative Market Research: An International Journal*, 3(2), pp. 62–73.

——— (2001). The education and training of entrepreneurs in Asia. *Education + Training*, 42(8/9), pp. 405–415.

Department of Families, Housing, Communities Services and Indigenous Affairs (FAHCSIA) (2013). *Closing the gap: Prime Minister's report 2013*. Retrieved from: http://www.fahcsia.gov.au/sites/default/files/documents/02_2013/00313-ctg-report_fa1.pdf (accessed: 26 July 2013).

Dockery, A. M. and Milsom, N. (2007). *A Review of Indigenous employment programs*. Perth: Curtin University.

Douglas, M. (2012). *Northern NSW health and disease in the Aboriginal community: Life stages, determinants, disease, service and workforce*. Lismore: University Centre for Rural Health.

Finlayson, J. (2007). *Organising for success: Policy report: Successful strategies in Indigenous organisations*. Canberra: Australian Collaboration Australian Institute of Aboriginal and Torres Strait Island Studies (AIATSIS).

Foley, D. (2004). An examination of Indigenous Australian entrepreneurs. *Journal of Developmental Entrepreneurship*, 8(2), pp. 133–151.

Fuller, D., Buultjens, J., and Cummings, E. (2005). Ecotourism and Indigenous micro-enterprise formation in Northern Australia: Opportunities and constraints. *Tourism Management*, 26, pp. 891–904.

———, Howard, M., and Cummings, E. (2003). Indigenous micro-enterprise development in Northern Australia: Implications for economic and social policy. *Journal of Economic and Social Policy*, 7(2), pp. 15–34.

Gillham, B. (2000). *Case study research methods*. London: Continuum.

Gray, M., Hunter, B., and Howlett, M. (2012). *Indigenous employment: A story of continuing growth*. Retrieved from: http://www.aihw.gov.au/uploadedFiles/ClosingTheGap/Content/Publications/2012/ctg-ip03.pdf (accessed: 19 July 2013).

Hesse-Biber, S. and Leavy, P. (2005). *The practice of qualitative research*. Thousand Oaks: Sage.

House of Representatives Standing Committee on Aboriginal and Torres Strait Islander Affairs. (HRSCATSIA) (2008). *Open for business: Developing Indigenous enterprises in Australia*. Retrieved from: http://www.aph.gov.au/house/committee/atsia/Indigenousenterprises/report/front.pdf (accessed: 26 July 2013).

Hunter, B. (1997). The determinants of Indigenous employment outcomes: The importance of education and training. *Australian Bulletin of Labour*, 23(3), pp. 177–192.

Ivory, B. (2003). Poverty and enterprise. In S. C. Carr and T. S. Sloane (eds), *Poverty and psychology: Emergent critical practice*. New York: Kluwer, pp. 251–266.

Kingsley, J., Phillips, R., Townsend, M., and Henderson-Wilson, C. (2010). Using a qualitative approach to research to build trust between a non-Aboriginal researcher and Aboriginal participants (Australia). *Qualitative Research Journal*, 10(1), pp. 2–12.

Kwamikagami (2013). *Bundjalung Nation map*. Retrieved from: http://en.wikipedia.org/wiki/File:Bandjalangic_languages.png (accessed: 30 July 2013).

Legge, J. and Hindle, K. (2004). *Entrepreneurship: Context, vision and planning*. Basingstoke: Palgrave Macmillan.

Liamputtong, P. (2007). *Researching the vulnerable: A guide to sensitive research methods*. London: Sage.

Lindsay, N. (2005). *Toward a cultural model of Indigenous entrepreneurial attitude*. Retrieved from: http://www.amsreview.org/articles/lindsay05-2005.pdf (accessed: 30 July 2013).

Lloyd, D. and Norrie, F. (2004). Identifying training needs to improve Indigenous community representatives input into environmental resource management consultative processes: A case study of the Bundjalung Nation. *Australian Journal of Environmental Education*, 20(1), pp. 101–113.

Malezer, L. (2008). *50,000 jobs target of corporate plan*. Retrieved from: http://www.aiatsis.gov.au/koorimail/issues/pdf/432.pdf (accessed: 30 July 2013).

McBryde, I. (1974). *Aboriginal prehistory in New England: An archaeological survey of northeastern New South Wales*. Sydney: Sydney University Press.

Mertens, D. M. (2005). *Research methods in education and psychology: Integrating diversity with quantitative and qualitative approaches*. Thousand Oaks: Sage.

Mitchell, S. (1995). Foreign contact and Indigenous exchange: Networks on the Cobourg Peninsula, North-Western Arnhem Land. *Australian Aboriginal Studies*, 2, pp. 44–8.

Moreton-Robinson, A. (2006). Towards a new research agenda? *Journal of Sociology*, 42(4), pp. 383–395.

Nguyen, N. (2013). *Early post-school outcomes for Indigenous youth: The role of literacy and numeracy.* Retrieved from: http://www.ncver.edu.au/publications/2308.html (accessed: 30 July 2013).

NSW Department of Education and Communities (2013). *Aboriginal Enterprise Development Officer Program (AEDOP).* Retrieved from: http://www.training.nsw.gov.au/programs_services/funded_other/acp/aedop.html (accessed: 26 July 2013).

Patton, M. (1990). *Qualitative evaluation and research methods.* Beverly Hills: Sage.

Pearson, C. and Helms, K. (2010). Releasing indigenous entrepreneurial capacity: A case study of the Yolngu clan in a remote region of Northern Australia. *Journal Global Business and Economics Review*, 12(1–2), pp. 72–84.

Pearson, N. (2000). *Our right to take responsibility.* Cairns: Noel Pearson and Associates.

——— and Kostakidis-Lianos, L. (2004). Building Indigenous capital-removing obstacles to participation in the real economy. *Australian Prospect*, 10.

Peredo, A. M., Anderson, R. B., Galbraith, C. S., Hoing, B., and Dana, L. P. (2004). Toward a theory of Indigenous entrepreneurship. *International Journal of Entrepreneurship and Small Business*, 1(1/2), pp. 1–19.

Rigney, L. I. (1999). Internationalisation of an Indigenous anti-colonial cultural critique of research methodologies: A guide to indigenist research methodology and its principles. *Journal of Native American Studies*, 14(2), pp. 116–117.

Royal Commission into Aboriginal Deaths in Custody (RCADC). (1991). *National Report 2.* Canberra: Australian Government.

Sharpe, M. C. (1985). Bundjalung settlement and migration. *Aboriginal History*, 9(1), pp. 101–124.

Shoebridge, A. (2009). Indigenous Entrepreneurship in Northern NSW. *Unpublished honours thesis.* Lismore: Southern Cross University.

Sofield, T. H. B. and Birtles, R. A. (1996). Indigenous peoples' cultural opportunity, spectrum for tourism (IPCOST). In R. Butler, and T. Hinch (eds), *Tourism and Indigenous peoples.* London: International Thompson Business Press, pp. 397–433.

Stark, J. (2013). *Diabetes threatens to wipe out Aborigines* Retrieved from: http://www.theage.com.au/news/national/diabetes-threatens-to-wipe-out-aborigines/2006/11/12/1163266413553.html (accessed: 30 July 2013).

Steering Committee for the Review of Government Service Provision (SCRGSP) (2011). *Overcoming Indigenous disadvantage: Key indicators – 2011.* Canberra: Productivity Commission.

Strauss, A. L. and Corbin, J. (2004). Open coding. In C. Seale (ed.), *Social research methods.* London: Routledge, pp. 303–306.

Sullivan, P. (2010). Government processes and the effective delivery of services: The Ngaanyatjarra Council and its regional partnership agreement. *Desert Knowledge CRC Working Paper 71.* Alice Springs: Desert Knowledge CRC.

Tashakkori, A. and Teddlie, C. (eds) (2003). *Handbook of mixed Methods in social and behavioral research.* Thousand Oaks: Sage.

Tindale, N. B. (1974). *Aboriginal tribes of Australia: Their terrain, environmental controls, distribution, limits and proper names.* Berkeley: University of California Press.

Trudgen, R. (2000). *Why warriors lay down and die.* Darwin: Aboriginal Resource and Development Services.

Ward, J. and Holman, D. (2001).Who needs a plan?. In C. Berglund (ed.), *Health research.* Oxford: Oxford University Press.

Whitford, M., Bell, B., and Watkins, M. (2001). Indigenous tourism policy in Australia: 25 years of rhetoric and economic rationalism. *Current Issues in Tourism*, 4(2–4), pp. 151–181.

Wood, G. J. and Davidson, M. J. (2011). A review of male and female Australian indigenous entrepreneurs: Disadvantaged past – promising future? *Gender in Management: An International Journal*, 26(4), pp. 311– 326.

PART II
INDIGENOUS ENTERPRISE

5

From Passive Consumers to Entrepreneurs: Building a Political Context for Economic Development in an Anishinabe Community, Quebec

Marie-Pierre Bousquet

Chapter Synopsis

When talking about salaried work, Native peoples of Canada are more readily associated with handouts than with entrepreneurship. In a context of dependence on the state, plus poor education, lack of capital, and non-ownership of their lands, Native peoples do not seem to have much to offer. Yet, in an environment so unconducive to innovation, there are nonetheless striking examples of people moving towards autonomy and empowerment. Pikogan, a small Anishinabe community of northwestern Quebec, has decided to take its destiny into its own hands: the band council organises and promotes initiatives such as Job Days, mentorship, and negotiations with companies. Drawing on data collected during a study about the colonization of the Abitibiwinnik (Pikogan band members), and including the transformation of their economy, I argue that these measures are a veritable act of decolonization; that is, the Abitibiwinnik are seeking to change the existing colonial structure of social and economic relations.

Introduction

A priori, to develop local economies in smaller communities, it takes at a minimum either money, experience, or something to attract investors: ideas, resources, skills, a well-trained workforce, etc. It is difficult, if not impossible, to imagine the development of entrepreneurship without one of these attractive forces. Quebec Native communities are rarely poles of attraction because they are often geographically isolated and the level of education of community members is generally very low. In 2006, according to Human Resources and Skills Development Canada, 34% of Natives aged between 25 and 64 did not have a high school diploma (compared to 15% for non-Aboriginals), and only 8% had a university degree (23% for non-Aboriginals).[1] In addition, outside major urban centres, regional economies are often fragile because they are undiversified and primarily dependent on the exploitation of natural resources. Add to this the fact that racism against Natives hinders their hiring, it is not surprising that Native people generally prefer working in Aboriginal organizations where they are free from such discrimination and encounter fewer differences in mentality. Finally, because of the *Indian Act,*[2] communities – whether they are recognised as a reserve or as a settlement[3] – are under the administrative and legal tutelage of the Ministry of Aboriginal Affairs. The main employer in the community is usually the band council, which receives its budget from the federal government and is a sort of super-municipality that manages all the services offered to the population: administration, housing, public works, health and social services, cultural, education, public safety, economic development, and even leisure.

Although these generalities have to be nuanced – Quebec Native communities are a very heterogeneous group – conditions are rarely conducive to the development of large-scale local initiatives.

Apart from the service sector, the areas where Native communities have been most active in the last 10 years are tourism (Iankova, 2005, 2008), arts and crafts, small business, construction, and employment in the forestry and mining industries (Boutet, 2010). We cannot forget, however, the gambling industry, represented by the casinos (Akwesasne) and online gaming (Kahnawake), the licensing of bingo[4] (e.g. Corporation Piekuakami Games Metueun Mashteuiatsh), and the First Nations Poker Trail (which began in 2006). Since part of this sector involves illegal activities, it is not the best example with which to illustrate the dynamic nature of contemporary Native economic development initiatives in Quebec. I will focus instead on the approach of a small Anishinabe community, Pikogan, which in my opinion is fairly representative of the way to think about economic development in a community of this type. I will argue that in a context so unfavourable to innovation – where half of the members of the communities are under the age of 25, and where workers earn on average two-thirds of the Canadian average wage[5] – it is still possible to increase autonomy and empowerment. To do this, Pikogan decided to take its destiny in hand: the band council organizes and promotes many initiatives, such as employment days, mentorship, a presence in the nearest Chamber of Commerce, and negotiations with companies. I analyse this set of initiatives – and especially those targeting mining companies – as a real attempt at decolonization, in the sense that the Abitibiwinnik are trying to change the structure of social relations. I base my analysis on data collected during a recent study on the colonization of the

---

1   Human Resources and Skills Development Canada website (http://www4.hrsdc.gc.ca/.3ndic.1t.4r@-fra. jsp?iid=29#M_4, accessed: 2 October 2012), referring to Statistics Canada. *Portrait de la scolarité au Canada, Recensement de 2006.* Ottawa, Statistique Canada, 2008 (no. 97–560-X2006001).

2   Enacted in 1876 and amended several times since, the *Indian Act* is a federal law that determines who is a Native in Canada, and establishes the rights of Natives who are legally recognized. This law derives from a colonial policy aimed at assimilating Natives.

3   A 'reserve' is federally owned land that is set aside for the use and benefit of a particular Native band. By contrast, a 'settlement' is land belonging to a provincial government, to a municipality, or even to a church, where a Native band is tolerated or even permitted to reside.

4   Note that the management of bingo on Native reserves is under federal and not provincial jurisdiction (e.g., not under the remit of Loto-Québec).

5   *'Justice pour les peuples autochtones – Voyons-y! Pauvreté chez les Autochtones'* Public Service Alliance of Canada (http://psac-afpc.com/issues/campaigns/aboriginal/aboriginalpoverty-f.shtml, accessed: 27 August 2012).

Abitibiwinnik since the late nineteenth century, specifically with regard to the transformation of their economy.[6]

Theoretical and Methodological Aspects

If one believes the theorists, whether Western or Native (of note, these categories are less than satisfactory), decolonization is far from being a fait accompli in Canada.

Yet, in the Canadian context, the term 'decolonisation' cannot refer to the definition given, for example, by Prasenjit Duara (2003: 2) when he talks about China: 'Decolonization refers to the process whereby colonial powers transferred institutional and legal control over their territories and dependencies to indigenously based, formally sovereign, nation-states.' Native Canadians, who lived through colonial oppression, are nonetheless part of a nation-state that controls their legal identity via the *Indian Act*, and that only in theory recognizes a right to Native self-governance. In practice, the only Native governments are band councils, tribal councils, and the Assembly of First Nations.

Band councils are creations of the *Indian Act* and fall under federal jurisdiction. Their jurisdiction is limited to the territory of the community (reserve or settlement) and not the territories for which band members recognize themselves as having rights (e.g., ancestral hunting territory).

Tribal councils are groups of First Nations that provide technical services and advice, particularly with regard to management and economic development. They also have political roles because they are mandated to protect aboriginal rights and advance the claims of the bands they represent. Non-profit organizations, tribal councils are usually funded by the Department of Aboriginal Affairs and Northern Development Canada.

The Assembly of First Nations, which has representatives from every province and territory, is an interest group that lobbies for the respect of Natives' rights, including the right to self-government and economic development. The Assembly receives most of its funding from the Ministry of Aboriginal Affairs.

Native political organizations in Canada must all negotiate with the federal government, to whom they are accountable. This places these organizations in financial conflicts of interest, since they must protect and represent the interests of their members while also complying with the requirements (and potentially contradictory interests) of the federal government, which controls the financing.

Decolonization in Canada cannot be thought of as a radical or even violent break with the colonial order – i.e. political, economic, social, intellectual and cultural – as conceived by Frantz Fanon (1961) and Edward Said (1988, 2000) in the context of nation-states. This view would mean that the decolonization of Native Canadians could only occur following their complete independence. Further, decolonization would have to involve the complete overthrow of the existing social order, which is not about to happen in Canada. Admittedly, Native intellectuals such as Devon Mihesuah (2003, 2004), Marie Battiste (2011), or Taiaiake Alfred (1999) have taken on the challenge of destroying Western imperialism, reconstructing identity, and restoring 'indigenisation' in Native thought, culture, spirituality, and education, including in the university. With or without independence, is it possible for Native communities to achieve total emancipation from colonial thought? This question is made all the more challenging when one considers the phenomenon of hybridisation: where does the colonial order end and the indigenous begin?

6   This research was supported by a grant from the Social Sciences and Humanities Research Council of Canada (SSHRC) and made possible by the ongoing collaboration of the population of Pikogan and the band council of the Abitibiwinni First Nation.

My goal here is not to investigate these questions. One of the basic meanings of colonialism is that it involves unequal power relationships. Decolonization would, therefore, imply the opposite: the establishment (or reestablishment) of equal relationships, or at least a structural change in relations with the colonists, accompanied by an improvement in the Aboriginal condition (Trépied, 2011). According to Poka Laenui (2000), who sees decolonization as more a social than a political process, there are five stages in the process of decolonisation: 1) rediscovery and recovery, 2) mourning, 3) dreaming, 4) commitment, and 5) action. According to Laenui (2000: 155), one of the *most crucial* phases is dreaming:

> True decolonization is more than simply replacing indigenous or previously colonized people into the positions held by colonizers. Decolonization includes the reevaluation of the political, social, economic, and judicial structures themselves and the development, if appropriate, of new structures that can hold and house the values and aspirations of the colonized people.

I could not say at what stage of decolonization the Algonquins are; as Laenui (2000: 152) states, these phases 'do not have clear demarcations from one to the next'. I think these stages can occur concomitantly, depending on individuals, groups, or contexts; they might also have begun to take place for a part of a group and not necessarily for another. In the case that interests me here, I would argue that not only have the Abitibiwinnik decided to dream of a better future that is independent of government funding and linked to a recovered pride, they have also decided to go from dreaming to action. They are creating new political, social, and economic opportunities, and so are seeking to change the existing colonial structure of social relations. As we shall see, the Abitibiwinnik began with two observations that I could summarize in two sentences: 'They [the whites] don't know who we are' and 'We don't know what we're capable of doing.' These two observations underlie all the steps they have taken in their process of decolonization.

My understanding of these observations is built on qualitative data collected during a three-year study in and with the community of Pikogan. The study had two parts:

1. An ethno historical analysis that sought to document the origins and functioning of bureaucratic colonialism amongst the Abitibiwinnik since the late nineteenth century. This included assessing the *marge de manœuvre* of the Abitibiwinnik in a social and economic system that had been imposed on them by the indirect action of the state through the employees of the Hudson's Bay Company, missionaries, and Indian agents.
2. A contemporary analysis that aimed to define when (and if) colonialism ended and opened the way for decolonization. Does the political rhetoric *marching towards autonomy/marche vers l'autonomie* and *taking charge of oneself/prise en charge* really make sense in the current system?

The data were collected in various ways, including archival research (mainly at the National Archives of Canada and in the local Pikogan archives) and semi-structured or open interviews with representatives of different generations of the Pikogan community. I drew upon interview data collected during previous studies, as I have conducted ethnographic field research in Pikogan since 1996. Finally, I examined regional newspapers, a mode of expression that the Abitibiwinnik have used actively for over a decade to express their desires, their discontent, their successes, and their openness for dialogue with surrounding non-Native communities.

Before analysing the results of the initial steps taken by Pikogan in the process of decolonisation, it is important to first understand their social, political, and economic context, including the ancestral territory, legal status, and land claims of this community. Following this description, I then examine the strategies used by Pikogan to dream of a viable economy and to appropriate a work culture that was imposed by capitalist market structures, making it their own and thus appropriate for Natives. In reflecting on the culture and values that the Abitibiwinnik are seeking to protect through their various economic initiatives, I return to my analysis and argue that, in Pikogan at least, there is a real attempt at changing the existing structure of social relations with the goal of becoming decolonized.

A History of Pikogan and its Economy

Pikogan is one of nine communities (six reserves and three settlements) identified as Anishinabek or Algonquin in Quebec.[7] The Pikogan reserve was founded in 1958 in the Abitibi-Témiscamingue region, north-western Quebec. The area was opened for colonization in the early twentieth century with the Gordon (1932–34) and Vautrin (1934–37) settlement plans – a response to the massive urban unemployment caused by the 1929 economic crash. These plans were set up by the federal and provincial governments to encourage city dwellers to return to the land.[8] The major cities in the region – all located on traditional Algonquin territory – are Amos (founded in 1914; 12,671 inhabitants in 2011), Val-d'Or (1930; 31,862), and Rouyn-Noranda (1917; 41,012).[9]

During the first half of the twentieth century, the Abitibiwinnik were still mostly semi-nomadic, living on a mixed economy of trapping and seasonal work. They were most often hired in the three sectors that are still the basis of the current regional economy: forestry and its derivatives (sawmills), mining, and agriculture to a lesser extent.

The decline of the fur trade in the early twentieth century, the traditional economy of the Anishinabek, forced them to change their means of subsistence and to move closer to the towns, villages, and work sites that were the primary source of employment, at least during the summer months; some Anishinabek stayed during the winter, renting barns in which to live (and sometimes to work) in exchange for work.

In 1956, the local Indian agent used band funds – with the agreement of the Abitibiwinni chief at the time – to purchase agricultural land near the town of Amos. In 1958, the federal government granted the legal status of reserve to this land. At the time, there was only one building on the site, the home of the farmer and former owner, Mr Blais; this building served as the band office, accommodation for one family, and occasionally for church services. The first houses on the reserve were built in 1964. Starting in 1958, the semi-nomadic members of the band gradually settled the site; they had no choice. The failing profitability of the fur trading posts had forced the closure of many, while agricultural colonization, the arrival of the railway, the opening of roads, and urbanisation had greatly reduced the Abitibiwinnik's access to their ancestral hunting grounds. Finally, from 1955 to 1972, the Abitibiwinnik were forced to send their children to the

---

7   Another Algonquin community that is officially recognized by the federal government is Pikwàkanagàn in Ontario. The use of the ethnonym Algonquin derives from a federal government classification that is somewhat arbitrary. The ethnonym Anishinabe is vernacular, but in practice applies to all those who understand the language of the Anishinabek, which is much larger than the Algonquin Nation, strictly speaking.

8   The colonization plans, implemented mainly by the clergy, provided financial incentives to urban families to clear and cultivate land in the Abitibi (Matthews, 1987). The Gordon plan was a relative failure because it had targeted industrial workers who were not farmers. The Vautrin plan tried to redress this error by targeting people who knew how to work the land. These plans allowed for the establishment of many villages.

9   See Statistics Canada, 2011 Census. Rouyn-Noranda (http://www12.statcan.gc.ca/census-recensement/2011/as-sa/fogs-spg/Facts-csd-fra.cfm?Lang=Fra&TAB=1&GK=CSD&GC=2486042); Amos (http://www12.statcan.gc.ca/census-recensement/2011/as-sa/fogs-spg/Facts-csd-fra.cfm?Lang=Fra&TAB=1&GK=CSD&GC=2488055); Val-d'Or (http://www12.statcan.ca/census-recensement/2011/as-sa/fogs-spg/Facts-csd-fra.cfm?Lang=Fra&TAB=1&GK=CSD&GC=2489008).

residential school in Saint-Marc-de-Figuery (15 km from Amos), with the result that parents who wanted to be close to their children had no choice but to settle on the reserve.

Reserve 'Amos no. 1' officially took the name of Pikogan in 1980, and over the years expanded from its initial 72 hectares to 91 hectares in 2008, when the federal government approved the addition of a further 187 hectares to the reserve, land that had been purchased by the band council in 1995 (for a total of approximately 278 hectares). In 2008, 869 people were registered members of the band, but only 536 lived on the reserve in the 148 existing homes (Guindon, 2008: 10). In the following years, the construction of a further 43 houses was planned, and many are already finished. Finally, 'space has also been planned for the commercial, industrial, recreational/ tourism development' (Guindon, 2008: 10).

This portrait of the community would be incomplete if I did not mention that the population of Pikogan is very young, with a median age of 24 years (2011 Census). If the current very high birth rate continues, the size of the population is expected to double by the middle of the twenty-first century. While this demographic dynamism leads to important resource needs – notably in infrastructure (houses, roads, etc.) – it also shows that the community has significant human resources. The vernacular language, Anishinabemowin, is still spoken, especially by those who are over 40 years of age, but the language of everyday life is French. However, the youth, in their social networks, seem more attracted by English as it enables them to communicate with a wider outside world. Also, part of the population is of Cree descent where English is the lingua franca (with Cree).

The Abitibiwinni Territory, Treaty No. 9, and the Beaver Preserve

Pikogan is only a small part of the ancestral Abitibiwinni territory. Indeed, before sedentarisation, the Abitibiwinnik had a vast territory from which they derived their resources; extending to Ontario in the west, James Bay in the north, the Mauricie in the east, and Val-d'Or in the south (hundreds of square kilometres). In line with the anthropological definition of 'semi-nomadism' – i.e. where group members return annually to a fixed location – the family groups that made up the Abitibiwinnik gathered each summer at Apitipik Point on Lake Abitibi, which overlaps the border between Ontario and Quebec. In the nineteenth century – following a change of policy regarding access to trading posts (hunters were forced to return to only one trading post, in order to build 'loyalty') and because of population declines due to epidemics – family territories (pieces of band territory) and their households became smaller.

In 1906, to end Native claims over northern Ontario, to make land available for the arrival of the transcontinental railway, and to legalize the Ontario–Quebec border, the Crown undertook to sign a treaty with the Native bands concerned, that is, Treaty No. 9. The treaty did not apply to territories outside Ontario. Nonetheless, the treaty directly affected the Natives of Lake Abitibi – that is, the Abitibiwinnik – whose territory overlapped the two provinces.[10] In 1908, after several hours of negotiations between the Treaty Commissioners and a newly elected chief and band councillors, and through the intermediary of an interpreter, the Abitibiwinnik acceded to the treaty in exchange for royalties of $4 per person per year, the establishment of day schools, and lands reserved for their use: 1 square mile per family of five (Frenette, 2006; Rankin, 2003). The Abitibiwinnik can still receive to this date $4 per person per year (the amount was not indexed); however, because the location of the land they were to receive was never specified, the Abitibiwinnik lost all of their

---

10   Quebec has a policy regarding the recognition of Native land rights that differs significantly from that of other Canadian provinces. The Quebec policy is derived from historical French policy that did not recognize the existence of indigenous title in its colonies. The Algonquin, if they wanted to negotiate land claims in Quebec, would first need to have recognised by the province that they have an ancestral title.

traditional territory in Ontario. The Treaty effectively cut the band in two, both physically and in terms of their legal identity. The Ontario Abitibiwinnik were settled in the reserve of Wahgoshig on the western edge of Lake Abitibi (200 km from Pikogan, and 3 hours by car), and listed as Ojibwa and not Algonquin. The Quebec Abitibiwinnik remained officially Algonquin and, while considered signatories to Treaty No. 9, received no reserve land from the Crown. The Pikogan reserve was not created under the terms of the Treaty, but with the money from the trust account of the Abitibiwinnik. In essence, the Abitibiwinnik paid for their own reserve.

The Abitibiwinnik began to complain in the nineteenth century about the encroachment of non-aboriginals on their hunting territory. In particular, the overexploitation by non-aboriginals of the most coveted fur, the beaver, saw its population decline dangerously. In Quebec, beaver trapping was twice banned (from 1897 to 1900 and from 1925 to 1935; e.g. Frenette, 1988: 169–70, 177). To protect their economy, the Algonquin First Nation demanded that their hunting territories be reserved for their exclusive use. Hunting reserves were created in 1928, including in the Abitibi for the Abitibiwinnik. In 1943, the provincial government transformed the Abitibiwinnik's hunting reserve into a beaver preserve of 78,930 square kilometres. Beaver preserves – of which there are 11 in Quebec – are divided into trap lines, and are restricted to particular groups or individuals.[11] Only Natives (including the Inuit) have the right to hunt fur animals, and only on their own preserves, provided that they meet quotas and report the number of beavers killed (at least in theory, because there has been no control since the 1970s).

The beaver preserve is currently the only protected part of the Abitibiwinni territory. But the fact that logging companies have the right to cut wood in the preserves threatens the environment of fur animals, and thus the viability of hunting and trapping that are still, to this day, essential parts of traditional activities and Abitibiwinnik identity. The Abitibiwinnik have therefore encouraged the training of their young people in the mapping and management of forest resources so that, under the *Forest Act*, they can negotiate with forestry companies who have a legal duty to consult Native communities. The rest of the Abitibiwinni territory in Quebec is now covered with fields, small towns, and lands that are under the control of municipalities, the region, the province, and sometimes even the Crown. Abitibiwinnik who wish to cross this land to develop income-generating activities such as adventure tourism are forced to pay for permits or obtain waivers.[12]

This presentation of Pikogan, its geographic area and its history, is not only contextual. As we will see, the Abitibiwinnik refer constantly to this territory which they never surrendered. Not only do they continue to use the territory, but they also claim the right to receive royalties from its use. The courts have so far proven an ineffective means for Quebec Natives to defend their claims; the only land claims that have led to a settlement concern land under treaty, such as the Murray Treaty for the Huron-Wendat or the James Bay Convention for the Cree. The Anishinabek Abitibiwinnik are the only group affected by Treaty No. 9, which is not supposed to be concerned with land in Quebec; and the legal difficulties that this creates further impedes the processing of Anishinabek claims. For other Native groups with files sitting on the shelves of the Secrétariat aux affaires autochtones in Quebec since the 1970s, the procedures have been lengthy and costly, and the few agreements signed with governments have been unsatisfactory.

---

11   Note that trap lines in beaver preserves constitute a system of wildlife management, and are based on the Anishinabe model of family hunting territories.

12   Pikogan has an adventure tourism business, Bercé par l'Harricana (Bousquet, 2008).

'Here, We do Nothing but Wait?'

In 1996, during a one-year stay in Pikogan, I noticed that for its inhabitants, the reserve was most often associated with boredom, inactivity, unemployment, and deprivation of liberty. As one of my informants, who was 50 years old, pointed out to me: 'Here, nothing is done. We do nothing but wait' (for the welfare or unemployment cheque). Like all other employed persons of the time, her life had been a succession of periods of employment and unemployment, but also different types of vocational training accumulated through various government programmes. The older unilingual Anishinabemowin, who had been born and raised in the forest, had worked mainly for mining and forestry companies, as workers or foremen. The subsequent generations, by contrast, were trained in an Indian Residential School (Bousquet, 2006) and then in schools in Amos, and had worked both inside and outside the reserve in various domains; these included work on farms raising mink, in construction, in the community police, cooking for tourist camps, in project management, in community radio, and in teaching. And, as with the previous generation, they had accumulated different types of skills through government training programmes, in library sciences, accounting, administration, etc.

Hardly anyone I met had a coherent or linear professional trajectory, aside from some employees of the band council, and few imagined that they might be able to have a long-term career that they liked and had really chosen. It was first necessary to earn money to live and to meet the urgent needs of a burgeoning young village, where all positions were to be filled in priority by members of the First Nation. I also noted among the younger members of the community a strong desire to do something for their families, combined with a desire to remain in the community if possible – or at least work with other Natives. Finally, I noticed that, in comparison with myself, for whom periods of unemployment where terribly stressful, the Anishinabek did not seem particularly stressed by unemployment; it was always possible to access social welfare, and to gain additional income through selling crafts, trapping, or through the occasional sale of homemade doughnuts. Betting on sports was also very popular. Finally, work was not specifically a source of pride, because this could be found elsewhere, for example, in traditional activities and in the act of raising children well.

Since the mid-1990s, members of succeeding Pikogan band councils have shared common goals: to change the Anishinabe work culture; retain those who go to study (ensure they return); create jobs outside the band council (the principal employer), and so become economically autonomous and no longer dependent on the government. This trend is generalized among all the First Nations of Quebec. Following an agreement with the government and in line with the federal programme 'Pathways to Success: Aboriginal Employment and Training Strategy' created in 1991, the Assembly of First Nations of Quebec and Labrador (AFNQL) signed in 1996 an agreement with Human Resources Development Canada 'transferring to the First Nations authorities full jurisdiction over the training and development of the aboriginal workforce'.[13] This lead to the creation of the Quebec First Nations Human Resources Development Commission which gradually opened regional offices throughout the province. Its Anishinabek branch, the Algonquin Abitibi Human Resources Development Commission, was established in the late 1990s and has an office in Pikogan.

---

13   First Nations Human Resources Development Commission of Quebec (http://www.cdrhpnq.qc.ca/about.htm), accessed 20 September 2012.

The Abitibiwinni Strategy

Abitibiwinnik strategy since the late 1990s unfolds on several fronts: land, human and social capital, politics, and diplomacy. They seem to want to implement the scheme developed by Anderson and Giberson in 2003 and reprinted in various publications on Aboriginal entrepreneurs:

After briefly describing all the initiatives put in place by the band council, I will focus on the work of the latter in the mining sector, as the process seems indicative of the desire for empowerment of the band, or at least of its leadership.

---

1. A predominantly collective one centered on the First Nation or community. For the purposes of:
2. Attaining economic self-sufficiency as a necessary condition for the preservation and strengthening of communities.
3. Control over activities on traditional lands.
4. Improving the socioeconomic circumstances of Aboriginal people.
5. Strengthening traditional culture, values and languages and the reflecting of the same in development activities.
    Involving the following processes:
6. Creating and operating businesses that can compete profitably over the long run in the global economy to:
    a) exercise the control over activities on traditional lands
    b) build the economy necessary to preserve and strengthen communities and improve socioeconomic conditions.
7. Forming alliances and joint ventures among themselves and with non-Aboriginal partners to create businesses that can compete profitably in the global economy.
8. Building capacity for economic development through: (i) education, training and institution building and (ii) the realization of the treaty and Aboriginal rights to land and resources.

Figure 5.1   **Aboriginal approach to economic development**

Source: Anderson and Giberson, 2003: 144.

The Land

The band council has reviewed the zoning of the reserve, which is divided into two parts: residential and commercial. Following the official expansion of the reserve in 2008, the commercial zone was also increased. At the moment (2012), there is only a convenience store/petrol station, but the commercial re-zoning has meant that Pikogan is able to welcome various initiatives, ranging from the establishment of small businesses to the installation of big box stores. As the Abitibiwinnik frequently shop at discount and department stores in Amos and Val d'Or, the idea is to keep in the community money that would otherwise be spent elsewhere, all while creating jobs. In addition, since 2008, Pikogan has provided an opportunity for community members to become homeowners. As reserves are lands owned by the Crown; residents have no property rights over their homes or land, except for usufruct, the right to live on the land and in the house. There are several possible scenarios, but Pikogan is among those reserves where people were only tenants of the houses built by federal funding with the assistance of the Canada Mortgage and Housing Corporation (CMHC/SCHL). This meant that Pikogan residents had no equity, and thus nothing to offer to banks as collateral if they wanted a loan. However, since 2008, any member of the band wishing to build a house on the reserve can do so, and obtain in exchange a certificate of possession from the band council.[14] As one councillor explained, this means that 'they will be able to borrow from financial institutions' (Guindon, 2008) which allows members of the community to consider other options, like starting a business venture. This change has been revolutionary in Pikogan.

Human and Social Capital

The band council has directed its initiatives at two audiences – the Abitibiwinnik and non-Natives – with the goal of convincing both of the same message: that the Abitibiwinnik have great potential and many capabilities. As one former chief told me in October 2010:

> Our people are capable, but they do not know what they are capable of. It's as if they are discouraged in advance. They do not know who they are. This is what we need to change. If we know who we are, if we know where we come from, then we know where we're going.

But the tasks are many: to make known to the Abitibiwinnik those employment opportunities that exist and allow them to dream that they can access them; to increase their awareness of the jobs that are available not only in their region but generally in Canadian society; and to encourage the young (and not so young) to study because, as chief Alice Jerome told a journalist in 2008, 'if we encourage young people to go to school, then they must be able to return to Pikogan to participate in its economic development' (Guindon, 2008).

The primary destination for post-secondary education is the Université du Québec en Abitibi-Témiscamingue (UQAT), small university founded in 1983 and based in Val-d'Or and Rouyn-Noranda, which also provides the opportunity for students from Amos to take courses via videoconference.[15] For those members of the community who have not completed high school, the band council encourages them to take adult education classes. Pikogan also created, in 2009, a forestry cooperative that 'aims to sub-contract forestry work from the major forestry companies in the region' (Lacroix, 2009). For many years, tens of Abitibiwinnik had received training in silviculture and forest management, but the impact on employment remained minimal. The formula of the cooperative, renamed a 'multi-stakeholder coop', was chosen not only for its effectiveness in building partnerships but also for the values conveyed by the Federation of Regional Development Cooperatives (Lacroix, 2009): the property of the coop is collective and power is exercised democratically, which corresponds to the traditional political ideals of the Abitibiwinnik. Pikogan also organizes 'opportunity days', where they present workshops and conferences to learn about different trades, to initiate projects, and to provide business mentoring services with the help of the Community Future Development Corporation

---

14   A certificate of possession is a particular title enshrined in the *Indian Act* which allows a certain level of property right to be granted by the Minister of Aboriginal Affairs or representative (e. g. the chief of a band council) to an individual living on a reserve. This property right is nonetheless limited because the possession can only be transferred to another member of the band or to the band council. Any transfer has to be approved by the Minister of Aboriginal Affairs (Schulze, 2006).

15   In 2009, UQAT inaugurated the First Peoples Pavilion. The university wants to be close to Native and Inuit communities and so 'offers programs respectful of aboriginal perspectives' (http://www.uqat.ca/services/premierspeuples, accessed: 1 October 2012).

(CFDC) Harricana, Amos. Pikogan is also aiming at a non-Native audience, since the band made the step to seek out support from various organizations, not just Native groups. In addition, and I will develop this aspect in the next section, the band wants to become known by the whites, and to valorise its culture and values which it refers to in all its written material aimed at a general public.

Politics and Diplomacy

Pikogan wanted to make sure to be represented at the Amos Chamber of Commerce, and one of the band councillors is now a board member. The band council, noting that private companies in the Abitibi-Témiscamingue in general have little or no Native employees (Cazin et al., 2006: 23), also wants to change the image that companies have of Natives. The band council therefore invites local company representatives to events that they organize to promote economic development. But, more importantly, the band council began a round of negotiations with companies, especially forestry and mining. Since the early 2000s, one of band council departments has focused on local resources, i.e. the ancestral territory of the Abitibiwinnik (including the beaver reserve and other stakeholders, such as municipalities). As the family lots of the beaver reserves are still used for traditional hunting and trapping, the band decided to establish a special department to negotiate with logging companies and so limit any damage to the local ecosystems. As already mentioned, the *Forest Act* allows for such an approach since it requires companies to consult with indigenous peoples. In the same line of thought, the board decided to negotiate directly with the mining companies. In 2011, the band council held its first conference on mining in Pikogan, to 'make known to the mining industry the history of the Abitibiwinni First Nation, but also of First Nations in general' (Proulx, 2011). For two days, companies were invited to operate kiosks (about the industry, employment opportunities, etc.), and a series of presentations were given by members of the band council on the history of Abitibiwinnik (including Treaty No. 9 and the creation of Pikogan), on indigenous rights, on employment, the myths and realities of the industry, etc. Following the important success of the first event, this experiment was repeated again in 2012 with similar results. Of note, in all the newspaper articles devoted to the subject (e.g. Proulx, March 2011; Guindon, 2012a, b), the chiefs and deputy chiefs (who changed between the two years) and councillors interviewed constantly repeated the same message: the Abitibiwinnik never surrendered their territory. They want to be recognized and treated as legitimate stakeholders by the mining industry, and to work with this industry when it is advantageous without having to go through the courts and obtain injunctions (Guindon, 2011). Specifically, they want their rights recognized by the companies that are exploiting the resources of their territory, so that they can '[share] the wealth they extract'; but they also 'want to develop harmonious relations' (Guindon, 2012b). Pikogan thus aims to distinguish itself from other First Nations in Canada who have had to resort to legal means to protect their territory and obtain royalties.

Protecting Culture and Values: But which Culture and which Values?

To cement this collaborative and cordial approach to relations with industry, the Abitibiwinnik began signing agreements in early 2012. In February, Pikogan and the Anishinabe community Timiskaming signed an agreement to collaborate in future negotiations with Aurizon Mines, and representatives of the company were invited to this very formal event (Rodrigue, 2012a). In

March, Pikogan and another Anishinabe community, Lac-Simon, signed an agreement with the Quebec government:

> which will establish the process for consultation and accommodation with the two Aboriginal communities in the development of mining projects in their respective territories. (Guindon, 2012c)

This was followed in May by an agreement of 'cooperation' between Pikogan, Lac-Simon (Guindon, 2012d) and the mining company Canada Lithium in order to:

> clarify various considerations such as education and training, employment opportunities, working conditions, business opportunities and financial compensation. (Guindon, 2012e)

Finally, in June Pikogan signed a reciprocity agreement with the bottling company Eaux Vives Water to lay the groundwork for future discussions on potential collaborations (Guindon, 2012e). Other signature projects are underway.

It may seem surprising that companies are signing agreements with Native communities. Unlike the *Forest Act*, the *Mining Act* does not require companies to consult with indigenous peoples. In addition, Quebec Natives have rather limited lobbying power when compared, for example, with those of British Columbia because the latter's land titles are not recognized. The territorial claims of most First Nations in Quebec have stalled. So, apart from their demographic dynamism – i.e. a burgeoning and youthful population (and thus potential workforce) – Quebec Native communities are not essential economic actors. A cynical, and I would argue superficial, analysis might be that signing agreements is simply excellent and cheap public relations for companies. Yet, this is to misunderstand the extent to which these agreements are mutually beneficial. For example, a visit by representatives of Brazilian mining companies to the Abitibi in June 2012, documented in a newspaper article (Rodrigue, 2012b), relates that the Brazilian officials were impressed by the management of relations between Natives and the mining sector, which was very different in Brazil; the province of Quebec was then cited as a model to follow. Moreover, companies have a significant corporate and financial interest in signing various types of agreement with Native communities. These agreements document the creation of a cordial working relationship with a key regional stakeholder, something that then can be taken to corporate boards of directors, and eventually to shareholders (including venture capital) to justify support and financial investment in new initiatives. In short, the Pikogan strategy, both short term and at the political level, is a win-win scenario for all involved.

The challenge facing Pikogan is to inscribe these processes in a comprehensive plan that protects and perpetuates the Abitibiwinnik culture and values. In this approach, it is necessary to educate the other, who is ignorant. The Abitibiwinnik had to develop brochures and give presentations to teach their history to non-Natives who, while they were at school, had learned an official history of Quebec that left little room for Natives and has completely erased regional Native histories. However, in the history of Abitibiwinnik, the Anishinabek are not colonized: they never ceded their land or their rights; they never ceased to be true to themselves and their way of thinking. On this point, the Abitibiwinnik radically subvert, and even overturn, the traditional relationship between Natives and non-Natives. It is the Abitibiwinnik who have become the teacher of their culture and values to an 'uneducated' non-Native student, who happens to be a corporate representative or a member of the local Chamber of Commerce. But which culture and which values are the Abitibiwinnik teaching?

At the signing of the Pikogan agreements, a particular decor was constructed for each event: flags of the various parties involved, miniature types, the four-colour medicine wheel, multicoloured blankets on the tables (south-western or Mexican style). The Anishinabek signatories wore feathered headdresses and items of traditional clothing (shirts, jackets, vests) with ribbons or fringes. The events were heavily ritualized, opening with a purification, or 'smudging', ceremony using sage and sweet grass, a prayer from the elders, handshakes that are duly photographed, traditional dances, and ending with an exchange of wampum. This protocol and its various elements are not typically Abitibiwinnik, although this does not mean these elements did not exist in Abitibiwinni culture. They are, in fact, all identifiable parts of the Pan-Indian movement, a political current with a spiritual connotation that unites all Natives around a common experience of colonization and dispossession (Boudreau, 2000).

The Pan-Indian movement is one that is in continual change or evolution. Its symbols and ceremonies have been adopted at different times (e.g. the feathered headdress was borrowed from the Plains Indians in the 1940s, thanks to Hollywood movies) and from various Native communities in Canada, in the United States, and in Latin America. Prayers are addressed to the Creator, and elders who recite these prayers may have different religious affiliations: Catholic, Anglican, or Pentecostal.[16] The key is that the prayer is given by an elder and in the vernacular language. Here, I will focus only on the wampum, which, with the signature of the written agreement, is the most important part of the ceremonies conducted by Pikogan with the other communities or with the various companies. Originally a necklace or a belt of sea shells used by the Algonquin (and other Algonquian groups in eastern North America) to seal political alliances, to pay a dowry, or to redeem a blood debt, the wampum created by the Abitibiwinnik for these agreements are leather rectangles embroidered with Algonquin words,[17] community logos (created in the 1970s or 1980s), and the logo of the other party to the agreement. The wampum has kept its original functions: to document an agreement by engaging the honour of the contracting parties; and a mnemonic function (symbols to remember the content of the agreement and the name of the parties). The reactivation of this diplomatic medium, the wampum, as part of agreement ceremonies in the 1990s has significant symbolic value. The overall atmosphere created by the Abitibiwinnik, which is certainly intentional, is one that obliges participants to be solemn and respectful. The various symbols and rituals deployed, and in particular the wampum, give the Abitibiwinnik complete control over the ceremony. Further, it empowers them so that they are seen and treated by government and industry as parties of equal standing when the agreement is enacted.

But why did the Abitibiwinnik choose a Pan-Indian protocol? I can venture several hypotheses. First, because non-Native Canadians, even if they are not familiar with Pan-Indianism, can at least identify the ceremony as Native. Second, because Pan-Indianism was born in the 1960s, part of the counter-culture movements aimed at overthrowing the relations of Western domination. Third, because it symbolises a new-found pride. The Abitibiwinnik culture, whether that of the semi-nomadic hunters and trappers or in the daily life of the contemporary reserve, is for many not sufficiently powerful, in part because the tradition was to think that the non-Native universe would be unlikely to impinge on the Native universe. Pan-Indianism rejects this view; it is instead founded on resistance and anti-colonialism.

A similar case can be seen with Abitibiwinnik values. Those values that they state in their brochures or on their website are not necessarily those that they would list in another context. They cite, for example, on the website of the Pikogan band council, 'complicity, teamwork and recognition of work well done' and 'politeness and courtesy'.[18] This is not to say that the Abitibiwinnik

---

16   For more information about Pan-Indian spirituality among the Abitibiwinnik and the cohabitation of this belief system with other religious movements see Bousquet (2007, 2009, 2012).

17   For example, on the wampum for the agreement between Pikogan and Timiskaming, the word *mamawi'idiwin* is written, which means 'unity' in Anishinabemowin (Rodrigue, 2012a).

18   See *Ses Valeurs*, Conseil de la Première Nation Abitibiwinni (http://www.pikogan.com/valeurs.html, accessed 2 October 2012).

are not polite and courteous, even if one could expand on differences in codes of etiquette between Natives and non-Natives which can cause misunderstandings. These values are rather those that the Abitibiwinnik want to internalise in the context of the modern work culture that they are trying to promote. Values are clearly not frozen in time; nor are they context insensitive. As shown by Stéphane Croussette (2008) in research on economic development among the Innu (culturally very close to the Anishinabek), modernity, the need for money, and a desire to acquire material goods create important tensions since the values inherited from the semi-nomadic life may be poorly adapted to the present context. For example, the difficulty that the Innu (and the Algonquin) have in accepting authority comes from a time of egalitarian communities based on mutual aid where 'everyone was boss' (Croussette, 2008: 55). Similarly, living in the present moment with no concern for tomorrow means that 'some members the community only work until they have enough money to buy the goods they desire' (ibid.), something also present amongst the Abitibiwinnik and possibly due to a lack of a financial culture.

The Pikogan band council is seeking to change these ways of being in the world, and in the workforce, by on the one hand giving warnings or even firing employees who do not follow the rules, and on the other hand diffusing these 'new' values via all the communication means at their disposal. Contemporary work values are subject to strong criticism from all those in the community who fear that the Abitibiwinnik ways of thinking will disappear in favour of non-Native values and ways of being. But the supporters of these new values argue that the Abitibiwinnik are a very small minority in the vast culture of capitalist labour, so it will be impossible to change relations with the whites if the Abitibiwinnik do not also work on changing themselves. Croussette (2008), in his study of the values of the Pessamit Innu in relation to work, refers quite rightly to the analysis by Albert Memmi (1985) of the values of the colonized, when explaining that the Innu accept their exclusion from the labour market on the grounds of cultural differences that make them unfit to participate (e.g. their supposed inability to arrive on time, so-called *Indian time*). In Pikogan, while this view of cultural differences as an explanation for their failure to integrate into the workforce may also be present amongst the population, the band council has decided to no longer tolerate such behaviour; being regularly late is now grounds for dismissal. The political representatives of the band have thus put themselves in opposition to these cultural archetypes that make the Abitibiwinnik inferior and keep them away from economic development. They are breaking – both politically and symbolically – this stereotyped role, one that they refuse to let community members continue to perpetuate.

Conclusion

In the context of administrative and financial dependency on the state, under-education, a lack of capital, and inability to own their land, the Abitibiwinnik did not seem to have much to offer. However, in this context that is so poorly conducive to innovation, the Abitibiwinnik demonstrate that progress towards autonomy and empowerment can still be possible. They have moved to change the context to one that is conducive to innovation. So while the band council is still one of the few employers in the community, they no longer want to be the sole or the main source of funds for implementing projects. They have launched initiatives, both rhetorical and practical, to break the habits of dependency created by colonialism. They have established policies that they spread through negotiation, dialogue, and education of non-Natives who they identify as partners and not as adversaries. This position of equality, where everyone has something to offer and something to gain, probably explains the positive reception of these approaches on the part of many companies. Finally, the band council no longer wants to depend on external institutions such as the courts to protect its territory and identify opportunities for financial benefit (e.g. royalties). Through its strategic approach, the band council has created a shared interest. This logic is fundamentally commercial and thus, while competitive, is not necessarily confrontational. In this active process, the band council finds itself able to tell the industry what to do, reversing the pattern of relationships to which the Anishinabek have been accustomed.

Passive consumers, the Abitibiwinnik want to show they also have the tools to become entrepreneurs. But before you can have entrepreneurship, you need a culture of employment. Abitibiwinnik leaders, and the majority of the population who support them, are well aware of the image of the welfare Native. As we have seen, their integration into the workforce has been anything but linear, something that is far from being exceptional among Quebec Natives (Boutet, 2010). The band council has therefore worked to build a culture and a political infrastructure that creates a positive environment for economic development. It would be wrong to see in this political project a subjugation to capitalist society and a dependence on the sirens of consumer society. The Abitibiwinnik want above all to be autonomous vis-à-vis the state. Of course, that means deployed by their political leaders will not garner unanimous support from the community, but the underlying project has their support. As explained by Gélinas (2008: 37):

> It's probably not a coincidence that what we observe today in the province are First Nations that want to establish a new form of partnership with the Quebec government, but not a partnership of the post-1930 type where they had to deal with what non-Native were willing to offer, but a partnership of the pre-1930 type in which, due to a number of tools (territories, royalties, guaranteed jobs, etc.), they would be able to direct, to a certain extent at least, their own development strategies. And if this approach seems to have worked quite well at the dawn of the Great Depression, it is reasonable to believe that it could be the same in the future. (my translation from French).

There is still some way to go for the Abitibiwinnik to see if their economic development plans will succeed. When people become employed and integrated into a workforce culture that is not their own – and when they also have the requisite human, social, cultural, and political capital – they can begin to take ownership of this work culture and eventually imagine new ways of working, and even new forms of entrepreneurship. This has become a reality for the Osoyoos band in British Columbia (Kayseas et al., 2006) and time will tell if this is also possible in the Abitibi, Quebec. But to return to Laenui's (2000) stages in the process of decolonization – 1) rediscovery and recovery, 2) mourning, 3) dreaming, 4) commitment, and 5) action – I think we can say that with confidence the Abitibiwinnik are well enrolled in the most important stage, that of dreaming of a better future; but they are also clearly moving to action, creating new political, social, and economic opportunities for their people. The Abitibiwinnik are in the process of addressing their two key challenges: 'making sure that the whites know who they are' and 'knowing what there are capable of accomplishing as a people'.

References

Alfred, T. (1999). *Peace, power, righteousness: An indigenous manifesto.* Toronto: Oxford University Press.
Anderson, R. B. and Giberson, R. J. (2003). Aboriginal entrepreneurship and economic development in Canada: Thoughts on current theory and practice. In C. H. Stiles and C. S. Galbraith (eds), *Ethnic entrepreneurship: Structure and process (International Research in the Business Disciplines, Volume 4).* Bingley: Emerald Group, pp. 141–67.

Battiste, M. (2011). Enabling the autumn seed: Toward a decolonized approach to Aboriginal knowledge, language, and education. In S. Burke and P. Milewski (eds), Schooling in transition: Readings in Canadian history of education. Toronto: University of Toronto Press, pp. 275–86.

Boudreau, F. (2000). Identité, politique et spiritualité: entretiens avec quelques leaders ojibwas du nord du lac Huron. Recherches amérindiennes au Québec, 30(1), pp. 71–85. (In French).

Bousquet, M. P. (2006). A generation in politics: The alumni of the Saint-Marc-de-Figuery School. In H. C. Wolfart (ed.), Papers of the thirty-seventh Algonquian conference. Winnipeg: University of Manitoba, pp. 1–17.

Bousquet, M. P. (2007). Catholicisme, pentecôtisme et spiritualité traditionnelle? Les choix religieux contemporains chez les Algonquins du Québec. In C. Gélinas and G. Teasdale (eds), Les systèmes religieux amérindiens et inuit: perspectives historiques et contemporaines. Quebec/Paris: Muséologie In-Situ/Harmattan, pp.155–66. (In French).

——— (2008). Tourisme, patrimoine et culture, ou que montrer de soi-même aux autres: des exemples anicinabek (Algonquins) au Québec. In K. Iankova (ed.), Le tourisme indigène en Amérique du Nord. Paris: Harmattan, pp. 17–41. (In French).

——— (2009). Régler ses conflits dans un cadre spirituel: pouvoir, réparation et systèmes religieux chez les Anicinabek du Québec. Criminologie, 42(2), pp. 53–82. (In French).

——— (2012). 'On a juste besoin d'être aimés': les bases de la tolérance religieuse chez les Anicinabek (Algonquins) du Québec. In M. P. Bousquet and R. R. Crépeau (eds), Dynamiques religieuses des autochtones des Amériques. Paris: Karthala, pp. 243–70. (In French).

Boutet, J. (2010). Développement ferrifère et mondes autochtones au Québec subarctique, 1954–1983. Recherches amérindiennes au Québec, 40(3), pp. 35–52. (In French).

Cazin, A., Ependa, A. and Sauvageau, A. (2006). Enquête sur les relations économiques entre les Autochtones et les entreprises de l'Abitibi-Témiscamingue. Chaire Desjardins-LARESCO. Abitibi-Témiscamingue: Université du Québec en Abitibi-Témiscamingue, p. 23. (In French).

Croussette, S. (2008). Le développement économique de la communauté innue de Pessamit. Mémoire présenté comme exigence partielle de la maîtrise en intervention sociale. Montreal: Université du Québec à Montréal, pp. 53–57. (In French).

Duara, P. (2003). Decolonization: Perspectives from now and then. New York: Routledge.

Fanon, F. (1961). Les damnés de la terre. Paris: Maspero. (In French).

Frenette, J. (1988). Le pays des Anicenabe, la revendication territoriale globale de la nation algonquine. Énoncé de revendication documenté et rédigé pour le Conseil de bande, réserve algonquine de Maniwaki, miméo. (In French).

——— (2006). Les Indiens du lac Abitibi et le traité 9 (1906). Retrieved from: http://www.gsdl.ubcic.bc.ca/collect/firstna1/index/assoc/HASH0139.dir/doc.pdf (accessed: 1 May 2013) (In French).

Gélinas, C. (2008). Les autochtones et le partenariat économique au Québec, 1867–1960. Recherches amérindiennes au Québec, 38(1), pp. 29–39. (In French).

Guindon, M. (2008). La réserve de Pikogan triplera sa superficie. L'Écho abitibien, 3 December. (In French).

——— (2011). Pikogan tend la main à l'industrie minière. Abitibi Express, 21 January. (In French).

——— (2012a). L'affirmation du territoire, la priorité pour Bruno Kistabish. Abitibi Express, 27 January. (In French).

——— (2012b). Pikogan durcit le ton à l'endroit des minières. Abitibi Express, 10 February. (In French).

——— (2012c). Projets miniers: Pikogan et Lac-Simon en voie d'être consultés et accommodés. Abitibi Express, 30 March. (In French).

——— (2012d). Canada Lithium s'entend avec Pikogan et Lac-Simon. Abitibi Express, 11 May. (In French).

——— (2012e). Pikogan négocie avec Eaux Vives Water, Abitibi Express, 26 June. (In French).

Iankova, K. (2005). Le tourisme autochtone au Québec. Globe: revue internationale d'études québécoises, 8(1), pp. 85–98. (In French).

——— (2008). Insertion de la réserve huronne dans l'espace urbain de la ville de Québec. Influences de la proximité de Québec sur Wendake. *Recherches amérindiennes au Québec*, 38(1), pp. 67–78. (In French).

Kayseas, B., Hindle, K. and Anderson, R. B. (2006). An empirically justified theory of successful indigenous entrepreneurship: case study of the Osoyoos Indian band. *Regional Frontiers of Entrepreneurship Research 2006: Proceedings of the 3rd Regional Frontiers of Entrepreneurship Research conference*. Auckland: AGSE, pp. 224–40.

Lacroix, G. (2009). *Pikogan veut sa place dans l'industrie forestière*. Retrieved from: http://www.hebdosregionaux.ca/abitibi-temiscamingue/2009/06/10/pikogan-veut-sa-place-dans-lindustrie-forestiere (accessed: 1 January 2013). (In French).

Laenui, P. (2000). Process of decolonization. In M. Battiste (ed.), *Reclaiming indigenous voice and vision*. Vancouver: UBC Press, pp. 150–60.

Matthews, G. J. (1987). *Historical atlas of Canada: Addressing the twentieth century, 1891–1961*. Toronto: University of Toronto Press, p 110.

Memmi, A. (1985). *Portrait du colonisé: Portrait du colonisateur*. Paris: Gallimard, pp. 117–20. (In French).

Mihesuah, D. (2003). *Indigenous American women: Decolonization, empowerment, activism*. Lincoln: University of Nebraska Press.

——— and Wilson A. C. (2004). *Indigenizing the academy: Transforming scholarship and empowering communities*. Lincoln: University of Nebraska Press.

Proulx, M. (2011a). Les Abitibiwinni veulent se présenter aux minières. *L'Écho abitibien*, 11 January. (In French).

——— (2011b). Pikogan courtise les mines. *L'Écho abitibien*, 28 March. (In French).

Rankin, J.-P. (2003). *Un long portage du traité 9 à l'autonomie gouvernementale*. Retrieved from: http://gsdl.ubcic.bc.ca/collect/firstna1/index/assoc/HASH01cf/a599fb87.dir/doc.pdf (accessed: 12 November 2014). (In French).

Rodrigue, R. P. (2012a). Entente historique entre Timiskaming et Pikogan. *Abitibi Express*, 3 February (in French).

——— (2012b). L'Abitibi s'exporte au Brésil. *Abitibi Express*, 7 June (in French).

Said, E. (1988). *Nationalism, colonialism, and literature: Yeats and decolonization*. Derry: Field Day.

——— (2000). *Culture et impérialisme*, trans. from French by P. Chemla. Paris: Fayard/Le Monde diplomatique.

Schulze, D. (2006). Le droit applicable au bail résidentiel dans les réserves indiennes. *Revue générale de droit*, 36, pp. 381–432. (In French).

Trépied, B. (2011). Recherche et décolonisation en Nouvelle-Calédonie contemporaine: Lectures croisées. *Revue d'histoire des sciences humaines*, 1(24), pp. 159–87. (In French).

6

Culture-Based Enterprise Opportunities for Indigenous People in the Northern Territory, Australia

Stephen T. Garnett, Beau J. Austin, Peter Shepherd, and Kerstin K. Zander[1]

Chapter Synopsis

Despite having ownership rights over large tracts of land, Indigenous people in remote and regional Australia have, until recently, had few employment opportunities available to them for participation in market-based economic activity. In the last few decades, however, several sources of income have arisen that enable the cultural and natural assets of these economically marginal traditional lands to be leveraged for economic participation. The first two, art and tourism, are now mature industries in which there has been substantial government and institutional investment. The third is provision of environmental services through management of the natural environment on traditional Indigenous lands, for which the wider settler society is willing to pay. This includes control of weeds and feral animals; management of fire to reduce carbon emissions; and, in coastal areas, surveillance as part of quarantine. Lastly, there are wildlife-based industries by which Indigenous people extend their historical exploitation of wildlife such as fruits, seeds, and animals into commercial markets. In this chapter, we describe the current extent of these economic opportunities in the Northern Territory of Australia, and compare them with each other and other sources of income. We conclude that policy enabling Indigenous people to engage in a portfolio of income-earning activities is likely to yield the most sustainable employment.

1   The authors would particularly like to thank Peter Whitehead for his many insights over the decades; Peter Yates for his advice on the current state of the bush-foods industry in the NT; and Brian Tucker for use of his art centre accounting data.

Introduction

The Northern Territory (NT) is sparsely populated, with just 230,000 people inhabiting 1,350,000 km² of land (Australian Bureau of Statistics, 2012a). Half of the land, including 80 per cent of the coastline, is owned by Indigenous people (Altman et al., 2007), who make up about 30 per cent of the population of the NT's non- Indigenous population (Australian Bureau of Statistics, 2012a). Away from the few large towns, the population is overwhelmingly Indigenous. This makes Indigenous people key stakeholders in northern Australia (Taylor, 2006; Altman et al., 2007), yet they have lower life expectancy, poorer health, lower rates of literacy and numeracy, higher unemployment, experience higher poverty, and poorer well-being than non-Aboriginal Australians (Department of Social Services, 2013a; Steering Committee for the Review of Government Service Provision, 2011).

Some key statistics are revealing that Indigenous Australians are half as likely to finish high school as non-Indigenous Australians, and only one-fifth of 20–24-year-olds continue on to university; employment rates for Indigenous Australians in remote and regional areas are around 52 and 51 per cent respectively, compared to 75 per cent for non-Indigenous Australians; Indigenous Australians have an average weekly income of $278 per week, compared to $473 per week for non-Indigenous Australians; Indigenous Australians are one-third as likely to be self-employed as non-Indigenous Australians; and just over one-third (36 per cent) of Indigenous Australians are home owners, compared to 71 per cent of non-Indigenous Australians (Department of Social Services, 2013b). In the NT, Indigenous unemployment in the booming capital is 12 per cent compared to the non-Indigenous rate of 4 per cent. Elsewhere in the NT comparable rates are 21 per cent and 8 per cent (Australian Bureau of Statistics, 2012a). An additional 77 per cent of Indigenous people are not looking for jobs in the formal economy (i.e. not in the labour force).

This is because, outside the towns, very few jobs are generated by the local economy; and there are high administrative barriers to entering the employment that is available and often inadequate physical infrastructure for many economic development options (Taylor, 2006). Ownership of land, in itself, has not proved sufficient in encouraging and achieving improved wellbeing for Indigenous Australians (Altman, 2007; Sutton, 2009; Langton, 2010).

Altman (2001a, b; 2007) and Altman (2005a, b) have shown that Australian Indigenous economies have – in addition to the public (government) and private sectors (the market) – an unusually high engagement with the customary economy. The customary sector includes activities such as hunting, gathering, and fishing for customary use as well as bartering and voluntary activity (Altman, 2001a, b; 2007). Customary (and non-customary) hunting and gathering makes the livelihoods of people more resilient; indeed in many cases makes them viable (Davies et al., 2008; Stafford Smith et al., 2008; Hunt et al., 2009).

However, the market sector remains an important component of the hybrid economy (Altman, 2006) and many Indigenous leaders have called for growth in private sector investment in Indigenous livelihoods (Dodson, 2007; Yunupingu, 2008; Mundine, 2010; Pearson, 2009). Ah Mat (2003) claims that investing in market sector development in Indigenous Australia is not only an economic imperative, but also a matter of moral import. Likewise, the Australian Government identifies increased economic participation in the private sector as a source of improved wellbeing for Indigenous Australians (Steering Committee for the Review of Government Service Provision, 2011; Department of Social Services, 2013b), and made it central to the Indigenous Economic Development Strategy 2011–2018 (Australian Government, 2011).

While such investment would be consistent with a renewed push for Australia to relocate much of its agricultural and pastoral endeavour to the north of the country (Northern Australian Land and Water Taskforce, 2009), monsoonal flood and drought (Woinarski et al., 2007; Northern Australian Land and Water Taskforce, 2009), poor soil (Orians and Milewski, 2007; Woinarski et al., 2007), and a lack of substantial local markets (Young, 1988; Altman, 2006) has meant that most conventional agricultural enterprises have so far failed. Conventional agriculture, even at a small scale, has also failed to involve Indigenous people. Thus, even for the few jobs available, there is very low participation (Gray and Chapman, 2006; Biddle et al., 2009) because many jobs are perceived as undesirable by Indigenous people (Altman and Sanders, 1991; Austin-Broos, 2006; McRae-Williams and Gerritsen, 2010).

However culture-based employment is an exception to this trend, with a variety of roles having widespread engagement. This includes arts and craft (Koenig et al., 2011; Attorney-General's Department, 2013), tourism (Fuller et al., 2005; Tremblay and Wegner, 2008), cultural and natural resource management (Altman et al., 2007; Luckert et al., 2007; Morrison, 2007; Sithole et al., 2008; Garnett et al., 2008) and wildlife-based enterprises (Austin and Corey, 2012; Zander et al., 2014). Reasons for this include the high flexibility of the work and the fact that it can be combined with traditional obligations (Altman and Sanders, 1991; Austin-Broos, 2006; McRae-Williams and Gerritsen, 2010). The aims of this chapter are to: 1) provide a synopsis of each of the four culture-based employment sectors, and 2) analyse their impact on employment opportunities for Indigenous Australians.

Creative Industries

Indigenous art and craft are the largest of the four culture-based employment sectors, both financially and in terms of the number of participants. Practised traditionally for millennia, there continues to be a high level of Indigenous involvement in the creative arts and other cultural activities (arts and crafts, music, dance or theatre, and writing or telling stories), especially in remote and regional areas (22 per cent of people had participated in the previous 12 months in 2008) compared with urban areas (16 per cent; Australian Bureau of Statistics, 2008). While this may have fallen away from even higher levels of engagement (27 per cent of people in both groups had been engaged in 2002; Australian Bureau of Statistics, 2006), the practice of a range of creative arts is now the basis of a mature industry. The many forms of Indigenous art shifted from being anthropological artefacts to valuable cultural commodities in the 1970s and now boast important advocacy bodies: the Association of Northern, Kimberley and Arnhem Aboriginal Artists (ANKAAA) and Desart. These are both funded under similar programmes to art centres and are recognised as the peak bodies.

The most recent valuation of the whole industry, in 2007, suggested a turnover of up to $500 million (Commonwealth of Australia, 2007). While returns from auctions of Indigenous art dropped from over $25 million in 2007 to less than $8 million in 2011 (ORIC, 2012), the auction market has little connection to the creators of the art and probably fluctuates independently. Although one analysis suggested that sales from Aboriginal art centres halved, on average, from $390,000 in 2007/08 to $189,000 in 2010/11 (ORIC, 2012), this is partly because more artists are operating independently of art centres (P. Shepherd pers. obs.). More detailed data available for 25 art centres suggests that the rapid rise in sales to 2007 has since remained fairly steady. Expenses, however, have risen and returns to artists fell to a third up to 2011 (B. Tucker unpublished data).

Overall, solid data on the Indigenous art industry are notably scarce: a recent literature review by Acker et al. (2013) identified gaps in the areas of market size, art centre operations, operation of the informal art market, characteristics and motivations of buyers, human resources, value chains and licensing. One of the problems with valuing the industry is its diversity. At the top of the market, the highest price paid for one work was $2.4 million, in 2007.[2] However, Indigenous art also encompasses the vast ill-defined production of tourist artefacts, not all of which is necessarily

2   *Warlugulong*, painted by Clifford Possum Tjapaltjarri, purchased in July 2007 by the National Gallery of Australia.

produced by Indigenous people; and, outside the art centre 40 per cent share of the market there is little transparency about returns to the actual artists, as revealed by a Senate inquiry into the industry in 2007 (Attorney-General's Department, 2013).

This resulted in a code of practice and the passing of the *Resale Royalty Right for Visual Artists Act* 2009, which provides 5 per cent royalty on sales of art worth over $1,000. Since its start on 9 June 2010 until 31 August 2013, the scheme has generated $1.9 million in royalties nationally for more than 700 artists, over 60 per cent of whom have been Indigenous (Copyright Agency, 2013). The Indigenous arts industry also receives substantial government support. The amount of assistance provided to artists and art centres through the Indigenous Visual Arts Industry Support (IVAIS) scheme – formerly National Arts and Crafts Industry Support – has risen from $8.7 million in 2007/08 to $11.1 million in 2013/14 (Office of the Registrar of Indigenous Corporations/ORIC, 2012; IVAIS, 2013), with additional support provided by other schemes as well as State and Territory governments.

In the NT most original Indigenous art has traditionally been sold either through these community-based art centres or galleries. There are a total of 42 Indigenous art centres in the Northern Territory: 11 in the Arnhem region; 12 in the Darwin/Katherine region; 5 on the Tiwi Islands; and 14 in central Australia (Aboriginal Art, 2013). Many of these art centres have close connections with galleries in the main urban centres, particularly Darwin, as well as selling art online or in centres away from the Northern Territory. They earn substantial revenue: the 18 centres with sales exceeding $100,000 per year in 2007/08 received a total income of $10.4 million, though this was only $4.3 million by 2010/11 (ORIC, 2012). They also received substantial support from IVAIS: in 2013, 22 centres in the NT were granted $100,000–150,000 a year for three years, with some additional funds for marketing and training (IVAIS, 2013). A city gallery typically returns about 60 per cent of the sale price to the artist, of which about 40 per cent is retained as a consignment fee, under agreement, by the art centre (P. Shepherd personal data). This amount varies, however, with some communities agreeing to larger consignment fees to aid development of the centre and its community programmes.

If, as is estimated, the art centre sales represent about a quarter of the sales arising from all forms of creative arts (Commonwealth of Australia, 2007), then the total earnings of Indigenous artists in the NT is about $20 million a year.

Employment resulting from this revenue is more difficult to estimate than the revenue itself. In 2011/13 Indigenous people in the NT identified the creative industries as their major form of employment (Australian Bureau of Statistics, 2012a). However an unknown number of people make money from the creative arts through occasional or casual sales without declaring it as their principal source of income. The sales records of art centres suggest that, on average, each centre may have about 100 artists on the books; but less than a fifth of these earn more than $10,000 per year, and only a few more than $30,000 (B. Tucker unpublished records).

While IVAIS funds are likely to be spent on employment of largely non-Indigenous art centre coordinators, overheads for artists are relatively low (e.g. Koenig et al., 2011). The rest of the income from art centre sales is likely to be distributed among the artists themselves, which very roughly translates into 400 jobs at $50,000 per year each.

Tourism

Australia's Indigenous peoples and their culture have long attracted tourists, sometimes with negative effects (Hinch and Butler, 2009). As part of the colonial process, Indigenous people have often been seen as curiosities by colonists who have then exploited Indigenous difference for profit. In Australia, however, Indigenous people have gradually reasserted control to create an

Indigenous tourism industry (Weaver, 2010). This form of tourism, where Indigenous people run their own businesses, or at least gain employment in the tourist industry, has long been held up as a potential source of income for Indigenous communities (Altman and Finlayson, 2003). Tourism is mentioned frequently in the National Indigenous Employment Strategy 2011–2018 (Australian Government, 2011), and increased Indigenous participation in tourism is one of the features of the key elements of the Tourism 2020 strategy (Department of Industry, 2013).

However, policies aiming to encourage the industry tend to be long on rhetoric but short on practical actions likely to promote sustainable tourism (Whitford and Ruhanen, 2010). There also tends to be an overestimation of demand for Indigenous tourism, and little understanding among Indigenous tour operators of what it is that tourists are seeking (Ruhanen et al., 2013). Nevertheless, given that 50 per cent and 70 per cent of Indigenous tourism businesses are located in remote or very remote areas respectively (Buultjens et al., 2010), drawing heavily on the local environment as part of their appeal, they are still seen as having great potential if supported appropriately (Buultjens and White, 2009).

To be defined as an Indigenous tourism visitor, one must have experienced Indigenous art, craft, and cultural displays, attended an Indigenous performance, or visited an Indigenous site or community. There is thus a very close link between the creative industries and Indigenous tourism, and the only elements of the tourist sector that can be unambiguously attributed to tourism alone relates to accommodation and tours. In 2011 just under half of the 5.8 million international tourists to Australia attended at least one cultural attraction while in Australia, spending $16 million on their trips. Of these people, 19 per cent experienced Australian Indigenous art/craft and cultural displays and 9 per cent visited an Aboriginal site/community (Australian Bureau of Statistics, 2012b). More ambitiously, Indigenous tourism visitors were estimated to have spent $7.2 billion in 2009, representing 12 per cent of total visitor expenditure in Australia (Tourism Research Australia, 2010).

Between 200,000 and 300,000 international Indigenous tourism visitors come to the NT each year, about a third of all the international Indigenous tourism visitors nationally and over two-thirds of all tourists visiting the NT. The NT also receives 100–200,000 Indigenous tourism visitors. While nationally both international and national Indigenous tourism visitors have fallen substantially from a peak in the mid-2000s, the number visiting the NT has remained fairly stable for a decade (Tourism NT, 2011).

Returns to Indigenous people and levels of employment in the industry are both very difficult to estimate. Some 18 per cent of international Indigenous tourism visitors took a tour with an Indigenous guide (Tourism NT, 2011), by inference possibly as many as 50,000 a year. For the domestic Indigenous tourists the equivalent figure is about 6 per cent (Tourism Research Australia, 2010), or about 10,000 tourists in the NT. Many of these tours are likely to have been be undertaken through the 27 tourism operators that identify Indigenous ownership or culture in their advertising material (see Table 6.1) which were found either through Tourism Australia's operator directory (nine), through a travel site like Trip Advisor (an additional 11), or through other web-based sources (an additional eight).[3] Twelve of these businesses are owned and run by individual Indigenous people and their families; nine are owned by Aboriginal corporations and employ guides on a casual basis; and eight are owned by non-Indigenous businesses but either employ Indigenous guides or pay a licence fee to operate on Indigenous land (this includes two listed by Tourism Australia 2013 that appear to employ no Indigenous people). Many name their Indigenous employees, or Trip Advisor blog posts name their guides, making it possible to estimate the number of individuals involved. In total, between them all, the businesses probably employ at most 70 Indigenous people (full-time equivalents) given that many of the guides are casual. This

---

3   Tourism Australia (2013) and http://www.tripadvisor.com.au.

is consistent with census figures for 2011 in which 45 Indigenous people identified tourism as their principle form of employment (Australian Bureau of Statistics, 2012a). However, the tourism businesses, particularly accommodation in Kakadu and at Uluru, also provide substantial returns to their communities or Aboriginal corporations, which can in turn employ additional Indigenous people in other roles. Tourism also provides some of the few opportunities away from Darwin for individuals and families to become involved in business as entrepreneurs (Tremblay, 2009).

Table 6.1 Indigenous tourist operations in the Northern Territory with a web presence in 2013 (excluding art centres and galleries) and their estimated levels of Indigenous employment (full-time equivalents/FTEs)

Tourist operator	Indigenous owned	Nature of employment	Estimated Indigenous FTEs
Aboriginal Australia Art and Culture Centre	Yes	Guides	1
Amuwarngka Cultural Tours	Yes	Guides	2
Animal Tracks		Guides	1
Arnhem Weavers	Yes	Family	6
Arnhemland Barramundi Nature Lodge		Guides	2
Arnhem Land Eco-Cultural Tours	Yes	Guides	5
Aussie Adventure		Guides	1
Ayal Aboriginal Kakadu Tours	Yes	Individual owner	1
Ayers Rock Resort	Yes	Guides	10
Banubanu Wilderness Retreat	Yes	Guides	0.5
Batji Tours	Yes	Individual owner	1
Bawaka	Yes	Individual owner	1
Davidson's Arnhemland Safaris		None	0
Gagudju Dreaming	Yes	Guides	10
Jungala	Yes	Guides	0.5
Kakadu Culture Camp	Yes	Individual owner plus family	4
Lirrwi Yolngu Tourism	Yes	Guides	2
Lord's Kakadu and Arnhemland Safaris		Guides	0.5
Munupi Wilderness Lodge		Guides	3
Nitmiluk Tours	Yes	Guides	10
Northern Territory Indigenous Tours	Yes	Individual owner plus family	1.5
Pudakul Aboriginal Cultural Tours	Yes	Individual owner plus family	6
Rainbow Valley Cultural Tours	Yes	Individual owner	1
RT Tours Australia	Yes	Individual owner	1
Sea Darwin	Yes	Individual owner	1
Urlpmerre Tours	Yes	Individual owner	1
Venture North Australia		None	0
Window on the Wetlands		Family	2.5
Total			**75.5**

Cultural and Natural Resource Management (CNRM)

Savannah lands in northern Australia require active management to retain the services they currently provide. The principal form of management is with fire, which has been practised traditionally for millennia (Press, 1987; Preece, 2002). Fire management is an integral part of the ecology of many species in the tropical savannahs. Under Indigenous management, fires were moderate in intensity compared to when they are unmanaged, canopies were protected, and soils maintained (Russell-Smith, 2002; Williams et al., 2002). Recently it has been found that traditional fire regimes have a smaller effect on greenhouse gas emissions than hotter, unmanaged fires (Russell-Smith et al., 2009). Since the arrival of Europeans to Australia a need has also arisen to control weeds and feral animals. Some 5 per cent of the Northern Territory flora (230 spp.) is exotic (Dunlop et al., 1995). Many of these species are an economic threat (Martin et al., 2006) and expensive to control: for example, at least $80 million was spent on rangeland weed control from 1996 to 2005 (Martin and van Klinken, 2006). Feral herbivores such as buffalo, camels, pigs, donkey and horses compete with grazing cattle and can have profound effects on water and biodiversity (Garnett et al., 2010), while feral cats are increasingly being blamed for declines in biodiversity (Woinarski et al., 2011).

Building on the 'Caring for Country' movement that arose in the 1990s (May, 2010), Indigenous people have increasingly been employed to provide the active management required to control these threats, largely through what are termed ranger groups. Commercial contract and payments for ecosystem services (PES) work undertaken by Indigenous land and sea management groups is conservatively estimated at $4–6 million per annum (Putnis et al., 2007).[4] The ranger programme is funded under the 'Working on Country' programme which has funding guaranteed until 2017. Besides the ranger programmes, there are some initiatives that offer payments for ecosystem services (PES), with greenhouse gas abatement being the most important and having the greatest potential (Heckbert et al., 2012). One of the earliest established programmes is the West Arnhem Land Fire Abatement (WALFA) project, under which the mining company ConocoPhillips pays $17 million over 17 years for Indigenous people to manage fire to reduce the area burnt in the late dry season, which also reduces greenhouse gas emissions. The concept of paying Indigenous people to provide ecosystem services has widespread support among Australian people (Zander and Garnett, 2011), although there is some danger that payments for land and sea management could reduce the amount carried out traditionally by people as part of their cultural responsibilities (Zander et al., 2013).

The programmes are an important source of Indigenous employment in remote communities. In 2011 there were 129 people who undertook various forms of natural resource management as their major form of employment (Australian Bureau of Statistics, 2012a), all but 23 away from Darwin. By 2013 the Australian Government currently funds 284 ranger positions in 60 ranger groups across the NT (Figure 6.1; Australian Government, 2013), and engagement in caring for country is now a key part of the Indigenous Economic Development Strategy 2011–2018 (Australian Government, 2011). A small number of additional people are employed through philanthropic funds or by businesses as part of environmental offset programmes, such as WALFA mentioned above.

---

4   The concept of PES and PES-like schemes, which include direct payments but also non-monetary rewards for the provision of ecosystem services (ES), has attracted considerable interest all over the world from both researchers and policymakers, as a market incentive based mechanism for achieving conservation objectives on private land (for example, Ferraro and Kiss, 2002; Pagiola et al., 2002; Muradian et al., 2010; van Noordwijk and Leimona, 2010).

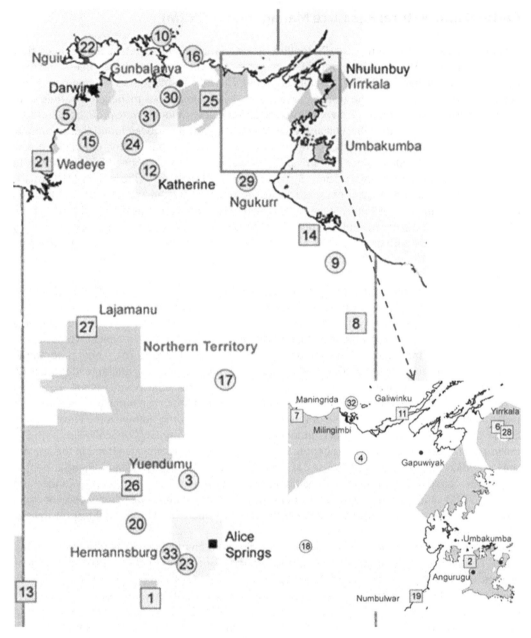

Figure 6.1   Ranger groups in the Northern Territory, Australia

Source: Department of the Environment, 2013.

Notes: 1: Anangu Rangers on Angas Down; 2: Anindilyakwa Rangers; 3: Anmatyerr Rangers; 4: Arafura Swamp Ranger Groups (3); 5: Bulgul Land and Sea Rangers; 6: Dhimurru IPA Rangers; 7: Djelk Rangers; 8: Waanyi Garawa Rangers; 10: Garngi Rangers; 11: Gumurr Marthakal Rangers; 12: Jawoyn Rangers; 13: Kaltukatjara Rangers; 14: Li-Anthawirriyarra Sea Rangers; 15: Malak Malak Land Management; 16: Mardbalk Marine Rangers; 17: Maru-Warinyi Ankkul Rangers; 18: Mimal Rangers; 19: Numbulwar Numburindi Amalagayag Inyung Rangers; 20: Anangu Luritjiku Rangers; 21: Thamarrurr Rangers; 22: Tiwi Islands Land and Sea Management; 23: Tjuwanpa Rangers; 24: Wagiman Guwardagun Rangers; 25: Manwurrk Rangers – Wardekken IPA; 26: Warlpiri Rangers; 27: Wulaign Rangers; 28: Yirrkala Rangers – Laynhapuy IPA; 29: Yugul Mangi Rangers; 30: Warnbi Rangers; 31: Werenbun Rangers; 32: Crocodile Islands Rangers; 33: Tjuwanpa Women Rangers.

Wildlife-Based Enterprises

Globally, people living on Indigenous-owned land rely heavily on enterprises based on the use of wildlife for livelihood creation and poverty alleviation (Davies and Brown, 2007; United Nations, 2010).[5] For the most impoverished, mainly in developing countries, these enterprises can be the sole source of livelihood (de Merode et al., 2004; Belcher et al., 2005; Heubach et al., 2011; van Vliet et al., 2012). In other areas, including Australia, animal- and plant-based enterprises are used to diversify sources of income and/or to facilitate social and cultural practices, as seen among Indigenous Australians (Altman and Cochrane, 2005; Austin and Garnett, 2011; Collier et al., 2011; Austin and Corey, 2012; Zander et al., 2014). Indigenous wildlife-based enterprises are potentially important because they harness some of the assets available to Aboriginal people living in remote and regional areas of northern Australia to create sustainable livelihoods, and have a tendency to strengthen, renew and/or revitalise associated cultural traditions.

Use of native plants and animals for commercial purposes represents an alternative land use to mainstream agricultural production that does not require substantial land modification or investments in infrastructure or chemicals. Utilisation of feral animals in particular can be seen as restorative rather than destructive, and therefore beneficial for natural resource management and biodiversity conservation. However, commercial use of native wildlife is relatively tightly regulated: while Indigenous people have rights to harvest wildlife for subsistence use (Bomford and Caughley, 1996; Davies et al., 1999), they are required to abide by all laws and regulations when that harvest is commercial (Cooney and Edwards, 2009). Nevertheless, as major landholders in northern Australia, Indigenous people are potentially well positioned to take advantage of the opportunities offered by wildlife-based enterprise.

Few have chosen to do so and there is no consolidated information on Indigenous wildlife-based industries, there being neither government agencies like Tourism Australia and Tourism NT or industry body like ANKAAA, Desart and perhaps other groups, although Aboriginal Bush Traders (2013) and the Northern Land Council have provided advice to potential operators. While numerous wildlife species have been identified as having significant commercial potential in Australia (Ramsay, 1994; ACIL Economics, 1997; Woodley, 1998; Whitehead, 2003; Griffiths et al., 2003, 2005; Gorman et al., 2006, 2008; Whitehead et al., 2006; Cooney et al., 2009; Cunningham et al., 2009; Fordham and Fogarty, 2010), there has been little effective commercialisation. In the NT we are aware of only four instances where Indigenous people are currently harvesting wildlife or feral animals on a commercial basis, although the returns are often small: crocodile eggs, feral buffalo, bush tomatoes and acacia seed. Enterprises aimed at selling turtle eggs and tarantula venom (Fordham and Fogarty, 2010) or mustering camels (Australian Broadcast Commission, 2013) were difficult obtain data for, probably because they are either too new or too small.

The Australian crocodile industry began in Queensland in the 1950s (Goulding et al., 2007). After a period of over-harvesting from the wild, the industry was regulated in the 1970s and the wild population in the NT has almost completely recovered (Fukuda et al., 2011). Indigenous people in the NT are currently involved through supplying eggs and hatchlings of saltwater crocodiles (*Crocodylus porosus*) to farms where they are grown for sale as meat or leather to both domestic and international markets. Eggs are collected from February to April, with some being hatched out in Indigenous communities before being supplied to farms. Much of the collection is by rangers, with traditional owners receiving a royalty payment for any eggs collected on their land. For one ranger group at Maningrida, the average annual income was $23,700 and the royalty payment $7,500 (Austin and Corey, 2012). While many of the large tidal rivers are now included

---

5   We use the definition of wildlife given by the Australian Government, which refers to both plants and animals (Woodley, 1998).

in this collection process (Fukuda et al., 2011), the income for Indigenous people is unlikely to be more than 10 times the amount described by Austin and Corey (2012).

Buffalo were introduced to Australia in the 1820s (Letts, 1982), with the wild population of buffalo in the NT estimated to be 150,000 and increasing (Bradshaw et al., 2007). Wild buffalo have been used commercially for more than a century for leather goods, meat, tourism, and for exporting live (Albrecht et al., 2009). Of these markets safari hunting is still popular (part of tourism but with little Indigenous employment, although some return to Indigenous corporations through licence fees) and live buffalo are still exported to Southeast Asia (Gorman et al., 2008) by the Gulin Gulin Buffalo Company (Austin and Garnett, 2011). This company had an average annual income of $640,000 for the period 1997–2008, paying an average of $43,000 p.a. in wages, largely to local people during the six-month mustering season, as well as an average of $102,000 p.a. to the local community through royalty payments for use of their traditional land for harvesting (Austin and Garnett, 2011; Collier et al., 2011).

The wild harvest of bush tomatoes (*Solanum centrale*) in the central desert has provided some return to central Australian Indigenous communities (Bryceson,2008; Cleary, 2009; Ryder et al., 2009), although there remain substantial ethical and legal issues relating to its commercialisation, particularly through horticulture (Holcolme et al., 2011; Lee, 2013). Indigenous desert-dwellers have harvested 4–20 tonnes of fruit from the wild per annum, depending on seasonal variation (Bryceson, 2008; Cleary, 2009), with individual communities sometimes having gaps between harvest of four years or more (Holcolme et al., 2010). Collectors receive $4–10/kg (Bryceson, 2008), making the monetary value of the harvest to Indigenous communities anywhere from $16,000 to $200,000 in a year.

The seeds of various Acacia species, sold as 'wattle seed', are harvested from the wild by Indigenous people, roasted and consumed as a spice added to other foods. Seed is also sometimes sold for environmental rehabilitation, sometimes at five times the price paid for edible wattle seed (P. Yates, personal communication). The amount collected varies from 0.5 to 5.0 tonnes/year depending on seasonal conditions, with collectors getting anywhere from $0.50 to $14.00/kg (Bryceson, 2008). Thus the total value of the harvest to all harvesters may vary from $250 to $70,000 in a year. In 2013, a good year for harvesting, the total value of seed bought was unlikely to have exceeded $40,000 (P. Yates, personal communication).

Employment in each of these industries is seasonal and at a relatively small scale. Six FTE positions are created through crocodile egg collection for two months per year at Maningrida (Austin and Corey, 2012). Gulin Gulin employs eight people for about six months, expanding to 15 for short periods of intense activity, mostly drawn from the local community (Austin and Garnett, 2011). The bush tomato industry might provide enough casual work for collectors to be the equivalent of one FTE, while wattle seed would support less than 0.5 FTE (P. Yates, personal communication). Thus the total Indigenous employment in these four persistent wildlife-based industries is almost certainly less than 15 FTEs per annum, although this figure is almost certainly spread across a much larger group of people working casually as resource availability and markets permit.

Overall Trends in Indigenous Participation in Culture-Based Enterprises

According to census data (Australian Bureau of Statistics, 2006, 2012a), Indigenous employment in Darwin increased by about 25 per cent in the five-year period from 2006 to 2011 (see Table 6.2). Away from Darwin, however – in the regional towns and remote areas where Indigenous people make up the majority of the population – there was an increase in the employment rate of just 3 per cent. However, the population growth rate in these areas is over 5 per cent, and over 20 per cent of Indigenous people in the labour force are already unemployed. By contrast, employment in the culture-based sectors increased by over 200 per cent away from Darwin, while that in Darwin city itself rose by 25 per cent from a low base. The biggest increase was in the number of people stating that the creative arts were their principal means of employment. However, the number of Indigenous people employed in both CNRM and tourism also more than doubled. The trends in wildlife-based industries could not be determined from the census as numbers are small, especially in terms of the category 'major form of income'.

The increase in employment was strongest for women, with male dominance in all three sectors declining over the five-year period. This trend was also apparent in the creative arts sector where women already dominated in 2006 so that, by 2011, there were twice as many women as men employed in this sector.

Table 6.2 **Trends in the number of Indigenous people employed in different industries in Darwin and outside Darwin in the Northern Territory, and in the ratio of males to females**

	Darwin		% change	Rest of the NT		% change	Female/male ratio		% change
	2006	2011		2006	2011		2006	2011	
CNRM	23	23	0	90	185	106	0.28	0.36	26
Tourism	5	15	200	24	30	25	0.20	0.44	122
Creative arts	8	7	-13	23	206	796	1.34	1.93	44
All culture-based employment	36	45	25	137	421	207	0.38	0.81	115
Total employment of Indigenous people in area	2712	3391	25	8921	9151	3	0.91	1.0	10

Source: Australian Bureau of Statistics, 2006, 2012.

Discussion

CULTURE-BASED EMPLOYMENT

The overall contribution of culture-based industries to employment is small compared to other forms of Indigenous employment. However, other forms of employment are not keeping pace with Indigenous population growth, even though most of the jobs are in government service delivery (particularly health and education; Australian Bureau of Statistics, 2012a). Judging by trends from 2006 to 2011, however, culture-based employment is increasing rapidly.

Of the four sectors examined here, the CNRM sector is currently the most vibrant. Not only has the number of Indigenous rangers doubled from 2006 to 2011 but there also appears to be substantial potential to increase the number of people employed further, particularly in the area of fire management to reduce greenhouse gas emissions (Heckbert et al., 2012). Public approval of the concept of paying Indigenous people to provide environmental services is high (Zander and Garnett, 2011) and the government has committed funds to support Indigenous CNRM until at least 2017 (Australian Government, 2013). Importantly, most of the employment and anticipated increase in CNRM employment has occurred in remote and regional NT, where official employment growth is lowest. However, the great promise for expanding CNRM into commercial carbon trading remains uncertain as government policies change.

By contrast, art and tourism are both mature industries. While the number of people stating in the census that they are engaged in the creative arts increased enormously between 2006 and 2011, the prices for art and the income of art centres across the NT appear to have stayed steady since the Global Financial Crisis (GFC). Similarly, while innovative product development by some art centres and communities (e.g. Tiwi Island football) has been paying off, the number of tourists engaging in some form of activity involving Indigenous people – including visiting art galleries or the Indigenous-owned facilities at Uluru and Kakadu – has fallen as the Australian tourism market shifts from Europe to Asia (Tourism NT, 2011). Whether there can be a shift to cater for the new tourism market remains to be seen. Also, while some tourism businesses started and run by individual Indigenous entrepreneurs appear to be thriving, the actual number of people employed is very small. For wildlife-based industries, the constraints that inhibit the development in any product-related business are likely to continue to limit expansion of the wildlife-based industry sector in the foreseeable future (Woodley, 1998), again despite some small successful enterprises (Austin and Garnett, 2011, Austin and Corey, 2012) and enthusiasm among Indigenous people to be involved in the sector (Zander et al., 2013).

However, it is a mistake to think of the sectors as separate. Each form of employment can be seen as contributing to a portfolio of income sources, a portfolio to which different types of income contribute according to the season. The seasonal contribution may vary through the year but, particularly in arid areas with unreliable rainfall, is also likely to vary significantly between years. This is integrally bound up in Altman's concept of the hybrid economy (Altman 2001a, b). Indeed, in places where culture-based enterprises are operating, it is almost impossible to tease out the different elements of the hybrid economy – the cultural, public and market sectors – because they are inherently interdependent. As an example, employment in CNRM enables people to visit and manage their own country.

While doing so they may engage in some wildlife-based enterprise (for example, collecting crocodile eggs or bush tomatoes), collect materials subsequently used in the creation of art works (bark, dyes, and so on), and may even be involved in guiding tourists on a casual basis. The renewed involvement with traditional country is also likely to contribute substantially to the cultural sector of the economy because more food can be obtained for domestic consumption by family and friends without entering the market economy. Indeed products that combine art and small quantities of bush produce for tourists have been produced for the high end of the market (Whitehead et al., 2006), and production of product for the creative arts market requires active NRM if it is to be sustainable (Forner, 2006; Koenig et al., 2007; Werner et al., 2008).

GOVERNMENT SUPPORT

It could be argued that most culture-based business and employment is more accurately described as being part of the state-based economy rather than driven by markets. Art centres receive substantial support to fund their coordinators, without which the industry would be much smaller; tourism is assisted by government-funded marketing; Indigenous CNRM is almost entirely government funded; and all the wildlife-based industries have received government funds at some stage. However, it can also be argued that most rural industries receive support through tax concessions and provision of infrastructure (ports, roads) that are essential for their business. Of the four sectors, the creative industries, tourism and wildlife-based industries sell product directly to the market, and their economics are driven by changes in private demand. Indigenous CNRM, however, has been largely reliant on direct government grants to pay salaries. However, unlike jobs in the government service sector, such as health and education, the Indigenous rangers provide services to buyers external to their communities – i.e. the Australian public as represented by the government. That the jobs also enable people to fulfil cultural responsibilities is fortuitous additionally, but is not the primary purpose of the funding. Further, there is substantial potential for Indigenous CNRM groups to enter new and expanding markets by providing greenhouse gas offsets for industrial pollution (Heckbert et al., 2012) if this is enabled by appropriate policy settings.

ENGAGEMENT IN ENTERPRISES AND ITS SOCIAL IMPACT

A critical feature of the culture-based enterprises is the enthusiasm with which Indigenous people engage in them (Armstrong et al. 2012; Zander et al., 2013), especially when compared to other opportunities (McRae-Williams and Gerritsen, 2010). Weber (1978 [1921–22]) described two fundamental rationalities that lead to economic participation: formal rationality and substantive rationality. In a Weberian sense, formal rationality refers to 'seeking efficiency', whereas substantive rationality involves 'adherence to an ideological system', which can include cultural and spiritual traditions or customs (Cleary, 2012). Cleary (2012) used a case study of bush tomato harvests by Indigenous people in the central Australian desert to demonstrate the meaning of these two terms in practice. Here, Indigenous people undertook customary harvests of bush tomatoes whether there was a market opportunity to sell this harvest or not, thus employing a substantive rationality in their harvesting activity. However, these same wildlife harvesters also behaved opportunistically, following a formal rationality, by selling their harvests to traders when market opportunities became available and thus generating a cash income. Holcombe et al. (2011) describe a similar situation for wattle seed.

Similar analyses can be applied to the engagement of Indigenous people in other culture-based enterprises. For instance, engagement of people in CNRM is driven largely by the opportunities that such employment provides to concurrently fulfil cultural obligations and educate their children (Zander et al., 2013). The ecosystem services provided seem to be a fortuitous by-product rather than the primary motivation for service provision. As noted by Yates (2009: 50) when discussing bush food collection:

> For Aboriginal people, the idea that their traditional foods could be a mere commodity is almost beyond comprehension … it is as though bush foods are an inseparable part of themselves. For the 'whitefellas', further down the value chain, such understandings … are at best thought quaint, and viewed as potential marketing tools.

The failure to appreciate the need for people to engage with culture and country as part of their employment may also explain the incongruous disconnect between pastoral properties needing labour and Indigenous communities next door with extremely high levels of un- and under-employment (Josif et al., 2007). For over a century Indigenous people across regional Australia were deeply involved in the cattle industry (McGrath, 1997) but changes to workplace practice reduced the cultural alignment that had previously connected people to the industry (May, 1994).

The relatively low levels of full-time equivalent employment in culture-based enterprises also belie the social benefit derived from involvement. Indigenous CNRM, for instance, has demonstrable benefits for health, education, social function and well-being (Burgess et al., 2009; Garnett and Sithole, 2009; Weir et al., 2011; Berry et al., 2010; Kingsley et al., 2013) to the extent that it has been argued that it could be a central organising principle of policy relating to remote Indigenous communities (Garnett et al., 2009). That is, support for Indigenous CNRM should be drawn not just from environment budgets but also from health, education, justice and other budgets since there are likely to be substantial savings in outlays to these sectors arising from people being supported to live and work on country (Campbell et al., 2011). Similarly, art centres are not only bringing in new funds to a community and expanding the size of the community economy as these funds are then circulated through the store and workshop, there are also 'well-being' benefits that are more difficult to measure – such as improvements in health, strengthening the community, improvements in school attendance and greater self-esteem of artists and their families. As one community group summarised it, being an artist was seen by many Indigenous people as a 'real job' offering a future as well as supporting the past, allowing people to develop pride, self-confidence and respect for others (P. Shepherd, personal communication). The art centres themselves were seen as being important for keeping both cultural objects and cultural stories for future generations; strengthening communities by supporting other organisations such as schools; and providing access to governance training and awareness of better ways to manage individual and community issues. Such pervasive benefits are harder to identify for non-cultural based employment initiatives.

Conclusion

Culture-based enterprises make a small but growing contribution to Indigenous employment in the NT, with the art industry creating the most income and CNRM showing the greatest potential for sustained growth. Absolute numbers are probably less important for assessing the contribution of these forms of enterprise and employment than the wider impact they have on the communities in which they occur.

While most other jobs have limited reach into community well-being, culture-based employment appears to have many co-benefits, particularly for remote communities, which in turn explains the high levels of engagement by Indigenous people in the NT. Importantly in a policy environment that is looking to increase Indigenous employment, they allow participants to develop 'western world' skills that then enable people to engage with the 'outside economy' on more equal terms. Their future, however, relies heavily on government support. Currently culture-based enterprises are strongly supported by government through management and marketing (creative arts and tourism) or purchasing services (CNRM). A failure to provide this support, however, would have a substantial impact on the well-being of Indigenous people living in remote and regional parts of the NT.

References

Aboriginal Art (2013). *Locations of art centres*. Retrieved from: http://www.aboriginalart.org/index.cfm (accessed: 28 December 2013).

Aboriginal Bush Traders (2013). *Aboriginal Bush Traders creates opportunities*. Retrieved from: http://www.aboriginalbushtraders.com (accessed: 28 December 2013).

ACIL Economics (1997). *Sustainable economic use of native birds and reptiles: Can controlled trade improve conservation of species?* Canberra: Rural Industries Research and Development Corporation.

Acker, T., Stefanoff, L. and Woodhead, A. (2013). Aboriginal and Torres Strait Islander Art Economies Project: Literature Review. *CRC-REP Working Paper CW010*. Alice Springs: Ninti One.

Ah Mat, R. (2003). The moral case for Indigenous capitalism. *Unpublished paper presented at the Native Title Conference: Native Title on the Ground*. Alice Springs, 3–5 June.

Albrecht, G. A., McMahon, C. R., Bowman, D. M. J. S. and Bradshaw, C. J. A. (2009). Convergence of culture, ecology and ethics: Management of feral swamp buffalo in Northern Australia. *Journal of Agricultural and Environmental Ethics*, 22, pp. 361–78.

Altman, J. (2001a). Aboriginal economy and social process: The Indigenous hybrid economy and its sustainable development potential. *Arena Magazine*, 56, pp. 38–39.

——— (2001b). Sustainable development options on Aboriginal land: The hybrid economy in the twenty-first century. *Discussion Paper No. 226*. Canberra: Centre for Aboriginal Economic Policy Research.

——— (2005a). Economic futures on Aboriginal land in remote and very remote Australia: Hybrid economies and joint ventures. In D. Austin-Broos and G. Macdonald (eds), *Culture, economy and governance in Aboriginal Australia*. Sydney: University of Sydney Press, pp. 121–134.

——— (2005b). Development options on Aboriginal land: Sustainable Indigenous hybrid economies in the twenty-first century. In L. Taylor, G.K. Ward, G. Henderson, R. Davis and L.A. Wallis (eds), *The power of knowledge: The resonance of tradition*. Canberra: Aboriginal Studies Press, pp. 34–48.

——— (2006). The future of Indigenous Australia: Is there a path beyond the free market or welfare dependency? *Topical Issue No. 9*.Canberra: Centre for Aboriginal Economic Policy Research.

——— (2007). Alleviating poverty in remote Indigenous Australia: The role of the hybrid economy. *Development Bulletin*, 72, pp. 47–51.

——— and Cochrane, M. (2005). Sustainable development in the Indigenous-owned savannah: Innovative institutional design for cooperative wildlife management. *Wildlife Research*, 32, pp. 473–480.

——— and Finlayson, J. (2003). Aborigines, tourism and sustainable development. *Journal of Tourism Studies*, 14, pp. 78–91.

——— and Sanders, W. (1991). Government initiatives for Aboriginal employment: Equity, equality and policy realism. In J. Altman (ed.), *Aboriginal employment equity by the year 2000*. Canberra: Centre for Aboriginal Economic Policy Research, pp. 1–18.

———, Buchanan, G. J. and Larsen, L. (2007). The environmental significance of the Indigenous estate: Natural resource management as economic development in remote Australia. *Discussion Paper No. 286*. Canberra: Centre for Aboriginal Economic Policy Research.

Armstrong, R., Morrison, J. and Yu, P. (2012). Indigenous land and sea management and sustainable business development in Northern Australia. *North Australian Indigenous Land and Sea Management Alliance (NAILSMA) Research Document*. Darwin: NAILSMA.

Attorney-General's Department (2013). *Senate inquiry into Australia's Indigenous visual arts and craft sector 2007*. Canberra: Ministry for the Arts, Australian Government. Retrieved from: http://arts.gov.au/indigenous/ivais/senate-inquiry-2007 (accessed: 28 December 2013).

Austin, B. and Garnett, S.T. (2011). Indigenous wildlife enterprise: Mustering swamp buffalo (*Bubalusbubalis*) in northern Australia. *Journal of Enterprising Communities: People and Places in the Global Economy*, 5, pp. 309–323.

Austin, B. J. and Corey, B. (2012). Factors contributing to the longevity of the commercial use of crocodiles by Indigenous people in remote Northern Australia: A case study. *Rangeland Journal*, 34, pp. 239–248.

Austin-Broos, D. (2006). 'Working for' and 'Working' among Western Arrernte in Central Australia. *Oceania*, 76, pp. 1–15.

Australian Broadcast Commission (ABC). (2013). *Camel muster master plan gets enterprise over hump*. Retrieved from: http://www.abc.net.au/news/2013–05–17/camel-muster-central-australia-aboriginal-council-meat-to-africa/4696332 (accessed: 28 December 2013.

Australian Bureau of Statistics (ABS). (2006). *Census 2006 – counting: Persons, place of usual residence*. Canberra: ABS.

——— (2008). National Aboriginal and Torres Strait Islander Social Survey. *Cat. No. 4714.0*. Canberra: ABS.

——— (2012a). *Census 2011 – Counting: Persons, place of usual residence*. Canberra: ABS.

——— (2012b). Arts and Culture in Australia: A Statistical Overview. *Cat. No. 4172.0*. Canberra: ABS.

Australian Government (2011). *Indigenous Economic Development Strategy 2011–2018*. Retrieved from: http://www.dss.gov.au/sites/default/files/documents/09_2012/ieds_2011_2018.pdf (accessed: 28 December 2013).

——— (2013). *Working on Country*. Retrieved from: http://www.nrm.gov.au/funding/woc/index (accessed: 28 December 2013).

Belcher, B., Ruiz-Perez, M. and Achdiawan, R. (2005). Global patterns and trends in the use and management of commercial NTFPs: Implications for livelihoods and conservation. *World Development*, 33, pp. 1435–1452.

Berry, H. L., Butler, J. R. A., Burgess, C. P., King, U. G., Tsey, K., Cadet-James, Y. L., Rigby, C. W. and Raphael, B. (2010). Mind, body, spirit: Co-benefits for mental health from climate change adaptation and caring for country in remote Aboriginal Australian communities. *New South Wales Public Health Bulletin*, 21, pp. 139–145.

Biddle, N., Taylor, J. and Yap, M. (2009). Are the gaps closing? Regional trends and forecasts of Indigenous employment. *Australian Journal of Labour Economics*, 12, pp. 263–280.

Bomford, M. and Caughley, J. (eds) (1996). *Sustainable use of wildlife by Aboriginal peoples and Torres Strait Islanders*. Canberra: Australian Publishing Service.

Bradshaw, C. J. A., Field, I. C., Bowman, D. M. J. S., Haynes, C. and Brook, B. W. (2007). Current and future threats from non-Indigenous animal species in Northern Australia: A spotlight on World Heritage Area Kakadu National Park. *Wildlife Research*, 34, pp. 419–436.

Bryceson, K. P. (2008). Value chain analysis of bush tomato and wattle seed products. *Research Report 40*. Alice Springs: Desert Knowledge Cooperative Research Centre.

Burgess, C. P., Johnston, F. H., Berry, H. L., McDonnell, J., Yibarbuk, D., Gunabarra, C., Mileran, A. and Bailie, R. S. (2009). Healthy country, healthy people: The relationship between Indigenous health status and 'caring for country'. *Medical Journal of Australia*, 190, pp. 567–572.

Buultjens, J. and White, N. (2009). *Indigenous tourism: The possibilities into the future*. Alice Springs: Desert Knowledge Cooperative Research Centre.

———, Gale, D. and White, N. E. (2010). Synergies between Australian Indigenous tourism and ecotourism: Possibilities and problems for future development. *Journal of Sustainable Tourism*, 18, pp. 497–513.

Campbell, D., Burgess, C. P., Garnett, S. T. and Wakerman, J. (2011). Potential primary health care savings for chronic disease care associated with Australian Aboriginal involvement in land management. *Health Policy*, 99, pp. 83–89.

Cleary J. (2012). Business exchanges in the Australian desert: It's about more than the money. *Journal of Rural and Community Development*, 7, pp. 1–15.

Cleary, J. (2009). Perspectives on developing new cooperative arrangements for bush-harvested bush tomatoes from desert Australia. *Working Paper No. 48*. Alice Springs: Desert Knowledge Cooperative Research Centre.

Collier, N., Austin, B. J., Bradshaw, C. J. A. and McMahon, C. R. (2011). Turning pests into profits: Introduced buffalo provide multiple benefits to Indigenous people of Northern Australia. *Human Ecology*, 39, pp. 155–164.

Commonwealth of Australia (2007). *Securing the future: Australia's Indigenous visual arts and crafts sector*. Canberra: Senate Standing Committee on Environment, Communication, Information Technology and the Arts.

Cooney, R. and Edwards, M. (2009). Indigenous wildlife enterprise development: The regulation and policy context and challenges. *Report to North Australian Indigenous Land and Sea Management Alliance (NAILSMA)*. Darwin: NAILSMA.

———, Baumber, A., Ampt, P. and Wilson, G. (2009). Sharing Skippy: How can landholders be involved in kangaroo production in Australia? *Australian Rangeland Journal*, 31, pp. 283–292.

Copyright Agency (2013). *Resale Royalty*. Retrieved from: http://www.resaleroyalty.org.au/about-resale-royalty.aspx (accessed: 28 December 2013).

Cunningham, A., Garnett, S. and Gorman, J. (2009). Policy lessons from practice: Australian bush products for commercial markets. *GeoJournal*, 74, pp. 429–440.

Davies, G. and Brown, D. (eds) (2007). *Bushmeat and livelihoods: Wildlife management and poverty reduction*. Oxford: Blackwell.

Davies, J., Higginbottom, K., Noack, D., Ross, H. and Young, E. (1999). Sustaining Eden: Indigenous community-based wildlife management in Australia. *Evaluating Eden Series No. 1*. London: International Institute for Environment and Development.

————, White, J., Wright, A., Maru, Y. and LaFlamme, M. (2008). Applying the sustainable livelihoods approach in Australian desert Aboriginal development. *Rangeland Journal*, 30, pp. 55–65.

de Merode, E., Homewood, K. and Cowlishaw, G. (2004). The value of bushmeat and other wild foods to rural households living in extreme poverty in the Democratic Republic of Congo. *Biological Conservation*, 118, pp. 573–581.

Department of Industry (2013). *Tourism 2020. Canberra: Australian Government*. Retrieved from: http://www.ret.gov.au/tourism/policies/nltts/nltts/Pages/default.aspx#about (accessed: 28 December 2013).

Department of Social Services (2013a). *Closing the gap on Indigenous advantage: The challenge for Australia*. Canberra: Australian Government. Retrieved from: http://www.dss.gov.au/our-responsibilities/indigenous-australians/publications-articles/closing-the-gap/closing-the-gap-on-indigenous-disadvantage-the-challenge-for-australia-2009 (accessed: 28 December 2013).

———— (2013b). *Closing the Gap Prime Minister's Report 2010*. Canberra: Australian Government. Retrieved from: http://www.dss.gov.au/our-responsibilities/indigenous-australians/publications-articles/closing-the-gap/closing-the-gap-prime-ministers-report-2010 (accessed: 28 December 2013).

Department of the Environment (2013). *Working on country funded projects*. Retrieved from: http://www.environment.gov.au/indigenous/workingoncountry/projects/index.html (accessed: 28 December 2013).

Dodson, P. (2007). Keynote address: Australia fair. *Impact*, Summer, pp. 8–11.

Dunlop, C. R., Leach, G. J. and Cowie, I. D. (1995). .*Flora of the Darwin region*. Darwin: Conservation Commission of the Northern Territory.

Ferraro, P. J. and Kiss, A. (2002). Direct payments to conserve biodiversity. *Science*, 298, pp. 1718–1719.

Fordham, A. and Fogarty, B. (2010). The viability of wildlife enterprises in remote Indigenous communities of Australia: A case study. *Working Paper No. 63*. Canberra: Centre for Aboriginal Economic Policy Research.

Forner, J. (2006). The globalization of the didjeridu and the implications for small-scale community based producers in remote northern Australia. *International Journal of Environmental, Cultural, Economic and Social Sustainability*, 2, pp. 137–148.

Fukuda, Y., Webb, G., Manolis, C., Delaney, R., Letnic, M., Lindner, G. and Whitehead, P. (2011). Recovery of saltwater crocodiles following unregulated hunting in tidal rivers of the Northern Territory, Australia. *Journal of Wildlife Management*, 75, pp. 1253–1266.

Fuller, D., Buultjens, J. and Cummings, E. (2005). Ecotourism and Indigenous micro-enterprise formation in northern Australia opportunities and constraints. *Tourism Management*, 26, pp. 891–904.

Garnett, S. T. and Sithole, B. (2007). *Sustainable Northern landscapes and the nexus with Indigenous health: Healthy country healthy people*. Canberra: Land and Water Australia.

Garnett, S. T., Sithole, B., Whitehead, P., Burgess, P., Johnstone, F. and Lea, T. (2009). Healthy country, healthy people: Policy implications of links between Indigenous human health and environmental condition in tropical Australia. *Australian Journal of Policy Review*, 68, pp. 53–66.

————, Woinarski, J. C. Z., Crowley, G. M. and Kutt, A. S. (2010). Biodiversity conservation in Australian tropical rangelands. In J. du Toit, R. Kock and J. Deutsch (eds), *Can Rangelands be Wildlands? Wildlife and Livestock in Semi-arid ecosystems*. London: Blackwell Scientific, pp. 191–234.

————, Woinarski, J. C. Z., Gerritsen, R. and Duff, G. (2008). *Future options for north Australia*. Darwin: Charles Darwin University Press.

Gorman, J., Griffiths, A. and Whitehead, P. (2006). An analysis of the use of plant products for commerce in remote Aboriginal communities of northern Australia. *Economic Botany*, 60, pp. 362–373.

Gorman, J. T., Whitehead, P. J., Griffiths, A. D. and Petheram, L. (2008). Production from marginal lands: Indigenous commercial use of wild animals in Northern Australia. *International Journal of Sustainable Development and World Ecology*, 15, pp. 1–11.

Goulding, B., Riedel, E., Bevan, A. and Warfield, B. (2007). Export markets for skins and leather for Australia's camel, crocodile, emu and goat industries. *Report for the Rural Industries Research and Development Corporation*. Canberra: Rural Industries Research and Development Corporation.

Gray, M. and Chapman, B. (2006). Some labour market measurement issues for Indigenous Australians. *Australian Journal of Labour Economics*, 9, pp. 5–16.

Griffiths, A. D., Philips, A. and Godjuwa, C. (2003). Harvest of Bombaxceiba for the Aboriginal arts industry, central Arnhem Land, Australia. *Biological Conservation*, 113, pp. 295–305.

———, Schult, H. J. and Gorman, J. (2005). Wild harvest of Cycasarnhemica (Cycadaceae): Impact on survival, recruitment and growth in Arnhem Land, northern Australia. *Australian Journal of Botany*, 53, pp. 771–779.

Heckbert, S., Russell-Smith, J. J., Reeson, A., Davies, J., James, G. and Meyer, C. (2012). Spatially explicit benefit–cost analysis of fire management for greenhouse gas abatement. *Austral Ecology*, 37, pp. 724–732.

Heubach, K., Wittig, R., Nuppenau, E.-A. and Hahn, K. (2011). The economic importance of non-timber forest products (NTFPs) for livelihood maintenance of rural West African communities: A case study from northern Benin. *Ecological Economics*, 70, pp. 1991–2001.

Hinch, T. and Butler, R. (2009). Indigenous tourism. *Tourism Analysis*, 14, pp. 15–27.

Holcombe, S., Yates, P. and Walsh, F. (2011). Reinforcing alternative economies: Self-motivated work by central Anmatyerr people to sell Katyerr (Desert Raisin, Bush Tomato) in central Australia. *Rangeland Journal*, 33, pp. 255–265.

Hunt, J., Altman, J. C. and May, K. (2009). Social benefits of Aboriginal engagement in natural resource management. *Working Paper 60*. Canberra: Centre for Aboriginal Economic Policy Research.

Indigenous Visual Arts Industry Support (IVAIS). (2013). *About Indigenous Visual Arts Industry Support (IVAIS)*. Retrieved from: http://arts.gov.au/indigenous/ivais (accessed: 28 December 2013).

Josif, P., Ashley, M. and Bubb, A. (2007). *Review of Indigenous Employment and Engagement in the Northern Pastoral Industry 2007*. Sydney: Meat and Livestock Australia.

Kingsley, J., Townsend, M., Henderson-Wilson, C. and Bolam, B. (2013). Developing an exploratory framework linking Australian Aboriginal peoples' connection to country and concepts of wellbeing. *International Journal of Environmental Research and Public Health*, 10, pp. 678–698.

Koenig, J., Altman, J. C. and Griffiths, A. D. (2011). Artists as harvesters: Natural resource use by Indigenous woodcarvers in Central Arnhem Land. Australia. *Human Ecology*, 39, pp. 407–419.

———, Altman, J. C., Griffiths, A. D. and Kohen, A. (2007). 20 years of Aboriginal woodcarving in Arnhem Land, Australia: Using art sales records to examine the dynamics of sculpture production. *Forests, Trees and Livelihoods*, 17, pp. 43–60.

Langton, M. (2010). *The resource curse. Griffith Review 28: Still the Lucky Country?* Retrieved from: http://griffithreview.com/edition-28-still-the-lucky-country/the-resource-curse (accessed: 28 December 2013).

Lee, L. S. (2013). Horticultural development of bush food plants and rights of Indigenous people as traditional custodians – the Australian Bush Tomato (Solanum centrale) example: A review. *Rangeland Journal*, 34, pp. 359–373.

Letts, G. A. (1982). History of water buffalo in Australia. In B. D. Ford and D. G. Tulloch (eds), The Australian Buffalo: A collection of papers. *Technical Bulletin No. 62*. Palmerston: Northern Territory Government.

Luckert, M. K., Campbell, B. M., Gorman, J. T. and Garnett, S. T. (2007). *Investing in Indigenous natural resource management*. Darwin: Charles Darwin University Press.

Martin, T. G. and van Klinken, R. D. (2006). Value for money? Investment in weed management in Australian rangelands. *Rangeland Journal*, 28, pp. 63–75.

———, Campbell, S. D. and Grounds, S. (2006).Weeds of Australian rangelands. *Rangeland Journal*, 28, pp. 3–26.

May, D. (1994). *Aboriginal labour and the cattle industry: Queensland from white settlement to the present.* Cambridge: Cambridge University Press.

May, K. (2010). Indigenous cultural and natural resource management and the emerging role of the Working on Country program. *Working Paper No. 65*. Canberra: Centre for Aboriginal Economic Policy Research.

McGrath, A. (1997). *Born in the cattle*. Melbourne: Allen and Unwin.

McRae-Williams, E. and Gerritsen, R. (2010). Mutual incomprehension: The cross-cultural domain of work in a remote Australian Aboriginal community. *International Indigenous Policy Journal*, 1(2), article 2.

Morrison, J. (2007). Caring for Country. In: Altman, J. and Hinkson, M. (eds), *Coercive reconciliation: Stabilise, normalise, exit Aboriginal Australia*. Melbourne: Arena, pp. 249–261.

Mundine, W. (2010). Wrong Mr Abbott, let's just get down to business. *The Drum Opinion*, 30 April 2010. Retrieved from: http://www.abc.net.au/unleashed/33878.html (accessed: 28 December 2013).

Muradian, R., Corbera, E., Pascual, U., Kosoy, N. and May, P. H. (2010). Reconciling theory and practice: An alternative conceptual framework for understanding payments for environmental services. *Ecological Economics*, 69, pp. 1202–1208.

Northern Australian Land and Water Taskforce (2009). *Sustainable development of northern Australia*. Canberra: Department of Infrastructure and Transport. Retrieved from: http://www.regional.gov.au/regional/ona/files/NLAW.pdf (accessed: 28 December 2013).

Office of the Registrar of Indigenous Corporations (ORIC). (2012). *At the heart of art: A snapshot of Aboriginal and Torres Strait Islander corporations in the visual arts sector*. Canberra: Australian Government. Retrieved from: http://www.oric.gov.au/html/publications/other/11_0327_Corp_Visual_Arts_Sector_v3-3.pdf (accessed: 28 December 2013).

Orians, G. H. and Milewski, A. V. (2007). Ecology of Australia: The effects of nutrient-poor soils and intense fires. *Biological Reviews of the Cambridge Philosophical Society*, 82, pp. 393–423.

Pagiola, S., Landell-Mills, N. and Bishop, J. (2002). Making market-based mechanisms work for forests and people. In S. Pagiola, J. Bishop and N. Landell-Mills (eds), *Selling Forest Environmental Services: Market-based Mechanisms for Conservation*. London: Earthscan, pp. 261–289.

Pearson, N. (2009). *Up from the mission: Selected writings*. Melbourne: Black.

Preece, N. (2002). Aboriginal fires in monsoonal Australia from historical accounts. *Journal of Biogeography*, 29, pp. 321–336.

Press, A. J. (1987). Fire management in Kakadu National Park: The ecological basis for the active use of fire. *Search*, 18, 244–248.

Putnis, A., Josif, P. and Woodward, E. (2007). *Healthy country, healthy people: Supporting Indigenous engagement in the sustainable management of Northern Territory land and seas: A strategic framework*. Darwin: CSIRO.

Ramsay, B. J. (1994). *Commercial use of wild animals in Australia*. Canberra: Australian Government.

Ruhanen, L., Whitford, M., and McLennan, C. (2013). Indigenous tourism in Australia: An analysis of international demand and supply. In *Proceedings of 1st World Conference on Hospitality, Tourism and Event Research and International Convention and Expo Summit 2013*. Bangkok: 25–28 May 2013, pp. 377–382.

Russell-Smith, J. (2002). *Pre-Contact Aboriginal and Contemporary Fire Regimes of the Savanna Landscapes of Northern Australia: Patterns, Changes and Ecological Processes*. Canberra: Department of Environment and Heritage.

Russell-Smith, J., Murphy, B. P., Meyer, C. M., Cook, G. D., Maier, S., Edwards, A. C. Schatz, J. and Brocklehurst, P. (2009). Improving estimates of savanna burning emissions for greenhouse accounting in northern Australia: Limitations, challenges, applications. *International Journal of Wildland Fire*, 18, pp. 1–18.

Ryder, M., Walsh, F., Douglas, J., Waycott, M., Robson, H., Singh, Z., De Sousa Majer, M., Collins, T., White, J. and Cheers, B. (2009). Sustainable bush produce systems: Progress Report 2004–2006. *Working Paper 31*. Alice Springs: Desert Knowledge CRC.

Sithole, B., Hunter-Xenie, H., Williams, L., Saegenschnitter, J., Yibarbuk, D., Ryan, M., Campion, O., Yunupingu, B., Liddy, M., Watts, E., Daniels, C., Christophersen, P., Cubillo, V., Phillips, E., Marika, W., Jackson, D. and Barbour, W. (2008). *Aboriginal land and sea management in the top end: A community-driven evaluation*. Darwin: CSIRO.

Stafford Smith, M., Moran, M. and Seemann, K. (2008). The 'viability' and resilience of communities and settlements in desert Australia. *Rangeland Journal*, 30, pp. 123–135.

Steering Committee for the Review of Government Service Provision (SCRGSP). (2011). *Overcoming Indigenous disadvantage: Key indicators 2011*. Canberra: Productivity Commission.

Sutton, P. (2009). *The politics of suffering: Indigenous Australia and the end of the liberal consensus*. Melbourne: Melbourne University Press.

Taylor, J. (2006). Indigenous people in the west Kimberley labour market. *Working Paper No. 35*, Canberra: Centre for Aboriginal Economic Policy Research.

Tourism Australia (2013). *Operator directory*. Retrieved from: http://www.tourism.australia.com/aboriginal/operator-directory (accessed: 28 December 2013).

Tourism Northern Territory (2011). *Indigenous Tourism*. Retrieved from: http://www.tourismnt.com.au/Portals/3/Indigenous%20Cultural%20Tourism%20YE%20Jun%2009–11%20.pdf (accessed: 28 December 2013).

Tourism Research Australia (2010). *Indigenous tourism in Australia: Profiling the domestic market*. Canberra: Tourism Research Australia.

Tremblay, P. (2009). The contribution of Aboriginal tourism to economic development: Making appropriate distinctions. In J. Carlsen, M. Hughes, K. Holmes and R. Jones (eds), *CAUTHE 2009: See change: Tourism and hospitality in a dynamic world*. Fremantle: Curtin University of Technology, pp. 951–976.

——— and Wegner, A. (2008). *Indigenous/Aboriginal tourism research in Australia 2000–2008: Industry lessons and future research needs*. Gold Coast: Sustainable Tourism Cooperative Research Centre. Retrieved from: http://www.crctourism.com.au/wms/upload/Resources/110018%20Tremblay%20IndigenousAboriginalTRA%20WEB.pdf (accessed: 28 December 2013).

United Nations (UN). (2010). State of the world's Indigenous peoples. New York: United Nations. Retrieved from: http://www.unpo.org/article/10586 (accessed: 28 December 2013).

van Noordwijk, M. and Leimona, B. (2010). Principles for fairness and efficiency in enhancing environmental services in Asia: Payments, compensation, or co-investment? *Ecology and Society*, 15(4), article 17.

van Vliet, N., Nebesse, C., Gambalemoke, S., Akaibe, D. and Nasi, R. (2012). The bushmeat market in Kisangani, Democratic Republic of Congo: Implications for conservation and food security. *Oryx*, 46, pp. 196–203.

Weaver, D. (2010). Indigenous tourism stages and their implications for sustainability. *Journal of Sustainable Tourism*, 18, pp. 43–60.

Weber, M. (1978 [1921–22]). *Economy and society: An outline of interpretive sociology*. Berkeley: University of California Press.

Weir, J. K., Stacey, C. and Youngetob, K. (2011). *The benefits associated with Caring for Country: Literature review*. Canberra: Department of Sustainability, Environment, Water, Population and Communities.

Werner, P. A., Prior, L. D. and Forner, J. (2008). Growth and survival of termite-piped *Eucalyptus tetrodonta* and *E. miniata* in northern Australia: Implications for harvest of trees for didgeridoos. *Forest Ecology and Management*, 256, pp. 328–334.

Whitehead, P. J. (2003). *Indigenous products from Indigenous people: Linking enterprise, wildlife use and conservation*. Paper presented to the Seizing our Economic Future Forum. Alice Springs: 6–7 March 2003.

Whitehead, P. J., Gorman, J., Griffiths, A. D., Wightman, G., Massarella, H. and Altman, J. (2006). Feasibility of small scale commercial native plant harvests by Indigenous communities. *Final report for the Joint Venture Agroforestry Program of the Rural Industries Research & Development Corporation, the Forest and Wood Products Research and Development Corporation and the Natural Heritage Trust*. Darwin: Key Centre for Tropical Wildlife Management and Rural Industries Research and Development Corporation.

Whitford, M. M. and Ruhanen, L. M. (2010). Australian Indigenous tourism policy: Practical and sustainable policies. *Journal of Sustainable Tourism*, 18, pp. 475–496.

Williams, R. J., Griffin, A. J. and Allen, G. E. (2002). Fire regimes and biodiversity in the savannas of north Australia. In R. A. Bradstock, J. Williams and A. M. Gill (eds), *Flammable Australia: Fire regimes and biodiversity of a continent*. Cambridge: Cambridge University Press, pp. 281–304.

Woinarski, J. C. Z., Legge, S., Fitzsimons, J. A., Traill, B. J., Burbidge, A. A., Fisher, A., Firth, R. S. C., Gordon, I. J., Griffiths, A. D., Johnson, C. N., McKenzie, N. L., Palmer, C., Radford, I., Rankmore, B., Ritchie, E. G., Ward, S. and Ziembicki, M. (2011). The disappearing mammal fauna of northern Australia: Context, cause, and response. *Conservation Letters*, 4, pp. 192–201.

Woinarski, J., Mackey, B., Nix, H. and Traill, B. (2007). *The nature of Northern Australia: Natural values, ecological processes and future prospects*. Canberra: Australian National University E-Press.

Woodley, J. (1998). *Commercial utilisation of Australian native wildlife*. Report of the Senate Rural and Regional Affairs and Transport References Committee. Canberra: The Committee. Retrieved from: http://trove.nla.gov.au/work/8845501?q&versionId=46551343 (accessed: 28 December 2013).

Yates, P. (2009). The bush foods industry and poverty alleviation in Central Australia. *Dialogue (Academy of the Social Sciences in Australia*, 28(2), pp. 47–56.

Young, E. A. (1988). Aboriginal Economic Enterprises: Problems and Prospects. In D. Wade-Marshall and P. Loveday (eds), *Northern Australia*. Darwin: Australian National University, pp. 182–200.

Yunupingu, G. (2008). Tradition, truth and tomorrow. *The Monthly*, December 2008-January 2009, pp. 32–40.

Zander, K. K. and Garnett, S. T. (2011). The economic value of environmental services on Indigenous-held lands in Australia. *PLoS ONE*, 6(8), e23154.

———, Austin, B. and Garnett, S. T. (2014). Indigenous peoples' interest in wildlife-based enterprises in the Northern Territory, Australia. *Human Ecology, Human Ecology*, 42, pp. 115–126.

———, Dunnett, D. R., Brown, C., Campion, O. and Garnett, S. T. (2013). Rewards for providing environmental services: Where Indigenous Australians' and western perspectives collide. *Ecological Economics*, 87, pp. 145–154.

7

Institutional Arrangements and Sustainable Livelihoods: The Experience of an Indigenous Community in Taiwan

Teresa C. H. Tao and Geoffrey Wall[1]

Chapter Synopsis

It is argued that sustainable development, while good in theory, is difficult to apply and that a sustainable livelihoods approach may offer better prospects of practical success. At the core of this approach are appropriate institutional arrangements for decision-making. However, the decision-making processes of indigenous groups are part of their culture and vary substantially from those of the majority society with which they must engage. This chapter examines the experience of a Cou community in Chashan, in the mountainous interior of Taiwan, as it has striven to diversify livelihoods through the incorporation of tourism. The important role of a prominent individual, inter-sectoral linkages and mechanisms for the distribution of benefits are highlighted. The case demonstrates the utility of a sustainable livelihoods approach and the importance of institutional arrangements for its successful implementation.

Introduction

Since the term 'sustainable development' was first publicised by the World Commission on Environment and Development (WCED) in the Brundtland Report in 1987 (*Our Common Future*),

1   Fieldwork in Chashan was partly supported by a grant to Dr Geoffrey Wall from the Social Sciences and Humanities Research Council of Canada. Special thanks are accorded to the Chashan residents in Alishan who shared their kindness, friendship, care, hospitality, and perspectives with us.

it has received widespread acclamation and has even been incorporated into the policies of international organisations and the legislation of many jurisdictions throughout the world. Nevertheless, it has not been easy to implement the concept (Sharpley, 2009). It is often not clear exactly what is to be sustained and at what scale, or whether the concept refers to a philosophy, a process, a programme or product, or all of these (Wall, 1997, 2002). Also, when sustainability is conceived as mediating tension between environment and economy, the role of culture is often underplayed (Wall, 1993).

As Wall (1991) has pointed out, *Our Common Future* does not make reference to tourism, and there has been confusion and disagreement over what the principles of sustainable development really are in the context of tourism and how they may be put into practice (Wheeller, 1993; Clarke, 1997; Stabler, 1997). The meanings attached to sustainable tourism have varied significantly, with little consensus among researchers and government institutions. According to McCool and Moisey (2008: 4–5), definitions of sustainable tourism can be grouped into three types:

1. *Sustaining tourism: how to maintain tourism business over a long time period.* This view is narrow and usually emphasises that the number of tourists visiting an area should be maintained or continue to rise. While maintaining the health of individual businesses may be a worthy social goal, this perspective does not necessarily recognise tourism as a tool to enhance local economic opportunities, protect cultural and natural heritage, and maintain a desired quality of life.
2. *Sustainable tourism: a kinder, gentler form of tourism that is generally small in scale, sensitive to cultural and environmental impacts and respects the involvement of local people in policy decisions.* This view recognises that there are finite biophysical and social limits to tourism development, and that tourism can overwhelm a community with negative social and environmental impacts. Thus, the interpretation of sustainable tourism is often close to that of ecotourism: small in scale, designed to benefit local people and protect the resources upon which tourism depends. A larger question, however, is the unnecessary and counterproductive distinction between sustainable and mass tourism. The aim should be to make all types of tourism sustainable.
3. *What should tourism sustain? Tourism as a tool for development.* This view sees tourism as a tool of social and economic development, not as an end in itself. In this sense, tourism is integrated into broader development programmes. Cultures are protected not solely for their value to the tourism sector, but also because of their intrinsic values and importance to their people (Robinson, 1999). This interpretation acknowledges that tourism may not be necessary for sustainable development and that it may be a legitimate goal to reduce tourism.

Interpretations 1 and 2 espouse a tourism-centric paradigm of sustainable tourism development: the term 'sustainable tourism' may be thought of as 'tourism which is in a form which can maintain its viability in an area for an indefinite period time' (Butler, 1993: 29).

The concern is with protecting the immediate resource base that will allow tourism development to be sustained (Hunter, 1995). This is a very narrow view because it assumes that tourism is a way of encouraging development to move in the direction of sustainability, which it may or may not do (Tao and Wall, 2009). In addition, applying sustainability principles to a single sector, such as tourism, ignores the fact that sectors compete for the use of scarce resources and a single sector could be sustained but, at the same time, sustainable development, when more generally conceived, could be undermined. Thus, a single-sector approach is inappropriate and sustainability is unlikely to be achieved through such a narrow perspective (Butler, 1998). Besides, it does not acknowledge the possibility that tourism might be introduced as an additional economic option and, through proper interaction with other economic activities, might contribute to the broader goals of sustainable development.

Regardless of the approach to sustainability that is adopted, implementation commonly founders on the lack of appropriate organisations and institutional arrangements to initiate and manage change in the direction of sustainability. Sustainability is a holistic concept but the responsibility for making decisions with respect to resource allocations is usually fragmented among numerous authorities. If tourism is to be a positive force, resources should be used wisely and it should not grow at the expense of other sectors. Mechanisms for managing the linkages between tourism and other sectors of the economy are required to ensure that the benefits and costs are distributed equitably. Otherwise, conflicts may arise, particularly if appropriate institutions are not in place to mediate the conflicts (Tao, 2006).

For indigenous groups specifically, cultural control is crucial. It not only means using their unique, often traditional, knowledge and expertise to provide cultural experiences to tourists, but also being able to organise tourism through their societal institutions (Tao and Wall, 2009). Few studies discuss in detail the institutional arrangements for tourism development that are guided by aboriginal culture. The following case study examines this topic.

Sustainable Livelihoods

Recognising that the notions of sustainable development and sustainable tourism have been deficient conceptually and in practical application, a sustainable livelihoods (SL) approach is proposed to examine the role of tourism in the communities in which it takes place. It is a people-centred paradigm that emphasises the inherent capacities and knowledge systems of local residents, and it is focused on community-level actions (Chambers, 1986; United Nations Development Programme/UNDP, 1999). One main idea of SL is the promotion of adaptive strategies, which are defined as 'the changes and adjustments people make in their livelihood systems in order to cope under difficult circumstances' (Helmore and Singh, 2001: 3).

They are rooted in local knowledge, combining traditional knowledge with appropriate elements from contemporary or external knowledge, assimilated into the community over time. A key feature of the SL approach is recognition that all human development and economic growth depends upon livelihoods – not jobs per se, but the wide, infinitely diverse range of activities that people engage in to make their living. The SL approach inherently incorporates the multi-sectoral character of real life, so that development work is better able to address actual problems as they exist at the community level. This approach also integrates environmental, social and economic issues into a holistic framework, providing an opportunity to promote the sort of cross-sectoral and cross-thematic approach that should be the hallmark of development work (Helmore and Singh, 2001; UNDP, 1999). In contrast to the single-sector emphasis of sustainable tourism, the SL approach provides a broader perspective to examine a wide range of tourism opportunities and their consequences for people's lives. There is a substantial literature on sustainable livelihoods, particularly concerning rural development (Adato and Meinzen-Dick, 2002; Carney, 1999; Chambers, 1986; Chambers and Conway, 1992; Hebinck and Bourdillon, 2001; Helmore and Singh, 2001; Lee, 2008), but very little has been written on SL in the context of tourism (Ashley, 2000; Tao and Wall, 2009).

Crucially, at the core of an SL approach is institutional processes and organisational structure (see Figure 7.1). As indicated above, in the absence of appropriate organisations and institutional arrangements, little is likely to be achieved.

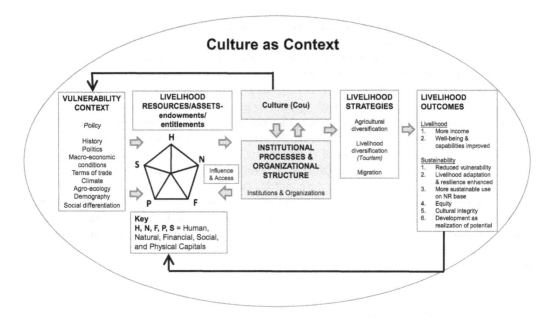

Figure 7.1   Sustainable livelihoods conceptual framework with tourism

Source: Adapted from Department for International Development (DFID), 1999; Scoones, 1998.

Institutions and Organisations

The term 'institution' has several meanings. It can be used as a synonym for 'organisation' or to refer to 'established human relationships within a society', 'typically composed working arrangements', 'routines, conventions and customs' or 'the way things are done' (DFID, 1999; Ostrom, 1992; Rasmussen and Meinzen-Dick, 1995). Some scholars make a distinction between organisations and institutions. Organisations are defined as groups of individuals bound together by some common purpose to achieve certain objectives (Ellis, 2000; Leach et al., 1999). Institutions are 'the rules of the game in society' and these include both 'formal rules and conventions and informal codes of behavior' (Ellis, 2000: 38; Leach, et al., 1999). Altman and Cochrane (2005) think that it is often hard to make a clear differentiation between institutions and organisations, and we do not attempt to do so in this chapter. Rather, the definition of Ostrom (1992) and Leach et al. (1999) is followed, and we view 'institution' as a set of 'rules in use' among individuals and groups. These rules shape the patterns of human behaviour and the results that are achieved (Ostrom, 1992).

Research Approach

A modified version of Scoones' SL framework (see Figure 7.1) is used as a conceptual framework to examine how tourism operates in a community, how tourism is linked to other sectors, and how the benefits are distributed. Chashan, Taiwan, which is a Cou indigenous community, is used to demonstrate the challenges of making and maintaining such links.

In the framework, tourism is a livelihood strategy linked to other sectors of the local economy. In Figure 7.1, particular emphasis is given to *institutions and organisations* because they bind together the processes of combining livelihood resources to pursue various strategies to realise different livelihood outcomes. *Processes and structures* mediate the complex tasks of achieving a sustainable livelihood (Scoones, 1998). *Culture*, in this case Cou culture, guides the institutional processes and the transformation of organisational structures, as indicated in the framework. Majority culture is the broad cultural context in which the minority group must operate.

Chashan, the study community, is located in Alishan Township in a remote area in the mountainous interior of Taiwan. It consists of three ethnic groups. According to a survey conducted in 2005, two-thirds of the population of Chashan are indigenous people (Cou 57 per cent, Bunun 10.7 per cent), while the other one-third are Han (31.4 per cent). The study site was chosen because people in Chashan depend upon multiple livelihood resources, and it is a good place to explore how the villagers have attempted to incorporate tourism into their existing livelihood activities in a rural economy. The livelihoods and priorities of individuals, households, and community are assessed, and the many positive and negative consequences of tourism initiatives are identified.

An additional aim is to understand tourism from an indigenous perspective. Cou culture has many implications for the way tourism development is being done. Thatched pavilions, which provide shaded places to relax, talk, and eat, are common to the cultures of the three ethnic groups and were selected by the village cadre as a symbol for tourism development. While the focus of the research is on the current situation in Chashan, an evolutionary perspective is adopted in the research so that the changes that gave rise to the present situation can be appreciated.

Field research was undertaken for a total of eight months from July 2004 to January 2005 and from November to December 2005, the second phase enabling the checking of data from the earlier phase and the filling of gaps. The sampling approach used in the first phase was progressive, evolving as the author became more familiar with the environment and was able to assess the number of individuals who could be approached given the time available. Data were collected through qualitative methods including direct and participant observation, and in-depth interviews with key village informants, village residents, government officials, academics, and NGO staff. Data were collected until information was repetitive and no new insights were being gained. The selection of interviewees followed two principles: targeting and spatial coverage. Initially, key leaders and village residents who had been involved in the initiation and establishment of Chashan Leisure Agricultural Area were contacted and interviewed. Then, since Chashan village is comprised of five diverse neighbourhoods, individuals from each neighbourhood were interviewed to ensure that the data fully represented the different voices of Chashan. Tourism activities are carried out in and around the village, and the majority of Chashan residents are involved in a variety of livelihood activities in addition to tourism. The collected data were analysed and a number of preliminary results appeared and further questions were raised. The initial results were shared with local residents through local presentations and a conference presentation to seek feedback in the second phase.

A total of 126 interviews were completed. In order to protect the anonymity of informants, specific informants are not identified below. However, unless otherwise stated, it can be assumed that the information was gained from interviewees in 2004 and 2005 and, in most cases, was corroborated by more than one person. Secondary data on indigenous people, and tourism in Taiwan and at the research site were also collected, including government documents and statistics, archival material, literary works, newspapers, and magazines. The number of important books and reports numbered more than 80.

The categories in the SL framework were used to guide data collection and analysis. Two forms of data analysis were conducted to gain different insights. Initially, types and patterns of activities and resource uses were examined. Different groups of informants' answers to research questions were also compared to quantitative data from reports (e.g., on community organisations). Second, components of the sustainable livelihood framework, particularly inputs, outputs and flows of livelihood resources, actors, and trends in the social environment were identified and linked to bring a dynamic element to the analysis.

Results

THE ROLE OF AN INDIVIDUAL

CA001 is a Bunun and married to a Cou. She was the former village head, an elder of Chashan Presbyterian Church and the former general executive of Chashan Community Development Association (CCDA). She was elected as the village head in 1996 and served in the position for eight years. She shared her concern about Chashan villagers' livelihoods and her plans from the past to the present as follows:

> [I]n the past we obtained more profit if we planted more plums; however, it came out that recently planting more means more loss. We cannot only rely on agricultural production nowadays. Some of our products overlap with those imported. When imported goods are better than ours, we cannot compete. The only solution is to combine recreation with agriculture, combining a taste of rich indigenous culture, natural environment and agriculture. A special process is necessary to enhance the quality of products as secondary economic activities. Through attracting visitors, we promote leisure agriculture through our services. Service is very important to promote our products. Thus they evolve to a more complex line in contrast with the past. Before you only needed to plant and take care of the crops; now you have production, processing, packaging, promotion and marketing. Promotion is not only a must in an outside market, but also in a local market to attract more people to come to the village.

CA001 initiated a plan to develop leisure agriculture (Chashan Village Office and Chashan Community Development Association, 1999). She started by encouraging villagers to return to a traditional lifestyle, being farmers, planting crops and raising livestock (2004). Then, progress was expected to continue with the improvement of the crop production environment, strengthening the skills of villagers so that local crops could be produced, processed, packaged, and promoted to become local specialities with added value for direct sale to customers (Interviewees CA001, CA002, 2004, 2005). She also encouraged each household to run a business on a small scale, such as a home stay, a food and beverage outlet or handicrafts, so that local specialities could be sold to tourists. To prevent monopolies, she gathered the members of the Presbyterian Church and established 'Strategic Alliances' in which each business/skill would be run by cooperating households so that all could make some profit. For example, if household A runs a home stay, household B runs an eatery and household C raises livestock and produces crops, then household C can supply its raw materials to household B to make dishes to serve tourists staying with household A (Interviewee CA001, 2004).

In the beginning (around 1998–99), she and other village cadres faced many challenges to promote the plan. For example, the majority of villagers were farmers; no one knew what a home stay was, and they were unsure whether tourists would come. As a result, most villagers were unwilling to spend time and money to prepare rooms or construct extra facilities (e.g. toilets) even though the Council of Indigenous Peoples (a government organisation that coordinates and plans indigenous affairs) provided partial subsidies to encourage the development of home stays. Only six households prepared extra rooms as home stays, including some village cadres and a few members of the Presbyterian Church (Interviewees CA001, CA002, 2004, 2005).

CHASHAN LEISURE AGRICULTURAL AREA (CLAA)

In 2001, CA001 and some village cadres went to the Council of Agriculture to apply to make Chashan into a leisure agricultural area. These areas are supported by national policies to promote domestic tourism in the hope that development of recreational agriculture and fisheries in rural villages will enhance the local economy and create employment opportunities. By shifting traditional agricultural practices to a combination of agriculture with tourism and education, abandoned farmland could be put to use again (Interviewees, CA001, CA002, 2004, 2005). The idea is demonstrated in Figure 7.2.

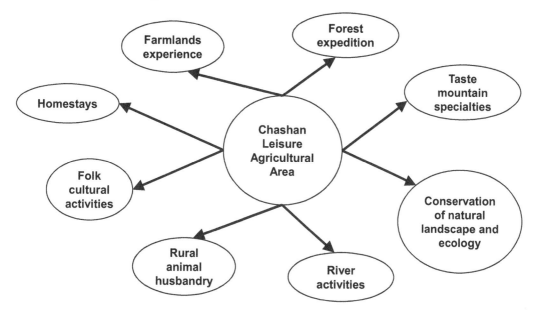

Figure 7.2   Integrated development of Chashan Leisure Agricultural Area (CLAA), Taiwan
Source: Li (n.d.: 1).

As CA001 (2004) commented, it is very difficult to have all of the components equally well developed. One aspect might be very strong (e.g. home stays), while the others might be very weak (e.g. rural animal husbandry). It was appreciated that not everyone in the village could be engaged in tourism, and that agriculture should be the foundation of tourism because it has long been the major livelihood activity in Chashan (see Table 7.1). CA001 commented that she does not like the term tourism (the meaning in Chinese is close to sightseeing) because it implies satisfying tourists' motivations of seeing 'other' cultures that are primitive and exotic, paying less attention to local people's benefits and feelings.

The chairman of the CLAA (Interviewee CA002, 2005) emphasised that the majority of Chashan residents sustained themselves from farming, so that too much emphasis on tourism would increase the gap between the rich and the poor. He claimed that funds from Alishan National Scenic Area Administration should not only be used to build trails and performance halls to attract more tourists, but should also be used to revitalise local agriculture; put abandoned farm land to use again; and upgrade and diversify the primary economic activity to secondary, tertiary, and even quaternary economic activities. In these ways, rural people might be better able to compete as Taiwan shifts from an industrial towards a service- and high-tech based economy. For example, taro sold raw is a primary activity; when cooked, it becomes secondary activity; when cooked, packaged and sold commercially, it becomes tertiary activity; when cooked and served as a dish to visitors who decide to buy a *well-packaged* taro product as a gift for friends, it becomes a quaternary economic activity. With an increasing number of visitors coming to Chashan, if local farmers' livelihoods could be supported by sales of canned bamboo shoots and by having visitors

Table 7.1   Economic activities of the Chashan population with work ability

			n	%
Total			288	
Not tourism-related	Migration	With productivity	84	29.2
		Without productivity	11	3.8
	Employment	Permanent jobs in Alishan area	22	7.6
		Odd jobs and labour (e.g. tea leaf picking, weeding, carrying fertiliser)	111	38.5
		Army	6	2.1
		Retail businesses	12	4.2
		Farming (crops and livestock), harvesting (bamboo and mountain products) for cash	100	34.7
		Hunting	12	4.2
		No work	13	4.5
		Unknown	7	2.4
Tourism-related		Tourism enterprises	42	14.6
		Tourism-related cash earning	20	6.9
		Sub total	62	21.5

Note: Based on interviews conducted in November 2005; the situation changes from time to time.

experience bamboo shoot harvesting, they might choose agriculture instead of unstable casual labour. It is not enough to supply home stays with locally produced crops and livestock because the quantity required is small and the demand is unstable.

The provision of education and assistance to Chashan farmers could lead to the creation of branded, well-packaged, agricultural products of high quality that consumers will buy for their own consumption and as gifts. Once the brand gains consumer acceptance, the increasing demand for agricultural products stirred up by tourism would create a future for Chashan agriculture. However, it is not easy to make people think of Chashan when they think of camellia oil, one of Chashan's agricultural specialities. Thus, farmers faced a number of challenges, including incorporating the service industry into their daily lives; upgrading economic activities from primary to tertiary and even quaternary; establishing a reputation for their agricultural products; and learning how to market them. All of these need funding, skills and professional assistance.

COMBINING TOURISM WITH AGRICULTURE

Agricultural products such as bamboo shoots, ginger and taro spoil easily (usually two days after harvest). They need to be processed and packaged to be sold to tourists (Interviewee CA003, 2004). Processing requires machinery, storage rooms and refrigerators. Chashan villagers do not have the money and skills to purchase, operate and maintain the machines. Besides, the sale of packaged agricultural products needs time, marketing skills, sales channels and stable markets. Villagers are short of the above assets and unwilling to bear the risk of lack of sales (CA002, 2004). Given the shortage of cash and urgent cash needs, villagers usually choose to sell the products directly to wholesalers from nearby towns at much lower prices because they can obtain cash immediately and, thus, solve the urgent difficulties of the moment. For example, fresh taro is sold to a nearby town at NT$4 (CAD$0.16)/kilo, while cleaned, chopped and packaged taro can be sold at NT$50 (CAD$2)/kilo (CA002, 2005). Villagers still choose the former because the latter takes much longer to get cash and involves a greater risk if the product is not sold. The prices offered by middlemen usually cannot even cover production expenses, and that is why many fields in Chashan are not in production (Interviewees CA002, CA003, CA006, CA007, 2004)

After Chashan was evaluated as one of several leisure agricultural areas, opportunities to market it as a tourist destination and to sell local agricultural products increased. CA001 and Ceayama (a music group run by Chashan Presbyterian Church) have often been invited to host or perform in international agricultural travel fairs. As a result, Chashan has gradually become better known and its home stay business has become more prosperous.

STRATEGIC ALLIANCES

The idea of 'Strategic Alliances' is based on the spirit of sharing and cooperation among small businesses. In order to increase the number of villagers involved in tourism, a village cadre (i.e. mainly the previous village head, CA001) provided their private property to the public to initiate a sharing mechanism (Luo, 2004). Supported by government funding, Chashan set up the following community facilities (on private property) and organisations: the Ceayama band (mainly composed of members of the Presbyterian Church); a parking lot; Mother Tain Eatery (mainly providing meals to visitors in home stays); and a performance square. The group of people who offered and shared common resources took 'sharing common resources' and 'cooperation' as their core values. This is reflected in the operation of the home stay business (Luo, 2004). In the early stage of tourism, when a tour bus came, tourists were divided among seven houses. Villagers not running home stays were divided into groups to provide different services – such as transportation, foodstuffs and meal preparation – to make cash. For example, membership of Mother Tian Eatery was divided into three groups: cuisine, mountain-plant use and logistics. The cuisine group only accepted reservations for meals in advance, so ingredients could be ordered from local residents, ensuring their freshness. The mountain-plant group used wild plants from the mountains to produce dishes and drinks, such as jelly fig, so customers could see the procedure of drink production, upgrading the primary economic activity to a tertiary one. The logistics group purchased livestock, agricultural products, and handicrafts produced by local residents and supplied them to Mother Tian Eatery and home stay proprietors. In this way, producers could sell their products on the spot and exploitation by middlemen was avoided.

Institutionalised division of labour gradually emerged and it had the following advantages: reduced operating costs; improved product quality; the establishment of a single contact for home stay reservations and the arrangement of visitors' transportation; preparation of meals; services of tour guides; and the performance of a night party (Luo, 2004). Quality was maintained because the different groups monitored each other. The mechanism relied heavily on trust and was strengthened when villagers saw that resources and benefits were shared fairly (Luo, 2004).

Nevertheless, as time went by, those home stays that provided the best service retained the most tourists, who became repeat customers and introduced their friends. A few individuals who had been successful in the home stay business wanted to expand by increasing the number of rooms, or secured large loans for guesthouses or to improve the quality of the accommodation or to build their own restaurants. As the businesses grew, they gradually separated themselves from the alliances. The ideals that CA001 advocated of having even benefit-sharing through work distribution and cooperation, and through developing the tourism industry on a small scale (250 visitors/day) and at a slow pace, gradually faded. Now, of 13 households who run home stays, only four are members of the Strategic Alliances. They are also members of the Presbyterian Church and continue to support the ideas of CA001, who is an elder of the church. The quality of their offerings is about the same, making it easier to reach consensus on prices.

Another reason for the unsuccessful operation of the alliances was the lack of clear statements concerning the inflow and expenditure of the government subsidies that require each home stay proprietor to contribute to the fund (Interviewees CA002, CA009, CB002, CE002, 2004; informal conversation, 2004). Originally, the home stays under the Strategic Alliances contributed part of their income to the institution as a common reserve fund for various purposes, such as maintenance of hiking trails and repair of scenic spots that had been damaged by typhoons. Villagers complained that CA001 collected the money but did not provide a clear explanation on how it was used. This was the major reason why CA001 was not re-elected as village head after eight years (informal conversation, 2004). A village cadre, CA002 (2004), indicated that CA001 did not take the funds; but, because she did not keep good track of every receipt and expenditure, she could not recount the details. This is a common problem in aboriginal villages where sound financial management and good accounting practices are rare. It was commonly expressed that CA001 tended to corner community resources and establish her own position prior to hearing the views of others when making decisions dealing with community affairs (Interviews, 2004, 2005).

The outcome of village elections shows that Chashan failed to adjust to all sorts of challenges. Criticisms often took the form of personal attacks, such as the leader does not make a clear distinction between public and private interests: the accounting system is not clear; power is divided arbitrarily, etc. This frustrated the leader, who took reciprocity as the starting point of her actions, and frustrated and disappointed the original leadership team. They took back their personal contribution to the public facilities, which further reduced the level of trust within the community (Luo, 2004).

DISPERSED RESPONSIBILITIES

Under the organisational structure of the CLAA (see Figure 7.3), several industries and tourism enterprises were proposed and developed: such as home stays; food and beverage outlets; processing of camellia oil and mountain tea; and song and dance groups. However, as a decreasing number of villagers engaged in agriculture and because of the lack of collective income to support the operation of the organisation, the groups had not operated for three years (Interviewee CA006, 2004). In the preceding two years, CA001 and the chairman of the organisation proposed charging a membership fee in the hope that, combined with subsidies from the Council of Agriculture, the organisation could continue to operate. At the time of the research in 2005, the number of members was 27 (Interviewees CA001, CA002, 2005).

CHASHAN COMMUNITY DEVELOPMENT ASSOCIATION

In addition to the CLAA, another major organisation is the Chashan Community Development Association (CCDA), which is the main contact for government organisations, such as Alishan National Scenic Area Administration, the Forestry Bureau and Alishan Township Administration. It was established in 1997. There were about 100 members in 2005 (CCDA, 2005). A membership fee (registration NT$300 (CAD$12)/person; annual fee NT$500 (CAD$20)/person) was charged

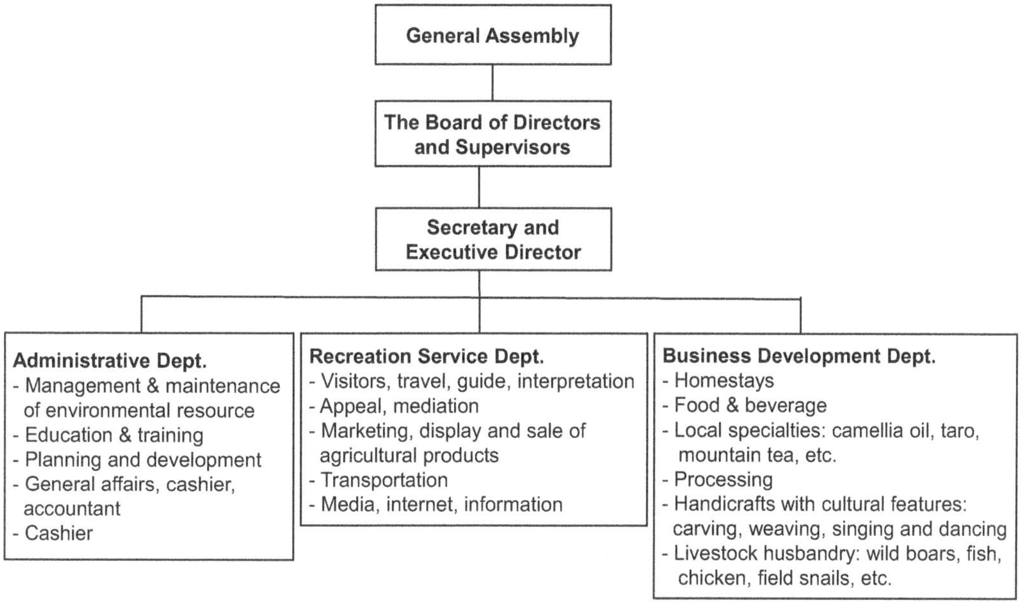

```
                        ┌─────────────────────────┐
                        │     General Assembly     │
                        └─────────────────────────┘
                                     │
                        ┌─────────────────────────┐
                        │   The Board of Directors │
                        │      and Supervisors     │
                        └─────────────────────────┘
                                     │
                        ┌─────────────────────────┐
                        │      Secretary and       │
                        │    Executive Director    │
                        └─────────────────────────┘
```

Administrative Dept.	Recreation Service Dept.	Business Development Dept.
- Management & maintenance of environmental resource - Education & training - Planning and development - General affairs, cashier, accountant - Cashier	- Visitors, travel, guide, interpretation - Appeal, mediation - Marketing, display and sale of agricultural products - Transportation - Media, internet, information	- Homestays - Food & beverage - Local specialties: camellia oil, taro, mountain tea, etc. - Processing - Handicrafts with cultural features: carving, weaving, singing and dancing - Livestock husbandry: wild boars, fish, chicken, field snails, etc.

Figure 7.3   Organisational structure of the Chashan Leisure Agricultural Area Development Association (CLAADA), as at November 2005

Source: Li (n.d.: 5).

for several years but this ceased in 2003. Since then, operation has depended on subsidies from several government organisations. As a result, its independence is weak and it tends to be directed by the government organisations (Interviewee CA002, 2004). Figure 7.4 shows the organisational structure of the CCDA. There are 15 board directors, including the chair, the general executive, and general affairs. In addition, there are five supervisors, including the chair. They are elected every three years through the General Assembly, not by customary procedures, by the members of the association who are over 20 years old. The chair of the board of directors is elected by the board of directors (CCDA, 2005). These 15 people have decision-making power with regard to some aspects of community development.

Under the organisational structure of the CCDA, a tourism enterprise promotion group was established (see Figure 7.4). At the time of research, however, only food and beverage and dance groups were in operation (CCDA, 2005). The groups and their business overlap with those of the Business Development Department of CLAADA. Half of the personnel of CCDA are also members of CLAADA. Responsibilities of each organisation are not assigned clearly, causing waste of community resources and manpower and making implementation of community affairs inefficient. For example, the government provided funding to build pavilions, but there was no consensus on which organisation is responsible for maintenance (Interviewee CA003, 2004). Many villagers expressed the need to merge the two organisations or improve communications between them (Interviewees CA003, CA008, CA009, CB004, CC001, CC002, 2004). Several such attempts have been made but have not succeeded (Interviewees CC001, CC002, CA009, 2004). As one board director (CA003, 2004) indicated concerning the importance of merging the two organisations:

> The promotion of tourism enterprises is one major task of [the] CCDA, but that is not enough. Tourism planning is more than to hold a pavilion festival. It cannot be separated from other

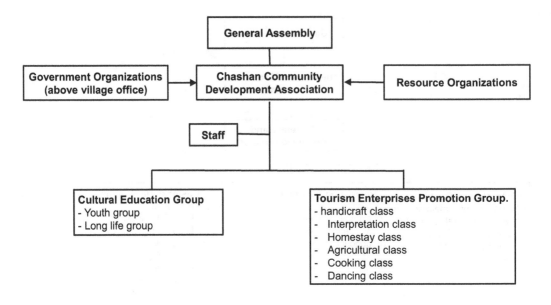

Figure 7.4   Organisational structure of the Chashan Community Development Association (CCDA)

Source: CCDA (2005: 26).

> *industries, such as how to package our agricultural products, how to use local crops and livestock to produce dishes to serve tourists in [the] home stays business ... .*

A main reason for the present situation is that when CA001 served as a village head, she was also the general executive of the CCDA and the leading cadre of CLAADA. She is a very capable person who has drawn many resources from different government organisations and put them into community construction through the village office, the CCDA and CLAADA. Nevertheless, her strong leadership did not create clear regulations and an efficient organisational system. When CA001 left the position, she did not pass on documents to the incumbent village head and the chair of the CCDA's board of directors. She is not sure if the successors will continue her ideas and plans, so she combined members of CLAADA and the Presbyterian Church to continue with her plan without communication with the CCDA and the village office (Interviewee CC001, 2004; informal conversation, 2004). Under the political administrative system, CLAADA is under the jurisdiction of the CCDA and it must go through the CCDA to apply for funds; but she often bypasses the CCDA to apply for funds from certain government organisations (Interviewee CC001, 2004). At present, there are three factions in Chashan – CLAADA, the CCDA and the village office – and villagers indicated that there is no common occasion to express their opinions and suggestions, and to discuss community issues collectively (Interviewees CA003, CA008, CA009, CB004, CC001, CC002, 2004). The Cou minister of the Presbyterian Church (CC001, 2004) expressed his concern as follows:

> *Some villagers do not rely on the Community Development Association and expand their own home stays and restaurants. Others possess the attitude of wait and see; they come to cooperate when things work well and, if not, they do things by themselves. However, minding your own business is not good to the tribe. Faction formation in a small village, no matter organisation or individual, is not good. So-called good is the link to Cou collective knowledge to manage a tribe as in the past. Decisions and knowledge are made and created collectively. So-called not good*

is a separation such that you would be unable to recognise this is a Cou village. We have been imprinted by traditional Cou structures, unless you intend to be separated from Cou identity … .

Another reason for factions is that the village consists of multiple ethnic groups (i.e. Cou, Bunun and Han) which have different social, cultural and historical backgrounds, so that ideas for the development of the village are not the same (Interviewees SA010, CE001, 2004). Several villagers commented that only a person with strong leadership qualities and with an open and tolerant heart would be able to unite diverse opinions to reach consensus (informal conversation, 2004).

USE OF THE SUSTAINABLE LIVELIHOOD FRAMEWORK

As highlighted in Figure 7.1, organisational structures and institutional processes combine livelihood resources and potentially allow tourism, as one of several livelihood strategies, to be pursued and different outcomes to be realised.

THE ROLE OF AN INDIVIDUAL

The previous village head played a prominent role in Chashan with her foresight and energy. Leadership is vital in any community and is particularly important in indigenous communities. This is an aspect of institutional arrangements even though it is not mentioned in the framework specifically. She had a good grasp of Cou traditional knowledge and guided the creation and use of resources to develop products and market the territory (e.g. agri-food products, regional cuisine and crafts) (Ray, 1998). She enabled residents in Chashan to be innovative with their 'traditional'knowledge, enabling tourism activities to be grown from within rather than developed from outside. She emphasised collective actions within the Cou people's clan system to harness local institutions for tourism development. The links between the new economic activities and traditional knowledge increased their endogenous strength and facilitated local control of development. By using her significant status in the Presbyterian churches, she put her ideas into practice through the social relations (important social capital) of the unofficial organisations of the churches. She encouraged and guided villagers to engage in tourism development. Such involvements and learning processes resulted in new identifications and tourism-related activities that have gradually become part of villagers' lives.

ORGANISATIONAL STRUCTURES

The SL framework also helps to promote understanding of the significance of organisational structure, social norms and institutions, in addition to leadership, when attempting to use tourism to diversify livelihoods. Chashan has three main organisations (i.e. village office, the CCDA, and CLAADA) but lacks clear rules for decision making. As a result, it is difficult to reach consensus and to control the development process.

In a fast-changing economy, the existing institutions were unable to keep up with the speed of tourism development. Increased tourism fame attracted a growing number of visitors. The acquisition of more public resources from outside the village, while welcome, placed increased pressure on the administration and the accounting system, as well on the distribution of power and benefits. Moreover, increasing interaction with outsiders (e.g. tourists, government organisations, planning firms) complicated an originally simple and quiet life in Chashan. Even though the CLAA Management Centre established limits on visitor numbers and introduced a pre-registration system as well as a reservation system for meals to manage growth, there have been many challenges. These will now be discussed.

LACK OF CONSENSUS AND THE FREE-RIDER PROBLEM

In the early stage of tourism development in Chashan, it was intended that benefits would be shared throughout the whole community across the differences of ethnicity, sub-clans and churches. However, many villagers have been suspicious of tourism operations. As the Cou minister of the Presbyterian Church indicated, three positions exist among villagers concerning the implementation of a benefit-sharing system. The first is the initiators of the institutions, such as labour division, who continue to endorse the collaboration mechanism. The second is those who wait and see: they watch the situation before deciding whether or not to cooperate. The third is those who do not participate at all. The lack of a communication platform between community organisations and individuals hampers progress.

The economic principle prevalent in the community is different from that of the capitalist market economy. The driving forces of the latter are maximisation of individual interests and cost effectiveness, while the former emphasises that the livelihoods of all community members should be sustained through various forms of cooperation (Luo, 2004). Even though the intention was to operate the community economy by expanding the range of cooperation based on trust, the external capitalist environment has had far-reaching impacts (Luo, 2004). For example, home stay proprietors (a small proportion of the villagers) and travel agencies are free riders who have taken advantage of the situation after Chashan became well known. Because of the increasing opportunities to make profits, the villagers who originally held a wait-and-see attitude began to operate businesses in ways that deviated from the concepts of limiting the number of visitors and making reservations for meals in advance. Two extreme views exist on limitation of the number of visitors. One advocates limitations to maintain service quality and reduce the impacts of tourism on original home stay proprietors, while the other hopes to increase the number of visitors in order to increase incomes. Rules are flouted in pursuit of personal interests and costs increase to those who operate in accordance with the rules (Luo, 2004). Bowles and Gintis (2002) indicated that the free-rider problem can be overcome if the community's members punish the 'anti-social' actions of others. Monitoring and punishing by peers in work teams, credit associations and partnerships are often effective means of attenuating the incentive problems that arise. Nonetheless, where the individual actions affecting the well-being of others are not subject to enforceable contracts, other problems emerge – such as refusal to cooperate, slandering of leaders, establishment of a new organisation to obtain external resources to continue one's objectives, and expansion of free riding on collective goods. The problems in Chashan originated from a lack of complete institutional arrangements that caused the original sharing mechanism to decrease progressively in effectiveness.

In such a situation, when a home stay is an individually run business, tourism can increase inequality within the village because a small proportion of better-off villagers are able to take advantage of common property and the tourism development trend (e.g., popularity of the leader and the band Ceayama). This contrasts with the spirit of sharing, as represented in Strategic Alliances. Conflicts started to appear between villagers who ran tourism enterprises and those who did not. The latter felt that the increasing number of tourists brought noise, traffic, and litter which disturbed their lives. Some villagers threatened to close the roads leading to the scenic spots, since most of these lands were owned privately and they had to clean up after tourists left but without any benefits. Other villagers complained that:

> We had an agreement before: the village does not belong to certain people. How can certain individuals not obey the agreement? Everyone should have some share of the benefits, but why do some people now make a lot of profits?

A home stay business relies on neighbourhood amenities and the surrounding environment (i.e. tranquillity, gardens, pavilions, local attractions and the agricultural products of other households). However, home stay businesses have not yet been well linked to local agriculture and other aspects of life, even though the original plan was to do so. The tourism development has been tourist-oriented rather than oriented towards the needs of villagers. Livelihood resources have been used to *sustain* tourism development. Cooperative mechanisms, such as the institution of labour division, have to be strengthened if tourism is to contribute more strongly to overall well-being.

INTER-SECTORAL LINKS

Even though Chashan's labour division institution has faced a number of challenges, its consideration of the majority of villagers' (farmers) benefits and the intention to make diverse connections between tourism and other economic activities (both intra-household and inter-household) has a number of advantages. One example is the revitalisation of declining agricultural and forest industries through agricultural diversification under the livelihood strategies component of the framework (see Figure 7.1). Abandoned orchards, bamboo fields and various farmlands have gradually been opened to visitors for them to participate in various recreational activities, such as picking fruit, involving them in the production process, and purchasing processed agricultural products. Visitors can also be involved in making bamboo-cooked rice. Recreational agriculture provides opportunities for economic diversification and offers new livelihood options that are close to the lifestyles of local people and contribute to the construction of a sense of place. This provides opportunities for more villagers to be involved in activities linked directly and indirectly to tourism and to reduce the risky characteristics of tourism.

Chashan's economic orientation is changing. After the local processed agricultural products, such as canned bamboo shoots, became well known and the demand for them increased, several community cadres discussed how to assist local villagers to produce them in larger quantities. This might inspire some households to work the abandoned agricultural land.

DIVERSIFIED LONG-TERM ADAPTIVE STRATEGIES IN CHASHAN

Without subsidies from government, and unwilling to bear debt risks of running a home stay business, many households are slowly starting to move in the direction of leisure agriculture. Some invited their friends to experience the harvesting of bamboo shoots. Some plan to run a café and combine it with planting vegetables and flowers. Some are starting to convert land to campsites and to use other existing industries as attractions, such as Gu fish watching and the sale of ginger-cane candy. Some have started to plant fruit trees. Fruit in an orchard can either be harvested and sold in a market or the space opened to tourists as a recreation orchard. In Chashan neighbourhood unit one, members of the True Jesus Church planned to invite all members of the churches in the closest city, Chiayi, to come to Chashan during the fruit harvesting season so that the home stay proprietors could have more business. Others started to plan their lands for their retirement and to incorporate leisure industry components into their plan, including the planting of trees and flowers; the design of trails and pavilions; and the raising of chickens, ducks, boars and sheep as attractions. Two households actively expanded the amount of livestock to accumulate physical capital which could be readily transformed into financial capital. Once the assets have been stabilised, they can secure a loan to build small log cabins and then need not worry about having no regular cash turnover.

Conclusion

It has been argued that sustainable development, while widely acclaimed, has not lived up to the expectations of its proponents. In part this is because the organisations and institutional arrangements are seldom in place to manage inter-sectoral linkages adequately. An SL approach addresses some of these deficiencies, and identifies the need for supportive institutional arrangements as a core requirement for the achievement of sustainable outcomes. However, this is more easily said than done, particularly for aboriginal communities whose traditional decision-making processes may differ from those of the majority society in which they are embedded. Tourism is a relatively recent activity in many such communities. When driven by the maximisation of individual interests in the context of a capitalist market economy, it is likely to undermine institutions with a communal mechanism based on collective knowledge guided by tribal culture and might lead to unsustainable outcomes (socio-culturally, economically and environmentally). The institutional processes and organisational structure component that is emphasised in the SL framework is particularly important in understanding the evolution of livelihoods after the introduction of tourism. It binds together the processes of combining resources to pursue various livelihood strategies and, ultimately, to realise different livelihood outcomes. Culture, in this case Cou culture as a focal point of the study, provides a guiding context for institutional processes and organisational structures. The culture of the majority provides a context in which the minority must operate; but community decisions have been made traditionally through processes that reflect aboriginal culture. However, as time went by, changes have occurred in uses and values of resources and activities. In other words, tourism presented challenges that required adjustments of traditional ways of making decisions. Hence, as shown in Figure 7.1, the links between culture and institutions operate in both directions. From a broader perspective, as a minority group with a culture that is different from the majority population, the whole framework is embedded in culture, for cultural difference from the majority is the context in which the Cou operate (Tao et al., 2010).

The strength of the SL framework, when incorporating tourism, is that it encourages the adoption of a broad perspective in the assessment of the consequences of tourism for different aspects of people's lives. The SL framework helps to encourage an improved understanding of tourism that goes beyond income generation, to consider the many other factors that people in different contexts define as contributing to their vulnerability or well-being. Contexts vary enormously, as do development processes. These processes are locally specific, shaped by history, cultural repertoires, economic and political relationships and the natural environment. Livelihoods are essentially contextual (Hebinck and Bourdillon, 2001). At the household level, tourism might be combined with other existing economic activities, contribute to the enlargement of a wage labour system or compete for the use of scarce resources; however, at the same time, at the community level, it may undermine traditional communal management systems. The case illustrates the utility of an SL approach; places empirical flesh on the bare conceptual bones of an

SL framework; and highlights the implications of minority and majority decision-making systems and their relationships.

References

Adato, M. and Meinzen-Dick, R. (2002). Assessing the impact of agricultural research on poverty using the sustainable livelihood framework. *FCND Discussion Paper-128*. Washington: International Food Policy Research Institute.

Altman, J. and Cochrane, M. (2005). Sustainable development in the indigenous-owned savanna: innovative institutional design for cooperative wildlife management. *Wildlife Research*, 32(5), pp. 473–480.

Ashley, C. (2000). The impacts of tourism on rural livelihoods: Namibia's experience. *Working Paper-128*. London: Overseas Development Institute.

Bowles, S. and Gintis, H. (2002). Social capital and community governance. *Economic Journal*, 112, pp. 419–436.

Butler, R. W. (1993). Tourism: An evolutionary perspective. In J. G. Nelson, R. Butler and G. Wall (eds), *Tourism and sustainable development: Monitoring, planning, managing*. Waterloo, ON: University of Waterloo, pp. 27–44.

——— (1998). Sustainable tourism: Looking backward in order to progress? In C. M. Hall and A. A. Lew (eds), *Sustainable tourism: A geographical perspective*. New York: Addison-Wesley, pp. 25–34.

Carney, D. (1999). Approaches to sustainable livelihoods for the rural poor. *ODI Poverty Briefing*. London: Overseas Development Institute.

Chambers, R. (1986). *Sustainable livelihood thinking: An approach to poverty*. Brighton: Institution of Development Studies, University of Sussex.

——— and Conway, G. (1992). Sustainable rural livelihoods: Practical concepts for the 21st century. *IDS Discussion Paper-296*. Brighton: Institution of Development Studies, University of Sussex.

Chashan Community Development Association (CCDA). (2005). *Handbook of the Fourth Annual (I) General Assembly of Chashan Community Development Association of Alishan Township in Jiayi County*. Minutes of the meeting. Unpublished manuscript. (In Chinese).

Clarke, J. (1997). A framework of approaches to sustainable tourism. *Journal of Sustainable Tourism*, 5(3), pp. 224–233.

Department for International Development (DFID). (1999). *Sustainable livelihoods guidance sheets: Section 2*. Retrieved from: http://www.eldis.org/vfile/upload/1/document/0901/section2.pdf (accessed: 27 November 2014).

Ellis, F. (2000). *Rural livelihoods and diversity in developing countries*. Oxford: Oxford University Press, p. 38.

Hebinck, P. and Bourdillon, M. (2001). Analysis of Livelihood. In P. Hebinck and M. Bourdillon (eds), *Women, men and work: Rural livelihoods in South-Eastern Zimbabwe*. Harare: Weaver, pp. 1–12.

Helmore, K. and Singh, N. (2001). *Sustainable livelihoods: Building on the wealth of the poor*. Bloomfield, CT: Kumarian.

Hunter, C. (1995). On the need to re-conceptualize sustainable tourism development. *Journal of Sustainable Tourism*, 3(3), pp. 155–165.

Leach, M., Mearns, R. and Scoones, I. (1999). Environmental entitlements: Dynamics and institutions in community-based natural resource management. *World Development*, 27(2), pp. 225–247.

Lee, M. H. (2008). Tourism and sustainable livelihoods: the case of Taiwan. *Third World Quarterly*, 29(5), pp. 961–978.

Li, Y.-Y. (n.d.). The Planning Report of Chashan Leisure Agricultural Area, Alishan Township, Jiayi. Unpublished manuscript. (In Chinese).

Luo, Y.-C. (2004). The evolution of 'Sharing': A preliminary discussion on Cayama (Chashan) community economy. *Working paper presented at the Tsou's humanities symposium – lectures/craft and architecture/*

literature and industry, November. Sponsored by Chinese Folk-Arts Foundation, Taipei; supervised by Jiayi County Government and Alishan National Scenic Area Administration, Jiayi, Taiwan. (In Chinese).

McCool, S. F. and Moisey, R. N. (2008). Introduction: Pathways and pitfalls in the search for sustainable tourism. In S. F. McCool and R. N. Moisey (eds), *Tourism, recreation and sustainability: Linking culture and the environment*, New York: CABI, pp. 1–15.

Ostrom, E. (1992). *Crafting institutions for self-governing irrigation systems*. San Francisco: Institute for Contemporary Studies.

Rasmussen, L. and Meinzen-Dick, R. (1995). *Local organizations for natural resource management: Lessons from theoretical and empirical literature*. Washington: International Food Policy Research Institute.

Ray, C. (1998). Culture, intellectual property and territorial rural development. *Sociologia Ruralis*, 38(1), pp. 3–20.

Robinson, M. (1999). Collaboration and cultural consent: refocusing sustainable tourism. *Journal of Sustainable Tourism*, 7, pp. 379–397.

Scoones, I. (1998). *Sustainable rural livelihoods: A framework for analysis*. Brighton: Institute of Development Studies, University of Sussex.

Sharpley, R. (2009). *Tourism development and the environment: Beyond sustainability?* London: Earthscan.

Stabler, M. J. (ed.) (1997). *Tourism and sustainability: Principles to practice*. Wallingford: CABI.

Tao, T. C. H. (2006). Tourism as a livelihood strategy in indigenous communities: Case studies from Taiwan. Unpublished PhD dissertation. Ontario: University of Waterloo.

——— and Wall, G. (2009). Tourism as a sustainable livelihood strategy. *Tourism Management*, 30(1), pp. 90–98.

———, Wall, G. and Wismer, S. (2010). Culture and sustainable livelihoods. *Human Ecology*, 29(1), pp. 1–21.

United Nations Development Programme (UNDP) (1999). *Participatory assessment and planning for sustainable livelihoods*. United Nations Development Programme: Sustainable livelihoods documents. Retrieved from: http://www.undp.org/sl/Documents/Strategy_papers/Participatory_A ssessment_for_SLSW.htm/PAPSL.htm (accessed: 10 September 2003).

Wall, G. (1991). Tourism and sustainable development. *Paper presented at annual meeting*, Kingston, ON: Canadian Association of Geographers.

——— (1993). International collaboration in the search for sustainable tourism in Bali, Indonesia. *Journal of Sustainable Tourism*, 1(1), pp. 38–47.

——— (1997). Sustainable tourism-unsustainable development. In J. Pigram and S. Wahab (eds), *Tourism development and growth: The challenge of sustainability*, London: Routledge, pp. 33–49.

——— (2002). Sustainable development: Political rhetoric or analytical construct. *Tourism Recreation Research*, 27(3), pp. 89–91.

Wheeller, B. (1993). Sustaining the ego. *Journal of Sustainable Tourism*, 1(2), pp. 121–129.

World Commission on Environment and Development (WCED). (1987). *Our common future (The Brundtland Report)*. London: Oxford University Press.

8

The Role of Elders in Indigenous Economic Development: The Case of Kaumātua on Māori Enterprises of Aotearoa/ New Zealand

Jason Paul Mika

Chapter Synopsis

The central theme of the chapter is to examine the role of elders in indigenous economic development. The experience of Kaumātua (elders) within Māori enterprises – commercial entities owned and operated by Māori – in Aotearoa/New Zealand, forms the case study. While elders remain an ever-present part of Māori enterprises, their role and value may not be widely understood, especially by a younger generation intent on having their turn at steering the proverbial *waka* (vessel) (i.e. our veritable enterprise). The chapter and associated research is based on kaupapa Māori research philosophy and practice, which is increasingly being applied to Māori entrepreneurship and business research (Gillies et al., 2007; Henry, 1999; Mika, 2013; Tinirau, 2004; Tinirau and Mika, 2012). This is research *by* Maori, *with* Māori and *for* Māori in terms of research benefits and is grounded in traditional Māori knowledge, culture and values (Pihama and Penehira, 2005; Smith, 1997; Smith, 1999).

Key issues to be discussed are: (i) who or what is a Kaumātua; (ii) what roles do Kaumātua perform within Māori enterprises; (iii) how do Kaumātua and others perceive their roles in Māori enterprises; and (iv) how do Kaumātua define Māori enterprise success? The chapter reviews the literature on the role of elders in indigenous economic development in traditional and contemporary settings. It is expected that the review elicits theory about why and how elders engage in entrepreneurial activity and the principles upon which their roles in indigenous enterprises are based. The chapter will incorporate findings from interviews with Kaumātua involved in Māori enterprises. The interviews will use an indigenous form of ethnography called 'collaborative storying' (Bishop,

1996), in which the researcher engages in an interactive conversation about the experiences of others with whom they may share whakapapa (family) and other connections.

Introduction

As a matter of tradition, when Māori first speak they introduce themselves by way of a proverb. This proverb is called a *pepeha*, which identifies who they are and where they come from. Reciting one's *pepeha* establishes one's place to speak. Secondly, it makes way for relationships to form with whom one is speaking, and from there understanding becomes possible. The following *pepeha* conveys my affiliation to Tūhoe:

> *Ko Mataatua te waka (The Mataatua is my ancestral canoe)*
> *Ko Toroa te tangata (Toroa was the captain of our canoe)*
> *Ko Tūhoe te iwi (Tūhoe is my tribe)*
> *Ko Hāmua te hapū (Hāmua is my subtribe)*
> *Ko Parekohe te maunga (Parekohe is my mountain)*
> *Ko Ohinemataroa te awa (Ohinemataroa is my river)*
> *Ko Waikirikiri te marae (Waikirikiri is my village courtyard)*
> *Ko Te Mana Mika te tīpuna (Te Mana Mika is my ancestor)*
> *Tīhei mauri ora! (I sneeze, 'tis the breath of life!)*

This chapter examines the role of elders in indigenous economic development. The chapter focuses on the experience of *Kaumātua* (elders) within Māori enterprises – commercial entities owned and operated by Māori, the indigenous people of Aotearoa, New Zealand – as a country-specific case. While Kaumātua remain an ever-present part of Māori enterprises, their role and value may not be widely understood or appreciated, especially by a younger generation intent on taking their turn at steering the proverbial *waka* (vessel), that is, our veritable enterprise (Ross, 1997). The chapter melds two intellectual domains: first, the theory and practice of Māori entrepreneurship; and second, the role of Kaumātua in traditional and contemporary society.

This immediately poses a challenge because the literature on the role of Kaumātua in Māori economic development is decidedly sparse – save several authors who devote some comment to the topic (see for example, Davies, 2011; Kawharu et al., 2012). Few studies are available, for instance, on the role of Kaumātua as 'older workers' and as owner-operators of Māori enterprises. Most writing on Kaumātua concerns their socio-economic, demographic and health status (Te Pūmanawa Hauora, 1996; Durie, 1999; Waldon, 2004), their traditional and contemporary roles as leaders (King, 1975; Mead, 1995; Walker, 2004) and their roles as keepers of traditional tribal knowledge (Buck, 1987; Davies, 2006, 2008; O'Regan and Rangipuna, 2009; Higgins and Meredith, 2013). The chief concern of this chapter, however, is the role of Kaumātua, not so much as entrepreneurs themselves, but in respect of the support they give to Māori entrepreneurs and Māori enterprises.

The central thesis of this chapter is that the traditional knowledge, wisdom and support provided by Kaumātua in Māori enterprises stands as a vital ingredient in the reinvigoration of the Māori economy. This is because of the capacity for Kaumātua to contribute traditional knowledge to Māori entrepreneurs and the Māori enterprises they run. In effect, Kaumātua serve as a living link between the past, present and future. Their cultural knowledge is essential to an emerging theory of Māori entrepreneurialism, a theory that posits Māori entrepreneurship as built upon indigenous values, customs and language, integrating Western entrepreneurship principles and practice in the pursuit of Māori development aims (Durie, 2002; Davies, 2011; Mika, 2013c).

The chapter illustrates the roles Kaumātua play in the Māori entrepreneurial process. It does this by recounting and discussing the experiences of several Kaumātua who have held leadership roles within tribal and non-tribal Māori enterprises at international, national, regional, and local levels. The Kaumātua profiled are Sir Tīpene O'Regan of Ngāi Tahu; Dame Georgina Kirby of Ngāti Rakaipaaka; and Mr Tāmati Cairns of Tūhoe, Raukawa, and Ngāti Kahungunu. Why these Kaumātua? Three reasons: (i) these are Kaumātua I respect and admire for their thinking, their manner and their contribution to Māori economic development; (ii) these are Kaumātua I have had the privilege of working with at one time or another; and (iii) they exemplify the diversity of contributions Kaumātua can and do make to Māori entrepreneurship. No doubt numerous other Kaumātua have made valuable contributions, which are recorded in the oral traditions of their tribes and in some cases in print (see for example, King, 1977; Harrison, 2002; O'Regan and Rangipuna, 2009; Turnbull, 2011), and I respectfully acknowledge them.

The chapter draws on a combination of first-hand interviews, transcribed speeches, and available literature to discuss the role of Kaumātua in Māori entrepreneurship. The chapter incorporates *kaupapa* Māori research philosophy and practice, which is increasingly applied to Māori entrepreneurship and business research (Henry, 1999; Tinirau, 2004; Gillies et al., 2007; Tinirau and Mika, 2012; Mika, 2013c). Kaupapa Māori research is research by Maori, with Māori, and for Māori and others in terms of the benefits of the research, and is grounded in *mātauranga* Māori (traditional Māori knowledge), *tikanga* Māori (Māori culture), and *te reo* Māori (Māori language) (Smith, 1997; Henry, 1999; Smith, 1999; Pihama and Penehira, 2005).

The kaupapa Māori cultural lens in which this chapter is written is reflected in the opening *pepeha* (proverb). This *pepeha* identifies me as a descendant of those who travelled from *Hawaiki* (distant homelands in the Pacific) to Aotearoa aboard the *Mataatua* canoe; settled in the mist-laden rainforest known as *Te Urewera*; and who intermarried with the locals and established their *mana* (power and authority) over that place under our eponymous ancestor, *Tūhoe* (Best, 1996; Nikora, 2003). One of the advantages of being an indigenous person is the sense of identity with which one is imbued by virtue of one's *whakapapa* (genealogy). Whakapapa helps keep one grounded, which is precisely what whakapapa means: to establish one's place in the world, in relation to the land and its people (Barlow, 1993; Mead, 2003). Whakapapa operates as an index of mātauranga Māori, a gateway to tribal histories, the legacies of one's ancestors (Buck, 1987; Nikora, 2003; Royal, 2005). The keepers of whakapapa, and therefore mātauranga Māori (Black et al., 2012), are our Kaumātua (Firth, 1973; Buck, 1987; Walker, 1990). I acknowledge my ancestors for the gifts they have left us, including our oral histories, traditions, values, and language.

The chapter begins by discussing Māori entrepreneurship. This is followed by a discussion of the role of Kaumātua in traditional and contemporary settings. The next section discusses the wisdom of three Kaumātua and their perspectives on Māori entrepreneurship. Finally, the chapter concludes with a discussion on the role of Kaumātua in Māori entrepreneurship and suggests areas for further research.

Māori Entrepreneurship

Māori entrepreneurship is a form of indigenous entrepreneurship (Foley, 2004; Dana and Anderson, 2007), which itself is a derivative of the general field of entrepreneurship (Davidsson, 2004; Hindle and Moroz, 2009). I define Māori entrepreneurship simply as the process by which a person or people of Māori descent start and operate a commercial enterprise. For our purposes, if the enterprise is 50 per cent or more owned and operated by Māori, then it may be regarded as a Māori enterprise (Battisti and Gillies, 2008; Mika, 2013a). However, Māori entrepreneurs may be found in non-Māori owned and operated enterprises too (Frederick and Henry, 2004; Tinirau and

Mika, 2012). Folely (2013) argues that less than equal ownership interest should qualify one as an indigenous enterprise otherwise a significant indigenous minority is excluded. The distinguishing feature is the degree of Māori ownership and control of the enterprise and the influence this has on the enterprise's culture and its approach to management and decision-making, though other factors do come into play (French, 1998). Māori enterprise is synonymous with Māori business; both in this chapter refer to a Māori commercial (profit-seeking) organisation.

Māori entrepreneurship and how it compares with non-Māori entrepreneurship has been the subject of public policy and academic research (see for example, Rotherham, 1991; Young, 1992; French, 1998; New Zealand Institute of Economic Research, 2003; Love and Love, 2005; Warriner, 2007). In public policy, discussion often falls back to the unresolved question of what is a Māori business (Statistics New Zealand, 2012). Answering this question is desirable because it would help classify and better measure the nature and extent of Māori business activity, which suffers from an absence of official data outside of the five-yearly census (Harmsworth, 2005; Statistics New Zealand, 2012; Mika, 2013a). In academia, defining Māori business presents the possibility of new knowledge about unique ways in which business occurs in Aotearoa (Henry, 1997; French, 1998; Love, 2004; Best and Love, 2011).

The debate about what sets Māori entrepreneurship apart seems to gravitate toward the view that Māori values, culture and customs are defining features (Durie, 2002; Davies, 2011). While the commerciality of Māori enterprises may be measured in the same terms as for any other ethnic group – that is, on the basis of an enterprise's profitability and survival – differentiation for Māori enterprises manifests in two main ways. First, as a result of internally driven micro-level variations such as: the manner in which business decisions are made; the selection of investment partners and investments; how employees are recruited, treated and managed; and how profits are used. Second are externally driven macro-level responses to Māori enterprises. These are observed within institutional arrangements relating to Māori assets like land and fisheries (Mahuika, 2006; Kingi, 2007), and the way in which Māori enterprises are perceived and treated by the general business community, both favourably (Jones et al., 2005; Te Puni Kōkiri, 2007a) and less favourably (Devlin, 2006; Dickson, 2010). These differences stem from cultural variations between Māori and non-Māori in business (Harmsworth, 2005; Te Puni Kōkiri, 2007b), which may be described as a 'Māori way' of doing business (Davies, 2011). What constitutes a Māori way of doing business is the subject of ongoing research, but a cogent theory of Māori entrepreneurialism is still emerging (see for example, Berwick, 1995; Tapsell, 1997; Ruwhiu, 2005; Henry, 2007; Tapsell and Woods, 2008; University of Otago, 2008; Knox, 2011; Tinirau and Mika, 2012). Some examples of Māori entrepreneurship practice and theory may help illuminate the matter.

Māori land-holding enterprises comprising various kinds of Māori trusts and incorporations operate within a legislative framework informed by Māori cultural values and practices (Mulligan et al., 2004; Spencer and Broughton, 2008). The legislative imperative is for the retention of Māori land by Māori because so much was lost through colonisation (Petrie, 2002). The expectations of an increasingly absentee ownership base (that is, owners who neither live on the land nor derive their livelihood from it) are for land retention because of the land's representation as a vestige of one's cultural and spiritual origins, and also for it to be economically productive (Maori Multiple Owned Land Development Committee, 1998; Jefferies, 2003; Davies et al., 2005; PricewaterhouseCoopers, 2013).

Māori enterprises in other sectors draw on Māori cultural values, practices and symbols as part of their products, services and operations (Jones et al., 2005). A conspicuous example of this is Māori tourism, particularly those enterprises that offer cultural experiences such as heritage tours, *hangi* (food cooked in an earth oven), cultural performances, and *marae* (village complex) visits (Barnett, 2001; Ryan and Higgins, 2006; Ministry of Tourism, 2008; New Zealand Māori Tourism

Council, 2008). With the establishment of Māori Television in 2004, Māori screen production companies are also increasingly producing programmes in *te reo* Māori (the Māori language), which employ Māori presenters and incorporate Māori cultural themes (Mika et al., 2005; Henry, 2011). Interestingly, Māori language programmes are popular with both Māori and non-Māori audiences (Stokes, 2004). Māori screen production enterprises are predominantly urban in nature, dealing with non-traditional Māori assets and issues. Māori culture in these contexts is evolving, finding new outlets among global markets (Māori Economic Development Commission, 1999; Warriner, 1999; Cash and Taurima, 2002; Allen, 2011).

Ella Henry combines Māori philosophy and entrepreneurship in a way that links Māori commercial activity with traditional Māori values and knowledge. 'Kaupapa Māori' describes 'traditional Māori ways of doing, being and thinking, encapsulated in a Māori worldview or cosmology' (Henry, 2007: 542). Thus, 'Kaupapa Māori entrepreneurship', according to Henry, is a form of 'social entrepreneurship'. That is, 'entrepreneurial activity ... underpinned by social objectives to improve the wealth and wellbeing for the community, rather than just the individual' (Henry, 2007: 542).

Keelan and Woods (2006) argue that there has been little recognition of the role that traditional stories have played in encouraging entrepreneurship within indigenous communities. To help bridge the gap, Keelan and Woods (2006) articulate a Māori approach to entrepreneurship that draws inspiration from the exploits of *Māui Tikitiki-a-Tāranga* (Māui, the son of Tāranga), an ancestral hero of Māori and Pacific traditions. They argue that stories of Maui's life and deeds, passed down over many generations through oral tradition, offer unique insights into the existence of and potential for Māori entrepreneurship. 'These stories are *kōrero tawhito* [ancient stories, italics in original] ... used to transmit to successive generations the philosophies, values, ideals, and norms of Māori society' (O'Sullivan and Mills, 2012: 2).

Keelan and Woods position 'Māuipreneurship' as a constitutive metaphor, which are metaphors that 'determine what makes sense and what does not' (for example, entrepreneurship drives economic development) (Klamer and Leonard, 1994: 40, cited in Keelan and Woods, 2006: 4). They do this by demonstrating how pervasive and integral Māui is to the Māori world view, as an ancestor and a benefactor of his people, and of humankind. Māuipreneurship as a heuristic metaphor is evident within descriptions of his character – Māui as a protagonist of superior skill, fearless in venturing into the unknown (a trait which ultimately spells his demise), but who is also regarded as somewhat of a prankster, reckless and devious at times. While acknowledging that these are not altogether wholesome attributes to be emulated by the modern entrepreneur, Keelan and Woods (2006) argue that, Māui's deeds offer important insights about entrepreneurial potential from an indigenous perspective.

The Role of Kaumātua

The status of Kaumātua, or esteemed elder in the Māori community, is not a self-appointed station but one that is 'bestowed' upon one by one's *iwi* (tribe) (Cairns, 2013: 3). Being a Kaumātua therefore represents a confluence of age and seniority (that is, birthright and longevity), both of which are valued cultural attributes among Māori. Age alone, however, does not qualify one to be a Kaumātua; experience also has some part to play, as one elder somewhat mischievously quips: 'some people are old and wise, and some people are just old' (O'Regan, 2009: 7). Another Kaumātua was asked how he defines Kaumātua and said:

> That's a difficult and easy question. One of the definitions is age. Another is age and experience.
> Another is age and knowledge. Another is age and your own whānau, hapū, iwi connection that

acknowledges that you have reached a particular plank in your life and you have the right to occupy or carry the name of Kaumātua by virtue of performance. (Cairns, 2013: 3)

In addition to age, experience and wisdom therefore, the role of Kaumātua is distinguished through consistent performance to a high standard as assessed by others. But what precisely does a Kaumātua do? The traditional role of Kaumātua is summarised by Higgins and Meredith (2013: 4):

Kaumātua, both male and female elders, were the leaders of the whānau [family]. Leadership was focused on the oldest members of the whānau, often as patriarch or matriarch possessing the wisdom and experience to guide the younger generations. Kaumātua made the decisions concerning the working of family land, the control and use of family property, and the rearing and education of children. They were the spokespersons for the whānau in rūnanga (tribal councils).

Kaumātua performed vital functions within tribal life of pre-European contact Aotearoa (pre-1769). This not only involved watching over children as parents toiled in the forests, rivers and seas (Buck, 1987), but also passing on to *mokopuna* (grandchildren) highly prized knowledge of ancestors, their deeds, their connection to celestial beings and the particular rituals, chants and songs which are used to retain and readily recall such knowledge (Melbourne, 1998; Raerino, 1999; Davies, 2006). However, of greater import is the mysterious quality – *ruānukutanga* (wisdom) – and the faculty to deploy it as required to secure the fortunes of the *whānau* (extended family), *hapū* (subtribe), and *iwi* (tribe) (Mika, 2009a; Nikora, 2009).

Kaumātua who were particularly blessed with foresight, knowledge and intellect accumulated over many years would be relied on for advice and wise counsel by *rangatira* (tribal chiefs) (Mead, 1994; Mead, 1995). The knowledge of Kaumātua would also be displayed publicly as oratory from the *paepae* (orator's bench) on the *marae*, the quality of which would add to the *mana* (prestige and standing) of the *hapū* and the *iwi* among *manuhiri* (visitors) (Tauroa and Tauroa, 1986; Rewi, 2010).

The period of colonial conquest in Aotearoa New Zealand from about 1835 to 1875 had a dramatic effect on Māori society (Moon, 1993; Durie, 2001; King, 2003; Walker, 2004). It was a period in which the Māori people suffered significant loss of land, life and resources through legislative manipulation, military might and commercial exploitation (Orange, 1987; Waitangi Tribunal, 1988, 1991, 1996, 2009; Melbourne, 1995). It was also a period in which Māori acquired a new language and the written word. Māori were exposed to Western knowledge, politics, commerce and technology, including Christianity, agricultural methods, tools and foods, muskets, tobacco and alcohol – both the virtues and the vices (Love and Waa, 1997; Petrie, 2002; Consedine, 2007). The large-scale loss of land and exclusion from the parliamentary process meant that tribal economies, some of which had surged in wealth on the supply of goods and services to nearby nascent but ever-growing settler populations, were rapidly undone (Schaniel, 1985; Hawkins, 1999; Consedine, 2007; Bargh, 2010). Over the colonial period, Māori moved away from subsistence-based economies and tribal capitalism, a form where the factors of production are communally owned and managed (Warren, 2009; Yates, 2009), to largely being participants in the wage-based economy of Aotearoa – a position which remains the dominant form of economic participation by Māori today (New Zealand Institute of Economic Research, 2003).

The thread to traditional knowledge and its capacity to galvanise Māori in unified resistance was severely fractured by legislation and its indiscriminate enforcement – for example, the Tohunga Suppression Act 1908 (Stephens, 2001) – and the sacrifice of Māori men in the First and Second World War (Ministry for Culture and Heritage, 2012a). The separation between Māori and traditional knowledge and its keepers, the Kaumātua, would be further exacerbated as a consequence of rapid urbanisation of the Māori people (Walker, 2004; Meredith, 2012). Over the space of 30 years, Māori went from a predominantly rural existence (with 65 per cent still living rurally in 1956) to a mainly urban populace (with 80 per cent living in urban centres by 1986) (Consedine, 2007; Taonui, 2012). Cultural bonds with the *hau kainga* (home people) which Māori had relied upon as an internalised guide for ethicality were weakened, and in many cases severed through city dwelling and suburbanity (Walker, 2004).

Urban Māori sought to reconstitute the cultural strengths of tribal life in the cities, congregating and socialising in workplaces with large Māori contingents, forming social and cultural clubs, sports teams, urban marae, and urban authorities. These were places in which to be Māori, to feel Māori, to think Māori and to speak Māori was natural, accepted, encouraged, and enriched (Walker, 2004; Consedine, 2007; Mika, 2008a; Meredith, 2012). Within this urbanised milieu, the role of Kaumātua in *te ao* Māori (Māori society) and *te ao hurihuri* (modern society) has arguably become more acute as Māori set out to reclaim their identity and reaffirm their *tūrangawaewae* (place to stand) (Durie, 2001; Walker, 2004).

Kaumātua who have managed to retain and practise traditional Māori knowledge, customs and language are highly sought after as a conduit to the old ways of knowing, doing and living. Kaumātua in this league are active as facilitators, navigators and conduits for Māori re-seeking, re-searching and re-establishing their cultural identity, cultural capacities, and the language of their forebears. Māori are now earnestly engaged in revitalising their language and customs through broadcasting (Matāmua, 2006), education (for example, *kohanga reo*, or Māori language preschools) (Reedy, 2000; Durie, 2005; Hook, 2006) and contemporary workplaces (Workman, 1995; Ngarimu, 2009). Moreover, Māori culture is increasingly being embraced by non-Māori, evident within elements of national identity, culture, and branding (Kalafatelis et al., 2003; Jones et al., 2005; Te Puni Kōkiri, 2007b).

Since the early 1990s, treaty settlements between Māori and the Crown for breaches of promises made under the Treaty of Waitangi of 1840 have injected the cultural renaissance among Māori with renewed impetus and reinforced the paramouncty of *iwi* in the rebuilding of tribal nations (Law Commission, 2002; Dodd, 2003; Dodd and Joseph, 2003; Gardiner, 2010; Finlayson, 2013). At the other end of the spectrum, *whānau* (extended families) have become a priority of Māori social policy in recent times (Durie et al., 2010). And within this movement, *whānau ora* (family wellbeing in an holistic sense) has emerged as a modern paradigm for supporting and empowering Māori to achieve their aims and address their social development needs (Mika, 2011; Hubbard, 2013; Ministry of Health, 2013; Te Puni Kōkiri, 2013).

Kaumātua are called upon by government to help them engage with Māori in sensitive and appropriate ways. In practical terms this may mean helping to build cultural competencies and some measure of responsiveness among officials when dealing with Māori people and Māori issues (Manatū Māori, 1991; Webster, 1998; Mika, 2006, 2008c, 2010b). Indeed, New Zealand's parliament established the role of *Kaumātua o Te Whare Pāremata* (elder of parliament) in 2000. The position was first held by Whānganui elder John Rangitihi Rangiwaiata Tahupārae, and then by his wife, Rose White-Tahupārae in 2009, following Tahupārae's passing in 2008 (Parliamentary Service, 2009). The Parliamentary Service's *Kaiwhakarite* (adviser), Kura Moeahu, describes the role of parliamentary Kaumātua:

> [T]here is a high demand for [t]ikanga Māori [Māori customs] elements to be incorporated into ceremonies held at Parliament and it will be [Rose's] role to oversee such ceremonies. ... the term [k]aumātua can refer to an older male or female who is selected to perform specific roles and functions on behalf of the people. Support and participation from appropriate persons to perform the various roles in accordance with tikanga Māori will be coordinated by the new [k]aumātua. (Parliamentary Service, 2009: 1)

The Wisdom of Kaumātua

There is much to be learned by the observance of Kaumātua: in the nature of their work (what they do); the quality of their performance (how they do it); and the impact of their contribution (what difference they make) to Māori enterprises. This section relates the experiences and wisdom of three Kaumātua. They are Sir Tīpene O'Regan, Dame Georgina Kirby, and Mr Tāmati Cairns, discussed in this order. The Kaumātua portrayed here are not without fault. On the contrary, they would readily admit to being subjected to criticism and to making mistakes. They do, however, share in common the courage to pursue what they believed to be right and just causes for Māori in their areas of expertise and practice. We begin with Sir Tīpene.

SIR TĪPENE O'REGAN

Sir Tīpene O'Regan is one of the most highly respected *rangatira* (tribal chiefs) and Kaumātua across Māoridom and more particularly among his people, the Ngāi Tahu of *Te Waipounamu*, the South Island (O'Regan, 2001). Born of a Ngāi Tahu mother, Rena Ruiha Bradshaw, and a Pākehā father of Irish descent, Dr Rolland O'Regan, Sir Tīpene was educated at St Patrick's College and Victoria University in Wellington. He spent much of his very early life in the company of his maternal grandmother in *Awarua* (Bluff).

Sir Tīpene devoted the greater part of his adult life to leading Ngāi Tahu and driving the tribe's treaty claims against the Crown in the courts and before the Waitangi Tribunal (1991). He was elected to the Ngāi Tahu Māori Trust Board in 1974 and retired as chairman with the board's transition to Te Rūnanga o Ngāi Tahu in 1996 (Christchurch City Libraries, 2013). He was the architect of the Maori fisheries settlements of 1989 and 1992 (Moon, 1998; Te Ohu Kai Moana, 2003; Walker, 2004) and finally achieved the landmark Ngai Tahu Treaty Settlement in 1998 (Ministry for Culture and Heritage, 2012b; Christchurch City Libraries, 2013).

Sir Tīpene has continued to occupy leadership positions in academia, business and Māori development. These have included a period as Assistant Vice-Chancellor Māori in the University of Canterbury and his continuing chairmanship of Ngā Pae o te Māramatanga, the Centre for Māori Research Excellence at the University of Auckland. He has recently retired from a 28-year term on the New Zealand Geographic Board, and in December 2013 completed a two-year term as co-chair of the Constitutional Advisory Panel – the initial phase of a general review of New Zealand's constitutional arrangements (Ngā Pae o te Māramatanga, 2012).

In April 2009, I was fortunate enough to be in the audience of a Māori fisheries conference in Napier at which Sir Tīpene O'Regan was delivering a keynote address. The conference theme was 'control or be controlled' and was clearly geared toward imploring tribal fishing enterprises to build a dominant position in commercial fisheries in Aotearoa New Zealand (Treaty Tribes Coalition, 2009). What struck me about Sir Tīpene's *kōrero* (speech) was his insistence that Māori had to design economic systems of their own rather than simply copy Western models, which hitherto had not worked for Māori. The intriguing question about this for me was what precisely a Māori economic system might look like. About the same time, the Tūhoe Fisheries Charitable Trust, for whom I was working; asked me to help organise the first Tūhoe Economic Summit. I immediately knew we had to have Sir Tīpene as the opening speaker to ensure thinking at the summit was bold and boundless.

Graciously, Sir Tīpene agreed to help, delivering a provocative and inspiring opening address at the Tūhoe Economic Summit on 17 July 2009 (Mika, 2009b). His presentation was replete with fundamentally important challenges for the development of all tribes, not just my own.

Figure 8.1   Sir Tīpene O'Regan

Source: An adornment, 2011.

The challenges Sir Tīpene posed were reflections of accumulated wisdom gathered from his old people and, by his own admission, from his mistakes as much as his successes (O'Regan, 2009). Tūhoe, like many other *iwi* (tribes) is in the process of settling its treaty claims with the Crown. Their challenge was, as Sir Tīpene suggests, to move from 'grievance mode' – where much of his tribe's history and culture had been about *te kereme*, the claim – to one focused on forward-looking tribal development; in effect nation building (Dodd, 2003). Sir Tīpene's metaphor for this transitional process is an analogy which compares claimants to a 'barking dog' that somehow manages to catch the passing car; that is, justice by way of a treaty settlement. Sir Tipene points to the dilemma tribes face in such circumstances: what is the dog to do with the car once it has finally been apprehended?

Another of the comments Sir Tipene made at the summit concerns the relationship between tribal centres and their connectivity with regional elements:

> Whilst you require overall unity to deal with the wider world, the elements within your iwi should form into their natural segments or corners, not competitively, but they must have their autonomy. I believe that requires some economic autonomy, but certainly political and cultural autonomy. So it's a collaboration between the centre and the region. I'm not talking of a separation. A collaboration that's based on function. If you develop all your economic strength at the centre and just send an annual payment out to your marae and annual dividend to individuals ... you just become a mokai [slave] of your central structure. What's worse ... all you've done is you've privatised welfare dependency. (O'Regan, 2009: 8–9)

Other aspects of Sir Tipene's address are worth considering as principles to support the development of post-settlement tribal enterprises:

- A change in thinking is required, one which is rooted in our cultural identities and histories but focused on the needs of present and future generations.
- Developing a clear sense of purpose and vision, which articulates whether iwi members want to be an iwi and if so, what kind of iwi they want to be.
- Having the courage to pursue a tribal vision and purpose knowing it is likely to upset the status quo.
- The permanency of iwi makes them an ideal investment partner, but also imposes an obligation upon iwi to look after all their members, not just the few.
- The need for a long term perspective to tribal development (50 to 100 years) but not to miss economic opportunities in the short and medium term;
- Designing our own institutions and economic systems whilst adapting rather than imitating Western models and methods.
- Finding a natural balance within iwi between functions rightly held by the centre and functions rightly held by the regions.
- Ensuring regional elements of iwi have a fair measure of economic, political and cultural autonomy to ensure they can engage constructively.
- The scarcity and importance of quality tribal leadership and the difficulty in finding, growing and selecting such leaders.
- Guarding against the dangers of incumbency, a problem which restricts democratic politics to a focus on being re-elected and staying in power.

Within these 'pearls of wisdom' there is no prescription for tribal economic success, and none was promised. Sir Tipene simply offers sign-posts about what iwi will need to consider as they make their way. Sir Tipene's advice does, however, accord with the notion that iwi are self-determining indigenous peoples (Durie, 1995; Smith, 1999; Mikaere, 2000; Aotearoa Independent Media Centre, 2011). As such iwi will need to devise visions, strategies, institutions, structures and economies that are inclusive and empowering, enhancing the autonomy, agency and potency of iwi members, individually and collectively.

DAME GEORGINA KIRBY

Dame Georgina is of Ngāti Rakaipaaka and Prussian descent and was made a Dame Commander (DBE) for services to Māori in 1994. Dame Georgina was president of the Māori Women's Welfare League from 1983 to 1987, a national organisation formed by Māori women in 1951 to advance Māori cultural development post-World War Two (Rogers and Simpson, 1993). Dame Georgina grew up in the family business, which was farming (Budvietas, 2011). Dame Georgina's father was a successful farmer who bought the seven surrounding farms, leaving this business to Dame Georgina and her siblings when he and their mother passed away. Dame Georgina disliked farming but concedes that 'if it hadn't been for that farm I probably wouldn't be where I am today, because I learnt all about business through my dad' (Budvietas, 2011).

Figure 8.2   Dame Georgina Kirby

Source: Government House, 2013.

I had the opportunity to work with Dame Georgina Kirby in May 2006, assisting Māori Women's Development Inc. (MWDI) to write Māori small business guides. Although aware of the MWDI, I was unfamiliar with the way the institution worked. Dame Georgina's work in fostering entrepreneurship among Māori women is an inspiring display of the kind of determination to help Māori in need for which the Māori Women's Welfare League is widely known and respected. Dame Georgina's philosophy is essentially that through entrepreneurship Māori women and men have the opportunity to provide for their families and to help them fully participate in the social and economic life of their communities.

In the early 1980s, Dame Georgina was asked by the government to speak in Kenya about business and why it was important for women in particular to go into business. After a subsequent speaking engagement in India, where she encountered one of the first women's business associations, Dame Georgina returned to New Zealand determined to set up something similar (Budvietas, 2011). Dame Georgina, with the support of the Māori Women's Welfare League, established MWDI in 1987. MWDI acts as a finance company, providing small loans to Māori women and men in business (Benedict, 2010; Mika, 2010a). Dame Georgina remarked that she would receive calls from *Pākehā* (New Zealanders of European descent) saying 'my wife is Māori, can I borrow some money? And I said, of course!' (Budvietas, 2011).

Dame Georgina, through her work as founder and chief executive of MWDI, has assisted thousands of Māori enterprises with finance, mentoring, advice and support. Ngaire Gallagher a Chartered Accountant from Ngāti Raukawa in Otaki, recalls the assistance that Dame Georgina provided her in establishing her accountancy practice:

> They helped with financing. And they also helped with advice, because what goes with that is you're able to contact them for advice and so on. But we used to go to their functions, conferences and things where you'd get a lot of good speakers. (Mika, 2013b: 1)

MWDI continues the legacy of Dame Georgina Kirby with its programme of finance and business support services under the leadership of chief executive Teresa Tepania-Ashton. MWDI provides small business loans of up to NZ$50,000 for eligible Māori enterprises, but operates as a lender of last resort for Māori who are unable to obtain business finance from other sources.

MR TĀMATI CAIRNS

Tāmati Cairns is an esteemed elder of the Tūhoe, Raukawa, and Ngāti Kahungunu tribes. I first met Tāmati Cairns and his late wife, Jane Cairns, in 1997 in Wellington. Tāmati was a leading figure in the Wellington section of our tribe known as *Tūhoe Ki Poneke* (the Tūhoe people of Wellington). However, it was not until October 2007 when Tāmati, then chair of the Tūhoe Fisheries Charitable Trust, called me to ask if I could facilitate a planning meeting of the trustees that we had the chance to work together. I also subsequently worked with Tāmati on various projects for Te Ata Hou, a kaupapa Māori-based educational trust which Tāmati and Jane administered.

Tāmati was born in a small community west of Taupō called Mōkai on his 'grandmother's and grandfather's lounge floor', so he was told. It was Tāmati's grandmother who took him to Ruatāhuna to be raised by his great-aunt and great-uncle of the Tūhoe tribe. For Tāmati, 'that would have been the beginning of [his] life's journey, being raised by the old people' (Cairns, 2013: 1). Tāmati found that 'both from a *hapū* [subtribal] perspective and a home perspective, [he] was very fortunate to be at the ankles ... of the old people that were about at that time'. Tāmati recounts some of his upbringing, schooling and early work life:

> We lived in a farm setting from a hapū [subtribe] perspective. And so everything we did on the farm reflected both the economy of what a farm would provide for a family and also what a farm would provide for the economy of the marae and the hapū. I saw such things as growing vegetable gardens, five rows for the family and two rows for the marae, one pig for the family, one pig for the marae. My primary schooling life was at Huiarau School. And my whakapono [faith] life was with the Presbyterian and the Ringatū faith. All of us who aspired to continue in education were fired off to boarding schools. I think I left home at the age of 12, 13 to [go to] boarding school. My school life ended and we were fired off to teachers training college. At boarding school it was all boys and at teachers training college it became two thirds women and one third men. And of course my life was in and around administration all the way up to the time I changed and became

Figure 8.3   Mr Tāmati Cairns

Source: Tūhoe Fisheries Charitable Trust, 2010.

> *a teacher in 1981. So my administration journey began back in 1967. And I worked in such places as banks, insurance companies, social welfare, forestry. When we moved to Wellington I became the manager of the Commercial Bank of Australia in Eastbourne. And that was a very interesting time because at that time Eastbourne was the centre of Pākehātanga (New Zealand European culture). And to have this Māori boy managing a bank I am sure would have been an oddity for the community at the time. But it was a good experience for me.*

In 2001, Tāmati went into business for himself as a self-employed consultant providing Māori cultural advice in the public and private sectors. This move was somewhat forced upon Tāmati with the closure of the university department where he worked. The experience in business is however one which Tāmati cherishes. Tāmati describes his experience in business:

> *It's through the business that you actually get to know your own people. And as a result of those engagements you'll carry on with that passion through your whole life. And your people know who you are; know where you are; know your strengths. That's business I think from a Māori perspective. It's a connection between the skill that you have and who you are and your connectedness to who you are both from a whakapapa [genealogical] perspective and from a business perspective. Tērā āhua [that sort of thing]. (Cairns, 2013: 3)*

For Tāmati, the most helpful thing to him in business was the support of his whānau, in particular his wife Jane. Tāmati suggests that: 'if your mind is at rest, then the whole gambit opens up for you and you're happy to engage in whatever challenge comes your way. … That's the "glue" for you in your business' (Cairns, 2013: 5). Tāmati considers that 'to be in business applies a different type of pressure, that if you don't release it, he raruraru nē hā [problems arise, don't they]' (Cairns, 2013: 4).

In Tāmati's view, the role of the Kaumātua is encapsulated in the concept of *taituarā*, which in Māori means support in all its forms and in its various contexts. This may extend to 'spiritual support, physical support, business support, social support, and family support' (Cairns, 2013: 3). The type of support delivered by Kaumātua varies depending on the needs of the situation. In a community setting in which a family is dealing with a serious social issue, Kaumātua may bring special knowledge in *karakia* (prayer); expertise in cultural processes of, for example, conflict resolution; and knowledge about who else can help and how to sensitively engage them (Mika, 2010b). Similarly in commerce, Tāmati believes the taituarā role of Kaumātua remains just as relevant.

Tāmati gives an example of taituarā in his role as Kaumātua to a Māori enterprise in the Mataatua district of the Bay of Plenty. There a Māori enterprise is seeking to do business with a Chinese enterprise in an agricultural venture. Tāmati is especially adept at reframing business processes into traditional Māori cultural constructs. Thus, Tāmati's role has to been to facilitate the business exchange by establishing a metaphorical corridor called the Whitau Sovereign Agreement, through which overseas business partners must pass before engaging with Māori in business (Mika, 2014). Tāmati explains that he heard the name *Whitau*, which means flax fibre in Māori, in a *kauhau* (sermon) of his church minister, Rev. Hariata Haumate, who had referred to a *whakataukī* (proverb) from another of our Tūhoe elders.

MRS MONA RIINI

The Whitau proverb is attributed to the late Mrs Mona Riini, wife of the late Rev. Sonny Riini. Mrs Riini was Moderator of Te Aka Puaho, the Māori Synod of the Presbyterian Church. Tāmati explains – as was conveyed to him by another of our iwi members who was present – that Mona was speaking to an international gathering at Te Maungarongo Marae in Ohope in 1981. Mona performed a *karanga* (ceremonial call of welcome) inside the house, before she spoke. This was unusual because the karanga is normally performed outside the meeting house to welcome guests.

As Mona began to address the group she laid out strands of whitau and invited participants to come forward, take a strand and return to their groups. They were then asked to return their whitau and share a thought with the *hui* (gathering). A *kuia* (female elder), named Te Ao, was seated by Mona's side. Te Ao took the whitau and wove a *whāriki*, a traditional flax mat, incorporating the ideas which people had shared. Mona then uttered the words of the Whitau proverb:

> *Rarangatia te whitau harakeke – weave a memory of the past; rarangatia te whitau wairua – weave a thought for today; rarangatia te whitau tāngata – weave a hope for tomorrow; rarangatia i rūnga i te aroha – weave a love for action and deed. (Cairns, 2013:6)*

As overseas businesspeople pass through the Whitau, Tāmati notes they will encounter an expression of who Māori are, their culture, their thinking, their spirituality and their expectations of their business partners (Cairns, 2013). They engage with Māori as a sovereign indigenous nation which exists in partnership with the Crown by virtue of the Treaty of Waitangi (Orange, 1987; Geare et al., 2005; Cairns, 2013) – hence, the naming of the acculturation device of the *whitau* as a *sovereign* agreement.

In another example, Tāmati describes how Te Ata Hou, a Māori educational and training organisation which he chairs, contributed to Tūhoe tribal developments in some rather ingenious and unconventional ways (Mika, 2012). On this occasion, Hinepūkohurangi Trust, a community organisation of the small rural settlement of Ruatāhuna, which was then chaired by Mr Rongonui ('Ron') Tahi, agreed to loan Te Ata Hou $30,000 to purchase computers and establish a training

Figure 8.4   Mrs Mona Riini

Source: Dale, 2003.

programme. With the task complete, Te Ata Hou was ready to return the funds. About this time, however, the government announced that it intended selling the Whakamarino Lodge located at Tuai on the shores of Lake Waikaremoana, near Ruatāhuna. The Electricity Corporation had built the lodge on traditional Tūhoe lands as a hostel for workers of the Waikaremoana hydroelectric power station (Waitangi Tribunal, 2009: 9).

Tāmati describes the part Te Ata Hou played in rescuing the lodge from falling into private hands:

> *We asked if we could continue to use these funds [the $30,000 loan] when the lodge came up. We didn't want the lodge to be lost to Tūhoe forever. So we entered the bidding and won it. We sent*

our American friend, a professor who has a great affection for Tūhoe and Tūhoe for him to do our bidding, complete with cowboy hat and Texan accent! We didn't want to let on that Tūhoe was bidding. It required a 10% deposit. We only had the Hinepūkohurangi money, which we used. We then argued with the government that they had no right to sell it. This was in October. By February the following year, the government established the 'resumption clause' – any surplus Crown land is offered back to potential claimants. When this happened, we gave back the lodge to the Crown, so it could be 'land-banked' for Tūhoe claims. (Mika, 2012: 4–5)

The story continues:

When this deal was over, the Ruatāhuna store came up for sale by auction. So Te Ata Hou and the Tūhoe Waikaremoana Māori Trust Board bid for the shop. We wanted the community to own their own store. We again used the funds from Hinepūkohurangi. We took out a loan with the Trust Board for the rest, which is now paid off. The shop is freehold. With its funds, Hinepūkohurangi became the third shareholder in the shop. So that original money helped set up two training programmes, stopped the lodge being sold and the buying of the shop! (Mika, 2012: 4–5)

Tāmati is clear that without the faith and the support of Hinepūkohurangi chair, Ron Tahi, Te Ata Hou would not have been able to accomplish all that it did to safeguard part of the tribal estate and help one of its communities achieve several development priorities.

The Role of Kaumātua in Māori Entrepreneurship

Māori entrepreneurship – the process of starting and running a Māori enterprise – is contributing to a growing and dynamic Māori economy. Traditional knowledge, wisdom and support provided by Kaumātua is helping Māori entrepreneurs revitalise the Māori economy, which in 2010 was estimated to be worth NZ$36.9 billion, up from $16.5 billion in 2006 (Nana et al., 2011). Not all Kaumātua may be inclined or equipped to participate in Māori entrepreneurship in this way, because such roles draw on the skill and expertise of Kaumātua in terms of Māori cultural knowledge, the Māori language and Māori institutional networks to do their work.

While Māori entrepreneurship and Western entrepreneurship are essentially the same in respect of the importance of profitability and positive cash flows over time, there are fundamental differences in terms of the nature of Māori assets, Māori values and the regulatory environment within which Māori enterprises operate. These differences point toward an emerging theory of Māori entrepreneurialism. The position argued in this chapter is that Māori entrepreneurship is founded upon indigenous values, customs and language, integrating Western entrepreneurship principles and practices in the pursuit of Māori development aims in ways which Māori determine are appropriate for them (Durie, 2002; Henry, 2007; Davies, 2011; Mika, 2013c).

Inculcating and maintaining differentiation within Māori enterprises and Māori entrepreneurship on the basis of traditional knowledge, values, and practices is unlikely to be successful without some degree of knowledge, competency and assurance. Where are Māori entrepreneurs to find such knowledge and the capacity to incorporate it meaningfully within Māori enterprises? While some may possess dual competencies in both Māori and Western cultural knowledge and practices, Māori entrepreneurs are likely to have to seek outside help. This is where the role of esteemed and knowledgeable elders comes into play – our Kaumātua.

Kaumātua are female and male elders who are recognised by their tribes as possessing valued traditional knowledge and experience and the capacity to effectively deploy this consistently within traditional and contemporary settings, including the entrepreneurial process. While age and experience are defining criteria, being a Kaumātua imposes a discipline and an obligation to provide appropriate cultural advice and support as the situation demands. Thus, age, plus knowledge and experience, and potentially wisdom, constitute criteria for Kaumātua status and their activity, *Kaumātuatanga*.

In modern times, Kaumātua continue to provide support, advice, and wise counsel to whānau, hapū, iwi, and Māori communities in rural and urban settings as Māori seek to restore their collective and individual social, cultural and economic wellbeing (Durie, 1999; Cairns, 2013). Some tribes do this by formally establishing Kaumātua councils to provide oversight of the tribes' governing bodies (for example, the Ngāpuhi tribe in the Northland region). Others engage Kaumātua as part of an ancillary advisory forum for advice on matters of *tikanga* (tribal custom) and *mātauranga-a-iwi* (tribal knowledge); for example, as part of a whakapapa committee to verify the genealogy of applicants to the tribal register (Mika, 2008b). Generally, however, Kaumātua are actively consulted by Māori enterprises particularly: 'when important decisions are at stake, as convincing Kaumātua of the merits of major transactions can prove decisive in Māori organisations as the voices of approving Kaumātua may help dispel shareholder unease' (Mika and O'Sullivan, 2014: 24).

There are at least three main ways that Kaumātua contribute to Māori entrepreneurship: (i) as entrepreneurs in their own right involved in the governance and management of Māori enterprises; (ii) as employees within Māori enterprises, typically as cultural advisers, though in some cases occupying other technical roles; and (iii) as cultural advisers (for example, as members of a Kaumātua council or as governors on a board of directors) in support of Māori entrepreneurs and Māori enterprises. This chapter focuses attention on the third of these roles of Kaumātua in Māori entrepreneurship. This latter role often arises because of whakapapa ties Kaumātua share with the enterprise, and in other cases Kaumātua may be engaged as advisers on either professional or voluntary terms.

Three Māori leaders were profiled as exemplars of the different ways Kaumātua contribute to Māori entrepreneurship. Sir Tīpene O'Regan is an example of a Kaumātua who has brought his combined capacities as a scholar, a leader and an esteemed elder to bear in tribal and nontribal Māori enterprises. Sir Tīpene's knowledge and experience in respect of Māori economic development presents a host of possibilities for further research. These include: (i) the design of Māori economic models and institutions; (ii) the future relationship between whānau, hapū, and iwi in Māori economic development; and (iii) developing Māori leaders for social and economic development. It is Sir Tīpene O'Regan's 'primary comment' about Māori economic development that I believe holds much promise for research:

> [Māori economic institutions] must be founded on a clear conceptual vision of what the group wants to be in the future. Thus, the Iwi aspirations as to the heritage, culture and identity and its perpetuation on an intergenerational basis must first be conceptualised, articulated and adopted. The economic design must be such as to enable that aspiration to be achieved. Everything follows from that moemoea [aspiration, dream]! (O'Regan, pers. comm., 2014)

Dame Georgina Kirby's passion for success among Māori women in entrepreneurship and the institution she and others established to support this derives from the pragmatic and nurturing response within the female fraternity of the Māori Women's Welfare League. Being raised within and around business also cultivated within Dame Georgina her view of entrepreneurship as a pathway for Māori to secure their families' fortunes.

Mr Tāmati Cairns draws on his upbringing within a remote rural Māori settlement, steeped in the Māori language and culture, to inform his foray into business and his leadership roles within Māori enterprises. Tāmati introduces a concept which effectively sums up the role of Kaumātua in Māori entrepreneurship – and that is taituarā, or support in all its forms. Taituarā allows Kaumātua to contribute in ways that reflect their knowledge and capacities, and to be acknowledged for this. Taituarā as performed by Kaumātua means Māori entrepreneurs have the possibility of obtaining the cultural support they require to establish and maintain the wealth and wellbeing of whānau, hapū, iwi, and Māori communities in business.

I have been struck by how much the manner in which all three Kaumātua went about their work resembles that of Māui Tikitiki-a-Tāranga (Māui, who was wrapped in the topknot of Tāranga, his mother). The similarity with our ancestor Māui is not so much in what Sir Tīpene O'Regan, Dame Georgina Kirby and Mr Tāmati Cairns did (the physicality of it), but how and why (the metaphysicality). Their actions and deeds exemplify what Keelan and Woods (2006: 2) call the 'Māuipreneur' – the combination of Māori values and entrepreneurial talent, in socially motivated, culturally grounded indigenous enterprises.

Two possibilities for research are: firstly, how are Kaumātua engaged within Māori enterprises, in terms of both the activity they perform and the terms and conditions on which they are engaged; and secondly, the nature and extent of Kaumātua as Māori entrepreneurs in their own enterprises, as examples of 'elder entrepreneurship', a growing phenomenon among developed economies such as ours (de Bruin and Dupuis, 2003; Rogoff, 2009).

Conclusion

This chapter set out to explore the role of elders in indigenous economic development, focusing on the experiences of Kaumātua (elders) in Māori enterprises of Aotearoa New Zealand. There is a hope that other indigenous scholars are encouraged to share stories on the part of their elders that they play in indigenous economic development. This study is a relatively novel addition to the mainstream and indigenous entrepreneurship literature.

Traditionally, elders in Māori society performed important roles as keepers of tribal knowledge, sources of wisdom in support of and as tribal leaders themselves, and overseeing child rearing. As the nature of Māori society changes, the role of Kaumātua is also changing. Kaumātua are helping modern-day Māori entrepreneurs make sense of Māori traditions as a way of doing business consistent with indigenous ethics and aspirations.

The balance of the Māori economy has shifted from a land-based, tribally owned one to an urban, wage-based entrepreneurial economy. Tribal Māori enterprises continue to administer and develop communally owned Māori assets built around primary industries of agriculture, fishing and forestry. Yet, a burgeoning breed of Māori entrepreneurs with strong urban roots is making their presence felt, particularly in service industries of property, construction, transportation, tourism and personal services. Whether operating close to their traditional homelands or in and around city precincts, Māori entrepreneurs are engaging Kaumātua as taituarā (support) in what they do. As taituarā, Kaumātua are connecting Māori entrepreneurs with their identity *as* Māori, and with this, bringing a sense of fulfilment and satisfaction with entrepreneurial endeavour, which money simply cannot buy.

References

Allen, J. (2011). *Te hoko ki tāwahi a ngāi Māori: Māori export competitiveness*. Wellington: Te Puni Kōkiri and New Zealand Institute of Economic Research.

An Adornment (2011). *Mountain Scene*. Retrieved from: file:///C:/Users/jpmika/Downloads/MS-2011–06–16-p11-Hilton-e-edition.pdf (accessed: 16 June 2011).

Aotearoa Independent Media Centre (AIMC). (2011). *Tamati Kruger on the negotiations, the raids and Mana Motuhake.* Retrieved from: http://www.indymedia.org.nz/article/79363/tamati-kruger-negotiations-raids-and-man (accessed: 26 March 2012).

Bargh, M. (2010). *Māori and parliament: Diverse strategies and compromises.* Wellington: Huia.

Barlow, C. (1993). *Tikanga Whakaaro: Key concepts in Māori culture.* Auckland: Oxford University Press.

Barnett, S. (2001). Manaakitanga: Maori hospitality: A case study of Maori accommodation providers. *Tourism Management,* 22, pp. 83–92.

Battisti, M. and Gillies, A. (2008). *Impact of Poutama Business Trust services on Maori businesses.* Wellington: Poutama Trust, New Zealand Centre for SME Research and Te Au Rangahau (Māori Business Research Centre).

Benedict, L. (2010). *Social lending: A tool for grantmakers, an opportunity for communities.* Wellington: Fulbright New Zealand.

Berwick, P. (1995). *Concepts of time and pastoral care within Maori businesses.* Palmerston North: Massey University.

Best, E. (1996). *Tuhoe, the children of the mist: A sketch of the origin, history, myths, and beliefs of the Tuhoe tribe of the Maori of New Zealand, with some account of other early tribes of the Bay of Plenty district.* Auckland: Reed.

Best, P. and Love, M. (2011). *Māori values for Māori business: Cultural capital in indigenous organisations.* Wellington: Victoria University of Wellington.

Bishop, R. (1996). *Collaborative research stories: Whakawhanaungatanga.* Palmerston North: Dunmore.

Black, T., Bean, D., Collings, W. and Nuku, W. (eds) (2012). *Conversations on Mātauranga Māori.* Wellington: New Zealand Qualifications Authority.

Buck, P. (1987). *The coming of the Maori.* Wellington: Maori Purposes Fund Board.

Budvietas, R. (2011). *Interview with Dame Georgina Kirby on the 100th anniversary IWD.* Retrieved from: http://www.youtube.com/watch?v=v3a7gUmIB1w (accessed: 26 March 2012).

Cairns, T. (2013). *Interview by J. P. Mika on the role of kaumātua in Māori entrepreneurship.* Palmerston North: Massey University.

Cash, M. and Taurima, W. (2002). *Tumatanui: The experience of the first indigenous wine company to export high quality wine from New Zealand (A bicultural research project).* Wellington: Open Polytech of New Zealand.

Christchurch City Libraries (2013). *Sir Tipene O'Regan 1939.* Christchurch City Council. Retrieved from: http://christchurchcitylibraries.com/Maori/People/O/Oregantipene/ (accessed: 29 November 2013).

Consedine, B. (2007). *Historical influences: Māori and the economy.* Wellington: Te Puni Kōkiri.

Dale, K. (2003). *Update: Moderator Te Aka Puaho.* Bush Telegraph: Presbyterian Church News update, October. Retrieved from: http://www.presbyterian.org.nz/fileadmin/our_newsletter/oct_2003/btoct03.pdf (accessed: 29 November 2013).

Dana, L. P. and Anderson, R. B. (eds) (2007). *International handbook of research on indigenous entrepreneurship.* Cheltenham: Edward Elgar.

Davidsson, P. (2004). *Researching entrepreneurship.* New York: Springer.

Davies, P. (2011). *Māori enterprise and capital markets: Towards a Māori commercial model.* Wellington: Te Puni Kōkiri.

———, Lattimore, R. and Ikin, K. (2005). Maori economic development: Overview and prospects. In J. E. Rowe (ed.), *Economic development in New Zealand: The dynamics of economic space.* Aldershot: Ashgate.

Davies, S. (2006). Kaumatuatanga: Roles of Kaumatua and future directions. *Australian Journal of Psychology,* 58, pp. 128–138.

——— (2008). Kaumātuatanga: The changing roles of kaumātua in Ngāti Rēhua: Future directions. *Unpublished master's thesis.* Hamilton: University of Waikato.

De Bruin, A. and Dupuis, A. (eds) (2003). *Entrepreneurship: New perspectives in a global age.* Aldershot: Ashgate.

Devlin, M. (2006). Ethnicity in business: The case of New Zealand Maori. In E. Rata and R. Openshaw (eds), *Public policy and ethnicity: The politics of ethnic boundary making*. New York: Palgrave Macmillan.

Dickson, I. (2010). *Maori enterprise and the New Zealand capital market: Report 2a scoping report*. Wellington: Māori Economic Taskforce and Te Puni Kōkiri.

Dodd, M. (2003). *Nation building and Māori development: The importance of governance*. Hamilton: University of Waikato.

————— and Joseph, R. (2003). Post-treaty settlement governance challenges: Independent dispute resolution for Ngati Awa. *Governance In Pacific States Development Research Symposium*. Fiji, 30 September–2 October.

Durie, M. (1995). Tino rangatiratanga: Maori self-determination. *He Pukenga Kōrero*, 1, pp. 44–53.

————— (1999). Kaumātuatanga reciprocity: Māori elderly and whānau. *New Zealand Journal of Psychology*, 28, pp. 102–106.

————— (2001). E taurangi tonu te hau: The winds of change forever blow: A Māori development trilogy. *Unpublished PhD thesis*. Palmerston North: Massey University.

————— (2002). The business ethic and Māori development. *Maunga Tu Maunga Ora Economic Summit 2002*. Hawera, New Zealand.

————— (2005). *Indigenous higher education: Māori experience in New Zealand: An address to the Australian Indigenous Higher Education Advisory Council*. Palmerston North: Massey University.

—————, Cooper, R., Grennell, D., Snively, S. and Tuaine, N. (2010). *Whānau ora: Report of the taskforce on whānau-centred initiatives*. Wellington: Office of the Minister for Community and Voluntary Sector.

Finlayson, C. (2013). *Tuhoe deed of settlement negotiations completed*. Wellington: Office of the Minister of Treaty of Waitangi Negotiations.

Firth, R.(1973). *Economics of the New Zealand Māori*. Wellington: Government Printer.

Foley, D. (2004). Understanding indigenous entrepreneurship: A case study analysis. *Unpublished PhD thesis*. Brisbane: University of Queensland.

Foley, D. (2013). Jus sanguinis: The root of contention in determining what is an Australian Aboriginal business. *Indigenous Law Bulletin, 8*(8), pp. 25-29.

Frederick, H. H. and Henry, E. (2004). Innovation and entrepreneurship among Pākehā and Māori in New Zealand. In Stiles, K. and Galbraith, C. (eds), *Ethnic entrepreneurship: Structure and process*. Oxford: Elsevier.

French, A. J. (1998). What is a Maori business: A survey of Maori business peoples perceptions? *Unpublished master's research report*. Wellington: Massey University.

Gardiner, J. (2010). Achieving enduring settlements. *PostTreatySettlements.org.nz*. Wellington: Victoria University of Wellington.

Geare, A., Cambell-Hunt, C., Ruwhiu, D. and Bull, R. (2005). *The New Zealand management supplement*. North Ryde, NSW: McGraw-Hill.

Gillies, A., Tinirau, R. S. and Mako, N. (2007). Whakawhanaungatanga: Extending the networking concept. *He Pukenga Kōrero: A Journal of Māori Studies, ,8*(2), pp. 29–37.

Government House (2013). *Celebrating women*. Wellington: Government House. Retrieved from: https://gg.govt.nz/content/celebrating-women-9 (accessed: 25 January 2014).

Harmsworth, G. (2005). *Report on the incorporation of traditional values/tikanga into contemporary Māori business organisation and process*. Palmerston North: Landcare Research and Mana Taiao.

Harrison, N. (2002). *Graham Latimer: A biography*. Wellington: Huia.

Hawkins, G. (1999). *Maori and business: A proud history*. Te Awamutu: Tu Mai.

Henry, E. (1997). Contemporary Maori business and its legislative and institutional origins. In J. Deeks and P. Enderwick (eds), *Business and New Zealand society*. Auckland: Longman Paul.

————— (1999). *Kaupapa Māori: Locating indigenous ontology, epistemology and methodology in the academy building the research capacity within Māori communities at Waikato University*. Hamilton: New Zealand Council for Educational Research.

—— (2007). Kaupapa Maori entrepreneurship. In L. P. Dana and R. B. Anderson (eds), *International handbook of research on indigenous entrepreneurship*. Cheltenham: Edward Elgar.

—— (2011). Māori entrepreneurship in the screen production industry in New Zealand. *Ngā Pae o Te Maramatanga Symposium on Optimising Māori Economic Development*. Wellington: 14–15 November.

Higgins, R. and Meredith, P. (2013). Kaumātua – Māori elders. *Te Ara: The Encyclopedia of New Zealand* (updated 16 April 2013). Wellington: Ministry for Culture and Heritage.

Hindle, K. and Moroz, P. W. (2009). Indigenous entrepreneurship as a research field: Developing a definitional framework from the emerging canon. *International Entrepreneurship and Management Journal*, 6(4), pp. 357–385.

Hook, G. R. (2006). A future for Māori education part I: The dissociation of culture and education. *MAI Review*, 1, article 2.

Hubbard, A. (2013). *Whanau Ora helps families recover. The Press*. Retrieved from: http://www.stuff.co.nz/the-press/news/8341612/Whanau-Ora-helps-families-recover (accessed: 5 March 2013).

Jefferies, R. (ed.) (2003). *Māori land use: National resource kit – Te Kete Mātauranga Whenua*. Opotiki: Māori Land Development Trust.

Jones, K., Gilbert, K. and Morrison-Brians, Z. (2005). *Māori branding: A report investigating market demand for Maori cultural elements*. Auckland: Mana Taiao.

Kalafatelis, E., Fryer, M. and Walkman, C. (2003). Survey of attitudes towards, and beliefs and values about, the Māori language. *Connecting Social Policy and Research Practice Conference*. Wellington: 29–30 April.

Kawharu, M., Tapsell, P. and Woods, C. (2012). Māori entrepreneurial behaviour: Lachmannian insights. *International Council of Small Business World Conference*. Wellington: 10–14 June.

Keelan, T. J. and Woods, C. (2006). Māuripreneur: understanding Māori entrepreneurship. *International Indigenous Journal of Entrepreneurship, Advancement, Strategy and Education*. Te Awamutu: Te Wānanga o Aoteaora.

King, M. (1977). *Te Puea: A life*. Auckland: Penguin.

—— (2003). *The Penguin history of New Zealand*. Auckland: Penguin.

—— (ed.) (1975). *Te ao hurihuri: The world moves on: Aspects of Maoritanga*. Wellington: Hicks Smith & Sons.

Kingi, T. (2007). *Māori land ownership and management in New Zealand: Pacific Land Program Case Study 4.4*. Palmerston North: Massey University.

Klamer, A. and Leonard, T. C. (1994). So what's an economic metaphor? In P. Miroirowski (ed.), *Natural images in economic thought: Markets read in tooth and claw*. Cambridge: Cambridge University Press.

Knox, C. (2011). Innovation and land based Māori business. *4th ISPIM Innovation Symposium*. Wellington: 29 November–2 December.

Law Commission (2002). *Treaty of Waitangi claims: Addressing the post-settlement phase*. Wellington: Law Commission.

Love, M. and Love, T. R. (2005). Māori and self-employment. In C. Massey (ed.), *Entrepreneurship and small business management in New Zealand*. Auckland: Pearson.

—— and Waa, P. (1997). Maori in the period of colonisation. In J. Deeks and P. Enderwick (eds), *Business and New Zealand society*. Auckland: Longman Paul.

Love, T. R. (2004). Uncovering the academic field of Māori business research. *Journal of Māori Business Research*, September, pp. 22–30.

Mahuika, M. (2006). Māori fishing. In M. Mulholland (ed.), *State of the Māori nation: Twenty-first-century issues in Aotearoa*. Auckland: Reed.

Manatū Māori (1991). *Review of the responsiveness of Te Tira Ahu Iwi 1991*. Wellington: Manatū Māori/Ministry of Māori Affairs.

Māori Multiple Owned Land Development Committee (1998). *Māori land development*. Wellington: Te Puni Kōkiri/Ministry of Māori Development.

Matāmua, R.(2006). Te Reo Pāho: Māori radio and language revitalisation. *Unpublished PhD thesis.* Palmerston North: Massey University.

Māori Economic Development Commission (MEDC). (1999). *An export strategy: A report by the Maori Economic Development Commission.* Wellington: MEDC.

Mead, A. (1994). Maori leadership: The waka tradition the crews were the real heroes. *Hui Whakapumau Maori Development Conference.* Palmersont North: 10–11 August.

Mead, H. M. (1995). *The mandate of leadrship and the decision-making process: A working paper for Te Puni Kōkiri.* Wellington: Te Puni Kōkiri.

——— (2003). *Tikanga Māori: Living by Māori values.* Wellington: Huia.

Melbourne, H. (1995). *Māori sovereignty: The Māori perspective.* Auckland: Hodder Moa Beckett.

——— (1998). *Hinepūkohurangi: He pūrākau nō roto o Tūhoe.* Wellington: Te Pou Taki Kōrero.

Meredith, P. (2012). Urban Māori – urbanisation. *Te Ara: The Encyclopedia of New Zealand* (updated 22 Sep 2012). Wellington: Ministry for Culture and Heritage.

Mika, J. P. (2006). *Maori responsiveness at Auckland regional women's corrections facility: Participant guide for staff.* Auckland: Department of Corrections and Puukaki Marae.

——— (2008a). *Business case for Ngā Whare Waatea Marae sustainable housing project.* Auckland: Manukau Urban Maori Authority.

——— (2008b). *Governance charter.* Rotorua: Tūhoe Fisheries Charitable Trust.

——— (2008c). *Towards Maori responsiveness for the foundation for youth development.* Auckland: Foundation for Youth Development.

——— (2009a). *A conversation with Tamaroa Raymond Nikora.* Hamilton: Author.

——— (2009b). *Report on the outcomes of the Tūhoe Economic Summit, Ohope.* Tāneatua: Tuhoe Fisheries Charitable Trust, 17–18 July.

——— (2010a). *Access to finance and banking services for Māori: A discussion paper.* Wellington: Te Puni Kōkiri.

——— (2010b). *Māori relationships toolkit: A practical guide for NZQA on facilitating effective engagement with Māori.* Wellington: New Zealand Qualifications Authority.

——— (2011). *Te Arawa Whānau Ora business case.* Rotorua: Te Arawa Whānau Ora.

——— (2012). *Case study: Te Ata Hou Trust.* Wellington: Te Ata Hou Charitable Trust.

——— (2013a). *Efficacy of using Poutama Trust's database for research on Māori business.* Wellington: Motu Economic and Public Policy Research and Poutama Trust.

——— (2013b). An interview with Ngaire Gallagher on the role of kaumatua in Māori entrepreneurship held on 7 November 2013. Palmerston North.

——— (2013c). What is the role of enterprise assistance in Māori entrepreneurship? A doctoral study of Māori entrepreneurs of Aotearoa New Zealand. *Meiji Business Review,* 60, pp. 137–159.

——— (2014). Manaakitanga: Is generosity killing Māori enterprises? In P. Davidsson (ed.), *Proceedings of the Australian Centre for Entrepreneurship Research Exchange Conference, UNSW, Sydney, Australia.* Brisbane: Queensland University of Technology, 4–7 February.

——— and O'Sullivan, J. G. (2014). A Māori approach to management: Contrasting traditional and modern Māori management practices in Aotearoa New Zealand. *Journal of Management and Organization,* 20(5), pp. 648–70.

———, Mckegg, K. and Smith, B. (2005). *Literature review: Research monitoring and evaluation model for Te Mangai Paho.* Wellington: Te Mangai Paho – Maori Broadcasting Funding Agency.

Mikaere, A. (2000). Māori and self-determination in Aotearoa/New Zealand. *Working Paper No. 5/2000.* Hamilton: University of Waikato.

Ministry for Culture and Heritage (2012a). *Impact:Māori and the Second World War.* Retrieved from: http://www.nzhistory.net.nz/war/maori-and-the-second-world-war/impact (accessed: 9 November 2013).

——— (2012b). *The Ngai Tahu claim: The Treaty in practice* Retrieved from: http://www.nzhistory.net.nz/politics/treaty/the-treaty-in-practice/ngai-tahu (accessed: 9 November 2013).

Ministry of Health (2013). *Report on the performance of general practitioners in Whānau Ora collectives as at September 2012*. Wellington: Ministry of Health.

Ministry of Tourism (2008). *Tourist activity: Māori cultural tourism*. Wellington: Ministry of Tourism.

Moon, P. (1993). *Māori social and economic history to the end of the nineteenth century*. Auckland: Huia.

———— (1998). The creation of the Sealord deal. *Journal of the Polynesian Society*, 107, pp. 145–174.

Mulligan, W., Mulligan, L. and Kimberley-Ward, N. (2004). *He mahi, he ritenga hei whakatinana i te tūrua pō 2004: Case studies. Māori organisations, business, governance and management practice*. Wellington: Te Puni Kōkiri and Federation of Māori Authorities.

Nana, G., Stokes, F. and Molano, W. (2011). *The asset base, income, expenditure and GDP of the 2010 Māori economy*. Wellington: Te Puni Kōkiri, BERL, and Māori Economic Taskforce.

New Zealand Māori Tourism Council (NZMTC). (2008). *New Zealand Māori Tourism Trade Manual 2008–2009*. Wellington: NZMTC.

Ngā Pae o Te Māramatanga/New Zealand's Māori Centre of Research Excellence (2012). *Annual report: Indigenous transformation through research excellence*. Auckland: Ngā Pae o te Māramatanga.

Ngarimu, K. (2009). *Māori Economic Workshop: Key themes*. Wellington: 28 January.

Nikora, T. R. (2003). *Ko wai a Tuhoe? statement of evidence of Tamaroa Raymond Nikora for Wai 36*. Wellington: Waitangi Tribunal.

———— (2009). *2nd Affidavit of Tamaroa Raymond Nikora*. Rotorua: Rangitauira.

New Zealand Institute of Economic Research (NZIER). (2003). *Māori economic development: Te ōhanga whanaketanga Māori*. Wellington: Te Puni Kōkiri.

O'Regan, H. (2001). *Ko Tahu ko au: Kai Tahu tribal identity*. Christchurch: Horomaka.

———— and Rangipuna, C. (2009). *Kura kaumātua: He hokika mahara/Recalling the memories*. Christchurch: Ake Associates.

O'Regan, T. (2009). Iwi economic development. In M. Te Pou (ed.) *Tūhoe Economic Summit*. Ōhope, 17–18 July.

O'Sullivan, J. G. and Mills, C. (2012). Using enterprise development stories to understand and encourage Maori entrepreneurship. *International Council for Small Business World Conference*. Wellington: 11–13 June.

Orange, C. (1987). *The Treaty of Waitangi*. Wellington: Allen & Unwin.

Parliamentary Service (2009). *New kaumātua for parliament appointed. Wellington, New Zealand Parliament*. Retrieved from: http://www.parliament.nz/en-nz/features/00NZPHomeNews070520091/new-kaum%C4%81tua-for-parliament-appointed (accessed: 9 November 2013).

Petrie, H. (2002). Colonisation and the involution of the Māori Economy. *XIII World Congress of Economic History*. Buenos Aires: University of Auckland.

Pihama, L. and Penehira, M. (2005). *Building baseline data on Maori, Whanau development and Maori realising their potential*. Auckland: Auckland Unisevices.

PricewaterhouseCoopers (PwC). (2013). *Growing the productive base of Māori freehold land*. Wellington: Ministry for Primary Industries.

Raerino, N. (1999). Pure and karakia as a window to Māori epistomology: Koi rō pure me karakia e oke ana. *Unpublished master's thesis*. Auckland: University of Auckland.

Reedy, T. (2000). Te reo Māori: The past 20 years and looking forward. *Oceanic Linguistics*, 39, pp. 157–68.

Rewi, P. (2010). *Whaikōrero: The world of Māori oratory*. Auckland: Auckland University Press.

Rogers, A. and Simpson, M. (eds) (1993). *Te tīmatanga – tātau tātau: Te Rōpu Wāhine Māori Toko i te Ora – early stories from founding members of the Māori Women's Welfare League*. Wellington: Williams.

Rogoff, E. G. (2009). The issues and opportunities of entrepreneurship after age 50. In S. J. Czaja and J. Sharit (eds), *Aging and work: Issues and implications in a changing landscape*. Baltimore, MD: Johns Hopkins University Press.

Ross, M. (1997). Entrepreneurs languish under tribal structure: Hereditary elders are not always the right people to drive a business. *National Business Review*, 28 February.

Rotherham, F. (1991). Doing business the Māori way. *National Business Review*, 30 August.

Royal, T. A. C. (2005). An organic arising: An interpretation of tikanga based upon the Māori creation traditions. *Traditional Knowledge and Research Ethics Conference*. Wellington: 10–12 June.

Ruwhiu, D. (2005). Creative counting: what makes indigenous business indigenous?. *International Association of Official Statistics Conference*. Wellington: 14–15 April.

Ryan, C. and Higgins, O. (2006). Experiencing cultural tourism: visitors at the Maori Arts and Crafts Institute, New Zealand. *Journal of Travel Research*, 44, pp. 308–17.

Schaniel, W. C. (1985). The Maori and the economic frontier: An economic history of the Maori of New Zealand, 1769–1840. *Unpublished PhD thesis*. Knoxville: University of Tennessee.

Smith, G. H. (1997). The development of kaupapa Māori: Theory and praxis. *Unpublished PhD thesis*. Auckland: University of Auckland.

Smith, L. T. (1999). *Decolonizing methodologies: Research and indigenous peoples*. London: Zed.

Spencer, S. and Broughton, P. (2008). *Māori commercial development for business*. Wellington: New Zealand Institute of Chartered Accountants.

Statics New Zealand (2012). *Tatauranga Umanga Māori: Consultation paper*. Wellington: Statistics New Zealand.

Stephens, M. (2001). *Victoria University of Wellington Law Review*. Retrieved from: http://lawisanass-wingate. blogspot.co.nz/2011/09/tohunga-suppression-act-1907.html (accessed: 9 November 2013).

Stokes, J. (2004). Non-Māori fans of Māori TV. *New Zealand Herald*, 25 June. Retrieved from: http://www. nzherald.co.nz/lifestyle/news/article.cfm?c_id=6&objectid=3574716 (accessed: 9 November 2013).

Taonui, R. (2012). Tribal organisation: The history of Māori social organisation. *Te Ara: The Encyclopedia of New Zealand* (updated 22 September 2012). Wellington: Ministry for Culture and Heritage.

Tapsell, P. and Woods, C. (2008). Potikitanga: indigenous entrepreneurship in a Maori context. *Journal of Enterprising Communities*, 2, pp. 192–203.

Tapsell, S. (1997). Is Maori management different? *Management*, 44(9), p. 46.

Tauroa, H. and Tauroa, P. (1986). *Te marae: A guide to customs and protocol*. Auckland: Reed Methuen.

Te Ohu Kai Moana (2003). *He kawai amokura: This report represents the full particulars of a model for the allocation of the fisheries settlement assets*. Wellington: Te Ohu Kai Moana.

Te Pumanawa Hauora (1996). *Oranga kaumātua: The health and wellbeing of older Māori*. Palmerston North: Massey University.

Te Puni Kokiri (2007a). *Ngā kaihanga hou: Maori future makers*. Wellington: Te Puni Kokiri.

——— (2007b). *Te tirohanga hou: Discovering the Māori edge*. Wellington: Te Puni Kokiri.

——— (2013). *Whānau Ora fact sheet*. Wellington: Te Puni Kokiri.

Tinirau, R. S. (2004). Te kōhao o te ngira: The eye of the needle – several research methods passing through one Kaupapa Māori orifice. *Qualitative Research in Business Symposium*. Auckland: Massey University, 3 December.

——— and Mika, J. P. (2012). Pinepine te kura: Nurturing Māori values and customs in business. *International Council of Small Business World Conference*. Wellington: 10–14 June.

Treaty Tribes Coalition (2009). Te Matau a Maui. *The 4th Annual Māori Fisheries Conference*. Napier: 6–7 April.

Tūhoe Fisheries Charitable Trust (2010). *Images of the trustees taken on the 17th June, 2010*. Tāneatua, New Zealand.

Turnbull, N. (2011). *Mā ngā uri ka ora: Growing healthy tamariki, whānau and hapū in Tūhoe communities*. Auckland: Health Research Council.

University of Otago (2008). *Maori business symposium: Intergenerational wealth: Re-igniting indigenous economies: Muramura ahi kaa ki uta, muramura ahi kaa ki tai*. Dunedin, 25–26 August.

Waitangi Tribunal (1988). *Report of the Waitangi Tribunal on the Muriwhenua Fisheries Claim: Wai 22*. Wellington: Waitangi Tribunal.

——— (1991). *The Ngāi Tahu report 1991*. Wellington: Waitangi Tribunal.

——— (1996). *The Taranaki report: Kaupapa Tuatahi, Wai 143*. Wellington: Waitangi Tribunal.

———— (2009). *Te Urewera: Pre-publication: Part I: Wai 894*. Wellington: Waitangi Tribunal.

Waldon, J. (2004). Oranga kaumātua: Perceptions of health in older Māori people. *Social Policy Journal of New Zealand*, December, pp. 167–180.

Walker, R. (1990). *Ka whawhai tonu matou: struggle without end*. Auckland: Penguin; rev. edn 2004.

Warren, K. T. R. (2009). *Once upon a tikanga:A literature review of early Māori business practice*. Palmerston North: Massey University.

Warriner, V. C. A. (1999). Is there a role for Māori cultural values in Maori exporting businesses? *Unpublished master's research report*. Palmerston North: Massey University.

———— (2007). The importance of traditional Maori values for necessity and opportunity: Maori entrepreneurs – iwi-based and individually owned. In L. P. Dana and R. B. Anderson (eds), *International handbook of research on indigenous entrepreneurship*. Cheltenham: Edward Elgar.

Webster, D. C. (1998). *Responsiveness to Māori*. Wellington: Wellington City Council and Māori Working Group.

Workman, K. (1995). Biculturalism in the public service: Revisiting Kaupapa. Department of Internal Affairs Maori Staff National Hui. Tapu Te Ranga Marae, Wellington: 27 April.

Yates, A. (2009). *Contemporary Māori business practices: A literature review*. Palmerston North: Massey University.

Young, C. (1992). *Māori business: What's the real story?* Auckland: NZ Business.

9

Factors Influencing the Creation of Enterprises and Success of Young Indigenous Entrepreneurs in Quebec and Labrador, Canada

Katia Iankova

Chapter Synopsis

Young Native families represent a growing and important segment of the population in the provinces of Quebec and Newfoundland and Labrador. Young Native entrepreneurs are of crucial importance for the economic development of Native communities in Canada due to their demographic weight and economic potential. The proposed work is targeted at better understanding the mechanisms of economic development in Native communities via the activities of young entrepreneurs. The objective is to identify the key factors of success for start-up businesses owned by Native youth in Quebec and Labrador, including interactions among family, friends and community that determine their sector of choice and characteristic activities. The project reflects recent tendencies of revival in aboriginal economies. The results of the research point out that the main factors of success for the young Native entrepreneurs of the two Canadian provinces, Quebec and Labrador, are: family and friends' support and encouragement; education and skills development; appropriate business networks; good understanding of the function of the funding bodies; good relationships with three levels of government – local, provincial and federal; training opportunities in and out of the communities; and last but not least, the creative and innovative spirit of the young Native businessmen and businesswomen.

Introduction

The proposed chapter reflects the results of a project started in 2009 and completed in 2010, and results in extending knowledge of indigenous economic development in Quebec and

Labrador, shedding light on the less studied field of the aboriginal economy, which in recent years has become of increasing importance for the First Nations themselves and for Canadian socio-economic development in general. Further, we hope to contribute to the understanding of the role of young Natives in this development and the economic inclusion of indigenous youth.

The primary objectives of the research are to (i) identify the factors for successful start-up businesses owned by Native youth in Quebec and Labrador; and (ii) identify the key obstacles to the creation of start-up enterprises. The research builds a knowledge base of the challenges faced by young Natives as they aspire to start and grow business enterprises. The targeted questions are: To what extent is there an influence from the community, friends and family in determining the choice of a business enterprise? What determines the economic sector of interest? How does the community and its relative proximity to urban centres affect decision-making?

Methodology

This study was funded by the Social Sciences and Humanities Research Council of Canada under the scheme of strategic grants: 'Northern Communities: Towards Social and Economic Prosperity'. With this project focusing on young Native entrepreneurs in Quebec and Labrador, we originated data that helped to produce a better understanding of the economic dynamic within the indigenous micro and small and medium enterprises (SMEs) started by young people belonging to the age group of 17–35 years old. This specific group is under-studied, but it is of crucial importance for the economic development of Native communities in Canada because of its demographic weight and economic potential. Young Native families represent a growing and important segment of the population in the provinces of Quebec and Newfoundland and Labrador. The research allowed an intercultural comparison and assessed the features common to the condition of indigenous entrepreneurship. This work also shed significant light on the less studied field of the Native economy, which in recent years has become of increasing importance for the First Nations themselves and for Canadian socio-economic development in general. The broad indigenous territory covered by the study and the bilingual character of the research made possible a cross-cultural comparison and identified particularities related to the ethnic affiliation and geographic position of the communities under study, which are situated in both urban and rural remote areas.

QUALITATIVE METHODS

The lack of scholarly research available on this topic informed our choice of qualitative research methods as the most appropriate for this project. This facilitated a deeper understanding of the successful indigenous businesses started by Native youth. Our previous research experience on topics related to aboriginal communities shows that qualitative research, and especially key-informant interviews, are the most appropriate approach regarding the specificity of research in aboriginal communities while giving very good results. The small size and the frequent cases of reticence of the communities needed a more personal approach as well as appropriate time to establish a relation of confidence and obtain optimal research results.

Semi-structured interviews were conducted with two types of key informant in the two provinces Quebec and Labrador for the period of time between the summers of 2009 and 2010. The languages of the interviews were French and English; the results are communicated in English for scholarly publications and in French and English for final reports, with the main findings returned to the communities.

1. Young entrepreneurs who have recently started a business from the communities of Kahnawake, Wendake, Mashteuiatsh, Chisasibi, Kuujjuaq in Quebec; and from Makkovik, Happy Valley – Goose Bay, Sheshatshiu, Natuashish, Makkovik, Hopedale, Postville and Nain in Labrador. The interview grid comprised questions about the economic and social conditions that encourage young people to create their own companies. Specific topics addressed (i) the reasons which motivate young people to create companies and which determine their choice of an economic sector; (ii) available financial, logistic, training and information resources and the lack thereof; (iii) the role played by the family and their social network in encouraging or discouraging young Native entrepreneurs to start a business.
2. Economic development agents from the band councils. These interviews supplemented the information derived from young Native entrepreneurs. The purpose of these interviews was to examine the point of view of the economic development professionals, which enriches the information obtained from aboriginal youth. Questions specifically addressed the community policies and programmes for support and employment of youth. They aimed at identifying key economic sectors and understanding the different realities in rural and urban communities.

Quebec and Labrador's Native Economic Realities

The economic growth of Quebec's indigenous communities is related to their geographical location relative to large economic provincial centres such as Montreal, Quebec City and Saguenay-Lac-Saint-Jean (Iankova, 2006). These centres significantly influence the development of smaller communities situated in their area. At the regional level, Wendake, Chisasibi, Kuujjuaq, Mashteuiatsh and Kahnawake – a network of five Native communities in Quebec – succeeded in building an infrastructure and creating successful economies during the last three decades. These initiatives required considerable government subsidies, following the signing of the James Bay Convention and the Peace of the Brave in 1975 and 2001 respectively.

With its strong demography of 4,000 people encompassing two communities, Cree and Inuit, Chisasibi represents a socio-economic node for Quebec's Cree communities. Similarly, Kuujjuaq unquestionably represents the northern capital of the Inuit of Nunavik and is their administrative and economic centre. In the future, Kuujjuaq is expected to play an important part in the urbanisation of the far north of Quebec province. It represents a strategic location in light of the possible opening of new northern maritime routes towards Europe and Russia (Hueber, 2002). Wendake is considered to be the capital of the American Indians of the province of Quebec. Situated 12 km from Quebec City centre, this community is one of the most prosperous within the province. It has a concentration of political power and major social institutions of Native communities living in Quebec (Noël, 1996). Mashteuiatsh, located in Saguenay-Lake-Saint-Jean, the economically most developed area in Quebec's Middle Nord, emerged as a local centre for the Innu-Montagnais communities and is considered the second most important node of regional development, after Wendake, for the French-speaking Native communities of Quebec. Kahnawake, with its 6,000 inhabitants, is located in the suburban area of Montreal. With socio-economic characteristics similar to those of Wendake, it is a central point for the Anglophone Amerindian communities of the south of Quebec.

The demographic and economic growth of these communities demonstrates the emergence of nodes of economic development among the indigenous peoples of Quebec. One of the obvious factors for their growth is the influence of the strong urban economy on reserves located near major cities (for example Wendake, Mashteuiatsh, Kahnawake). For reserves like Chisasibi or Kuujjuaq, located in remote areas far away from large cities, other factors come into play, in particular their demographic weight, government policies on regional development, and the conventions signed between the federal and provincial governments and the First Nations (Iankova, 2007).

Labrador's economy has been built around the resources of land and sea: the fishery, mining industries and hydro-electricity projects have been major contributors to Labrador's economy. Although the cod fishery has been closed since 1992, the fishery remains the most important employer for coastal communities. Recently, forestry and tourism have been taking over the economy (Destination Labrador, 2014). The Native communities populating Labrador belong to the Inuit and Innu nations, and are living in scattered small communities mainly located along the Atlantic coast. The biggest community is Nain; however, the Nunatsiavut government designated a smaller community as their capital – Hopedale, which is located considerably more in the south. The population of Labrador who declared indigenous identity was estimated to be 23,450 people, and the Native population living in the territories governed by the Nunatsiavut communities in 2013 were counted as consisting of 2,687 people (Statistics Canada, 2006). Most of the Native economic development projects are driven by the local government of the Nunatsiavut, which was constituted in 2005 and allowed the Inuit of the province to self-govern. The designation of the Torngat provincial park in 2006 opened new opportunities for eco, cultural, adventure and educational based tourism (Park Canada, 2008). In these communities are present some small industries such as construction, tourism, environmental services, retail, interior design, arts and crafts (Nunatsiavut Government, 2014).

Native Entrepreneurial Strategies and Youth

Data concerning the place of Native youth in economic development are very fragmentary. Studies conducted by government institutions such as Statistics Canada (2002) focus largely on general economic trends (e.g. demographics, employment data), but do not treat specifically the role of young people in economic renewal. There are several works which examine various aspects of aboriginal entrepreneurship. Wuttunee (1992) and Bherer et al. (1989) discuss the factors influencing the success of indigenous companies in Canada, but without specific reference to young entrepreneurs.

According to the results of the Harvard Project of aboriginal management, successful business depends on having adequate start-up funds, a supply of skilled workers, smart management, adequate infrastructure and a strong business network of aboriginal and non-aboriginal partners (Cornell, 2006). Proulx (2005) investigates the cultural and economic rebirth of Quebec's First Nations indicated by the increasing number of companies in the tertiary sector: administration, transport, construction, finances, computing and tourism. In addition to these sectors, the traditional activities of hunting and fishing still contribute to the economy and the maintenance of social stability of the Inuit societies of Northern Quebec (Martin, 2003). However, these activities have lost popularity among many young people, having more significance for identity affirmation than economic importance.

DEMOGRAPHIC IMPORTANCE

The indigenous population is increasing twice as quickly as the whole of the Canadian population: 56 per cent of the indigenous population is less than 24 years old, compared to 35 per cent of the

Canadian population (Lévesque et al., 2001). According to Industry Canada (1998), the majority of Native contractors are between 17 and 35 years of age; in this age segment, the business spirit is very pronounced. Young Natives are nearly 2.5 times more likely to become entrepreneurs than the average young Canadian. One reason for this interest in business is that, compared with the preceding generations, today's Natives are more likely to complete their secondary and university studies. Certain colleges and universities in Quebec and Canada offer special training for them, which facilitates their integration into the academic community and the success of their university studies (Assemblée National du Québec, 2007). This also gives them confidence and the initial tools necessary to later start their own business. Young, dynamic and educated, many of them return after graduation to their communities and start their own companies or are engaged immediately in community government (Iankova, 2006).

Between 2004 and 2014, the Ministry of Indian and Northern Affairs set up programmes aimed to help young Natives acquire work experience and improve their job-seeking skills (Aboriginal Affair and Northern Development, 2014). These special programmes have helped several indigenous youths from Ontario, Alberta, Manitoba, Saskatchewan, Labrador and Yukon to create their own companies in the domains of restaurant management, biopharmaceutical products, trade, visual arts and fashion. Two of these companies belong to young Natives from Quebec and Labrador: Randy Edmunds from Makkovik, owner of the hotel and restaurant Adlavik Inn; and Tammy Beauvais de Kahnawake, a fashion designer inspired by the Mohawk culture (Aboriginal Business Canada, 2007). A problem as identified by successful young aboriginal entrepreneurs is the lack of aftercare or guidance once their businesses become operational (Northern Development Ministers Forum, 2010). According to Redalph and Nielsen (1997), quoted by Swinney and Runyan (2007), common indigenous cultural values include high collectivism and low individualism, whereas entrepreneurial values are described as high in individualism and low in collectivism. Entrepreneurs may have an entrepreneurial orientation, favouring growth and profits; or a small business orientation, favouring quality of life and emotional attachment to the business (Swinney and Runyan, 2007). On the other hand, one stream of researchers describes the model of community-based enterprises as a successful fit to traditional Native values. Indeed, the experience with the creation of cooperatives was a tradition in Inuit communities of Quebec in the 1970s and 1980s (Iankova, 2006). According to Peredo and Chrisman (2006), the character of community-based enterprises is influenced by previously developed skills and experiences. They emphasise the need to simultaneously achieve social, economic, environmental and cultural goals. It also serves as an umbrella for local development, providing conditions for individual enterprise development.

The studies on youth are separately evolved from the economic studies. Literature abounds with studies concerning social issues such as violence, suicide, and alcohol and drug abuse. However, in the last five years researchers have started to be interested in the link between youth and community development. Johnston-Nicholson et al. (2004) as well as Rose and Giles (2007) discuss the concept of the 'six Cs' of positive youth development: competence, confidence, character, connection, caring and contribution. Rose and Giles (2007) investigated the role of the Alberta future leaders programme, and found that the six Cs are integral for both the short- and long-term benefit of youth personal development as leaders. We considered these concepts in developing the interview guide.

Indigenous Economy

The structure of the indigenous economies in Quebec and Labrador interestingly reminds one of the socialist types of economies because they are highly centralised, community profit driven, and state funded. The public sector is the biggest and the most powerful sector among the economic activities. Projects including general infrastructure and residential buildings have been booming in the last 10 years as the Canadian indigenous communities, because of the demographic pressure of growing communities, lack housing (sometimes families of 8–10 people live in the same house), and need public spaces such as community centres, hospitals and general infrastructure such as roads, sewerage and a potable water supply. Other types of community-owned companies operate in the hydro-electrical and forestry businesses, museums, centres of interpretation, administration, accommodation and tourist services. Cooperatives are more frequent in the Middle and Great North – especially popular are the food stores.

Private businesses are in the minority in the big economic picture, and would compete with difficulty against the powerful public economy. The private businesses find their niche in such activities as general stores, services, small industries such as petrol stations, accommodation, arts and crafts boutiques, crafts shops, performing art groups, restaurants, restored traditional villages, etc.

Tourism appeared to be one of the most preferred economic activities for the Native communities in Quebec, and is certainly most aspirational for those in Labrador as these communities perceive it to be a possible driver of economic development for their territories. During previous studies related to tourism, it was observed that there were very few young entrepreneurs in this sector, but there was a significant level of interest among young people to create business opportunities. The recreation, hospitality and catering sectors are some of the most attractive economic sectors for public and private indigenous investments (Iankova, 2005). Other sectors that appeal to Native peoples include transport, trade, the food industry based on the indigenous culinary tradition, arts and crafts, cultural events such as pow-wows, and the clothing industry or 'Native fashion'. Sports accessories, psychopharmacology and the treatment of certain diseases using traditional indigenous knowledge also represent areas of economic interest to indigenous peoples (Iankova, 2006).

Youth and Entrepreneurship: Factors of Success and Obstacles

The Native youth has a great sense of business; however, they lack experience, information and knowledge of how to start and sustain a business. As the most important and significant factor for start-up businesses, the respondents pointed out the moral support of their families, relatives and friends. In many of the cases, the families also financially supported the young entrepreneurs. For example, one of the interviewees recognised that her family allowed her to use the family house to start her small business and transform it into a Bed and Breakfast (B&B). This support is crucial as, among the indigenous communities in Quebec and Labrador, the 'capitalist' initiatives are viewed very often in a negative way by some or the majority of the community. Especially sensitive are the elders. One of the interviewees, an elder member, stated 'Money – they are evil thing coming from the white[s], they spoiled us and corrupted our values of sharing and mutual help'. This clash of perceptions is particularly strong and also expressed by some young entrepreneurs stating that in traditional societies such as the Natives, where the word of the elders has a weight and value of an unwritten law:

> It is very difficult to find our place in the sun and make our way in the community. By the time that our voice will be heard, we will be old and then we will not have so much energy and ideas to change the world..

Young entrepreneurs complained about being victims and being ostracised by their respective communities accusing them of suffering from the 'apple syndrome' – being red outside but white inside; in other words, having the red skin of indigenous people but having the white mentality of business orientation ('moneymaking'), which is akin to the white dominant society. Some of the youth shared their disappointment in the fact that many generations already express a backward mentality of perceiving themselves as being victims of the white man, without having overcome this resentment and being able to move forward in their lives. This has an impact on the youth's morale and the pace with which they carry out their businesses.

The intergenerational clash in business is particularly pronounced when it is related to the cultural and art businesses. One of the interviewees from Wendake, for example, complained that she needed the approval of the elders for her company producing traditional masks. Traditionally the masks are related to the evil and good spirit protectors of the community:

> All was well when I started to make the masks in traditional way as I was though by my elder pairs. However, when I wanted to innovate, to use some Japanese techniques and more modern materials, I faced huge resistance and I was banned to sell them in the community, accusing me that I was betraying the tribal traditions and spirit of my culture.

This resistance to innovative practices, although it cannot be generalised, is very pronounced in some localities and stops new ideas from emerging. At the same time, in the souvenir shops in the communities, cheap imitations of indigenous art produced in Mexico or China are for sale. When asking the shop owners whether this lack of authenticity bothered them, they answered that they make good money out if it and that 'the tourists are looking for cheap souvenirs as gifts'. The prevalent opinion was that as long as the origin is displayed on the label, they are honest with their customers. However, some of them were concerned about this false representation of their culture; and the big problem that they see coming is to compete today with the new sophisticated technologies that are able to 'exactly copy an original Inuit art and sell it ten times cheaper than an Inuit artists would do'. This is a big challenge for the local artists to place their original productions; but, as one of the managers stated: 'there are customers of any product and there always will be people that will be ready to pay more for an authentic Inuit art'. In fact, many of the local artists work in collaboration with art galleries in the cities in the south such as Montreal, Quebec City Corner Brook and St. Jones, where their art is sold much faster than in their communities. The problem is that the art galleries take too big a percentage (40 per cent) of the final price, 'only because they are geographically better situated'. In the most remote areas of Labrador, in Nain for example, some artists prefer to sell their products by directly contacting the visitors in the hotels or restaurants; but again this is a successful strategy only in the biggest Inuit community in Labrador, Nain, and in their capital, Hopedale. Most popular among tourists are Inuit jewellery and small statuettes from soapstone or Labradorite, a beautiful and unique stone that can be only found in Labrador. These are some of the reasons that young artists in Quebec and Labrador decide to 'play solo' and sell their products using social media advertising and creating websites connecting them to a larger international pool of customers selling via online payment systems such as PayPal and credit cards. Being more skilled in IT, or having friends within the community who study IT, they can innovate through new technologies.

Education and technical skills were the second biggest factor leading to the success of a start-up business. Not all of the respondents had university or college degrees. In fact, a quarter of them only had high school education; however, all of them recognised that a formal education or informal training is most helpful for business success as it gives them competitive advantages: first the knowledge necessary to start a business; but also all the skills learned at school for management and marketing the ideas and products and services derived from it. But university is recognised as not only beneficial for the skills related to the subject but also for the network that students would build during their university/college studies. A network with other indigenous and non-indigenous fellows is pointed out as important for their start-up business ideas as 'this circle of fellow friends would evolve to a network of business partners'. In indigenous communities in Canada, education is not at the top of the indigenous value systems. According to the respondents from the band councils and university officers, around half of the students at every level drop out of school. While this tendency is worrying, one of the student liaison officers, a Native herself, commented on it in a more positive way and tried to highlight a different angle to interpret the situation:

> Yes it is true that 50% drop school and Uni, but the other 50% stay, and those who stay, they return to their communities where they fill the numerous vacancies in the administration and management of their communities, others will start businesses and succeed.

The opportunities for training in existing businesses in the reserves were pointed out as another additional strategy for starting a new business. In fact the collectivism, still very strong in the mentality of indigenous people, implies mutual help and transmission of knowledge from elder to youth. This appears to be an opportunity for a kind of 'internship', a training within existing and well-established businesses in the reserves in order to provide some tools to start an enterprise. For example, a fine cuisine restaurant owner in Chisasibi told us that he 'helped a youngster to start a pizza place as he needed a support'. To my question whether he did not see the new business as a competition, he answered that 'there is enough bread for both of us', and also that the young businessman was not related with family ties to him. The partnership rather than the competition was underlined by all of the participants of the study as one of the key strategies in the indigenous business world.

Access to relevant information, namely to specific professional programmes and sources of funding, was another big factor leading to the commencement and the survival of a new business. The structure of existing channels of information communication is top-down – the programmes' funding comes from the two levels of government, federal and provincial; it arrives at the band council and is supposed to be communicated for the attention of all members of the community. It was stated, however, that not everyone has access to these governmental programmes for training or funding projects, as the information is not spread equally and only a fraction of the community knows about it. That is why it is very important to 'have connections' with the 'powerful of the day' in order to benefit from them. Favouritism and nepotism therefore appear to be among the worst obstacles hampering business development and healthy competition. The young entrepreneurs pointed out that some of the communities' members are advantaged and others disadvantaged and even discouraged by the band council from starting a business; but the abovementioned game of allocating information and grants selectively to relatives and friends of the local management and political powers cannot be generalised to all of the studied communities.

One of the interviewees, a young businesswoman from Labrador (with a high school level of education), shared that she was seeking help from an economic development agent in her community; but as she did not find the local officer very committed and engaged with her request, she ended up learning by herself with the aid of materials found on the internet on how to write a CV and make her own business website. In some of the cases, the sources of funding are clear; but the obstacle the entrepreneurs hit was that their business activities would not easily be funded by the banks as their businesses, being tourism and hospitality, are considered a high risk because of seasonality; and the fact that they could not guarantee the business in exchange for their house mortgage, as 99 per cent of the houses of the indigenous members living in reserves are state (community) owned, and are public property, therefore cannot be gauges in exchange for business loans.

Conclusion

Indigenous businesses need to evolve in today's globalised economy; and young entrepreneurs, more open than preceding generations, are better prepared for these realities. Better educated and comfortable with new technologies, they increasingly integrate them in their business models and operations. Innovative techniques in product development, marketing, advertisement and sales are used to increase their competitive advantages by connecting them to the global markets and thus giving them the chance to overcome the geographical remoteness. Creating websites connected to the main internet search engines increases the visibility of their businesses; credit card online payment systems are another favourite innovation that they adopt, especially for beauty and art products, the hospitality sector and music. For delivery they use the national mail services or international companies. Facing many internal problems of development, mainly related to the acceptance and approval of their own communities, the young Natives' businesses are striving to expand. Those who succeed in surviving during the first few years of their establishment usually persist and stabilise, operating successfully on the national and some on the international level. With a strong drive and motivation, young Natives in Quebec and Labrador are launching businesses in the new tertiary and creative industries sectors. Surprisingly, for the indigenous communities the young women are more business-oriented than the young men. This is a phenomenon that goes counter-current to the main tendency in Canada. During our project we could not find the reasons for this, having different, mostly anecdotal explanations from the young businesswomen like 'our men are good for nothing and are too lazy'. It is clear that the dynamic among young women is very strong and the friendship ties are tight. Nevertheless, serious and deeper further research is needed to understand the reasons behind these facts. The indigenous entrepreneurial realities and the young entrepreneurs' strategies are two topics which are very new and under-researched and deserve the attention of future studies, especially with the connection to creativity and innovation that they are capable of showing as business models and new products. They should be placed in the larger framework of global economic realities and new developments in business strategies.

References

Aboriginal Affair and Northern Development (2014). *Employment*. Retrieved from: https://www.aadnc-aandc.gc.ca/eng/1100100033784/1100100033788 (accessed: 19 November 2014).

Aboriginal Business Canada (ABC) (2007). *Profils des clients*. Retrieved from: http://strategis.ic.gc.ca/eic/site/abc-eac.nsf/fra/h_ab00075.html (accessed: 1 December 2013). (In French).

Assemblée nationale du Québec (2007). La réussite scolaire des autochtones. *Rapport et recommandations*. Quebec: Commission de l'éducation. (In French).

Bherer, H., Gagnon, S. and Roberge, J. (1989). *Wampoum et lettres patentes. Étude exploratoire de l'entreprenariat autocthone*. Quebec: Université Laval. (In French).

Cornell, S. (2006). Indigenous peoples, poverty and self-determination in Australia, New Zealand, Canada and the United States. *Joint Occasional Paper on Native Affairs-2006–02*. Tucson: Native Nations Institute for Leadership, Management, and Policy.

Destination Labrador (2014). *Labrador economy*. Retrieved from: http://www.destinationlabrador.com/guide/labrador_economy.htm (accessed: 11 November 2014).

Hueber, R. (2002). De nouveaux défis pour l'Arctic canadien. Le Nord canadien: le défi au changement. *Les cahiers du CRIC*, 6, pp. 30–35. (In French).

Iankova, K. (2005). Le tourisme autochtone au Québec. *Globe: revue internationale d'études québécoises*, 8(1), pp. 85–98. (In French).

——— (2006). Le tourisme et le développement économique des communautés autochtones du Québec. *Recherches amérindiennes au Québec*, 36(1), pp. 69–78. (In French).

——— (2007). Le tourisme urbain en milieu autochtone. Le cas de Wendake, une communauté amérindienne au Québec. *Unpublished PhD thesis*. Montreal: Université de Québec à Montréal (UQAM). (In French).

Industry Canada. (1998). *Les entrepreneurs autochtones du Canada: progrès et perspectives*. Retrieved from: https://www.ic.gc.ca/eic/site/eas-aes.nsf/vwapj/srmem199806f.pdf/$FILE/srmem199806f.pdf. (accessed: 1 December 2013). (In French).

Johnston-Nicholson, H., Collins, C. and Holmer, H. (2004). Youth as people: The protective aspects of youth development in after school settings. *Annals of the American Academy of Political and Social Science*, 591, pp. 55–71.

Lévesque, C., Trudeau, N., Bacon, J., Monpetit, C., Cheezo, M.-A., Lamontagne, M. and Sioui-Wawanoloath, C. (2001). *Les femmes autochtones et l'emploie: défis et enjeux des programmes d'employabilité au Québec. Recherche en matière de politique*, Ottawa: Condition féminine Canada. (In French).

Martin, T. (2003). *De la banquise au congélateur: mondialisation et culture au Nunavik*, Quebec: Université Laval. (In French).

Noël, M. (1996). *Amérindiens et Inuits, Saint-Laurent*. Quebec : Trécarré. (In French).

Northern Development Ministers Forum (2010). *Aboriginal youth entrepreneurship success factors and challenges*. Retrieved from: http://www.chnook.org/wp-content/uploads/2012/01/Aboriginal-Youth-Entrepreneurship-2010.pdf (accessed: 19 November 2014).

Nunatsiavut Government (2014). *Business: Building on our future*. Retrieved from: http://www.nunatsiavut.com/business/ (accessed: 1 December 2013).

Park Canada (2008). *Establishing Torngat Mountains National Park of Canada*. Quebec: Park Canada.

Peredo, A.-M. and Chrisman J. J. (2006). Toward a theory of community-based enterprise. *Academy of Management Review*, 31(2), pp. 309–328.

Proulx, M.-U. (2005). *La renaissance autochtone. L'annuaire du Québec 2006*. Montreal: Fides, pp. 521–529. (In French).

Rose, A. and Giles, R. A. (2007). Alberta's future leaders program: A case study of Aboriginal youth and community development. *Canadian Journal of Native Studies*, 27(2), pp. 425–450.

Statistics Canada (2002). *Profils des communautés de 2001. Diffusé le 27 juin 2002. Date de modification: 2005–11–30. No. 93F0053XIF au catalogue de Statistique Canada*. Retrieved from: http://www12.statcan.ca/english/Profil01/CP01/Index.cfm?Lang=F (accessed: 1 December 2013). (In French).

——— (2006). *Provincial/territorial distribution of aboriginal identity population: Census of population, 2006*. Retrieved from: http://www.statcan.gc.ca/pub/89–645-x/2010001/c-g/c-g004-eng.htm (accessed: 1 December 2013). (In French).

Swinney, J. and Runyan R. (2007). Native American entrepreneurs and strategic choice. *Journal of Developmental Entrepreneurship*, 12(3), pp. 257–273.

Wuttunee, W. A. (1992). *In business for ourselves: Northern entrepreneurs: Fifteen case studies of successful small Northern businesses*. Montreal: *McGill-Queen's University Press*.

PART III
SUSTAINABILITY AND INDIGENOUS TOURISM

10

Entrepreneurship in an Indigenous Community: Sustainable Tourism and Economic Development in a Newly Inscribed UNESCO World Heritage Site

Jin Hooi Chan, Ying Zhang, Tom McDonald, and Xiaoguang Qi

Chapter Synopsis

In June 2013, the Honghe Hani Rice Terraces in China were inscribed as a UNESCO World Cultural Landscape in recognition of their breathtaking beauty and the centuries-long sustainable relationship between the environment and indigenous communities stewarded by unique cultural and religious practices. Based on intensive fieldwork, this chapter discusses the environmental issues currently facing the rice terraces and communities, and the possible effects and implications following the UNESCO inscription. The chapter provides a comprehensive review of the intertwined social, cultural and environmental factors within the site, including out-migration, tourism development and the role of government, sustainability, governance, and entrepreneurship of the local indigenous community. The chapter argues that tourism development and the subsequent World Heritage Site inscription have overwhelmingly brought important effects for local communities, particularly while local communities display an enormous amount of ingenuity in addressing existing challenges and adapting to new opportunities. The benefits of development should be more widely distributed among the communities. This chapter thus highlights the critical role of providing the indigenous community with access to resources such as knowledge, skills and finance to enable greater involvement and participation, while making the case for acknowledgement of the different forms of participation and ownership.

Introduction

Indigenous tourism refers to tourism activity in which indigenous people are directly involved either through control and/or by having their culture serve as the essence of the attraction. The factor of control is a key one in any discussion of development, and tourism development is no exception to this rule. (Hinch and Butler, 1996: 9)

On 22 June 2013, the Cultural Landscape of the Honghe Hani Rice Terraces was granted World Heritage Site (WHS) status by the United Nations Educational, Scientific and Cultural Organization (UNESCO, 2013). The WHS is located in Yuanyang County, Honghe State in remote and mountainous terrain in the south of China's Yunnan province, bordering Vietnam. The area is an autonomous prefecture of the Hani and Yi ethnic minority groups, with its own distinctive socio-cultural practices and religions, in addition to those drawn from the main Chinese ethnic group, the *Han*.

More than anything else, the inscription marks a time when the site has garnered a high level of attention both inside China and worldwide, and it is also likely to be a pivotal point in the ongoing development and transformation of the area. In particular, the inscription highlights the likelihood that tourism will become an even more significant force of change in the economic, socio-cultural, and physical environment of the site. Tourist arrivals at the site had already experienced an explosive increase in the two years prior to the inscription, and this trend is generally predicted to continue to accelerate following WHS inscription (UNESCO, 2010; Herbert, 2001; Hall and Piggin, 2003; Yang et al., 2010). There have been a number of studies on various changes World Heritage Sites experience following their inscription (Hall and Piggin, 2001; Kim et al., 2007; Leask and Fyall, 2006; Rakic and Chambers, 2008; Ying and Zhou, 2007), with particular attention on tourism development, tourism management and conservation management which examined developments from the tourists' perspective (Jimura, 2011). However, only a few studies (e.g. Jimura, 2011) have concentrated on examining the impacts or changes in local communities.

Our focus on the potential effects of the new WHS status does not aim to ignore the fact that over a few years during the process leading to the inscription there were many concerted efforts in crafting policies for conservation, promotion, and management of the site. These include the publication of 'Measures for the Administration of the Conservation of Hani Rice Terrace No. 1' on 20 October 2011 by the Office of Honghe State People's Government and 'Guideline for Conservation Management of Hani Rice Terrace' on 1 July 2012 legislated by the Standing Committee of the Twelfth People's Congress of the Honghe State and Yunnan Province. Nonetheless, this moment provides a key junction at which to reflect on the history of the site, and the opportunities and challenges facing the area and local communities today, and to consider what direction the site may take in the future.

This chapter argues that the effect that WHS status can have on local communities is overwhelmingly important and cannot afford to be ignored. As in the case of the Honghe Rice Terraces, these impacts may often directly threaten the preservation of the site itself as well as generating new opportunities to address existing problems in the local communities. Taken as a whole, these positive effects need to be facilitated and nurtured to ensure they benefit local communities; but a number of important negative factors also need to be addressed to avoid further complications and irreversible damage. This chapter demonstrates that the contradictory effects of WHS status reflect the cultural complexity of the communities, as well as their dynamics with the newcomers, with which they draw their boundaries. We documented cases of how local people learnt new knowledge, skills, and entrepreneurial behaviours, which were brought in from other areas by newcomers such as tourists, tourism-related entities, or returning locals working in the cities. We propose that the local indigenous communities should be the nucleus of any development in shaping the future of this WHS.

This chapter realises the ingenuity of the local community in adapting to the new-found status of their locale as demonstrated by a number of successful cases with transformative effects on individuals. Although the benefits of development should be more widely distributed among the communities unfortunately this is impeded by the lack of access to resources such as knowledge, skills and finance. As such, we call for more involvement and participation between different actors in the Hani Rice Terraces to maximise opportunities for the transfer of knowledge between different agents, while realising that 'participation' may take a myriad forms – some more overt than others – which may include greater involvement and representation in carving the direction of the development; engagement in the economy; access to appropriate training and education; or the continuation of the ability to practise certain cultures or traditions. In addition to the local communities, various levels of local government, the state-appointed WHS operator, tourism operators, and the tourists themselves also play important roles to ensure a shared sustainable future for the WHS.

The chapter first describes the background of the site and the methodology deployed in this research. We then discuss the challenges and consequences of a serious change in the local communities, i.e. out-migration of young people. Next we analyse the key challenges of sustainable tourism development in the WHS to the natural environment and the indigenous society; and then how tourism is working to allay the fearsome negative effects of manpower draining. We analyse two cases – a government-entrusted destination operator and an indigenous entrepreneur – to see how changes were brought about and challenges to move ahead in the WHS. We then provide a summary of the analysis and conclusions.

The aim of this chapter is not to make a set of concrete recommendations and proposals for implementation, but instead to highlight several important issues pertaining to sustainability of the rice terrace, the economy of the communities, and tourism.

Background of the Research Site

The rice terraces are located within the WHS in Yuanyang County, Honghe Prefecture. They encompass some 16,603 hectares of core area and 29,501 hectares of buffer zone in the county – around latitude 102° 40' E, longitude 23° 05' N (UNESCO, 2013) – where there is an extensive concentration of magnificent rice terraces along the northern slopes of the Ailao Mountains (see Figure 10.1). There are 82 villages with a total population of about 50,000 in the area. The inscription as a WHS obviously represents a key moment in the history of this unique site, where this spectacular man-made rice ecosystem has existed for circa 1,300 years,[1] supported by an integrated cultural and religious concept of harmonious coexistence of the natural environment, villages, and the rice terraces.

The Ailao Mountain range runs northwest to southeast along the southern bank of the Hong River, which originates in Yunnan, flows through Vietnam, and drains into the Gulf of Tonkin. The highest point of the Ailao Mountains is more than 3,000 metres above sea level, and the majority of the peaks are over 2,000 metres. In the core area of the WHS, the upper slopes of the mountain (altitudes above 1,800 metres) are primarily forested, while the terraced rice fields are distributed in slopes from 700 to 1,800 metres. The slopes of the Ailao Mountains are generally very steep (see Figure 10.2). For instance, the slopes of the terraces at Pugaolao village (see Figure 10.1) range from 15 to 20 degrees.

---

1   This estimate is based on *Manshu*, a geographical report written at the end of the Tang Dynasty (AD 618–970) documenting minority ethnic groups practising ingenious forms of mountain farming in southern Yunnan. Unfortunately, this record lacks details of the exact location and type of ethnic minority. More reliable records on rice terraces and irrigation channels however only appeared during the Ming dynasty (AD 1368–1644) (Shimpei, 2007).

Figure 10.1   Honghe Hani Rice Terraces of Pugaolao village, Duoyishu, China
Source: Photographer Dehou Zhou, 2013.

Figure 10.2   Steep slopes of rice terraces at Laohuzui
Source: Photographer Dehou Zhou, 2013.

Different altitudes along these mountain slopes are occupied and cultivated by different ethnic communities. At the upper and middle slopes, the villages of *Hani* and *Yi* ethnicities are mostly sandwiched between the forested peaks and the paddy terraces. Thai villages are mainly concentrated at the lower alluvial plain of the Hong River. The altitudinal distribution of vegetation and the ethnic landscape are depicted in Figure 10.3.

This study concentrated on the rice terraces of the *Hani* and *Yi* ethnic groups in Yuanyang. *Hani* tend to cultivate and live at higher altitudes (from 1,400 to 1,800 metres), while *Yi* dwell and work on the terrace slopes below 1,600 metres (as shown in Figure 10.3). The difference in altitude has at least two geographical significances: average temperature and water resources. On the rice terraces an elevation difference of 1,000 metres could cause up to a 5.5 degree Celsius difference in average temperature. *Yi* farmers in Laohuzui – an ethnic *Yi*-dominated valley in spectacular rice terraces within the WHS – said that they had converted the traditional red rice variety to the modern improved white rice variety with a higher yield. However, the white variety is not growing well in the *Hani* terraces, which are at a higher altitude.

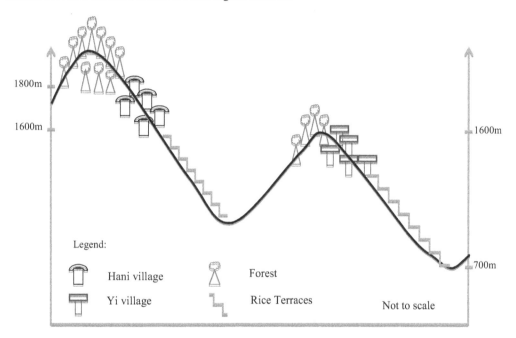

Figure 10.3 Schematic of altitudinal distribution of forest, villages, and rice terraces

Water, on the other hand, is an abundant resource in the area, with *Hani* land blessed with a forested mountain peak at an altitude higher than 1,800 metres. The sub-tropical region of Yunnan has two distinct seasons: a rainy season (May–October) with ample rainfall of over 1,800 millimetres annually; and a severe dry season. Owing to the humid, tropical climate of the area, water from the valleys at the base of the mountains evaporates and travels upwards, where the cooler air that surrounds the cloud forest at 1,800 metres causes the water to condense, turning into precipitation. Other than preventing erosion and landslides, the cloud forest also functions as a natural 'sponge', storing rainwater and ensuring year-round flow of springs and streams, which sustains the *Hani*'s rice terraces and villages located further down the mountain slopes.

Irrigation of the land below is achieved through a complex web of man-made drainage channels that distribute water from the mountain streams into the rice terraces. The terraces are themselves constructed out of compacted earth, which is moulded into mounds, creating long, thin, basin-like fields into which rice is planted. There is an overflow point somewhere in the rice terrace, which allows the water to flow down into the lower fields.

The irrigation system has also affected the structure of social life in the area, with the *Hani* establishing a democratic social system to manage the irrigation systems. Representatives from each household, led by elected irrigation foreman (*yiroharapo*), are responsible for the maintenance, operation, and appropriate distribution of water among the villagers by using water gates (*yika*). Apportioning water to different rice terraces in the proper way is particularly important for maintaining a fair system of distributing production resources during the dry season (Shimpei, 2007). In addition, through this complex web of intricate canals and sluices, each family channels wastewater that is produced from the household and domesticated animals and stored in small ponds beside homes to their own rice terraces as organic fertiliser. This endeavour has to be well coordinated among the villagers in order to avoid same-day discharge.

Most strikingly, these geographically significant features and environmental services have been well preserved for generations under the support of the socio-religious belief of the *Hani* people, which is precisely the reason cited for the area's inscription as a UNESCO World Heritage Cultural Landscape (UNESCO, 2013). There are a number of detailed anthropological studies on the culture and religion of the *Hani* people and of their rice terraces (e.g. Bouchery, 1996; Mao, 1991; Wang, 1999; Lu, 2011). We will not repeat these accounts at length here, but only wish to highlight the relevant cultural-religious aspects pertaining to the human–environment relationship. For instance, Bouchery (1996: 103) elucidated the establishment of a forested sanctuary housing the spirits whom the villagers enter into some sort of contractual relationship with at the formation of a new *Hani* settlement. Lu (2011) explains *Hani* religious elements of forest worship, and attributes these practices to the well-conserved forest, resulting in an ample water supply for the villages and rice terraces.

Although such anthropological accounts are extremely revealing of local cosmological and ideological understandings, equally we should not over-romanticise the life and the cultural landscape of *Hani* and *Yi* peasants through exotic accounts, which can sometimes ignore the physically demanding terrace agricultural practices and the extreme economic hardship experienced by some in the communities.

The indigenous communities and rice terraces face a unique set of challenges that place them in an especially precarious position. These challenges differ substantially from many other WHS (i.e. places of architectural interest, ancient cities) but with great similarity to the challenges of the Philippine Cordilleras rice terraces – a precedent to be reflected later in this chapter.

Research Methodology

We are all tourists. (Mintz, 1977: 59)

Minzu University of China sponsored our research team comprising three experienced Chinese and international scholars, two Chinese research assistants, and a local interpreter-guide who undertook intensive fieldwork in the *Yuanyang* rice terraces in June and July 2013. We met a wide variety of stakeholders in the site, including various levels of representatives from the Yunnan Expo Yuanyang Hani Terrace Tourism Development Co. (*Shibo-Yuanyang*), who have been entrusted by the government to develop and manage tourism activities in the WHS. We also met with owners and employees of a wide range of tourist accommodation in the scenic area, ranging from large state-owned, enterprise-backed hotel operations to small guesthouses.

We conducted 200 hours of audio-recorded interviews with local residents and community leaders from a number of villages, and with government officials from village, town, and county level. The interviews were mostly conducted in standard Chinese Mandarin (*Putonghua*); however, on occasion, our guide helped as interpreter, particularly when we interviewed local villagers who were unable to speak Putonghua. In addition to verbal interviews, we collected tourism and social related statistics from local agencies, took photographs, conducted observations, and engaged in unrecorded discussions in order to gain a better understanding of the site and the dynamics in the community.

Out-Migration and Declining Numbers of People Engaged in Rice Terrace Farming

The rice terraces and their socio-environmental co-existence are the primary reasons why UNESCO bestowed the World Cultural Landscape Heritage status, and the terraces are also the main attraction for tourists. As discussed above, despite being breathtakingly beautiful, these rice terraces are also incredibly fragile and the communities are encountering several unprecedented challenges in their efforts to preserve them. In this section we analyse the problems faced by the communities due to the high rate of out-migration of young people.

REASONS FOR OUT-MIGRATION

Many of the young people that we spoke to in the scenic area who were thinking of leaving or had previously left tended to cite finding employment as the main reason for migration to outside areas. In fact, local community leaders place the proportion of young people leaving the area at around 80 per cent. This has partly been caused by the migration of young people to the outside area, with the problem further compounded by other local people moving out of agriculture into other more profitable local industries, chiefly tourism-related sectors.

What then are the main reasons for out-migration? The arduous nature of rice cultivation in the terraces, combined with the relatively low earnings, has meant that in recent years the number of local people choosing not to engage in rice terrace farming has been growing quite significantly. The terrain is rough, with more than a 400 metre drop (approximately 100 'storeys' of terraces) in altitude from the village at the top of the terraces to the lowest terrace. The terraces are also extremely fragile and require incredibly high levels of constant maintenance with the input of hard labour. Moreover, there is minimal scope for mechanisation in this type of terrain. Since household farm size is small, single households are typically unable to cultivate large fields, in addition to constraints on land resources on the mountain slopes.

The output of the rice terraces hardly matches the input of household labour. The annual yield of rice is generally low, with only one harvest per year for the non-engineered traditional variety of red rice. *Yi* farmers in the Laohuzui area of the WHS changed their traditional varieties to modern white rice varieties in the 1970s but the *Hani* chose not do so, owing to the white rice varieties not growing well at the higher altitudes of the *Hani*'s terraces. Many villages complained that the harvest is generally barely sufficient for a household's annual consumption.

Most farmers need to supplement their 'household income' through animal husbandry, e.g. by raising pigs and ducks, along with fish and other sources of protein from the inundated rice fields. The animals are mostly left to roam the village, with the waste they produce creating a further set of problems: it raises hygienic concerns, and is particularly seen by tourists and government officials as damaging the aesthetic value of the villages.

IMPLICATIONS OF OUT-MIGRATION

The communities in the rice terraces are living agents who carry 'codes of culture', along with their knowledge and experience of terrace agriculture, which maintain the balance of co-existence with the natural environment. Therefore, the fragility of the current state of these communities due to out-migration is, of course, an issue of particular concern, which directly impacts upon the preservation of the rice terraces. Literature has documented many cases of rural out-migration, in China and globally, and discussed the implications (Connelly et al., 2010). A parallel example is the rice terraces of the Philippine Cordilleras, formerly listed as an endangered heritage site by UNESCO (2001), in response to the rice terraces and irrigation system becoming degraded and being unrepaired. Some *Ifugao* villages in the area abandoned rice planting on the terraces, converting to cash-earning vegetables or migrating out of this rural mountain to the 'modern world' in order to find a better livelihood.

Some watersheds also experienced deforestation and erosion. Villalon (2012) suggests that the main shortcoming in earlier management practices was the relevant national authorities who, while conserving the terraces as a monument, failed to see them as a living site with the complexity of maintaining traditional values under the pressures of modernisation and economic hardship experienced by the community.

The pressures and degrees of out-migration experienced in Honghe WHS as discussed in the earlier part of this section occur for similar reasons to those of the Philippine Cordilleras. Subsequently, we therefore examine the implications of out-migration on the economy and sustainability of the Honghe rice terraces, with reflection on the contemporary issues of rural out-migration under the larger context of Chinese society.

With the declining number of individuals involved in rice terrace farming, the remaining agriculturalists have been stretched to cultivate the existing land. Most importantly, they are left with far less time to carry out maintenance and construction of the rice terrace walls. Local farmers explained to us the significant issues relating to maintaining the terraces.

In addition, the migration of individuals to the outside world is a cause for concern precisely because of the challenges that arise with regard to the transmission of *Hani* 'culture'. Particularly with regard to agriculture, as was mentioned before, the reluctance of young people to remain in the local area has meant that fewer of these people possess the skills and knowledge required to maintain the rice terraces.

THE INEVITABILITY OF OUT-MIGRATION AND THE BENEFITS OF MIGRATION

However, relates to in with national trends, and that in many cases migration (and particularly for young people) can also be positive and is as much about the transformative effects on the self as it is about employment, with migration offering opportunities for new experiences; access to and consumption of new goods; and romantic relationships and freedom from parents that are not available in the local area (Jacka, 2005).

It is worth remembering that some external migration is perhaps somewhat inevitable and can, at times, be extremely beneficial to both migrants and the region they migrate from. For example, the economic migrant brings back cash earned with their labour in the city and reinvests in the village, for instance by constructing homes or guesthouses. There is much evidence to suggest that in China much migration is this type of circular migration, with migrants eventually returning to their place of origin, bringing with them new skills and ideas from outside (Connelly et al., 2010; Zhang, 1999). For instance, the diffusion of a solar hot water system in the villages is partly due to the migrants who adopted the idea and have economic power to install it for their families in the villages. Its adoption has, on the one hand, altered the villagers' showering habits. On the other hand, it provides badly needed hot water for preparing animal feed, and therefore reduces the consumption of firewood harvested from the precious water-holding forest.

It is nonetheless important to note that more local employment opportunities, training, and entertainment for young people may help to stem the flow of persons away from the area. In the next two sections, we shall examine the potential of tourism and the opportunities available to transform not only individuals but also the structure of employment and economic activities in the area.

Tourism Development and Sustainability

The status of World Heritage Site attracts a substantial number of visitors, and almost every site is a significant tourism destination (UNESCO, 2010). It has been well regarded as a complementary tool for economic and social development in indigenous and rural communities, whether within a WHS or not, by many researchers, practitioners, politicians, government bureaucrats, and relevant communities themselves (Briedenhann and Wickens, 2004; MacDonald and Jolliffe, 2003; Ying and Zhou, 2007).

However, just as there are opportunities, there are threats from the expansion of tourism too. A threat to the Yuanyang rice terraces could come simply in the form of increasing visitor numbers and increasing touristic exploitation of the rice terraces and their culture. The numbers of tourists visiting the terraces has increased markedly in recent years, and is expected to do so even more in the future due to the widely publicised inscription as an UNESCO World Cultural Landscape, as well as improvements in transport infrastructure, including a new access road to the site and muted talk of an airport for Honghe, the county seat. *Shibo-Yuanyang* has built an official entrance to the site at Qingkou along the main road to the county capital, Nansha, and former capital Xinjie town.

The number of visitors captured by the official entrance ticket sales to the WHS clearly suggests an exponential increase over the past five years. Prior to inscription as a WHS, the number of people entering the scenic area recorded by *Shibo-Yuanyang* has increased from 32,000 in 2009 (when it was first recorded) to over 140,000 annually in 2012: about three times the local population, with a total of RMB 6.7 million in entrance fees collected.[2] The County Tourism Office and *Shibo-Yuanyang* predict a substantial increase in tourist arrivals in the coming years. The exponential increase in tourist numbers has strongly indicated the potential mounting challenges in managing the WHS sustainably.

Firstly, the increased visitor numbers have brought a set of significant environmental challenges and resource pressures. These include an increase in the amount of solid waste and litter left behind by visitors – not only that which is correctly disposed of but also that which is discarded by the roadside and in the WHS. Based on the interviews conducted, there were recurring concerns about the need to improve collection of solid waste; however, this could be planned and managed accordingly without much difficulty. The main challenge would be the pressure on proper disposal of the collected waste – such as land availability and pollution potential of landfill – or any other treatment pathways.

---

2   Income from ticket sales in 2012 was RMB 6.7 million, with a total of 132,000 people purchasing an entry ticket. There are several types of ticket with different prices, and about 10,000 people are exempt from payment (e.g. government officers). Estimated tourist income from food and accommodation providers was RMB 450,000 in 2010 rising to RMB 1.8 million in 2012, catering for 43,739 customers (data from the County Tourism Office triangulated with data from *Shibo-Yuanyang*). The figures suggest a substantial tourist income for this rather remote mountain region.

The increased number of visitors in the settlements in the WHS also places unique demands on the infrastructure that supports tourism: for instance, increasing demands for tap water (currently fed by untreated spring water in most villages) and the competing demands for water during the dry season, which coincides with the annual peak tourist season. Other important amenities required are those such as electricity and hot water for washing, and problems with dealing with sewage and wastewater at a site lacking a properly integrated sewage processing system.

With the increasing popularity of this WHS, we noted increasing pressure on the property market. Even in the very first few days of UNESCO inscription at the time we arrived at the WHS, the interviewees informed us of the increasing number of enquiries for renting properties to be refurbished as guesthouses, which also leads to the increasing pressure on rents.

It is nearly impossible for any small entrepreneur to obtain permission for the construction of new buildings within the WHS. The local government prohibits new building, and the site's Guideline for Conservation Management strongly discourages any constructions by imposing regulatory approval hurdles as well as instituting stringent controls on retrofitting any existing building.

However, the guideline falls short of regulating renting of traditional dwellings in the WHS. Some villagers – who see a good business opportunity in providing accommodation to the increasing number of tourists – rent their dwellings to individuals and businesses, mostly newcomers to the WHS. In addition, it is not unreasonable to foresee a gradual expansion of this kind of rental arrangement under this optimism in the tourism sector. All guesthouse owners we interviewed said that they were fully booked during the peak season. Indeed, some of their guests have to put up with sleeping on whatever space is available in the guesthouse.

As rental is normally under long-term contract (usually 10–20 years) with a flat rate, it is susceptible to future dispute, particularly when the market rate for rent increases sharply due to the limited supply of properties in the WHS. Furthermore, if such renting arrangement in the WHS becomes truly widespread, it also runs the risk of effectually 'buying-out' the villagers from their own hometowns. Despite renting out dwellings providing a stable income for the villagers, they have to move to the neighbouring town away from the rice terrace ecosystem. We noticed a few tightly locked guesthouses during our fieldwork, which only open for business during the peak tourist season. In the extreme case, there is a possibility that villages could become 'ghost villages' only populated by tourism operators and tourists seasonally. This type of tourism gentrification is not uncommon in many tourist areas around the world. There has been discussion of 'relocating' the entire village to a nearby vicinity, but this has not been implemented as no suitable land has been identified.

The 'hollowing out' of villages renders a blanched landscape not only thin in cultural value, but also prone to environmental degradation. Villagers are the lifeline of the rice terraces, and the carriers and transmitters of the *Hani*'s culture and religion. Gentrification might not deter tourist arrivals in other vicinities but the sustainability of the landscape would be in question without the villages.

Tourism has also brought with it specific sets of touristic material culture familiar from other parts of China. Xinjie, the main town accessing the scenic area, now features multiple large, luxury hotels, shops, restaurants and karaoke bars. This is clearly a mixed blessing. On the one hand, all these institutions create jobs for local people to serve tourists and bring considerable money into the local economy. On the other hand, the increase in the tourist trade also tends to take more people away from agriculture, further underlining the precarious nature of the rice terraces. The architecture and styles of these developments can sometimes jar considerably when placed against the local landscape, although there have been limited efforts to create forms of hotel that fit more sympathetically into the local environment – such as by limiting the use of concrete for building and reintroducing thatched roofs into the rural landscape – but these remain the exception rather than the rule.

Economy of Tourism and its Agencies

The sustainability of tourism activity in many heritage sites is of great concern to UNESCO. Apart from many conservation challenges, there are questions raised on tourism development in indigenous areas in regard to the distribution of economic benefit and socio-environmental costs to the local community. Tourism academics have long advocated that community participation or involvement is conducive to ensuring fairness in benefit distribution and therefore sustainability in tourism development (Briedenhann and Wickens, 2004; Garrod et al., 2012).

There is, however, a lack of inclusion of rural residents in the decision-making process of tourism development (Prentice, 1993), particularly in developing countries. It has also been argued that community democratic participation could be both manipulated and difficult to implement due to institutional constraints in developing countries (Tosun, 2000; Ying and Zhou, 2007).

In this section, we explore the above concerns about tourism development in this newly inscribed WHS. We firstly provide a case of how the government appointed a site operator, *Shibo-Yuanyang*, to work on concerns sych as sharing benefits with local communities, providing employment, and engaging local communities in the tourism activities in the WHS. Then we discuss a case of a life-transforming experience of an indigenous entrepreneur, highlighting the possibilities of improving not only out-migration but also the socio-economy of the locals.

Government-Appointed Site Operator

The government-appointed site operator plays an important role in promoting tourism economy in many destinations in China, moving away from direct state management of protected sites, and ensuring the sustainability of the WHS. The local government appointed the Yunnan Expo Yuanyang Hani Terrace Tourism Development Company (*Shibo-Yuanyang*) to develop and manage tourism activities in the WHS. *Shibo-Yuanyang* was established in 2008 as a joint venture of the Yunnan World Expo Tourism Holding Group (*Yunnan Shibo Lvyou Konggu Jituan*) and the Yuanyang county state-owned asset management company (66.6 and 33.3 per cent respectively). The group is a well-established state-owned tourism conglomerate based in the capital of Yunnan province. It brings not only a vast network of supporting industries along the tourism value chain but also extensive experience in developing and managing tourism destinations.

Building on the experience of running various tourism destinations across the province, *Shibo-Yuanyang* understands very well the necessity to share the fruits of tourism development and economic incomes with the indigenous communities. One of the top managers of *Shibo-Yuanyang* emphasised that the company's purpose is to share the benefit of tourism development with the locals:

> *I say we are one – bonded together in an organic way. We also shoulder some responsibility to take care of the locals. I can't say it will be poverty eradication, but it is mutual development and sharing the benefit of [tourism] development ... in the meantime the locals will also be involved in the tourism development. (translated from Chinese)*

Sharing of development benefits could be achieved in a number of ways. The company collects entrance fees from tourists – and data has shown that fees have increased substantially; 5 per cent of the collection is to be used for indigenous community development. Unfortunately, this 5 per cent of income is injected into the pot of local government finance without being clearly earmarked – or at least it has not been seen as so, commented a community leader. Of course, at this early stage of tourism development the investment from local government might be much higher than the 5 per cent collection as claimed by the government official. This unspecified budgetary arrangement is unfortunately very common in China (Li et al., 2008). Nonetheless, transparency of budget management could possibly enhance the working relationship among the stakeholders. Moreover, it will help in the understanding of the financial sustainability of the WHS to ensure not only sharing of benefits with the local communities but also providing funds for the proper conservation and maintenance of the site (Steckenreuter and Wolf, 2013). Lack of funding for conservation of the site – either from the overtly low collections or from the government – has resulted in substantial deterioration of the quality of value the site has to offer, as observed by Li et al. (2008) and Zhang (2002).

The company also sees the importance of providing employment and training to the local communities. They noted a few cases of local people gaining more experience of catering to tourists and increasing responsibility. For instance, two of the newly promoted local executives were sent to the provincial capital to market the destination. When asked about local recruitment, a manager said that:

> Apart from a few of us [senior managers] who come from the provincial capital, about 95 per cent of middle managers are locals. We also continuously provide training to the locals, take them to other tourist destinations to observe and learn, as well as share our experience with them. (translated from Chinese)

Nevertheless, it is more challenging working with the wider communities. Despite efforts in promoting interaction with indigenous people, the company does not have a professional specialising in community participation. Their efforts are ad hoc and their roles are ambiguous (even to themselves), as the responsibility of community development rests within the overarching state apparatus at various levels of government, from prefecture to village level. A manager commented as follows:

> We also continually provide training to the local people. We take them to other tourist destinations to learn about development experience there. We also share our experience with them. We meet with the village organisations – the village committee, the local people, at least once a year … However, the local people and community development are the responsibility of the village committee and the government. We cannot do much. (translated from Chinese)

There are of course some conflicting interests in implementing certain measures to promote tourism by the company. For instance, the company has purchased a fleet of electric minibuses in order to provide environmentally friendly eco-transport for every visitor entering the WHS. However, this measure, even though well intended, has received objection from existing minivan operators in the WHS who pick up tourists in the neighbouring towns. Those operators are either small guesthouse owners or supply tourists to these guesthouses. By the time our research team left the site in July 2013, both parties had yet to arrive at an amicable solution. We believe that it would have been easier to find a solution through better involvement of various stakeholders, and their interests being taken on board in the decision-making process of purchasing the electric minibus.

Indigenous Entrepreneurship in the Tourism Sectors

> To me, cultures were never fixed, enclosed units or homogeneous, integrated entities. (Bruner, 2005: 9)

The involvement of indigenous people in the tourism sector has always been seen as a way of improving the livelihood of local people and transferring the benefits of tourism development to them. There are cases of indigenous entrepreneurs who run restaurants and guesthouses, and provide transport services, as minivan drivers or owners, or as tour guides. Here, we present a case study of a young indigenous entrepreneur whose life has been transformed by the arrival of tourists.

Marshall is a young married man of *Hani* ethnicity in his mid-twenties who, in co-operation with his family, runs two guesthouses in his home village within the WHS.[3] Their second guesthouse had opened a few months before we undertook our fieldwork. Marshall explained to us that his decision to become a tourism entrepreneur was by no means a carefully planned out one, but rather highlighted several key points in his life where interactions with others helped him become more aware of the entrepreneurial way of life and inspired him to follow this course of action.

Marshall related that he had struggled in formal education, having only reached the fourth year of primary school before giving up studying. He used to skip classes to ask tourists for money, and recalled how one day a local woman who ran a restaurant told him not to ask tourists for money because it would make them uncomfortable. Instead she told him to sell boiled eggs or rice noodles to the tourists. So, from that time, Marshall started selling around 100 boiled eggs per day. He recalled his sales pitch during that period:

> I would not say 'Uncle, Auntie, can you buy my eggs?' Instead I would say 'Uncle, auntie, can you swap your money for my eggs, I want to go and pay my tuition fees!'

He carried on selling eggs to tourists until he was into his teens, but during this time also started to guide visitors around the different areas and villages of the WHS, helping carry photography equipment for the tourists. Through this period of interaction with tourists, he gradually came to know better what kind of experiences they wanted and requirements they had. For instance, he learnt not only what kind of scenery most of the tourists wanted to see and where the best spots for photography were, but also photographic skills. He had soon become one of the most popular tourist guides within the WHS. With his many returning customers and friends, new ideas developed:

> At the time I started to guide tourists, the tourists would say 'Marshall, how about we have lunch at your house?!' I would be very happy … after eating they would say that it was fine and they wouldn't go to other places; instead they would stay for the night at the house, the business slowly started in this way.

In this example a key diffusing agent of touristic knowledge are the visitors themselves, who bring with them into the WHS sets of expectations and requirements garnered from touristic experiences that they have had elsewhere. Clearly being able to interact with these visitors helped Marshall develop more innovations in the local tourism sector, and has led to greater integration of the locals in the tourism sector within wider national and international industries.

Owing to the lack of adequate parking near their home, Marshall undertook a 15-year lease on a new property in the village. This has been a significant commitment for Marshall, and for the initial rent and decoration he and some friends invested hundreds of thousands of Chinese Yuan. In addition, there is an annual rent of tens of thousands. He was very worried about the amount he had committed to; however, these fears have been allayed by the outcome of the WHS application. Marshall described being absolutely elated upon hearing that the rice terraces had received their

---

3   The entrepreneur's real name has been changed in order to protect the subject of the research.

inscription, confirming his belief that the number of visitors was bound to increase year-on-year. As such, Marshall very much sees his future as remaining in the rice terraces:

> In reality there is no need to leave here. I just want to remain in this beautiful place. It doesn't matter if I earn a lot of money or not; if I were to leave, I would miss home so much. My ideal is to follow the development of tourism here.

Marshall does not see competition as a problem, and cites the Lijiang and Dali areas of his province as good examples of how tourism can develop well, with what he judges to be every family in those places participating in the tourist industry. He explains that he would be happy to share his knowledge about conducting tourism operations with other people from the area to help them also succeed in the tourism industry. Marshall acknowledges the help of others in his application. He explains that many people in the village are preparing to enter the tourism industry, and that he, like many other families, received a grant worth tens of thousands of Yuan as part of a government 'beautiful home' programme to beautify their homes. In addition, he also highlighted being able to receive an interest-free grant from the government to work on his new project.

Conclusion

> Tourists travel to consume 'experiences which are different from those typically encountered in everyday life'. (Urry, 1990: 1)

Irrespective of whether John Urry is right about the expectation of Chinese or international tourists – despite this expectation being complex, multi-faceted, and in flux – a tourism-based economy of the indigenous people in the WHS could only be sustained if the local residents are willing partners in the process. Further, Allen et al. (1988) propose that the indigenous people's attitudes toward tourism and their perceptions of its impact on their life and community must be understood and continually assessed.

Firstly, the difficulty in community participation in rural tourism in China has been documented in particular as 'not easily' implemented (Ying and Zhou, 2007; Wang et al., 2010; Yang et al., 2013). Even though there are various levels of community participation in the WHS, there are a few possible improvements – such as more concerted efforts and involvement of community participation professionals. In addition, in order to avoid conflict, such as the electric minibus case in the WHS, we propose that early involvement of the indigenous people in the decision-making process might be able to diffuse potential disagreement to arrive at an amicable solution.

We have demonstrated in the above case that it is crucial not only that fairness of benefit distribution must be done, but also that fairness must be *seen* to be done – the criteria of transparency. Ying and Zhou (2007) have proposed that some sorts of property rights have to be formally legislated where the rights of tourism development and operation as well as its subsequent distribution of benefits are clearly defined for all stakeholders, be they the communities, the governments, or the external capitals. In our case study, we have noticed the efforts in benefit distribution, providing employment and training as well as entrepreneurial opportunities. But, in agreement with Ying and Zhou (2007), we have yet to see any clarity in terms of the issues of rights and (perceived) fairness of benefit distribution. Who has the exclusive right to the scenery of the rice terraces and the cultural elements of the *Hani* people?

In the case of the *Hani*'s entrepreneurs, we have demonstrated the possibility of successful self-transformation in improving the livelihood of indigenous people in tourism. As in Franz Boas' concept of fluidity and dynamism of culture, we see that willing changes occurred in the interaction between the indigenous people and the tourists. The exchange of indigenous people and tourists is nonetheless beyond solely an economic transaction. By cultivation of entrepreneurial spirit of the indigenous people, there is the potential for substantial economic contribution, which is crucial for the continuity of rice terrace livelihood and culture, and possibly for reducing out-migration. Notably, the life transformation experience of Marshall is not only pulling him out of poverty but also fulfilling from his own perspective. It is inspirational for the indigenous communities, particularly for the young children who are selling things or begging from visitors at many tourist destinations throughout the developing world. In addition, what endeared us most to Marshall was that he seemed to have a completely different notion of property right based on trust and sharing. This is in contrast to the notion of legislated property rights for power and benefit distribution discussed by Ying and Zhou (2007). How could we reconcile and move forward with these competing logics? This remains to be understood.

According to Malinowski (1961: 25), the chief goal of an anthropologist was 'to grasp the native's point of view, his relation to life, to realise his vision of his world'. Similarly, in the quest for development, the chief goal of researchers, government officials, planners, *Shibo-Yuanyang*, newcomers, tourists, and the indigenous people themselves is to understand the needs and vision of the indigenous communities, and then to provide the necessary resources, support, and training for them to realise their aspirations. It must be acknowledged that these two groups of newcomers – *Shibo-Yuanyang* and small guesthouse and business owners – brought new resources, ideas, and investment into the community. Most of those are transferable, and we witness local entrepreneurs – among them local returners who once left to work in the cities – seizing opportunities and imitating business models and ideas as they learn to start their own businesses and run their own establishments.

References

Allen, L. R., Long, P. T., Perdue, R. R. and Kieselbach, S. (1988). The impact of tourism development on residents' perceptions of community life. *Journal of Travel Research*, 27(1), pp. 16–21.

Bouchery, P. (1996). The relationship between society and nature among the Hani people of China. In B. Formoso (ed.), *The link with nature and divine mediations in Asia*. Oxford: Berghahn, pp. 99–116.

Briedenhann, J. and Wickens, E. (2004). Tourism routes as a tool for the economic development of rural areas: Vibrant hope or impossible dream? *Tourism Management*, 25(1), pp. 71–79.

Bruner, E. M. (2005). *Culture on tour: Ethnographies of travel*. Chicago: University of Chicago Press.

Connelly, R., Roberts, K., and Zhenzhen, Z. (2010). The impact of circular migration on the position of married women in rural China. *Feminist Economics*, 16(1), pp. 3–41.

Garrod, B., Fyall, A., Leask, A. and Reid, E. (2012). Engaging residents as stakeholders of the visitor attraction. *Tourism Management*, 33(5), pp. 1159–1173.

Hall, C. M. and Piggin, R. (2001). Tourism and world heritage in OECD countries. *Tourism Recreation Research*, 26(1), pp. 103–105.

——— (2003). World heritage sites: Managing the brand. In A. Fyall, B. Garrod, and A. Leask (eds), *Managing visitor attractions: New direction*. Oxford: Butterworth-Heinemann.

Herbert D. (2001). Literary places, tourism and the heritage experience. *Annals of Tourism Research*, 28(2), pp. 312–333.

Hinch, T. and Butler, R. (1996). Indigenous tourism: A common ground for discussion. In R. Butler and T. Hinch (eds), *Tourism and indigenous peoples*. London: International Thomas Business, pp. 3–21.

Jacka, T. (2005). *Rural women in urban China: Gender, migration, and social change*. Armonk, NY: Sharpe.

Jimura, J. (2011). The impact of World Heritage Site designation on local communities: A case study of Ogimachi, Shirakawa-mura, Japan. *Tourism Management*, 32(2), pp. 288–296.

Kim, S. S., Wong, K. K. F. and Cho, M. (2007). Assessing the economic value of a world heritage site and willingness-to-pay determinants: A case of Changdeok Palace. *Tourism Management*, 28(1), pp. 317–322.

Leask, A. and Fyall, A. (2006). *Managing World Heritage Sites*. Oxford: Butterworth-Heinemann.

Li, M., Wu, B. and Cai, L. (2008). Tourism development of World Heritage Sites in China: A geographical perspective. *Tourism Management*, 29(2), pp. 308–319.

Lu, C. (2011). *Hani Nonggeng Wenhua [Hani Traditional Farming Culture]*. Luxi: Dehong Minzu. (In Chinese).

MacDonald, R. and Jolliffe, L. (2003). Cultural rural tourism, evidence from Canada. *Annals of Tourism Research*, 30(2), pp. 307–322.

Malinowski, B. (1961). *Argonauts of the western Pacific: An account of native enterprise and adventure in the archipelagos of Melanesian New Guinea*. New York: Dutton.

Mao, Y. (1991). Hani Titian Wenhua Lun [Hani Rice Terrace culture]. *Nongye Kaogu [Agricultural Archaeology]*, 23, pp. 191–298. (In Chinese).

Mintz, S. M. (1977). Infant, victim, and tourist: The anthropologies in the field. *Johns Hopkins Magazine*, 27, pp. 54–60.

Prentice, R. (1993). Community-driven tourism planning and residents' preferences. *Tourism Management*, 14(2), pp. 218–227.

Rakic, T. and Chambers, D. (2008). World heritage: Exploring the tension between the national and the 'universal'. *Journal of Heritage Tourism*, 2(3), pp. 145–155.

Shimpei, A. (2007). Agricultural technologies of terraced rice cultivation in the Ailao Mountains, Yunnan, China. *Asian and African Area Studies*, 6(2), pp. 173–196.

Steckenreuter, A. and Wolf, I. D. (2013). How to use persuasive communication to encourage visitors to pay park user fees. *Tourism Management*, 37, pp. 58–70.

Tosun, C. (2001). Challenges of sustainable tourism development in the developing world: the case of Turkey. *Tourism Management*, 22(3), pp. 289–303.

United Nations Educational, Scientific and Cultural Organization (UNESCO). (2001). *Convention Concerning the Protection of the World Cultural and Natural Heritage, WHC-01/CONF.203/24*. Paris: UNESCO.

——— (2010). *Convention Concerning the Protection of the World Cultural and Natural Heritage, WHC-01/34. COM/INF.5F.1*. Paris: UNESCO.

——— (2013). *Honghe Hani Rice Terraces inscribed on UNESCO's World Heritage alongside an extension to the uKhahlamba Drakensberg Park*. Retrieved from: http://whc.unesco.org/en/news/1044 (accessed: 15 September 2013).

Urry, J. (1990). *The tourist gaze: Leisure and travel in contemporary societies*. London: Sage.

Villalon, A. (2012). Continuing living traditions to protect the rice terraces of the Philippine Cordilleras. In K. Taylor and J. L. Lennon (eds), *Managing cultural landscape: Key issues in cultural heritage*. Oxford: Routledge, pp. 291–307.

Wang, H., Yang, Z., Chen, L., Yang, J., and Li, R. (2010). Minority community participation in tourism: a case of Kanas Tuva villages in Xinjiang, China. *Tourism Management*, 31(6), pp. 759–764.

Wang, Q. (1999). *Titian Wenhualun [Rice Terrace Culture]*. Kunming: Yunnan University Press. (In Chinese).

Yang, C-H., Lin, H-L. and Han, C-C. (2010). Analysis of international tourist arrivals in China: The role of World Heritage Sites. *Tourism Management*, 31(6), pp. 827–837.

Yang, J., Ryan, C., and Zhang, L. (2013). Social conflict in communities impacted by tourism. *Tourism Management*, 35, pp. 82–93.

Ying, T. and Zhou, Y. (2007). Community, governments and external capitals in China's rural cultural tourism: A comparative study of two adjacent villages. *Tourism Management*, 28(1), pp. 96–107.

Zhang, H. X. (1999). Female migration and urban labour markets in Tianjin. *Development and Change*, 30(1), pp. 21–41.

Zhang, W. (2002). *Tourism management model for World Heritage Site situated cities*. Beijing: Peking University Press. (In Chinese).

11

Developing a Sustainable Indigenous Tourism Sector: Reconciling Socio-Economic Objectives with Market-Driven Approaches

Lisa Ruhanen, Char-lee McLennan, and Michelle Whitford

Chapter Synopsis

In Australia, an increasing awareness of Indigenous culture has led to a growth in the supply of activities and experiences which are often owned and/or managed by Australia's Aboriginal and Torres Strait Islander peoples. Yet, Australia's Indigenous tourism sector is problematic, and too regularly the sector experiences declining demand, a range of supply side challenges including access to start-up finance and capital, recruiting and retention of appropriately skilled labour, underdeveloped and inconsistent product, and mismatches between experiences sought and product offered. While there has been growth in the development of new Indigenous tourism businesses and tourism products in recent times, Buultjens and White (2008) suggested that many Indigenous businesses find it difficult to achieve sustainability. Given this context, this chapter presents the findings of business case studies conducted with 41 Indigenous tourism operators in Australia. The interviews explored business operators' perceptions of the issues, opportunities, and challenges associated with operating a tourism business. The findings of the study provide insights into the gamut of issues confronting Indigenous tourism business operators.

Introduction

Like many countries around the world, tourism is one of Australia's key economic sectors: worth A$98 billion in direct visitor expenditure; employing some 5 per cent of Australia's workforce; and generating 8 per cent of the country's export value. Despite the continuing high value of the Australian dollar and the increased number of emerging destinations in the Asia Pacific region, the number of international arrivals to Australia in 2012–13 grew to a record 6.3 million visitors

(Tourism Research Australia, 2013). In the state of Queensland, tourism is similarly important to the economy. Tourism contributes some A$22 billion to the state economy and accounts for 7.8 per cent of Queensland's gross domestic product (GDP) (Tourism and Events Queensland, 2013). A key platform of the current Queensland State government is the development of a four-pillar economy focused on tourism, agriculture, resources, and construction (Newman, 2012).

Australia's tourism product offering is diverse, and the country's cultural heritage is an integral part of the product portfolio (Sustainable Tourism Cooperative Research Centre, 2008). A key component of Australia's cultural heritage is the country's Indigenous population; Australia's Aboriginal and Torres Strait Islanders are the oldest living cultures in the world. Indigenous culture is considered by the nation's tourism bodies to be one of the factors that contribute to the uniqueness of destination Australia, and is seen to provide a unique array of cultural experiences for visitors and a point of difference in a competitive and crowded international market place (Tourism New South Wales, 2006). Indeed, the national tourism body, Tourism Australia, promotes 'Aboriginal Australia' as one of the seven key Australian 'experiences' that have potential to encourage international travellers to visit Australia.

Similarly at the sub-national level, Australian states and territories have been attempting to develop and grow their Indigenous tourism product. Most of Australia's states and territories incorporate Indigenous tourism experiences to some degree in their product mix, with states such as Queensland, Northern Territory and Western Australia in particular tending to put more emphasis on these types of tourist experiences, largely due to the higher proportion of Indigenous Australians residing in these states/territories.

In Queensland, the state tourism authority, Tourism and Events Queensland (TEQ), claims that Torres Strait Islander and Aboriginal cultures provide Queensland with two distinct Indigenous cultures and a significant opportunity to build a strong advantage over competitor destinations. The authority has developed the *Indigenous tourism Program 2010–2013*, which focuses on the establishment and marketing of sustainable Indigenous experiences and destinations, and the integration of Indigenous people into all facets of mainstream tourism (Tourism and Events Queensland, 2013a). The purpose of the programme is to provide a plan of action outlining TEQ's involvement in Indigenous tourism that identifies:

- opportunities and impediments to grow Indigenous tourism in Queensland;
- the scope of TEQ involvement in Indigenous tourism, including marketing and development;
- the vision, objectives, strategies, and annual priority activity to address identified impediments and realise opportunities; and
- how TEQ will consult, interact, and coordinate activity with partners and stakeholders.

The programme's aims are set within the vision of presenting Queensland's Indigenous people as the traditional custodians of Australia while providing sustainable Indigenous tourism businesses and signature experiences. It has been a long-held approach of the organisation to promote the participation of Indigenous peoples in the mainstream tourism industry rather than facilitating the development of a culturally focused, niche product.

Thus TEQ recognises the importance and benefits of incorporating Indigenous peoples and their cultures into the state's broader visitor experiences to grow destination appeal (Tourism and Events Queensland, 2013b). There are, however, inherent challenges underpinning this approach which is articulated in Indigenous tourism strategies developed by Queensland (and other Australian states/territories). A particularly challenging issue centres on the utilisation of tourism as a sustainable, socio-economic development opportunity for Indigenous peoples. The problem here lies in the fact that there has been a significant decline in demand for Indigenous experiences since 2005 (Brereton et al., 2007; Fuller et al., 2005; Tourism Research Australia, 2011). Research by Ruhanen et al. (2012) shows that the potential market for Indigenous tourism experiences in Australia is only 2 per cent of visitors; that is, just 120,000 of the 6+ million international visitors to Australia. This is in spite of concerted marketing efforts by national and state tourism authorities, dating back to the 1990s, to develop and promote Australia's Indigenous tourism experiences to the market.

A further challenge, and the one that is the impetus for this study, is the suggestion that there is little differentiation in Australia's Indigenous tourism product offerings. According to Cave et al. (2007), the avid support for Indigenous tourism development by those eager to realise the potential socio-economic benefits and commercial success it can provide to Indigenous peoples has led to the funding of new tourism products that replicate current products. They claimed that this has negatively impacted the profitability of the existing products, and has not necessarily secured financial sustainability for the Indigenous tourism operators and employees. Arguably, this socio-economic agenda must be reconciled with market-driven approaches. Indeed, identifying and promoting unique experiences and points of differentiation are keys to enhancing the cultural tourism experience, differentiating states and regions around the country (Amoamo, 2011; Bunten, 2010), and remaining competitive in a global market. Failure to do so will arguably compromise the sustainability of Indigenous tourism enterprises and, ultimately, the socio-economic objectives sought for Indigenous peoples through tourism.

This chapter presents an applied case study of Queensland, and reports on a study driven by both academic and practical objectives. Responding to claims in the literature that the socio-economic objectives of Indigenous tourism have been pursued with such ardour that the market viability of the product has been overshadowed (Cave et al., 2007), the study seeks to explore whether a lack of differentiation exists in the Australian Indigenous tourism market place and discusses the extent to which this may be compromising the sustainability of Indigenous tourism enterprises. Concomitantly, the study was driven by practical objectives with a government agency seeking to understand their position in the Indigenous tourism market in Australia. Thus the objectives of the study were to: 1) catalogue the scope and type of Indigenous products and experiences offered throughout the country to identify points of differentiation; and 2) explore Queensland's point of difference in the Indigenous tourism market place vis-à-vis other Australian states and territories.

Indigenous Tourism

The past several decades has seen increasing interest in Indigenous culture and history. Accordingly, more countries have attempted to gain leverage via their Indigenous populations and provide a point of differentiation in the global market place, while concomitantly offering new or enhanced socio-economic development opportunities for Indigenous peoples and/or communities. Countries such as the United States, Canada, and New Zealand have all developed and promoted, to varying degrees, a tourism product based around their Indigenous populations. In Canada, as early as the 1860s, Nepal (2005) reported traveller interest in the country's First Nations people. Canada continues to place emphasis on the development of Indigenous economic enterprises, with tourism being viewed as a key source of First Nation economic strength (Anderson, 2002; Anderson et al., 2006). Similarly in New Zealand, the Maori peoples have been involved in tourism in various forms since the 1800s (Butler and Hinch, 2012). Additionally, ethnic minorities in South-East Asian countries such as Thailand, Cambodia, Laos, Vietnam, and Myanmar have long offered art and craft based tourism products (Cohen, 2000; Notzke, 2006). Indigenous peoples in the northern regions of Norway, Sweden, Finland, and Russia have also been embedded in tourism promotional materials. In the southern and eastern states of Africa, wildlife management, including hunting, takes place with Indigenous community participation; and in parts of South

Africa there has been the marketing of tourism routes in an attempt to offer a point of difference (Briedenhann and Wickens, 2004).

INDIGENOUS TOURISM IN AUSTRALIA

Similarly, this has been the case in Australia, where Aboriginal and Torres Strait Islander culture is promoted to both domestic and international visitors. From the nineteenth century, it was recognised that there was interest in Aboriginal culture (Brereton et al., 2007; Kleinert, 2009). As early as the 1840s, South Australian settlers were interested in and willing to pay to see corroborees (Ryan and Huyton, 2000). Art and craft based products were offered by businesses in the 1950s; and in Australia's north, Indigenous tourism began in the 1960s with the establishment of a number of activities, including the Indigenous company Aboriginal Arts and Crafts (Altman, 1993; Whitford et.al., 2001).

Indigenous development and land rights became national issues in Australia in the 1970s; and, as governments at both national and state level exhorted the need for sustainable pathways for Indigenous involvement in the national economy, Indigenous tourism was put forward as a vehicle to achieve this goal (Ryan and Huyton, 2000a, b; Buultjens et al., 2010). Recognising the contribution of Indigenous culture to tourism, the Northern Territory (NT) created the first Aboriginal tourism development position in the NT Tourist Commission in 1984 (Schmiechen, 2006). The 1990s saw a heightened focus on Indigenous culture and lifestyles as a tourism product, particularly in the Northern Territory (Mercer, 2005). While the culture of Indigenous people was considered a key product, it was also recognised that there were opportunities for adventure tourism on lands only accessible by local Indigenous clans (Dodson and Smith, 2003). However, this form of development was impeded to some degree by remoteness, cost of transportation, small populations, and weak economies of scale (Dodson and Smith, 2003).

Indigenous tourism as a sector was formalised following the release of the 1997 *National Aboriginal and Torres Strait Islander Tourism Industry Strategy*, which provided further impetus for Indigenous tourism to become an integral, albeit niche, part of Australia's domestic and international tourism product (Office of Aboriginal Affairs, 2007; Tourism Queensland, 2004; Northern Territory Tourism, 2008). Culture is the predominant focus of Indigenous tourism product and includes a wide range of activities including heritage tours, arts and crafts, performing arts, nature-based experiences, cultural centres, and adventure tours and cruises, amongst others (Northern Territory Tourism, 2008; Western Australia Tourism, 2011; Whitford and Ruhanen, 2010). Indeed, it has been suggested that for many international visitors, Australia's Indigenous culture is what makes Australia truly unique and offers a much-needed competitive advantage in an increasingly competitive international market place (Tourism New South Wales, 2006).

INDIGENOUS TOURISM AS A POINT OF DIFFERENCE IN THE MARKET

According to Porter (1990), the success of a product is dependent on the creation of a unique competitive advantage. This competitive advantage is seen as being derived from resources that are valuable, rare, and not easily reproduced (Barney, 1991). The need for destinations to create a competitive advantage has become critical as today's tourists are increasingly discerning and competition in the market place is at an all-time high (Dwyer and Kim, 2003). Thus, as tourism destinations trend towards similarly styled experiences and products (e.g. multinational hotel chains), it is the local cultures and heritage of a destination that offer one of the few points of differentiation. Indeed, local and cultural distinctions are among the few opportunities to create competitive advantages in a global tourism market place (Notzke, 2006). Indigenous culture, specifically, is often seen as a further point of difference, as Indigenous peoples are seen to generate fascination amongst non-Indigenous people (Butler and Hinch, 2012).

A number of studies have explored the use of Indigenous culture as a point of difference. For instance, McIntosh (2004) investigated the use of Maori culture as a point of difference for New Zealand, finding that even if Indigenous culture was not the primary reason for visiting the country, it still forms an important part of the visit and was considered to be a 'point-of-difference' for a trip to New Zealand. While McIntosh determined that tourists did increase their understanding of the Maori culture, the actual level of learning was shallow. That is, tourists desire a 'romanticised' version of the culture, generally in the form of a one-off experience that is not essential to the trip itinerary. Importantly however, the researchers cautioned that Indigenous culture will likely attract no more than a niche group, as only a small number of both domestic and international travellers are genuinely interested (Carr, 2004; Ryan, 1997; Ryan and Huyton, 2000a, b). For instance, Ryan and Huyton (2000a) found that fewer than half of the domestic and international visitors to Katherine in the Northern Territory of Australia have an interest in Aboriginal culture, with that interest usually being just a part of broader interest in the Northern Territory as a whole.

Nevertheless, Australia's Aboriginal and Torres Strait Islander cultures do provide tourists with a unique opportunity to experience aspects of a 40,000-year-old culture (Buultjens et al., 2005). This was identified in the 2003 *Tourism White Paper* released by the Australian government, which noted that Indigenous tourism was a niche market that could offer competitive advantages for the country (Department of Industry, Tourism and Resources, 2004). Today, most Australian tourism marketing campaigns contain Indigenous Australian images in their attempt to sell the country to international and domestic tourists (Nielsen et al., 2008), as Indigenous culture has been identified as 'one of seven key experiences which underpin Tourism Australia's global marketing activities' (Tourism Research Australia, 2011: 1). Yet Tourism Australia's efforts have not been without their critics. For instance, Pomering and White (2011: 171) argued that Australia's national tourism agencies 'persist in featuring a contrived or staged, Indigenous identity in their campaigns'. Numerous Australian Indigenous tourism operators have voiced similar criticisms. Arguably the development and use of such contrived imagery serves only to homogenise the product (amongst other things). In turn, this dissipates and/or loses the very essence of what makes the product unique in the first instance and, concomitantly, negates the product's capacity to provide a point of differentiation.

This study was driven by the practical objectives of a government agency seeking to understand their position in the Indigenous tourism market in Australia and, in particular, the extent to which their Indigenous tourism product provided a point of differentiation for the state. Thus the aim of this study was to explore whether a lack of Indigenous product differentiation exists in the Australian tourism market place and the extent to which this may be compromising the sustainability of Indigenous tourism enterprises. The study also responds to claims within the literature that the socio-economic objectives of Indigenous tourism have been pursued with such ardour that the market viability of the product has been overshadowed – a build it and they will come approach (Cave et al, 2007; Ruhanen et al, 2012). Thus the objectives of the study were to 1) catalogue the scope and type of Indigenous products and experiences offered throughout the country to identify points of differentiation; and 2) explore Queensland's point of difference in the Indigenous tourism market place vis-à-vis other Australian states and territories.

Method

To address the aims and objectives of the study, a mixed-model approach was implemented, including undertaking 1) an audit of Indigenous tourism businesses in Australia, and 2) a visitor perception survey. A mixed-model approach allowed for the research questions to be better understood and fully explored (Hanson et al., 2005; Mertens, 2003); provided support for the validity of the study (Denzin, 1989; Denzin and Lincoln, 1994; Kvale, 1996); reduced personal and methodological bias (Huberman and Miles, 1994; Miles and Huberman, 1984); and allowed for a more holistic approach. Importantly, the results from one method supported, expanded, and justified the results of the other method (Goodyear et al., 2005; Hanson et al., 2005).

AUDIT OF INDIGENOUS TOURISM PRODUCTS AND SERVICES

An audit of Indigenous tourism products and services in Australia was undertaken in phase one of the study. The objective was to catalogue the scope and type of Indigenous products and experiences offered throughout the country to identify points of differentiation. This audit was undertaken for each of the eight states and territories in Australia via a desk-based search, including trawls through webpages identified in a Google search, in addition to searches of the Tourism Australia and state tourism authority websites and business directories. A consumer-focused Indigenous travel guide for Australia was also used – *Australia Walkabout: Travel Experiences in Aboriginal and Torres Straits Islands* (Crawshaw, 2009).

The combined search tools elicited a total of 536 businesses in Australia. Although the database was current at the time, it may be that some businesses are no longer in operation. A further limitation is that although extensive and thorough, the search may not have identified all businesses, and thus the catalogue results should be treated as a sample rather than a population.

The data was input into Excel and catalogued by business name, location, region, state, contact details, business description, type of product, web reference, and year the business was established. Location of the business was coded to tourism region based on Australian Bureau of Statistics classifications and correspondence files (Cat. 9503.0.55.001). Businesses were coded by business or service type, and so themes were identifiable as the business would often have the theme in its business. For example, Didgeri Air Art Tours could easily be coded to 'tours' and Marrawuddi Gallery as 'gallery'. Others could be identified and coded from the description in their business listing. Businesses were only catalogued by one code. For example, a cultural centre that also included an art gallery was coded as 'cultural centre'.

VISITOR PERCEPTION SURVEY

The second stage of the research involved a scoping survey of visitors at a Queensland tourism attraction. The attraction is a wildlife park and one experience within the park is an Aboriginal dance performance. Surveys were distributed to visitors by a team of four data collectors at the conclusion of the dance performance. The objective of the survey was to investigate visitors' perspectives of the Indigenous tourism product offerings in Australia generally, and Queensland specifically. A total of 131 respondents completed the survey over a four-day period. Potential participants were approached and invited to complete a self-administered questionnaire. The study deliberately sought to survey tourists who had participated in some form of Indigenous tourism, thus the strategy was to recruit participants at the conclusion of the Aboriginal dance performance. Analysis of the survey results was undertaken in Stata v.12, which is a statistical software package. Due to the small sample size, analysis was confined to descriptive analysis and t-tests. Table 11.1 presents an overview of the respondents who participated in the survey.

Although the survey was designed as a scoping study, it is an acknowledged limitation that for various budgetary and logistical constraints the survey was not replicated at other sites

Table 11.1   Respondent profile for visitor perception survey of a Queensland tourism attraction

Visitor type	International	33%
	Domestic	67%
Gender	Male	37%
	Female	63%
Length of stay	Day trip	23%
	>2 weeks	41%
	2–4 weeks	26%
	<4 weeks	10%
International country of residence	UK/Europe	28%
	USA/Canada	10%
	Japan	15%
	China	10%
	Other Asia	20%
Domestic state of residence	Queensland	48%
	New South Wales	26%
	Victoria	20%

throughout Australia, or with a larger sample incorporating other sites throughout the state. It is recognised that those respondents who had not had, or would not have, an Indigenous experience in Queensland (or indeed in Australia) could offer valuable insights into the potential deficiencies in Queensland's offerings. Future research should incorporate a range of other approaches to data collection, including pre- and post-visitation perceptions and visitor/non-visitor perceptions.

Results

INDIGENOUS TOURISM BUSINESS AUDIT

This study identified a total of 536 Indigenous tourism businesses, products, and services at the time of sampling in late 2011. Of these, 26% were located in the Northern Territory, followed by Western Australia (20%) and Queensland (17%); and together these three states account for 63% of all Indigenous tourism product in Australia (see Table 11.2). Previous studies have identified that half of Australia's Indigenous tourism businesses are located in remote or very remote areas (Buultjens and White, 2008). Yet the results of this study were somewhat higher, as 69% of Indigenous tourism businesses were located in regional and rural areas of Australia and 31% of Indigenous businesses were located in capital cities (Brisbane, Darwin, Perth, Adelaide, Melbourne, Sydney, Canberra, and Hobart). Indeed the top Indigenous tourism product regions, ranked by number of products, were all regional and rural locations: Alice Springs and the Red Centre (12%); Australia's North West (12%); Darwin and the Arafura Coast (6%); Kakadu Arnhem (6%); and Tropical North Queensland (5%) (see Table 11.3).

Businesses were coded by primary type and 27 different product categories emerged. All 27 coded products are presented in Table 11.4 to give an indication of the full range of products available. Tours were the predominant Indigenous tourism product: a third of all Indigenous

Table 11.2   Australian Indigenous tourism businesses by state

State/Territory	Number of Businesses	% of Total Businesses
Northern Territory (NT)	138	26
Western Australia (WA)	108	20
Queensland (QLD)	90	17
New South Wales (NSW)	80	15
Victoria (VIC)	48	9
South Australia (SA)	36	7
Tasmania (TAS)	19	3
Australian Capital Territory (ACT)	16	2
Total	**535**	**100**

Table 11.3   Australian Indigenous tourism products by tourism region

Region	State	Obs	%
Alice Springs and Red Centre	NT	66	12.3
Australia's North West	WA	65	12.2
Darwin and Arafura Coast	NT	34	6.4
Kakadu Arnhem	NT	31	5.8
Tropical North Queensland	QLD	29	5.4
Cape York and Top End	QLD	28	5.2
Experience Perth	WA	26	4.9
Sydney	NSW	26	4.9
Central and North Coasts	NSW	25	4.7
Adelaide Region and Wetlands	SA	23	4.3
Melbourne City	VIC	20	3.7
Australian Capital Territory	ACT	16	3.0
South Coast and Highlands	NSW	13	2.4
West and Outback NSW	NSW	12	2.2
Brisbane	QLD	11	2.1
Outback Queensland	QLD	10	1.9
Australia's South West	WA	7	1.3
Flinders and the Desert	SA	6	1.1
South Tasmania and Hobart	TAS	6	1.1
West Coast Victoria	VIC	6	1.1

tourism experiences offered in Australia are tours. Galleries (14%), arts and crafts (11%), and cultural centres (7%) were the other top product categories identified.

An analysis of Indigenous product offerings across the Australian states/territories showed that New South Wales, Queensland, and Western Australia had the most diverse Indigenous tourism product offerings with 17 different product categories. This was followed by the Northern Territory (15), Victoria (14), South Australia (9), Tasmania (7), and the Australian Capital Territory

Table 11.4   **Indigenous tourism products in Australia**

Rank	Type of product	Obs	%
1	Tours	174	33
2	Gallery	75	14
3	Art and craft	58	11
4	Cultural centre	36	7
5	Accommodation	31	6
6	Festival, fair, and cultural event	24	4
7	Dance and performance	21	4
8	Workshops and education	16	3
9	Museum	15	3
10	Walks	10	2
11	Cruise	9	2
12	National Park	9	2
13	Agritourism	8	2
14	Restaurant and cooking	8	2
15	Camping	7	1
16	Bush tucker garden	5	1
17	Indigenous attraction	4	1
18	Indigenous resource	4	1
19	Radio and media	4	1
20	Community stay	3	0
21	Fishing charter	3	0
22	Interpretative centre	3	0
23	Ecotourism	2	0
24	Health and wellbeing	2	0
25	Wildlife park	2	0
26	Retail	1	0
27	Visitor centre	1	0

(5). Two product categories, 'tours' and 'galleries', were identified in all states/territories. Similarly, with the exception of the Australian Capital Territory, all states/territories had Indigenous cultural centres, while 'accommodation' and 'museums' were identified in six of the eight states/territories.

PERCEPTIONS OF INDIGENOUS TOURISM VISITORS

To explore perceptions of Indigenous tourism product differentiation amongst the visitor market, as well as Queensland's point of difference vis-à-vis other Australian states and territories, a visitor survey was completed by 131 Indigenous tourism respondents. As noted in the methodology, all these tourists had viewed an Indigenous dance performance within a Queensland tourism attraction.

A series of background contextual questions were posed to the participants about their interest in, and engagement with, Indigenous tourism experiences in Australia. Some 93% of the respondents agreed (52% strongly agreed) on a five-point Likert scale that they like to 'learn about the culture and lifestyles of local people when travelling'. Thus, when the respondents were asked to rank the eight Indigenous tourism experiences in terms of their importance to their visit to Australia, they indicated that experiencing Aboriginal culture was the most important Indigenous tourism influence. The same experience items were used for respondents to indicate how well they perceived Queensland's Indigenous tourism products, where 1 is 'very poor' and 5 is 'exceptional'. The respondents could select 'don't know', and 28 respondents did so. Two sample mean comparison tests revealed that Queensland's Indigenous tourism products were perceived to be significantly underperforming except in terms of 'experiencing contemporary Indigenous culture' and 'experiencing Indigenous lifestyles in cities/urban areas'.

Respondents were asked whether they had experienced/would experience a range of different Indigenous tourism products/services during their visit to Australia and/or which of these they would like to experience. They were then asked to indicate whether they would/will choose Queensland to have these particular experiences. The most likely and/or desired Indigenous experience was 'song and/or dance performance', yet only around half of these respondents stated they would choose Queensland as the state in Australia to undertake this experience (see Figures 11.1 and 11.2). Given that the respondents had all experienced a dance performance in Queensland in order to be included in the study, it is clear that Queensland is not necessarily the first choice in which to undertake this experience, but it is the more convenient location.

'Tours/guided walks' and 'Indigenous wildlife parks' were some of the most popular experience categories identified by respondents, but only 37% of respondents planned to undertake either activity in Queensland. 'Art gallery/arts and crafts' were identified by half of the respondents, but just over half of these planned to engage in this activity while in Queensland. A further limitation of the survey instrument was that there was not sufficient space to explore further where the respondents planned to participate (if at all) in such experiences.

The respondents indicated which states/territories in Australia they primarily associate with Indigenous tourism. Allowing for multiple responses, the vast majority of domestic respondents

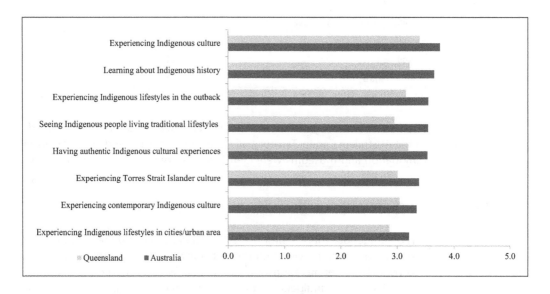

Figure 11.1   Importance to visitors of types of Australian experience

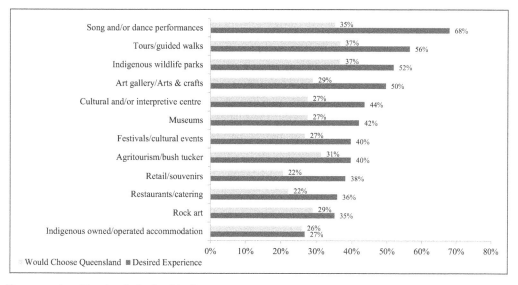

Figure 11.2   Tourists's desired indigenous experiences in Australia and whether they would be undertaken in Queensland

stated the Northern Territory (75%) and just over half identified Queensland. Surprisingly, given the prevalence of Indigenous tourism product (see Table 11.2), far fewer identified Western Australia (see Figure 11.3). International visitor respondents were more likely to state Queensland (41%), followed by New South Wales. For both domestic and international visitors, a geographical bias would have been at play in these responses, further influenced by the fact that the survey was issued in Queensland and the respondents had just participated in an Indigenous tourism performance. Further, the fact that international visitors identified New South Wales would have been influenced by the market's familiarity with a third of all tourists visiting that state (Destination New South Wales, 2013).

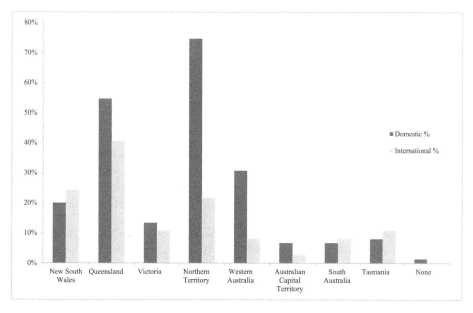

Figure 11.3   Australian states/territories primarily associated with indigenous tourism

It is important to note here that the study was scoping in nature, and so the results should be viewed as such. The findings do suggest that Queensland is generally not seen as a destination to participate in a range of Indigenous tourism experiences. This result is disconcerting given that the respondents were, at the very time of the survey, participating in an Indigenous tourism experience in Queensland. If anything it would have been expected that the respondents would have over-represented the importance of Queensland. It may be that the respondents did not intend to have any further Indigenous tourism experiences while in Queensland and so ranked the items lower on the scale; or, as noted earlier, that Queensland was not their first choice but instead a more convenient location. Despite this, international visitors were more likely to associate Indigenous tourism with Queensland, while domestic visitors perceive the Northern Territory to be the key Indigenous tourism destination in the country.

Conclusion

Tourism, as a viable and sustainable economic development option for Indigenous Australians, is arguably under threat. Even without considering a myriad supply side challenges facing Indigenous tourism operators (e.g. low product awareness, inconsistent product delivery, negative media attention, etc.), the continued decline in visitor demand from an already low potential visitor pool raises cause for concern and presents a considerable challenge (Ruhanen et al., 2012).

Another challenge identified in this study is the apparent homogenisation of Indigenous tourism product in Australia. Cave et al. (2007) warned that the arduous pursuit of tourism to meet Indigenous socio-economic agendas has led to a compromised product mix which, according to the results of this study, constitutes a largely undifferentiated 'mix'. Poor product mix will surely impact on the sustainability of both existing and new entrants to the market that will inadvertently destabilize the reason for pursuing tourism as a socio-economic development objective for Indigenous peoples in the first instance.

Arguably, it is only if and when this and other significant challenges are overcome that tourism can be utilised as an effective vehicle to facilitate the development of socio-economic opportunities for Indigenous peoples, particularly for those in regional and rural parts of the country. Most of the country's Indigenous tourism product (69%) is located in regional or remote centres – including the Northern Territory centres of Alice Springs, Uluru, Darwin, Kakadu and Arnhem land, northern Western Australia, and far northern Queensland. The prevalence of tourism businesses in these regional and remote areas of Australia potentially provides socio-economic development opportunities for Indigenous peoples living in locations where there are few to no other development options available to regions. Yet the regional and remote areas of Australia face particular challenges with access to markets (i.e. visitors to Australia primarily frequent the eastern states of the country) and affordability (i.e. in terms of transportation costs and in destination services), amongst others. This is certainly the situation in Queensland's far northern regions (i.e. Torres Strait and Cape York), which are heavily constrained by the tyranny of distance and affordability but could, and arguably should, offer visitors a unique, environmentally and culturally rich Indigenous product.

Yet the results of this study suggest that this is unlikely to occur as, on the whole, the Indigenous tourism product on offer in Australia is becoming increasingly standardised. For instance, in terms of product differentiation across the country, of the 27 product categories coded, the majority (65%) fall into four categories: tours (33%), galleries (14%), arts/crafts (11%), and cultural centres (7%). Tours and galleries were identified in all states/territories, as were cultural centres (with the exception of the Australian Capital Territory). Given the size of the Indigenous tourism visitor market (e.g. some 120,000 international visitors), combined with the lack of product differentiation identified in this study, we need to acknowledge the concerning implications for the sustainability of Indigenous tourism enterprises and pose some fundamental questions. For instance, will a visitor (either domestic or international) be either able to and/or inclined to differentiate between the cultural subtleties of an Indigenous tour in Arnhem Land of the Northern Territory or an Indigenous tour in Melbourne, Victoria? How many Indigenous tourism experiences are visitors seeking and/or willing to partake in while in Australia? The statistics suggest that many visitors will not participate in one Indigenous tourism experience let alone several around the country. Thus if a visitor participates in a tour in one state they are unlikely to do an Indigenous tourism tour in another state during their trip. Indeed, they are unlikely to have another Indigenous experience at all. Is this due to the lack of product differentiation throughout the country or are there other factors at play, and what are they?

In relation to the positioning of Indigenous tourism experiences in Queensland then, there are two key points from the findings of this study. Firstly, it is imperative that Queensland actively seeks ways to differentiate its Indigenous tourism product. This study found that Queensland's Indigenous tourism product is underrepresented in certain product types such as Indigenous cruise experiences, Indigenous health and wellbeing, restaurant and cooking, and retail. Indeed across Australia, there are few examples of Indigenous agritourism, bush tucker gardens, camping, dance and performance, fishing charters, workshops, and education. Further, a large proportion of identified businesses in Queensland were tour operators and galleries, which primarily cater to risk-averse and/or older travellers. There is opportunity then to increase Indigenous tourism attractions in Queensland that align with Tourism Australia's market segment called 'Experience Seekers'. This requires developing products that appeal to consumers who are:

- Experienced travellers who have taken previous international holidays and as such will have higher expectations in terms of quality, value, and service standards. They may also feel more comfortable to engage in independent travel itineraries and are often averse to tours.
- More predisposed toward activities and pursuits that enhance them as individuals, whether through understanding or learning new things. There may be opportunities to capitalise on increased interest in Indigenous spirituality and environmental concerns (Drew, 1994; Flannery, 1998).
- Knowledgeable consumers who will investigate options thoroughly. Promotion and marketing channels should reflect their propensity for non-traditional and mainstream media. Current affairs, topical, and special interest programmes have been identified which may present opportunities to promote Indigenous product offerings in Queensland (Tourism Australia, n.d.).

Secondly, Queensland should pursue its strategic objectives around 'mainstreaming' Indigenous tourism. If after further research we find that visitors probably will not seek multiple Indigenous experiences during their visit, then the best opportunity to gain socio-economic leverage from the tourist dollar is to incorporate Indigenous participation into mainstream products (e.g. tours of local natural attractions or accommodation that is owned or operated by Indigenous peoples). Moving away from an overt cultural product should assist in differentiating the product and offer more beneficial socio-economic opportunities in a market that is arguably reaching saturation and decline.

From demand perspectives, it has been found that while tourists are interested in the cultural points of difference from their own culture, Indigenous culture is generally not considered a dominant tourism product but rather a complementary aspect of a core product (McIntosh, 2004). Thus, as Cave et al. (2007) suggested, Indigenous operators might be better identifying their unique cultural differences and incorporating these aspects of their culture within mainstream tourism products to gain competitive advantage. Similarly, Buultjens et al. (2005) argued that the Australian Indigenous tourism market is relatively immature and would gain advantages by linking with other products such as ecotourism. The integration of Indigenous tourism in the mainstream tourism industry, as discussed previously, is a current strategic objective of Tourism and Events Queensland. Further research is needed to quantify the extent to which this is actually taking place in practice and the outcomes and successes for those Indigenous tourism businesses. Moreover, this audit only sought to quantify Australia's Indigenous tourism product; but, as some researchers argued, competitive advantage can also be effectively achieved through a greater focus on product quality (Lobo, 2008). Negative perceptions or images may also significantly impact a product's competitiveness as it impacts consumer's decision making (Konecnik, 2004; Lee et al., 2002). Therefore, future empirical research should investigate issues and differences regarding product quality and visitor perceptions.

In summary, and based on a purely quantitative review of product offerings, Queensland currently has no significant point of difference to other states/territories in Australia. However, based on these findings, there is no state or territory in Australia that could currently claim a point of differentiation with their Indigenous tourism product on offer. This study also raises key implications pertaining to marketing Indigenous tourism products more broadly, as it brings into question whether it is possible to truly differentiate the 'stand-alone' Indigenous tourism product across Australia. According to Cave et al. (2007), the development of cultural tourism products by minority groups in New Zealand displayed a tendency to emulate existing cultural-based attractions because they draw on familiar cultural attractions and settings, social and spatial proximity, and proven business success formulas. To successfully differentiate the product then, future research is required to determine if it may be necessary to not only take a more localised approach to Indigenous tourism development but to also dovetail the product with mainstream experiences and/or attractions.

This chapter has presented a case study of Indigenous tourism in Queensland, Australia. Exploring the lack of differentiation amongst Indigenous tourism product from both supply and demand perspectives has provided interesting and valuable insights into the sustained use of tourism as a socio-economic development tool for Indigenous peoples. While we are not suggesting that the findings of this study are generalisable, on the basis of this study's findings it can be concluded that current approaches in Australia to Indigenous tourism development which rely on a fairly narrow range of products are unlikely to deliver the socio-economic outcomes desired by the hundreds of businesses working in this sector across Australia. Arguably, without differentiation the market – which is saturated and in decline – will continue to wane. Strategies such as those used by TEQ to embed Indigenous tourism in the mainstream tourism industry appear to be one option to reverse this trend. Yet, in supporting such an approach, it must be acknowledged that not all Indigenous peoples care to embark on the road to tourism business development for purely socio-economic objectives, but are instead driven by socio-cultural outcomes such as cultural maintenance and preservation. This scoping research has demonstrated that there is much latitude for further investigation of these issues to ensure the continual development of 'road maps' that will provide appropriate and effective pathways for those Indigenous peoples wanting to navigate enhanced socio-economic outcomes via the tourism industry.

References

Altman, J. C. (1993). Where to now? Some strategic Indigenous tourism policy issues. Paper presented at the *Proceedings of the Indigenous Australians and Tourism Conference*. Darwin, June, 1993 (pp. 51–55).

Amoamo, M. (2011). Tourism and hybridity: Re-visiting Bhabha's third space. *Annals of Tourism Research*, 38(4), pp. 1254–1273.

Anderson, R. B. (2002). Entrepreneurship and Aboriginal Canadians: A case study in economic development. *Journal of Developmental Entrepreneurship*, 7(1), pp. 45–65.

———, Dana, L. P. and Dana, T. E. (2006). Indigenous land rights, entrepreneurship, and economic development in Canada: 'Opting-in' to the global economy. *Journal of World Business*, 41(1), pp. 45–55.

Barney, J. (1991). Firm resources and sustained competitive advantage. *Journal of Management*, 17(1), pp. 99–120.

Brereton, D., Memmott, P., Reser, J., Buultjens, J., Thomson, L., Barker, T., O'Rourke, T. and Chambers, C. (2007). *Mining and Indigenous tourism in Northern Australia*. Gold Coast: Sustainable Tourism Cooperative Research Centre.

Briedenhann, J. and Wickens, E. (2004). Tourism routes as a tool for the economic development of rural areas: Vibrant hope or impossible dream? *Tourism Management*, 25(1), pp. 71–79.

Bunten, A. C. (2010). More like ourselves: Indigenous capitalism through tourism. *American Indian Quarterly*, 34(3), pp. 285–311.

Butler, R. and Hinch, T. (2012). *Tourism and Indigenous peoples*. Oxford: Taylor and Francis.

Buultjens, J. and White, N. E. (2008). Indigenous tourism: The possibilities into the future. *Proceedings Desert Knowledge Symposium 2008 – Developing Desert Directions: Rethinking the Future*. Alice Springs, 3–6 November. Darwin: Desert Knowledge CRC.

———, Gale, D. and White, N. E. (2010). Synergies between Australian Indigenous tourism and ecotourism: Possibilities and problems for future development. *Journal of Sustainable Tourism*, 18(4), pp. 497–513.

———, Waller, I., Graham, S. and Carson, D. 2005. Public sector initiatives for Aboriginal small business development in tourism. In C. Ryan and M. Aicken (eds), *Indigenous tourism: The commodification and management of culture* Oxford: Elsevier.

Carr, A. (2004). Mountain places, cultural spaces: The interpretation of culturally significant landscapes. *Journal of Sustainable Tourism*, 12(5), pp. 432–459.

Cave, J., Ryan, C. and Panakera, C. (2007). Cultural tourism product: Pacific Island migrant perspectives in New Zealand. *Journal of Travel Research*, 45(4), pp. 435–443.

Cohen, E. (2000). *The commercialized crafts of Thailand: Hill tribes and lowland villages: Collected articles*. Honolulu: University of Hawaii Press.

Crawshaw, I. (2009). *Australia Walkabout: Travel Experiences in Aboriginal and Torres Straits Islands*. Potts Point, NSW: Cactusmedia.

Denzin, N. (1989). *The research act: A theoretical introduction to sociological methods*. Englewood Cliffs, NJ: Prentice Hall.

——— and Lincoln, Y. (1994). *Handbook of qualitative research*. Thousand Oaks: Sage.

Department of Industry, Tourism and Resources (2004). *Tourism white paper*. Canberra: Commonwealth Government.

Destination New South Wales (NSW). (2013). *Travel to New South Wales*. Retrieved from: http://www. destinationnsw.com.au/__data/assets/pdf_file/0016/212182/Total-NSW-snapshot-YE-Jun-13.pdf (accessed: 17 November 2013).

Dodson, M., and Smith, D. E. (2003). *Governance for sustainable development: Strategic issues and principles for Indigenous Australian communities*. Canberra: Australian National University.

Drew, P. (1994). *The coast dwellers*. Ringwood: Penguin.

Dwyer, L. and Kim, C. (2003). Destination competitiveness: Determinants and indicators. *Current Issues in Tourism*, 6(5), pp. 369–414.

Flannery, T. (1998). *The explorers*. Melbourne: Text Publishing.

Fuller, D., Buultjens, J. and Cummings, E. (2005). Ecotourism and Indigenous micro-enterprise formation in northern Australia: Opportunities and constraints. *Tourism Management*, 26(6), pp. 891–904.

Goodyear, R. K., Tracey, T. J. G., Claiborn, C. D., Lichtenberg, J. W. and Wampold, B. E. (2005). Ideographic concept mapping in counseling psychology research: Conceptual overview, methodology, and an illustration. *Journal of Counseling Psychology*, 52, pp. 236–242.

Hanson, W. E., Creswell, J. W., Plano-Clark, V. L., Petska, K. S. and Creswell, J. D. (2005). Mixed methods research designs in counseling psychology. *Journal of Counseling Psychology*, 52(2), pp. 224–235.

Huberman, M. and Miles, M. (1994). Data management and analysis methods. In N. Denzin and Y. Lincoln (eds), *Handbook of qualitative research*. Thousand Oaks: Sage, pp. 428–444.

Kleinert, S. (2009). *Aboriginal enterprises: Negotiating an urban aboriginality*. Canberra: Australian National University. Retrieved from: http://press.anu.edu.au/apps/bookworm/view/Aboriginal+History+Volume+34,+2010/5611/ch07.xhtml (accessed: 17 July 2011).

Konecnik, M. (2004). Evaluating Slovenia's image as a tourism destination: A self-analysis process towards building a destination brand. *Brand Management*, 11(4), pp. 307–316.

Kvale, S. (1996). *Interviews: An introduction to qualitative research interviewing*. Thousand Oaks: Sage.

Lee, G., O'Leary, J. T., and Hong, G. S. (2002). Visiting propensity predicted by destination image. *International Journal of Hospitality and Tourism Administration*, 3(2), pp. 63–92.

Lobo, A. C. (2008). Enhancing luxury cruise liner operators' competitive advantage: A study aimed at improving customer loyalty and future patronage. *Journal of Travel and Tourism Marketing*, 25(1), pp. 1–12.

McIntosh, A. J. (2004). Tourists' appreciation of Maori culture in New Zealand. *Tourism Management*, 25(1), pp. 1–15.

Mercer, D. (2005). The 'new pastoral industry'? Tourism and Indigenous Australia. In W. Theobald (ed.), *Global tourism*, Oxford: Elsevier, pp. 140–162.

Mertens, D. M. (2003). Mixed methods and the politics of human research: The transformative-emancipatory perspective. In A. Tashakkori and C. Teddlie (eds), *Handbook of mixed methods in social and behavioural research*. Thousand Oaks: Sage, pp. 135–164.

Miles, M., and Huberman, M. (1984). *Qualitative data analysis: A source book of new methods*. Newbury Park: Sage.

Nepal, S. (2005). Limits to Indigenous ecotourism: An exploratory analysis from the Tl'azt'en territories, northern British Columbia. In C. Ryan and M. Aicken (eds), *Indigenous tourism: The commodification and management of culture*. Amsterdam: Elsevier, pp. 111–126.

Newman, C. (2012). *We will grow a four pillar economy*. Retrieved from: http://www.thepremier.qld.gov.au/plans-and-progress/plans/6-months-july-dec-12/four-pillar-economy.aspx (accessed: 9 October 2013).

Nielsen, N., Buultjens, J. and Gale, D. (2008). *Indigenous tourism involvement in Queensland*. Gold Coast: Sustainable Tourism Cooperative Research Centre.

Northern Territory Tourism (2008). *Five Year Tourism Strategic Plan: A plan to guide the success of the Northern Territory tourism industry 2008 to 2012*. Darwin: Northern Territory Government.

Notzke, C. (2006). *The stranger, the native and the land: Perspectives on Indigenous tourism*. Concord, ON: Captus.

Office of Aboriginal Affairs (2007). *Aboriginal tourism development plan for Tasmania*. Hobart: Department of Premier and Cabinet.

Pomering, A. and White, L. (2011). The portrayal of Indigenous identity in Australian tourism brand advertising: Engendering an image of extraordinary reality or staged authenticity? *Place Branding and Public Diplomacy*, 7(3), pp. 165–174.

Porter, M. E. (1990). *The competitive advantage of nations*. New York: Free Press.

Ruhanen, L., Whitford, M. and McLennan, C. (2012). *Demand and supply issues in Indigenous tourism: A gap analysis*. Canberra: Indigenous Business Australia.

Ryan, C. (1997). *The tourist experience: A new introduction*. London: Thomson.

Ryan, C., and Huyton, J. (2000a). Who is interested in Aboriginal tourism in the Northern Territory, Australia? A cluster analysis. *Journal of Sustainable Tourism*, 8(1), pp. 53–88.

———— (2000b). Aboriginal tourism: A linear structural relations analysis of domestic and international tourist demand. *International Journal of Tourism Research*, 2(1), pp. 15–28.

Schmiechen, J. (2006). *Indigenous tourism research agenda: Key directions for the future 2005–2008*. Gold Coast: Sustainable Tourism Cooperative Research Centre.

Sustainable Tourism Cooperative Research Centre (2008). *Culture and heritage tourism: Understanding the issues and success factors*. Gold Coast: STCRC.

Tourism and Events Queensland (TEQ). (2013a). *Tourism facts and figures*. Retrieved from: http://www.tq.com.au/research/summary-visitor-statistics/summary-visitor-statistics_home.cfm (accessed: 12 December 2013).

———— (2013b). *Indigenous tourism program 2010–2013*. Retrieved from: http://www.tq.com.au/fms/tq_corporate/special_interests/indigenous/TQ%20Indigenous%20Tourism%20Program%202010–2013%20-%20Factsheet%20DEC10.pdf (accessed: 12 December 2013).

Tourism Australia (n.d.). *A uniquely Australian invitation: The experience seeker*. Retrieved from: http://www.tourism.australia.com/home.aspx?redir=en-au/ (accessed: 9 October 2013).

———— (2013). *Our target market*. Retrieved from: http://tourism.australia.com/markets/the-experience-seeker.aspx (accessed: 12 December 2013).

Tourism New South Wales (2006). *Principles for developing Aboriginal tourism: Based on consultations with Aboriginal communities*. Retrieved from: http://archive.tourism.nsw.gov.au/Sites/SiteID6/objlib13/principles_for_developing_aboriginal_tourism.pdf (accessed: 4 February 2008).

Tourism Queensland. (2004). *Indigenous tourism strategy: Including Indigenous people in tourism*. Brisbane: Queensland Government.

Tourism Research Australia. (2011). *Snapshots 2011: Indigenous tourism visitors in Australia*. Canberra: Department of Resources, Energy and Tourism.

———— (2013). *State of the industry 2013*. Retrieved from http://www.tra.gov.au/documents/State_of_Industry_FULLv9.pdf (accessed: 12 December 2013).

Western Australia Tourism. (2011). *Making a difference, 2011–2015: Aboriginal tourism strategy for Western Australia*. Perth: Western Australian Government.

Whitford, M. and Ruhanen, L. (2010). Australian Indigenous tourism policy: Practical and sustainable policies? *Journal of Sustainable Tourism*, 18(4), pp. 475–496.

————, Bell, B. and Watkins, M. (2001). Australian Indigenous tourism policy: 25 years of rhetoric and rationalism. *Current Issues in Tourism*, 4(2–4), pp. 151–181.

12

An Assessment of Community-Based Ecotourism Impacts: A Case Study of the San/Basarwa Communities of the Kalahari, Botswana

Naomi Moswete and Brijesh Thapa

Chapter Synopsis

Community-based ecotourism via community-based natural resource management (CBNRM) is relatively new in Botswana, especially in the Kalahari region. Generally, in Botswana, there is paucity of empirical research with respect to the examination of social and economic benefits of tourism within the wider local communities. This issue is evident in remote communities, specifically among the San/Basarwa of the Kalahari region. Hence, the purpose of this study was: 1) to explore the level of tourism awareness and ecotourism knowledge; and 2) to assess the socio-economic impacts of community-based ecotourism on the San/Basarwa communities residing closer to the Kgalagadi Transfrontier Park (KTP) in the greater Kalahari region in western Botswana. The research findings were encouraging for the KTP adjacent communities and the San/Basarwa in particular, as they indicated high awareness and knowledge of ecotourism-related resources within their villages. Community-based tourism industry benefits many Indigenous individuals in various ways, and the San/Basarwa people are no exception. Although this case study uncovered the positive effects of tourism on the San/Basarwa community, there are still issues that need to be addressed if tourism is to be further developed and beneficial.

Introduction

Tourism has been identified by the government of Botswana as a vital tool for development, and has so far become the second most important sector after minerals, especially diamonds (World

Travel and Tourism Council/WTTC, 2007). In 2012, tourism contributed 9.1% of total employment (61,000 jobs), many of which were in hotels, safari-based facilities, travel agents, airlines, and other leisure-related industries (WTTC, 2013). Historically, tourism in Botswana has been related to safaris for international hunters, especially in the Ngamiland-Okavango regions (Gumbo, 2002; Selby, 1991), while some visitors have frequented the Kalahari Desert (Thomas and Shaw, 1991). The hunting as well as the wildlife-based tourism legacy of the industry has been sustained over the past few decades, with an exclusive focus on affluent international tourists (Barnes, 2001; Moswete and Mavondo, 2003; WTTC, 2007). With such a limited product and target market, the tourism industry is 'enclave' in its approach, particularly in the Okavango Delta region (Mbaiwa, 2005). Enclave tourism is where activities offered tend to be concentrated in remote areas, and the types of facilities and their physical location fail to take into consideration the needs and wishes of the local people (Akama and Kieti, 2007; Britton, 1982; Ceballos-Lascurain,1996).

Given the characteristics and limited regional impact of enclave tourism development, it is only recently that the government has emphasised greater attention to the socio-economic impacts of community tourism on the livelihoods of rural and remote area communities. Generally, there is increasing recognition of the importance of 'responsible tourism',[1] as it is known to generate social and economic benefits for local people and remote area dwellers (Akama and Kieti, 2007; Barnes, 2001), and also contribute to the conservation and preservation of cultural and natural resources (Mbaiwa, 2005; WTTC, 2007, 2013).

For example, there has been a recent emergence of and interest in community-based ecotourism (Botswana Tourism Organisation, 2003; Government of Botswana, 2003), which has been modelled on the community-based natural resource management (CBNRM) framework (Arntzen et al., 2003; Johnson, 2009; Mulale, et al., 2013) and the principles of sustainable tourism (Aronsson, 2000). Community-based ecotourism (CBE) implies that a community is:

> caring for its natural resources in order to gain income through tourism, and is using that income to better the lives of its people; it involves conservation, business enterprises, and community development. (Sproule and Subandi, 1998: 215)

In Botswana, since tourism occurs in the peripheral areas, communities are encouraged to initiate community-based tourism (CBT) by forming community-based organisations (CBOs). Thus, CBT are:

> tourism initiatives that are owned by one or more communities, or run as joint venture partnerships with the private sector with equitable community participation, as a means of using natural resources in a sustainable manner to improve their standard of living in an economic and viable way. (Government of Botswana, 2007).

Based on this approach, several local communities have established CBOs (also known as Trusts) in their villages/communities (Mulale, 2005), and the majority of successful CBT projects are wildlife/safari based, with a few related to cultural heritage (Barnes, 2001; Mbaiwa, 2013; Sebele, 2010). Also, rural dwellers who have participated in CBT/CBE enterprises generally live adjacent to protected areas (Arntzen et al., 2003; Government of Botswana, 2001).

However, even with the growth of such alternate types of tourism development, there has been a paucity of empirical research with respect to the social and economic benefits of tourism within the

---

1   Responsible tourism maximises the benefits to local communities; minimises negative social or environmental impacts; and helps local people conserve fragile cultures and habitats or species. Cape Town Declaration on Responsible Tourism, http://www.responsiblecapetown.co.za.

wider local communities (Arntzen, 2003; Mbaiwa, 2004; Moswete et al., 2009; Ndubano, 2000; Sebele, 2010). This issue is evident in remote communities, specifically among the San of the Kalahari region,[2] where most research has generally been concentrated on culture, language, history, geography, soil, and geology (Hitchcock, 1991, 1997; Hitchcock and Brandenburgh, 1990; Thomas and Shaw, 1991). Overall, there has been very little research conducted with regard to community-based ecotourism initiatives and associated economic benefits on the San communities in the greater Kgalagadi region (Hitchcock, 1997; Moswete et al., 2009). Hence, the purpose of this study was: 1) to explore the level of tourism awareness and ecotourism knowledge; and 2) to assess the socio-economic impacts of community-based ecotourism on the San/Basarwa of the Kalahari in western Botswana.[3]

Methodology

THE STUDY SITE

According to the Kgalagadi District Development Committee (2003), the Kgalagadi district covers a large proportion of the Kalahari Desert in the southwest of the country. It is composed of two sub-districts, the north and south (both situated within the Kalahari Desert ecosystem), and forms part of the first formally declared transfrontier park in southern Africa – Kgalagadi Transfrontier Park (KTP).[4] KTP is positioned between Botswana and South Africa, and shares dual ownership and management between the two governments. As a transfrontier protected area, KTP was created from the merging/adjoining of two protected areas – Gemsbok National Park in Botswana (28,400 square kilometres) and the Kalahari Gemsbok National Park in South Africa (9,591 square kilometres) (South African Park Board and Department of Wildlife and National Parks (1997). This park has become vital in terms of conservation of flora and fauna as well as to the rural communities that reside close to it.

DATA COLLECTION

The population of the San/Basarwa in Botswana is relatively small, and they reside in most parts of the country (Government of Botswana, 2001). The study sample was drawn from nine villages and settlements located close to KTP (Botswana side) based on national map references, National Settlement Strategy (2002), and the KTP management plan (see Figure 12.1). Five communities in north and four in south Kgalagadi were selected. Overall, there were eight ethnic groups residing in the respective communities, comprised of San/Basarwa (N=53), Baherero (20), Banama (3), Bangologa (106), Batlharo (157), Bakgalagadi (210), 'coloureds' (98), and other groups (98). However, for the purpose of this chapter, only the San/Basarwa sample was used for the analysis.

Data was collected using interviewer-administered household questionnaires from residents. Household heads aged 18 years and older were contacted and requested to participate. Due to the high rate of illiteracy in the study area (Arntzen, 2001; Government of Botswana, 2003), the interviewer asked the questions verbally and subsequently completed the questionnaire. Other methods were employed to get additional information and perspectives, such as in-person

---

2   The San – also known as the Basarwa – are considered the first people of Botswana, or *indigenous* people.

3   It should be noted that components of this chapter were derived from a larger study that examined stakeholder perspectives on the potential for community-based ecotourism development in the Kalahari region.

4   A relatively large area that straddles frontiers (boundaries) between two or more countries and covers a large-scale natural system encompassing one or more protected areas.

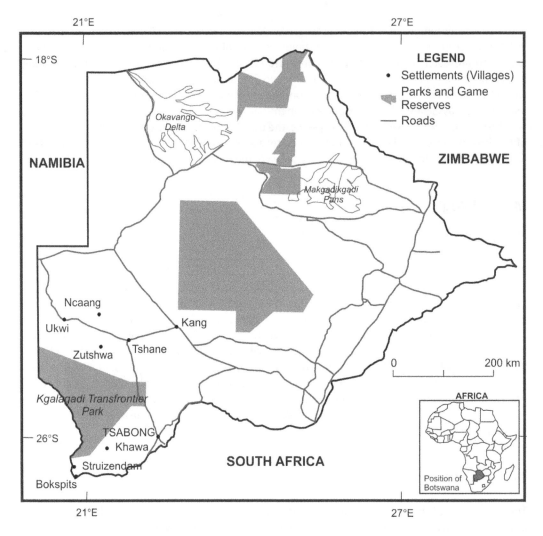

Figure 12.1   Map of Botswana showing the study site and sampled villages

Source: Created by Koorutwe, 2009.

interviews with key officials at local and national level. Purposive sampling was used to select respondents (e.g. park manager, land board member, secretary, tribal administrator, district economic planner, wildlife wardens). In addition, participant observation was also used to gather information during fieldwork in 2009, and partially also in 2012 by the lead author.

Results

PROFILE OF RESPONDENTS

The residents represented villages in Kgalagadi North (Ncaang, Ngwatle, Ukhwi, and Zutshwa), while others were from Kgalagadi South (Khawa, Bokspits, Struizendam, and Tsabong). Males comprised 51%, while 49% were female. The youngest respondent was 19 years of age, and the oldest 78. Collectively, 45% were in the age group 18–30; 21% in the 31–40 group; 15% in the 51–70 group; and only 3.7% were amongst the 71 years and older cohort. Literacy levels varied: 21% had attained primary school education: 36% secondary/high school; and 43% noted lack of formal schooling and were illiterate.

With respect to occupation, 28% worked in the arts and crafts sector, and 26% were involved in elementary jobs that included safari campsite caretakers, cleaners, animal trekkers during hunting expeditions, and night watchmen. Community residents had part-time jobs which were mainly provided by district council support programmes, such as drought relief projects – where they participated in the construction of dams and village shelters for meetings. In addition, about 34% were noted to be self-employed, 38% had part-time jobs, and 17% were unemployed.

TOURISM AWARENESS

The level of awareness of tourism was assessed through 11 statements to which respondents had to answer Yes, No, or Don't Know. Some of the highlights include an overwhelming majority (96%) indicated awareness of the availability of accommodation establishments in their area (e.g. guest houses, lodges, campsites), while 45% of the residents were aware that visitors to the Kalahari region visited the area for recreation and tourism. Also, 94% of respondents felt that ecotourism was important for their community. However, while KTP provides opportunities for community development projects in the area, 50% noted lack of benefits. Also, 47% of the residents sampled were not aware of the existence of a cultural village for tourism in the Kgalagadi district, but 92% indicated that there were campsites for tourists to stay at when visiting their area (see Table 12.1).

Table 12.1   Tourism awareness of the San/Basarwa in the Kgalagadi region of Botswana (%)

Items/statements*	Yes	No	Don't know
There are guest houses/lodges/campsites for visitors in my village	96	2	2
There are campsites for visitors and tourists to use when in my village	92	8	0
Many visitors to KTP stay in my district	62	23	15
Many Batswana visit my district strictly for meetings, funerals, and business	79	19	2
Many people from the Kalahari region visit my district for recreation/tourism	45	38	17
Community campsites outside KTP accrue more money from visitors	42	21	37
Revenue from community-based tourism benefits many people in my village	38	50	12
KTP provides opportunities for community development programmes/projects	34	48	18
There is a cultural village for tourism in my district	32	47	21
Ecotourism is important to my community	94	6	0
Community-based ecotourism is essential for my community	92	6	2

Note: * 53 San/Basarwa heads of households were interviewed.

ECOTOURISM KNOWLEDGE

Six statements were used to assess residents' knowledge about ecotourism based on a *True, False,* or *Not Sure* format. The San/Basarwa appeared to be knowledgeable about ecotourism, as 96% indicated that it entailed the sustainable use of wildlife resources; on the other hand 87% acknowledged that ecotourism was about sustainable harvesting of veldt products (grass, herbal teas, and medicinal plants). Also, 92% noted that ecotourism promoted the preservation of cultural traditions. However, a sizeable number did not know whether ecotourism encouraged local participation in planning and decision-making activities: 32% indicated that they were not sure, and 8% responded that it was untrue (see Table 12.2).

Table 12.2   Ecotourism knowledge shown by the San/Basarwa of the Kgalagadi region, Botswana (%)

Items/statements*	True	False	Not sure
Ecotourism encourages conservation of natural resources	87	0	11
Ecotourism promotes preservation of cultural traditions	92	0	8
Ecotourism encourages local participation in planning and decision-making activities	60	8	32
Ecotourism ensures economic benefits for local communities	74	5	21
Ecotourism encourages sustainable use of wildlife in local communities	96	0	4
Ecotourism promotes sustainable harvesting of veldt resources	87	4	8

Note: * 53 San/Basarwa heads of households were interviewed.

Types of Community Ecotourism Benefit

SOCIO-ECONOMIC BENEFITS AT COMMUNITY LEVEL

The CBNRM policy of 2007 explains community-based ecotourism as small-scale tourism enterprises which are community owned and managed with minimal negative impacts and maximum economic benefits for local people and their natural and cultural environments (Government of Botswana, 2007). CBE enterprises which operate in the natural environment are widely regarded as key drivers for job growth, wealth creation, and economic empowerment, particularly in impoverished rural areas in most developing nations.[5] In this study area, community-based tourism initiatives were started through CBNRM, and have enabled the development of community-based organisations (CBOs), also known as Trusts. The San/Basarwa who live in these areas are part of the communally owned CBO-based tourism. Table 12.3 shows a compilation of classification of names, location, and status of operation.

---

5   Community-based ecotourism (CBE) are ventures which are environmentally sensitive; aim to ensure local people's high level of control over activities taking place; and a significant proportion of the benefits go directly into the local community coffers.

Table 12.3   List of CBNRM-based CBOs (Trusts) in the Kalahari region of Botswana

Trust/CBO	District	Registered	Active	No. of villages	Population (2001)
Koinaphu Community Trust	Kgalagadi	Yes	Yes	3	2,512
Lehututu Community Conservation Trust	Kgalagadi	Yes	-	1	1,778
Mahumo Community Trust	Kgalagadi	Yes		3	1,045
Maiteko Tshwaragano Development Trust	Kgalagadi	Yes	-	1	525
Nqwaa Khobee Xeya Trust	Kgalagadi	Yes	Yes	3	835
Qhaa Qing Development Trust	Kgalagadi	Yes	Yes	1	-
BORAVAST Development Trust	Kgalagadi	Yes	-	4	1,500
Khawa Kopanelo Development Trust	Kgalagadi	Yes	Yes	1	623
Maiteko Tshwaragano Development	Kgalagadi	Yes	-	1	581
TSAMAMA Development Trust	Kgalagadi	Yes	Yes	3	-

Source: Van der Jagt and Rozemeijer, 2002; Mbaiwa, 2013.

Income

The San/Basarwa, through their CBOs, derive income from community-related tourism. A sizeable number of residents have benefitted through revenue generation from safari-based tourism activities. In general, safari-based tourism has assisted communities financially through the generation of revenue from trophy hunting and accommodation (guest houses, campsites). Additional income results from hunting expeditions, walking safaris, animal trekking and skinning, veldt production and sale, and meat sales. Following a hunt, the safari operator generally gives meat to the CBO/Trust based on business agreements, and revenues generated through the sale of the meat accrue.

Social services

Income from tourism has supported the purchase of vehicles, which benefits the members of the community. Several of the active CBOs/Trusts have bought off-road vehicles for day-to-day use by the community. For instance, the Khawa Kopanelo Development Trust in Kgalagadi South, Nqwaa Khobee Xeya Trust in the south own land cruiser open vans (LANDflow Solutions, 2005). These vehicles have become very useful as they are used for funerals; to ferry sick people to nearby towns for medical attention; to ferry water and provisions at times of death or other community activities (e.g. village meetings), etc. Residents also indicated that when there is death in the family the CBO/Trust contributes money towards the purchase of food.

Reinvestment of revenue from community tourism

As part of the Kalahari communities' partnership with CBOs/Trusts, the San/Basarwa people also benefit from developments that are built in their communities. In some of the villages and settlements sampled, the CBO/Trust had built a tannery. For instance, Nqwaa Khobee Xeya Trust had a guest house and campsite in Ukhwi and a campsite and tannery in Ngwatle. Similarly, the Qhaa Qing Development Trust in Zutshwa owned a developed campsite, craft shop, and guest house. Thus, when tourists visit and use campsites and lodgings – and participate in other tourism activities – revenue is accrued for the entire community. This form of tourism in the remote areas of the country and among the small San/Basarwa populations is able to contribute towards alleviating poverty and reduce dependence on the government.

SOCIO-ECONOMIC BENEFITS AT THE INDIVIDUAL LEVEL

Arts and crafts

The San/Basarwa were most likely to be involved in handicraft businesses – the production and sale of arts/crafts such as belts, wristbands, earrings, necklaces and handbags – and this had a direct impact to their households and the general welfare of families. In fact, when asked about their source of income, about 32% were noted to derive cash via arts and crafts (see Figure 12.2 and 12.3).

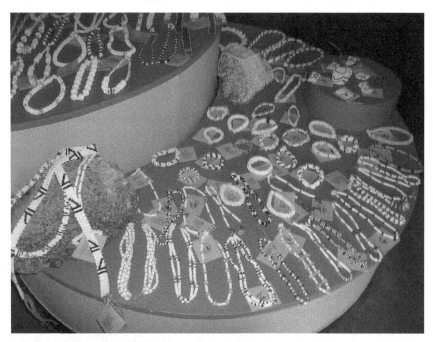

Figure 12.2   San/Basarwa craft outlet in Gantsi village in the Kalahari

Figure 12.3   A San/Basarwa craftswoman from Ncaang village in the Kalahari with items made from ostrich eggshell

Employment creation

Community-based tourism creates employment opportunities, especially for rural residents. In Botswana, CBO/Trust-tourism projects create employment prospects in remote regions where, were it not for tourism, there would be no jobs. According to Schuster (2007) there were 8,000 local people employed in CBO-tourism in Botswana, mainly in jobs in rural towns and villages (cited in Mbaiwa, 2013; also Mulale, 2005). In this study, significant numbers of individual San/Basarwa men and women were involved in CBNRM tourism-related enterprises and benefitted from them. Safari-based CBE has opened up employment opportunities in the remote Kalahari. Most residents work as animal trekkers and skinners during the hunting season as they accompany charismatic species hunters and provide services as guides. Individuals are paid at the end of the month or the hunt if hired by a safari operator. They also receive monetary tips from international hunters they escort, as well as meat and other benefits that include, for some, friendship. Other individuals derive benefits by selling handicrafts, herbal teas, and other veldt products (e.g. devil's claw, a plant of the sesame family). In some villages and settlements communities have built craft outlets where individuals are able to sell their goods to tourists staying at campsites or guest houses.

CONSERVATION AND PRESERVATION OF RESOURCES

Many of the San/Basarwa have come to appreciate CBNRM community ecotourism and understand wildlife conservation and other heritage resources. Previous studies have revealed that residents who derived socio-economic benefits from conservation tourism become supportive of conservation programmes and ecotourism in their areas (Ormsby and Mannie, 2006). The San/ Basarwa are masters of hunting in the harsh environments of the Kalahari as they have long survived on meat and wild foods. However, because of community conservation-based tourism there has been a decrease in illegal hunting of wild animals in the study area (Moswete et al., 2009), as the local people have begun to appreciate the value of wild animals.[6] Indeed, when asked if KTP should be protected for the survival of wildlife, 92% were in favour of the conservation of wild animals in the park (see Moswete et al., 2012). Similarly, 81% admitted that they were happy to have their village next to KTP; about 73% of residents were supportive of KTP as a transboundary park; and 23% opposed/strongly opposed it.

Although many local residents identified favourably with the park (KTP), according to key officials, a sizeable number of San were not hired by the park – only a few were (Moswete, 2009). However, as part of the village CBO, they too have opportunities to be employed equally and derive other social benefits. The San/Basarwa cultural revival can be observed through community tourism, especially in music, dance, and handicrafts. The preservation of their culture in music and dance has led the San/ Basarwa to develop pride and appreciate their uniqueness compared to the rest of Botswana (Moswete et al., 2012). Indeed, tsutsube (songs and dance movements with hand clapping) is unique to the San/ Basarwa of Botswana – i.e. not found in any other ethnic group in the country (see Figure 12.4).

Figure 12.4   San music and dance performance at the Kuru festival in Gantsi, Kalahari
Source: K. Setlhabi.

In the recent past, and after the formation of the Ministry of Arts and Culture, Botswana is beginning to see most of the small remaining population of the San/Basarwa taking part in presidential traditional music and dance competitions without feeling ashamed. They have

6   Personal communication with the Khawa village chief, 2012.

participated and won prizes (cash) at local and national events in the country. Hitherto, there was conservation of their unique language, music and dance, arts and craft motives, dress and way of life as hunters and gatherers. This has been appreciated highly as the entire younger generation in the country is exposed to and learn about the culture – heritage – of the San/Basarwa.

Conclusion

Studies have shown that local residents who accrue more socio-economic benefits from tourism tend to have a high level of awareness of the industry; hence, strong support exists in favour of tourism-related developments in their communities (Moswete, 2009; Scovronick and Turpie, 2009; Sirakaya et al., 2002). In the context of this study, findings were encouraging for communities adjacent to KTP, the San/Basarwa in particular, as they indicated high levels of awareness and knowledge of ecotourism-related resources within their local communities. In addition, and based on discussion with some village leaders, the majority of both local and national officials believed that cultural-heritage resources were in abundance and that they could be further utilised for communally owned ecotourism projects (Moswete, 2009).[7] Furthermore, the results indicated the important role played by the Department of Wildlife and National Parks: community extension by holding residents' workshops that over the years have managed to reach out to the small population of San/Basarwa to educate them about community-based ecotourism as a business via the CBNRM – Botswana's new approach to developing community tourism in the remote parts of the country.

Community-based tourism industry benefits many indigenous individuals in various ways (Johnson, 2009; Saarinen and Niskala, 2009; Scovronick and Turpie, 2009; Mbaiwa, 2008, 2013), and the San/Basarwa people of the Kalahari in southwestern Botswana are no exception (Moswete, 2009). Although this case study uncovered the positive effects of tourism on the San/Basarwa community, there are still issues that need to be addressed if tourism is to be further developed and more beneficial. Despite the fact that community-based ecotourism via CBNRM has opened up socio-economic opportunities in the study area, the San/Basarwa still face with the challenge of deriving adequate benefits from it.

Some of the CBO-tourism has not been generating satisfactory cash benefits, especially since in 2009 the government reduced CBO/Trust hunting quotas by excluding some prestigious species, such as lions, favoured by affluent international hunters. This has translated into community-based projects generating insufficient income for the poorer segments of the community – especially in communities with a high population of San/Basarwa.

The government's recent hunting ban is a drastic step that would adversely affect those who have been part of CBO/Trust tourism in marginal areas, where without tourism people would be forced into poverty and dependency on government handouts. Generally, an impact on benefits (income) distribution is still a challenge as many receive less tourism income than anticipated. According to Muchapondwa and Stage (2013), generally the poorer segments of the population in Botswana appear to receive a smaller share of tourism income compared to their share of overall income. Yet, it can be concluded that community-based tourism tends to benefit most of those who reside in remote areas and have established CBNRM- CBOs (Mbaiwa, 2013).

A general review of the tourism multiplier effect of community-based ecotourism in the sampled San/Basarwa villages shows a weak trend, since tourism benefits have not been used adequately to address poverty issues. A significant number of San/Basarwa still derive support

---

7   Cultural heritage resources include: monuments, historic structures, cultural landscapes, music and dance, food, architecture, etc. (Moswete et al., 2009).

in the form of government handouts. However, in general, tourism has brought changes to these communities as individuals who are involved in and benefit from community CBO-based ecotourism are able to support their families. Accordingly, CBNRM-tourism and the district councils' drought relief projects (known as *Ipelegeng*) provide the most needed employment and income to many members of the community, thus reducing poverty for some families. Most families and individuals are involved in the production and sale of arts and crafts. This means that people are able to earn income from sales of their products to both local and international visitors to their area. This also applies to conservation and the preservation of cultural skills, talents, and knowledge (arts and crafts) as the young generation can learn from their parents.

Tourism in communities neighbouring KTP is still in its infancy. The San/Basarwa residents who have knowledge of tourism are those living in villages with community-based organisations. Hence, there is the need to educate the residents about the business of tourism and how they could diversify the product from safari hunting into a year-round product of wildlife and cultural tourism. The park (KTP) is not well known; however, with suitable exposure and sustainable marketing more visits by local and international tourists would be possible. Also, when planned infrastructure is in place, community-based ecotourism or park-based tourism is likely to improve, with benefits spreading to the poorest segment of the Kalahari population – the San/Basarwa.

References

Akama, J. S. and Kieti, D. (2007). Tourism and socio-economic development in developing countries: a case study of Mombasa Resort in Kenya. *Journal of Sustainable Tourism*, 15(6), pp. 735–748.

Arntzen, J, W. (2001). The impacts of government policies on rangelands conditions and rural livelihoods: global change and subsistence rangelands in Southern Africa. *Working Paper No. 4*. Gaborone. Centre for Applied Research.

——— (2003). An economic view on wildlife management areas in Botswana. *Occasional Paper No. 10*. Gaborone: IUCN/SNV CBNRM Support Programme.

———, Molokomme, D. L., Terry, E. M., Moleele, N., Tshosa, O. and Mazambani, D. (2003). Main findings of the review of community-based natural resources management in Botswana. *Occasional Paper No. 14*. Gaborone: IUCN/SNV CBNRM Support Programme.

Aronsson, L. (2000). *The development of sustainable tourism*. New York: Continuum.

Barnes, J. I. (2001). Economic returns and allocation of resources in the wildlife sector of Botswana. *South African Journal of Wildlife Research*, 31(3–4), pp. 141–53.

Britton, S. G. (1982). The political economy of tourism in the third world. *Annals of Tourism Research*, 9, pp. 331–358.

Botswana Tourism Organisation (BTO). (2011). *Botswana eco-tourism best practices manual*. Gaborone: Botswana Tourism Board (BTB) Secretariat.

Ceballos-Lascurain, H. (1996). *Tourism, ecotourism and protected areas*. Gland: IUCN.

Government of Botswana (GoB), (2001). *Botswana national atlas: department of Surveys and Mapping*. Gaborone: Government Printers.

——— (2003). *National Development Plan 9 2003/04–2008/09. Ministry of Finance and Development Planning*. Gaborone: Government Printers.

——— (2007). Community based natural resource management policy. *Paper No. 2 of the Botswana Government*. Gaborone: Government Printers.

Gumbo, G. B. (2002). The political economy of development in the Chobe: peasants, fishermen and tourists, 1960–1995. *Unpublished MA dissertation*. Gaborone: University of Botswana.

Hitchcock, R. K. (1991). Tourism and sustainable development among remote area population in Botswana. In L. Pfotenhauer (ed.), *Tourism in Botswana*. Gaborone: Botswana Society, pp. 161–172.

———— (1997). Cultural, economic and environmental impacts of tourism among Kalahari Bushmen. In E. Chambers (ed.), *Tourism and culture: An applied perspective*. Albany: State University of New York Press, pp. 93–128.

———— and Brandenburgh, R. L. (1990). *Tourism, conservation, and culture in the Kalahari Desert*. Retrieved from: https://www.culturalsurvival.org/ourpublications/csq/article/tourism-conservation-and-culture-kalahari-desert-botswana (accessed: 1 February 2013).

Johnson, S. (2009). State of community-based natural resources management (CBNRM). *Report of the Botswana National CBNRM Forum*. Gaborone: Kalahari Conservation Society.

Kgalagadi District Development Committee (KDDC). (2003). *Kgalagadi District Development Plan 6: 2003–2005*. Gaborone: KDDC.

LANDflow Solutions (2005). *Kgalagadi communal areas land management plan, 2005–2020*. Gaborone: Ministry of Local Government.

Mbaiwa, J. (2004). The success and sustainability of community-based natural resource management in the Okavango, Botswana. *South African Geographical Journal*, 86(1), pp. 44–53.

———— (2005). Enclave tourism and its socio-economic impacts in the Okavango Delta, Botswana. *Tourism Management*, 26, pp. 157–172.

———— (2008). Tourism development, rural livelihoods and conservation in the Okavango Delta, Botswana. *Unpublished PhD thesis*. College Station: Texas A&M University.

———— (2013). Community-based natural resource management (CBNRM) in Botswana. *Final Draft CBNRM Status Report of 2011–2012*. Gaborone: CBNRM.

Moswete, N. (2009). Stakeholder perspectives on the potential for community-based ecotourism development and support for the Kgalagadi Transfrontier Park in Botswana. *Unpublished PhD thesis*. Gainesville: University of Florida.

Moswete, N. and Mavondo, F. (2003). Problems facing the tourism industry of Botswana. *Botswana Notes and Records*, 35, pp. 69–78.

————, Thapa, B., and Child, B. (2012). Attitudes and opinions of local and national public sector stakeholders towards Kgalagadi Transfrontier Park, Botswana. *International Journal of Sustainable Development and World Ecology*, 19(1), pp. 67–80.

————, Thapa, B., and Lacey, G. (2009). Village-based tourism and community participation: a case study of Matsheng villages in southwest Botswana. In J. Saarinen, F. Becker, H. Manwa, and D. Wilson (eds), *Sustainable tourism in Southern Africa: local communities and natural resources in transition*. Bristol: Channelview, pp. 189–209.

Muchapondwa, E. and Stage, J. (2013). The economic impacts of tourism in Botswana, Namibia and South Africa: is poverty subsiding? *Natural Resources Forum*, 37, pp. 80–89.

Mulale, K. (2005). The structural organization of CBNRM in Botswana. *Unpublished PhD thesis*. Ames: Iowa State University.

————, Matema, C., Funda, X., Slater-Jones, S., Njovu, D., Kanguechi, G., Hay, D., and Crookes, V. (2013). *Community-based natural resource management in Southern Africa: an introduction*. Bloomington, IN: AuthorHouse.

Ndubano, E. (2000). The economic impacts of tourism on the local people: the case of Maun in the Ngamiland-Sub District. *Unpublished PhD thesis*. Gaborone: University of Botswana.

Ormsby, A. and Mannie, K. (2006). Ecotourism benefits and the role of local guides at Masoala National Park, Madagascar. *Journal of Sustainable Tourism*, 14(3), pp. 271–287.

Saarinen, J. and Niskala, M. (2009). Local culture and regional development: the role of OvaHimba in Namibian tourism. In P. Hottola (ed.), *Tourism strategies and local responses in southern Africa*. Wallingford: CABI, pp. 61–72.

Schuster, B. (2007). *Proceedings of the 4th National CBNRM Conference in Botswana and the CBNRM Status Report*. IUCN Botswana, Gaborone: 20–23 November 2006.

Sebele, L. S. (2010). Community-based tourism ventures, benefits and challenges: Khama Rhino Sanctuary Trust, Central District, Botswana. *Tourism Management*, 31(1), pp. 136–146.

Selby, H. (1991). Hunting as a component of tourism in Botswana. In L. Pfotenhauer (ed.), *Tourism in Botswana*. Gaborone: Botswana Society, pp. 370–380.

Sikaraya, E., Teye, V., and Sonmez, S. (2002). Understanding residents' support for tourism development in the Central Region of Ghana. *Journal of Travel Research*, 41, pp. 57–67.

Scovronick, N. C., and Turpie, J. K. (2009). Is enhanced tourism a reasonable expectation for transboundary conservation? An evaluation of the Kgalagadi Transfrontier Park. *Environmental Conservation*, 36(2), pp. 149–156.

South African Park Board and Department of Wildlife and National Parks (1997). *Kgalagadi Transfrontier Park Management Plan*. Gaborone: Botswana.

Sproule, K. and Subandi, A. (1998). Guidelines for community-based ecotourism programs: Lessons from Indonesia. In K. Lindberg., M. Wood, and D. Engeldrum (eds), *Ecotourism: A guide for planners and managers*. North Bennington, VT: International Ecotourism Society, pp. 215–235.

Thomas, D. S. G. and Shaw, P. A. (1991). *The Kalahari environment*. New York: Cambridge University Press.

Van der Jagt, C. and Rozemeijer, N. (2002). Practical guide for facilitating community based natural resources management (CBNRM) in Botswana. *CBNRM Support Programme Occasional Paper No. 8*. Gaborone: SNV, IUCN.

World Travel and Tourism Council (WTTC). (2007). *Botswana: The impact of travel and tourism on jobs and the economy*. London: WTTC.

——— (2013). *Botswana: Travel and tourism economic impact*. Retrieved from: http://www.wttc.org/ (accessed: 20 January 2014).

13

Aboriginal Culture in Indigenous Tourism Management in Central Australia

Benxiang Zeng and Rolf Gerritsen

Chapter Synopsis

This research analyses the role of 'culture' in Indigenous tourism management in Central Australia. Indigenous culture is a major driver of Indigenous tourism development and plays a key role in Indigenous tourism establishment and management. Yet culture is a diffuse concept that has both 'high' culture and 'low' culture aspects. Culture also has both supply-side and demand-side elements – mostly centred on 'authenticity'. These may not be compatible, which will inhibit successful cultural tourism. One incompatibility that is 'cultural' is the disjunction between western business management models, with their distinction between the 'personal' and 'business', as against the Indigenous fusing of the personal and business. Case studies from Central Australia show some enterprise successes. These suggest that 'low' cultural components – including kinship, eldership, land ownership and sociality, and partnership – are important determinants on the supply side of Indigenous tourism business management. Improving the compatibility of these factors with western-cum-modern 'cultural components', such as organisational leadership and rational management, could benefit both Indigenous people and other stakeholders in the Indigenous tourism industry. Indigenous tourism management policies should pay more attention to harnessing cultural differences and securing 'culturally-ready' tourism management.

Introduction

Internationally, tourism has developed as a leading economic sector for many developing peripheral regions (Bunten, 2010; Moscardo, 2005). Additionally, in some staples (single commodity export) of regional economies, it is seen as an economic alternative to obtaining local economic independence, although in practice this may be problematic (Carson and Carson, 2011). Tourism has been a significant contributor to the Australian economy, and Indigenous cultural tourism is expected to play a similarly important role in economic development, particularly in

Indigenous areas and remote communities (Tourism Research Australia, 2010). In some remote regions in Australia, tourism is being recognised as one of the main drivers of local economic activity. For example, Central Australia has seen the development of a large-scale tourism economy, with around 600,000 tourists and around $600 million of annual tourist expenditure (Tourism Northern Territory, 2010, 2011). Tourism and its associated activities provide 24.8% of the area's gross regional product (GRP), making it the most tourism-dependent region in Australia (Tourism Research Australia, 2011a). This is a major activity, considering that the total population is small (Alice Springs, 28,000; the region, 40,000). However, tourism in the region is not necessarily focused solely upon Indigenous tourism, although at least 30% of the regional tourism revenue can be attributed in some way to the attractions of Aboriginal culture (Zeng et al., 2010).

Generally we can accept that substantial Indigenous entrepreneurship in the tourism industry is likely to bring about widely dispersed economic benefits as well as development benefits, particular to the Indigenous participants. These include greater self-reliance, self-confidence, and an increased sense of well-being (Neblett and Green, 2000). Nonetheless, there are impediments to be overcome in achieving successful, long-term Indigenous tourism in remote Australia.

Since the mid 1990s, Australian Indigenous tourism has been officially promoted and extensively marketed. The number of tourism businesses which provide Indigenous tourism products and services to Indigenous tourism visitors boomed in the period from the mid 1990s to the early 2000s. Compared with other visitors, Indigenous tourism visitors spend more money purchasing Indigenous cultural products and services than do mainstream tourists (Tourism Research Australia, 2010). The key issue is to ensure that Indigenous people can benefit in some way from these tourism activities. As many analysts have noted, cultural tourism can allow the diversification of livelihoods for Indigenous people (Mbaiwa, 2009). So, a prima facie economic reason exists for governments and Indigenous people to welcome tourism. In Australia that case is even stronger because, for example, the country has little that is singular about its built environment. But Australia's Indigenous culture is internationally distinctive. Aboriginal culture is important in differentiating Australian uniqueness from its international competitors in the tourist market (Morse, 2000).

Notwithstanding that Indigenous tourism has been supported by governments and other key stakeholders, this tourism sector has been declining since 2005, both in terms of total Indigenous tourism visitor numbers and in its relative share of Australian tourism industry. International visitors are the major contributor to Indigenous tourism visitation in Australia. In 2005, the number of international Indigenous tourism visitors peaked (at 915,000) and then began declining, to 689,000 in 2010. Domestic overnight Indigenous tourism visitor numbers peaked in 2006, when 700,000 domestic overnight trips were recorded. Since then this number has been declining. In 2010, the total was 306,000, the lowest level since 1999 (see Figure 13.1).

In recent years (2006–2010) the total number of Indigenous tourism visitors in Australia has decreased by 10.37% annually on average. International visitors in this category decreased annually at a rate of 4.89%, and domestic overnight visitors in this category decreased much more significantly, by an average annual rate of 18.69% (see Table 13.1).

Following the significant declines in Indigenous tourism visitor numbers and visit nights, total expenditure by Indigenous tourism visitors has also been decreasing in recent years. In 2010, total expenditure stood at $3.79 billion, 10.6% less than in 2009. Since 2006, there has been an average annual decrease of 5.9% in total expenditure by Indigenous tourism visitors (see Table 13.1). Although this expenditure is not on Indigenous tourism activities alone, this continuous decline does imply a decline in expenditure on Indigenous culture related activities and services.

While the Australian tourism industry as a whole has mostly maintained its long-term growth, the Indigenous tourism share has declined since 2005. Generally the trends for international, domestic, and total Indigenous tourism visitors had similar change patterns with their numbers and their shares in total tourism visitors (see Figure 13.2).

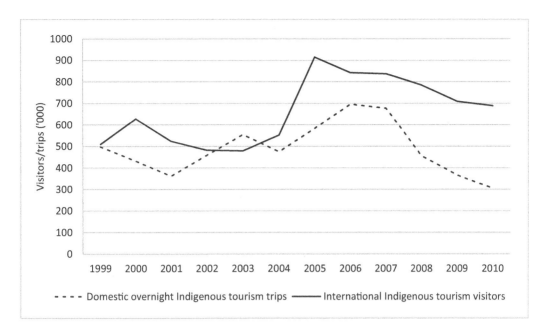

Figure 13.1   Domestic and international overnight Indigenous tourism visitors in Australia, 1999–2010

Source: Tourism Research Australia 2011a, b.

Table 13.1   Indigenous tourism visitors, nights, and average expenditure in Australia, 2006–2010

	2006	2007	2008	2009	2010	Change 2009/10 (%)	Average annual change 2006–2010 (%)
International							
Visitors (000)	842	837	785	709	689	-2.82	-4.89
Average expenditure per visitor ($)	4,240	4,477	4,777	5,057	4,800	-5.08	3.15
Visitor nights (million)	42	41	42	40	38	-5.00	-2.47
Average expenditure per night ($)	85	92	90	90	88	-2.22	0.87
Total expenditure ($ billion)	3.6	3.7	3.7	3.6	3.3	-8.33	-2.15
Domestic overnight							
Trips (000)	700	677	456	367	306	-16.62	-18.69
Average expenditure per visitor ($)	1,757	1,706	1,571	1,746	1,604	-8.13	-2.25
Visitor nights (million)	7.1	5.6	4.8	3.1	2.5	-19.35	-22.97
Average expenditure per night ($)	174	205	149	205	194	-5.37	2.76
Total expenditure ($ billion)	1.23	1.15	0.72	0.64	0.49	-23.44	-20.55

Table 13.1   Indigenous tourism visitors, nights, and average expenditure in Australia, 2006–2010 (*concluded*)

	2006	2007	2008	2009	2010	Change 2009/10 (%)	Average annual change 2006–2010 (%)
International and domestic overnight							
Visitors/trips (000)	1,542	1,514	1,241	1,076	995	-7.53	-10.37
Average expenditure per visitor/trip ($)	3,132	3,203	3,562	3,941	3809	-3.34	5.01
Visitor nights (million)	49.1	46.6	46.8	43.1	40.5	-6.03	-4.70
Average expenditure per night ($)	98	104	94	98	94	-4.87	-1.24
Total expenditure ($ billion)	4.83	4.85	4.42	4.24	3.79	-10.61	-5.88

Source: Tourism Research Australia, 2011b.

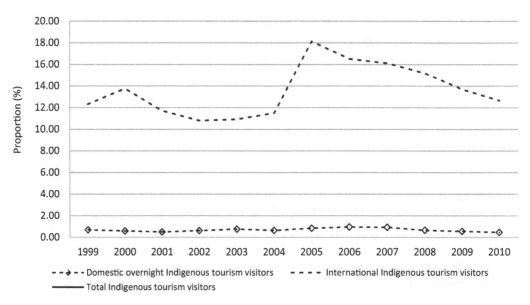

The trend of proportion of Indigenous tourism visitors in total visitors (1999-2010)

- - ◆ - - Domestic overnight Indigenous tourism visitors   - - - - International Indigenous tourism visitors
——— Total Indigenous tourism visitors

Figure 13.2   Share of Indigenous tourism in the Australian tourism industry, 1999–2010

Sources: Tourism Research Australia, 2011a, b.

The proportion of international tourists participating in Indigenous tourism declined from 18% in 2005 to 13% in 2010, while domestic tourists participating in Indigenous tourism declined from 0.9% in 2006 to 0.5% in 2010 (Table 13.2 and Figure 13.2). These declines began before the Global Financial Crisis (GFC).

The continuous decline in Indigenous tourism suggests that Indigenous-focused tourism enterprises performed worse than the Australian tourism industry as a whole.

Without doubt there is global demand for Indigenous tourism experiences and a growing interest in the values, knowledge, and traditions of Indigenous cultures (Peeler, 2004).

Table 13.2   Changes in Indigenous tourism participation

	Domestic overnight			International			Total		
	Indigenous tourism visitors	Total visitors	Proportion (%)	Indigenous tourism visitors	Total visitors	Proportion (%)	Indigenous tourism visitors	Total visitors	Proportion (%)
1999	498	72,981	0.68	510	4,143	12.31	1,008	77,124	1.31
2000	432	73,771	0.59	628	4,567	13.75	1,060	78,338	1.35
2001	362	74,585	0.49	524	4,475	11.71	886	79,060	1.12
2002	459	75,339	0.61	482	4,463	10.80	941	79,802	1.18
2003	554	73,621	0.75	479	4,385	10.92	1,033	78,006	1.32
2004	475	74,301	0.64	552	4,797	11.51	1,027	79,098	1.30
2005	584	69,923	0.84	915	5,046	18.13	1,499	74,969	2.00
2006	696	73,564	0.95	842	5,099	16.51	1,538	78,663	1.96
2007	677	73,800	0.92	837	5,197	16.11	1,514	78,997	1.92
2008	456	70,491	0.65	785	5,167	15.19	1,241	75,658	1.64
2009	367	66,077	0.56	709	5,175	13.70	1,076	71,252	1.51
2010	306	67,402	0.45	689	5,441	12.66	995	72,843	1.37

Source: Tourism Research Australia, 2011b.

Indigenous tourism in Australia seems attractive and has received a lot of official support, but it still keeps declining. There have been various explanations for this phenomenon. Conventional explanations include the operating environment of the tourist market; business impediments; insufficient capital and over-sufficient regulation; the confused focus of the industry; structural disadvantage (Indigenous tourism occurs mostly in remote areas that are expensive to access) ; the negative impact upon lifestyles and livelihoods; and the development of cultural products and services such as mis-represented and exploited culture (Gerritsen and Zeng, 2011; Ryan and Aicken, 2005; Smith, 2009). All these interpretations reveal to some extent the problems the industry has faced. Some of these issues apply also to the tourism industry generally and not necessarily solely to Indigenous tourism. Therefore, they are unconvincing explanations for the relative decline of the Indigenous tourism industry in comparison with the Australian tourism industry as a whole.

Some recent studies have focused on underlying traditional cultural and social factors. Whitford and Ruhanen (2010) suggested that since the late 1990s, while Australian governments have developed a number of policies relating to Indigenous tourism, these policies exhibited a propensity for a top-down approach to Indigenous tourism development and failed to display the flexibility required to deal with the diversity of the social, economic, and cultural circumstances of Indigenous Australians. Gerritsen and Zeng (2011) identified another reason for the relative decline of the sector: that is the problem of Indigenous township/community-centred tourism (often associated with art centres). They posited that the decline there was in part a consequence of both overloading tourism enterprises with community development roles as well as wider Indigenous opposition to post-2007 governmental community development policies. The recent (post-GFC) decline in international sales of Aboriginal art may also be a factor here, as the art centre is usually a core element of a community tourism enterprise. The Aboriginal disaffection hypothesis suggested by Gerritsen and Zeng (2011) was partly demonstrated during the recent (August 2012) Northern Territory election, when the Aboriginal vote, after almost 35 years of attachment to the Labor Party, rejected that government and voted for the opposition Conservatives (Gerritsen, 2012; Sanders, 2012). The Gerritsen-Zeng hypothesis touched cultural components in Indigenous tourism management, and raised a necessity to investigate the cultural aspects in Aboriginal tourism business management.

Although there have been many explanations for the decline of Indigenous tourism in Australia in recent years, the problematic role of culture in management has not been sufficiently addressed in the research. More research is needed to clarify the argument that different cultural perspectives on tourism development and cultural attitudes and motivations toward business management will significantly impact on Indigenous tourism management. This chapter argues that while cultural components are a driving force for Aboriginal tourism development in Central Australia, they have to be knowledgeably managed if they are not to impact deleteriously on the *management* of Aboriginal tourism businesses. In that sense we are looking at a conundrum, not of attraction but of management of that attraction.

Literature Review

The term 'culture' has traditionally been referred to, by 'metaphorical extension', as a representation of the process of cultivation or improvement within society (Levine and Janowitz, 1971). During the course of analysis, distinctions have been made between 'high' and 'low' culture. High culture supposedly denotes 'all that is best' of what has been written, created, or thought in the world (Williams, 1974). In academic circles, high culture is a 'set of cultural products' held in the highest esteem by society (Gans, 1999; Tuchman and Fortin, 1989). Low culture emphasises morality but limits itself to familial and individual norms and values.

Their own culture is extremely important to Australian Aboriginal people. They also have a distinction (in practice, if not theory) between 'high' culture and 'low' culture. 'High' culture is sacred/ceremonial knowledge that is highly secret and retained by a small number of qualified senior men and women. This can affect a tourism venture if it reveals knowledge to inappropriate people, goes onto land where they have no permission to be, or strays near a place that is important for sacred/ceremonial reasons (Myers, 1982). Transgressions such as this are extremely serious and can lead to an Aboriginal community banning such a tourism venture, even at some cost to itself.

Aboriginal 'low' culture is also a system of norms and values, but it is very different from the mainstream European-derived culture of most Australians (Meggitt, 1962; Myers, 1986). Aboriginal culture incorporates a unique attachment to place, a wider idea of family that means not just blood-related kin but also affines in particular social relations (what they term related 'skin' classifications). The *weltanschauung* or way-of-being in life is too complex to outline here but, to take one example, it features 'demand-sharing' values that contradict the deferred gratification endemic in societies in capitalist systems (Peterson, 1993).

Culture affects attitude, including attitudes toward new venture creation and development (Baskerville, 2003; Lindsay, 2005). Developing a better understanding of differences between Indigenous entrepreneurship and non-Indigenous entrepreneurship can lead to more culturally sensitive entrepreneurial education, training, and development programmes that reflect an economic development approach desired by Indigenous communities. Thus, where entrepreneurship from a non-Indigenous perspective is focused upon the commercialisation of innovation, Indigenous entrepreneurship is associated with creating, managing, and developing new ventures by Indigenous people for the benefit of Indigenous people (Hindle and Lansdowne, 2005). Underpinning these benefits are strong desires for self-determination and the preservation of heritage (Anderson, 1999; Hindle and Lansdowne, 2005). Indigenous people prefer to develop entrepreneurial strategies that originate in and are controlled by the community, as well as being acceptable within Indigenous culture (Anderson et al., 2004; Robinson and Ghostkeeper, 1987).

Lindsay (2005) developed a complex Indigenous entrepreneur attitude model that included cultural aspects. This suggested that the attitude of Indigenous entrepreneurs is influenced by Indigenous cultural values and practices. Moreover, culture not only affects attitude; it also affects perception and behaviour, which are also relevant to the study of entrepreneurship in Indigenous settings. As such, the development of any Indigenous entrepreneurship models that focus on such variables needs to reflect an Indigenous cultural context. Australian Indigenous social and economic values can be sharply different from conventional (western) attitudes to 'business' and 'work'. Unlike capitalist societies, Aboriginal cultural values do not separate work and life (McRae-Williams and Gerritsen, 2010).

Cultural values and practices need to be reflected in the content, delivery, and marketing of Indigenous tourism programmes (Radcliffe and Laurie, 2006). It cannot be assumed that similar entrepreneurship strategies can be effective in all cultural environments. For example, Horn and Tahi (2009) investigated rural Māori tourism business development and found that a range of cultural factors play important roles in their tourism business establishment and operation. These are the cultural demands that rural Māori have on their time; the ways in which cultural practices clash with commercial practice; the expectations that rural Māori have of business development; the ways in which land ownership operates; and the historical factors that have left rural Māori marginalised and in a position of trying to recover what they have lost.

Culture is at the core of Indigenous tourism development. There has been extensive research focusing on the development and promotion of cultural products and services for Indigenous tourism businesses. For example, Manyara et al. (2006) propose a new, postcolonial model of tourism development involving small Indigenous enterprises and promoting cultural products to new markets. Carter and Beeton (2004) analysed the complexity of cultural expression, arguing that the 'physical' manifestations of culture (e.g. art and music) are often a 'product' for tourism, especially for Indigenous tourism. Nevertheless, complexities in culture and cultural expression create difficulties in developing/marketing cultural products whilst protecting local traditional cultures – the so-called 'commodification of culture' problem (Johnston, 2006; Finkel, 2008; Zeppel, 2010).

Current knowledge regarding the motivations for Indigenous tourism development is deficient, although it can be inferred that economic incentives are the driving force for tourism development. However, in addition to economic incentives, social, cultural, political, and environmental factors are strong determinants for many Indigenous communities interested in pursuing tourism as a development option (Colton, 2005).

Nonetheless, the driving force of Indigenous tourism has come from demand by tourists to see the 'other' – cultures that are often regarded as being wild, primitive, and exotic or, at a minimum, substantially different from their own. At the present time, the scale and speed of growth of such tourism is spreading into formerly ignored peripheral and remote areas that are the home areas of Indigenous populations not previously exposed to such development (Butler and Hinch, 1996). Could Indigenous people benefit from such tourism through increased economic independence accompanied by a higher degree of self-determination and cultural pride? Attempts to answer this question should be based on an understanding of whether tourism activities in which Indigenous people are directly involved are controlled by them, as well as whether their culture serves as the essence of the attraction. The literature reveals that most disadvantageous tourism developments occur when tourism is imposed on Indigenous communities and is under external control (Butler and Hinch, 1996; Colton, 2005; Smith and Robinson 2006). Supporting Gerritsen and Zeng's (2011) worries about overloading Aboriginal tourist enterprises with community development roles, recent observers have worried about the effect on its traditions of increasing state control over Aboriginal art production (Rothwell, 2013).

There has been some discussion on the drivers of Indigenous tourism development, both in Australia and internationally. Many factors have been recognised as impelling Indigenous tourism, such as economic-cum-regional development; Indigenous participation and empowerment; demand from tourists; and cultural aspects, including customary law and local traditions (Colton, 2005; Butler and Hinch, 1996; Galla, 2006; Shire of Halls Creek, 2011).

Culture is usually described as a driving force and a goal for development as well as a key factor impacting on every stage of the development process (Galla, 2006). Sustainable development relies upon recognition of the value of cultural diversity within communities (regardless of socio-economic status) and committed individuals (de Varine, 2006).

Understanding what constitutes an Indigenous culture and endeavouring to sustain it are formidable challenges because culture is not static (Tai, 2007). And at any one time, not all persons in any Indigenous group may define or value all elements of that culture in the same way. Thus senior men may prioritise spiritual tradition and sacred sites, while women will focus upon retaining traditional ecological knowledge and transmitting this to the younger generation. In Australia, there has been little exploration of the roles within tourism enterprises of culture and especially the 'low' culture components – such as eldership, generational succession, traditional knowledge heritage, and so on. This chapter tries to provide some analysis of the implications of Indigenous culture in Indigenous tourism business management. Questions such as 'What is the role of Indigenous culture in Indigenous tourism management?' are rarely directly examined in the literature, which seems instead to focus upon the impacts of tourism on Indigenous culture. From the following four cases, our research tried to provide such evidence.

Case Studies

In some regions in Australia, Aboriginal cultural values have been applied as the core values of local tourism development. In Western Australia's Shire of Halls Creek, the local tourism development strategy highly values local cultures, heritage and community character, and respect for customary law and traditional owners as core values and driving forces for tourism development (Shire of Halls Creek, 2010). Yet in the same region of far Northwest Australia tourism enterprises have been seen as having a negative cultural and spiritual impacts upon Aboriginal people (Smith, 2009). Should we then be pessimistic about the benefits to Indigenous people of cultural tourism?

This research uses some case studies in Central Australia to provide evidence to support the argument that, where cultural compatibility is a driving force in the management of Aboriginal tourism projects, it becomes an important determinant in influencing the success of that tourism.

OWNERSHIP, CULTURAL RECOGNITION, AND EMPLOYMENT

We analysed available case data downloaded from the database of Australian Indigenous Tourism (2011a). The data for 151 Indigenous tourism operators was analysed: 107 out of 151 (i.e. 71%) are owned or co-owned by Indigenous people – directly by individuals/families or indirectly by communities or Indigenous corporations (see Table 13.3). Most of these businesses are running guided cultural tours where Indigenous people (owners or employees) are involved as guides. This suggests that Indigenous people have very strong willingness to participate in, manage, and control the tourism activities where Indigenous culture would be prime products.

Only 63% of Indigenous owned or co-owned businesses are directly managed by Indigenous people. There is still a relative high percentage (37%) of such businesses being managed by non-

Table 13.3   Ownership and employment of Indigenous tourism businesses in Australia

Ownership	Management	Number of businesses	Indigenous employees (n)	Non-Indigenous employees (n)	Indigenous employees (%)
Indigenous owned	Indigenous managed	66	358	70.5	83.55
	Non-Indigenous managed	8	78	44	63.93
	Non-identified management	16	134	166	44.67
	Subtotal 1: Indigenous-owned businesses	90	570	280.5	67.02
Co-owned (Indigenous and non-Indigenous	Co-managed (Indigenous and non-Indigenous)	2	6	8	42.86
	Non-Indigenous managed	12	207.5	180	53.55
	Non-identified management	3	6	24.5	19.67
	Subtotal 2: Co-owned businesses	17	219.5	212.5	50.81
Total-Indigenous owned and co-owned		107	789.5	493	61.56

Source: Australian Indigenous Tourism, 2011b.

Indigenous people. This suggests that Indigenous people still lack 'western/modern' management skills (e.g. accounting and logistics) and need support from outside. In many cases they choose to control the businesses on their lands and based on their culture via ownership rather than direct involvement in the daily management. However, such management may exclude Aboriginal social perspectives intrinsic to their notion of life management (Johnson et al., 2007; McRae-Williams and Gerritsen, 2010). Plausibly, the sustainable management of Indigenous tourism enterprises may require the incorporation into their organisation of Indigenous values of social organisation (Bunten, 2010).

Another interesting fact derived from the data is that Indigenous owned and managed businesses employ more Indigenous people, while non-Indigenous managed businesses tend to employ fewer Indigenous people. Although there is not enough information to explain this phenomenon, it might indicate shortages of management and general workforce personnel for some Indigenous tourism activities. Alternatively, it may reveal that when the enterprise is Indigenous managed, Indigenous skills and attributes are better recognised.

This latter point supports the conclusion that benefits from Indigenous tourism to Indigenous people may extend beyond economic profits for the individual to multiple social and economic advantages for entire communities (Anderson, 1999; Hindle and Lansdowne, 2005) – but only so long as Indigenous values are central to such enterprises and the Indigenous people have substantial control over the management of the enterprises, via ownership or direct operation.

KINSHIP, ELDERSHIP, AND ELITE MARKETING IN UMPIYARA CULTURAL CAMP

Umpiyara Cultural Camp was set up by an Anangu family in the Mutitjulu community, near the famous Central Australian monolith called Uluru (also known as Ayers Rock). The camp officially started in early 2011. Although it is too early to conclude that it is successful, this project has already shown some of the uniqueness of an Aboriginal tourism business.

The proprietors have a strong vision to break the negative reliance on welfare by creating economic independence and cultural succession for their family and their kin. They intend to pass on this independence to future generations; the elders in the family have inspired the whole family to participate in the business. Their vision will be achieved by sharing their culture with visitors. This small tourism business was formed on a kinship basis, and is led by a younger family member. They share their cultural-educational camp with diverse groups, comprising both interested international and national groups who want to visit the Anangu's traditional country. The camp is culturally based and targets small groups to organise different 'special-interest' camps – such as a cultural camp, a women's camp, and a school student camp. The campsite is located in the middle of the bush, around 15 km from the Yulara township.

This small family business applies a unique triple driving forces model: elders, elites, and scholars. Elders in the family inspire and teach the younger generations and drive the formation and implementation of tourism business. Elite (i.e. well-educated) family members promote and market the traditional cultural and natural activities to a wide range of target markets, who are encouraged by the elite to be interested in and committed to Indigenous cultural sharing and country conservation. The in-depth involvement of Aboriginal scholars with a kinship to the family occurred throughout the project's implementation.

The family understands that they are on a learning curve so far as tourism enterprise is concerned and that they need to learn from doing. The business started with small programmes and targets, to gain management experience and to train and inspire family members to be involved in tourism. The number of tourists is also strictly controlled, at 25 persons at most per camp. This reduces the danger of commodification and fetishisation of their product.

This project had been well prepared. Planning included budgeting, activity design, and proper facility preparation (such as toilets, tents, swags, and water supply). The group also secured initial governmental support to engage external consultants to establish their market. The project has been also aiming at the official eco-tourism standard accreditation, a target that has marketing advantages.

The project leaders are also thinking beyond the enterprise itself. The strategy is to provide a training base for younger generations in the family. The younger family members are also encouraged to work for other businesses in the region once they feel confident enough through the learning from doing process in their own family's enterprise. So the enterprise has wider social development effects. Further, through this the family kin-based business intends to move towards a partnership with the broader community.

The successful initiation of this small family business suggests that it is important to understand that the management structure is built on a cultural base, and the management principles focus upon traditional cultural conservation and cultural sharing. More importantly, the management structure and strategy are based on Indigenous culture and concepts of sociality and sharing of authority. Both 'high' and 'low' cultures play important roles in business establishment and management.

LEADERSHIP AND PARTNERSHIP: COMMUNITY-BASED INDIGENOUS TOURISM DEVELOPMENT

The Central Land Council (a statutory body representing traditional owners of Aboriginal lands in Central Australia) has been engaging local Aboriginal people to be involved in the Federal Government's Indigenous Protected Area (IPA) programme.

In Central Australia, Aboriginal communities considered tourism as a means to social, rather than economic, development. They saw tourism as a very good way to get their children 'onto country', as they did not want them to lose their identity and culture. The communities had firm ideas for tourism development on their lands, and reasonable understanding about tourism. They were conscious of access issues, such as keeping tourists away from sites of sacred significance; road houses being provided for fuel supplies; travel safety; money boxes for camping sites; and appropriate signage for tourists travelling to Aboriginal communities. They were also conscious that they needed a project plan and some initial external help and funding support. They wanted to establish partnerships with the local Central Australian tourism industry, governments and local businesses to set up and manage Aboriginal tourism enterprises.

With regard to tourism products and services, they were aware of the attraction of their culture and lands. They proposed to share with tourists experiences such as 'telling in the bush' (broadly explaining the ecology and how they make use of it and the significance of 'country' for themselves), as well as activities such as making digging sticks and then going out for honey ants – 'going out country and coming back for *inma*' (an Aboriginal dance).

Aboriginal communities expressed their desire to keep control over the tourism development run on their lands and/or based on their culture. While ownership was considered as one of the most important issues in their tourism development, they wanted to take leadership in tourism development and management. They welcome and are keen to facilitate tourism development on their country, but they were worried about 'whitefella'-controlled tourism, as 'blackfellas want to lead the show'.

This case suggests that leadership is one of the most important concerns for Aboriginal people in proposing a tourism business, as they think that taking leadership is the best way to maintain their cultural core in any development. Once they are at a leadership position, they are willing to establish a partnership with other stakeholders.

JUNGALA TOURS: BALANCING COMMODIFICATION AND CULTURAL CONSERVATION

The Jungala tourism enterprise is a long-established Aboriginal-owned and operated business based in Alice Springs, in Central Australia. It operates a number of activities, such as bicycle-based tours of the township's Arrernte sites of significance and guided walking tours of the Larapinta Trail (an increasingly famous trekking trail through the West MacDonnell Ranges near Alice Springs). In a sense the Aboriginal owner-operators of this business are a trusted elite group of organisers of a wider group of Aboriginal persons (as in our Umpiyara Cultural Camp case study). In this context we mean 'elite' in the sense of cultural intermediaries.

One activity that the enterprise operates is to take school groups (usually from schools based in the large cities of Australia's eastern seaboard) on walking tours through 'country'. These tours are led by traditional owners of that country who, during these camping treks, 'explain the country' (in their terms). This 'explaining' means that they educate the school groups on the meaning of the country to their people, such as the use their people made of the country for food and spiritual nourishment. They explain how their people adapted to the vagaries of a harsh and variable climate, where short-term abundance would be replaced by hardship and resource shortage. By the end of the three-day trek, the school groups are invariably emotionally involved with the experience and their hosts.

The presentation of the Indigenous to the 'other' creates a stylisation and simplification of the Indigenous culture, often to the extent (as we have noted earlier) of over-simplification or even fetishisation of the Indigenous culture or environment (Igoe, 2010). The Jungala tourism activity described here avoided such appropriation, and instead produced appreciation. From the Aboriginal traditional wwner point of view the result they achieved – sympathetic understanding and validation – was as important as the business economics of the process.

So this cultural tourism product operated on two levels. On the one hand the Aboriginal managers operated a normal, small capitalist business. But their product was not inanimate. Their walking tour guides were not just employees. These 'employees' wanted recognition 'for their story', i.e. understanding of their way in the world, both as a people and as individuals. The brilliance of the enterprise, as an Aboriginal cultural tourism product, was that it operated at those two levels.

Key Findings

From the above case studies, some important findings are derived. Central Australian Aboriginal people are interested in cultural tourism, although they usually have little conventional managerial experience. They are eager to learn to run tourism businesses and prefer to achieve that by 'learning from doing'. This suits the Aboriginal style of knowledge acquisition more than formal classroom-style learning (Eickelkamp, 2011). Like the mainstream industry, Aboriginal tourism pursues economic benefits. But successfully managed Aboriginal cultural tourism enterprises are sensitive to broader 'cultural' issues, such as 'respect' or passing on their culture to the younger generations. This means that these social objectives may be even more important than simple economic benefit.

Cultural factors – some 'low' cultural components (such as eldership, kinship, ownership and cultural expression) in particular – are the major driving forces in Aboriginal tourism management, especially at the early stage of tourism business development. Leadership and partnership are always important for a successful transition from a family-based Aboriginal tourism business to a mainstream tourism business.

Cultural tourism presents a dilemma for Central Australian Aboriginal people: they welcome external help and support, including funding, knowledge and skills (by establishing a partnership), but they are worried about the possible loss of their cultural authenticity (i.e. ownership) and independence (i.e. leadership).

Conclusion

'Culture' is a diffuse concept that has both 'high' and 'low' aspects. Culture also has both supply-side and demand-side elements – mostly centred on 'authenticity' – that may not always be compatible. Such incompatibilities may inhibit successful cultural tourism, especially among the Aboriginal people of Central Australia. One incompatibility that is 'cultural' is the disjunction between western business management models, with their distinction between the 'personal' and 'business', as against the Aboriginal fusing of the personal and business.

Family-based businesses are probably an ideal option for Aboriginal tourism development in its initial stage. This is because they are based on traditional modes of social organisation (kinship and eldership) as well as a strong traditional knowledge transmission system, such as story telling generation by generation. However, a broader base (i.e. community-based tourism) is necessary for a sustainable Aboriginal tourism industry.

A transformation from a traditional eldership to a broader leadership is critical. Eldership generally reflects traditional structures and depends on the elder's wisdom and reputation. It is a knowledge system with a confined subject matter (i.e. elders cannot speak outside their range of ritual authority or their 'country'). The next stage is the transfer from such eldership into a collective leadership based on knowledge, capability and responsibility; or, as in the Jungala case here, a partnership between the two forms of management.

Indigenous elite groups necessarily play an important role in Indigenous tourism development, especially in tourism marketing, through their knowledge, social networks and their reputation. They are the ideal cultural intermediaries because they straddle both worlds (Negus, 2002). However, deriving from this observation, two issues deserve concern. Firstly, it must be realised that since many such elites have been away from their own country for a long time; this might negatively affect their understanding of local cultures, as well as their acceptance by local communities. Therefore, it is important for these elites to re-establish the linkage with local communities both regarding their cultural identities and learning their own cultures from local people. Secondly, the possibility of 'elite capture' must be taken a consideration. Therefore, the transformation from purely family-based enterprises to better involve a wider community is important. In Aboriginal terms, that involves *two-way* (i.e. Aboriginal and western/modern) interaction and respect.

External support, particularly from government and the mainstream tourism industry, is important for developing successful Indigenous cultural tourism enterprises. Since the late 1990s, Australian governments have developed a number of policies relating to Indigenous tourism. However, the policies failed both to appreciate the diversity and complexities of Indigenous peoples' cultures and to address the role of Indigenous culture in tourism development, especially in relation to tourism management. Also, the activities of the mainstream tourism industry sometimes raise fears amongst Indigenous people for the authenticity of the product. This is as much an issue of respect for Aboriginal people as an issue of false competition. External support for successful Indigenous tourism needs to include general managerial capacity building. But more attention is required to incorporate cultural differences into the operation of cultural tourism enterprises.

Indigenous cultural tourism is not only an economic activity but also (possibly more importantly) an empowerment process (Whitford and Ruhanen, 2010). In this process Australia's Indigenous people and their culture ('low' culture, in particular, in the sense of customary laws, traditional knowledge and social norms) should be recognised and incorporated into 'management'. Compatibility between Indigenous culture and modern western culture (i.e. management and marketing) is crucial. As seen in our case studies, successful and sustainable Aboriginal cultural tourism enterprises need to be able to accommodate both modern business management and sustainable social and cultural management deriving from Aboriginal values and norms. Together with welfare reform, these approaches will generate better Aboriginal empowerment and employment outcomes.

References

Anderson, R. B. (1999). *Economic development among the Aboriginal peoples of Canada: Hope for the future.* Toronto: Captus University Press.

Anderson, R. B., Hindle, K., Giberson, R. J. and Kayseas, B. (2004). Understanding success in Indigenous entrepreneurship: An exploratory investigation. In *AGSE 2004: Regional frontiers of entrepreneurship research 2004: Proceedings of the first annual regional entrepreneurship research exchange*. Hawthorn: Swinburne University of Technology, Australian Graduate School of Entrepreneurship, pp. 83–100.

Anderson, W. (2009). Promoting ecotourism through networks: Case studies in the Balearic Islands. *Journal of Ecotourism*, 8(1), pp. 51–69.

Australian Indigenous Tourism (2011a). *Australian Indigenous tourism database*. Retrieved from: http://www.Indigenoustourism.australia.com/ExportFile/2011113173322.csv (accessed: 6 September 2012).

——— (2011b). *Operators (Download)*. Retrieved from: http://www.Indigenoustourism.australia.com/nitpm.asp (accessed: 6 September 2012).

Baskerville, R. F. (2003). Hofstede never studied culture. *Accounting, Organizations and Society*, 28(1), pp. 1–14.

Bunten, A. C. (2010). More like ourselves: Indigenous capitalism through tourism. *American Indian Quarterly*, 34(3), pp. 285–311.

Butler, R. and Hinch, T. (eds) (1996). *Tourism and Indigenous peoples*. London: Thomson Business.

Carson, D. A. and Carson, D. B. (2011). Why tourism may not be everybody's business: The challenge of tradition in resource peripheries. *Rangeland Journal*, 33(4), pp. 373–383.

Carter, R. and Beeton, R. (2004). A model of cultural change and tourism. *Asia Pacific Journal of Tourism Research*, 9(4), pp. 423–442.

Colton, J. W. (2005). Indigenous tourism development in Northern Canada: Beyond economic incentives. *Canadian Journal of Native Studies*, 1, pp. 185–206.

de Varine, H. (2006). Ecomuseology and sustainable development. *Museums and Social Issues*, 1, pp. 225–231.

Eickelkamp, U. (2011). *Growing up in Central Australia: New anthropological studies of Aboriginal childhood and adolescence*. New York: Berghahn.

Finkel, R. (2008). The commodification and management of Culture. *Journal of Tourism and Cultural Change*, 5(3), pp. 221–223.

Galla, A. (2006). *Museums in sustainable heritage development: A case study of Vietnam*. Retrieved from: http://www.intercom.museum/documents/4–1galla.pdf (accessed: 6 September 2011).

Gans, H. J. (1999). *Popular culture and high culture: An analysis and evaluation of taste*. New York: Basic Books.

Gerritsen, R. (2012). *Was the NT election outcome a shockwave or a regional ripple?* Retrieved from: http://theconversation.com/was-the-nt-election-outcome-a-shockwave-or-a-regional-ripple-9138 (accessed: 6 September 2012).

——— and Zeng, B. (2011). Market opportunity plus aspirations and capacity should lead to success: Why not so for Australia's Indigenous tourism industry? *International Journal of Culture and Tourism Research*, 4(1), pp. 43–60.

Hindle, K. and Lansdowne, M. (2005). Brave spirits on new paths: Toward a globally relevant paradigm of Indigenous entrepreneurship research. *Journal of Small Business and Entrepreneurship*, 18(2), pp. 131–141.

Horn, C. and Tahi, B. (2009). Some cultural and historical factors influencing rural Maori tourism development in New Zealand. *Journal of Rural and Community Development*, 4(1), pp. 84–104.

Igoe, J. (2010). The spectacle of nature in the global economy of appearances: Anthropological engagements with the spectacular mediations of transnational conservation. *Critique of Anthropology*, 30, pp. 375–397.

Johnson, J., Cant, G., Peters, E. and Howitt, R. (2007). Creating anti-colonial geographies: Embracing Indigenous peoples' knowledge and rights. *Geographical Research*, 45(2), pp. 117–120.

Johnstone, A. (2006). *Is the sacred for sale? Tourism and Indigenous peoples*. London: Earthscan.

Levine, D. N. and Janowitz, M. (1971). *Georg Simmel: On individuality and social forms*. Chicago: University of Chicago Press.

Lindsay, N. (2005). Toward a cultural model of Indigenous entrepreneurial attitude. *Academy of Marketing Science Review*, 5, pp. 1–17.

Manyara, G., Jones, E. and Botterill, D. (2006). Tourism and poverty alleviation: The case for Indigenous enterprise development in Kenya. *Tourism Culture and Communication*, 7(1), pp. 19–37.

Mbaiwa, J. (2009). Cultural tourism and livelihood diversification: The case of Gewihaba caves and XaiXai village in the Okavango Delta, Botswana. *Journal of Tourism and Cultural Change*, 7(1), pp. 61–75.

McRae-Williams, E. and Gerritsen, R. (2010). Mutual incomprehension: The cross cultural domain of work in a remote Australian Aboriginal community. *International Indigenous Policy Journal*, 1(2), pp. 1–11.

Meggitt, M. (1962). *Desert people: A study of the Walbiri Aborigines of Central Australia*. Sydney: Angus and Robertson.

Morse, J. (2000). International demand. In *National Indigenous Tourism Forum Proceedings Report: Tourism – the Indigenous Opportunity*. Canberra: Commonwealth Department of Industry, Science and Resources.

Moscardo, G. (2005). Peripheral tourism development: Challenges, issues and success factors. *Tourism Recreation Research*, 30(1), pp. 27–43.

Myers, F. (1982). Always ask: Resource use and land ownership among Pintupi Aborigines of the Australian Western Desert. In N. Williams and E. Hunn (eds), *Resource managers: North American and Australian hunter-gatherers*. Canberra: Australian Institute of Aboriginal Studies, pp. 173–195.

Myers, F. (1986). *Pintupi country, Pintupi self: Sentiment, place and politics among Western Desert Aborigines*. Washington, DC: Smithsonian Institution.

Neblett, J. and Green, M. (2000). *Linking development, Indigenous entrepreneurship and tourism, with special reference to Barbados*. Retrieved from: http://www.siue.edu/GEOGRAPHY/ONLINE/neblett.htm (accessed: 20 July 2011).

Negus, K. (2002). The work of cultural intermediaries and the enduring distance between production and consumption. *Cultural Studies*, 16(4), pp. 501–515.

Peeler, L. (2004). *Giinagay: A newsletter celebrating Indigenous Australian culture*. Retrieved from: http://www.Aboriginaltourism.com.au/media.asp?data=06080F0B4D4C4F4979505350564D4C (accessed: 18 November 2011).

Peterson, N. (1993). Demand sharing: Reciprocity and the pressure for generosity among foragers. *American Anthropologist*, 95(4), pp. 860–874.

Radcliffe, S.A. and Laurie, N. (2006). Culture and development: Taking culture seriously in development for Andean Indigenous people. *Environment and Planning D: Society and Space*, 24(2), pp. 231–248.

Robinson, M. and Ghostkeeper, E. (1987). Native and local economies: A consideration of economic evolution and the next economy. *Arctic*, 40(2), pp. 138–144.

Rothwell, N. (2013). Fragile picture of future. *The Australian*, 9 August, p. 15.

Ryan, C. and Aicken, M. (2005). *Indigenous tourism: The commodification and management of culture*. London/Amsterdam: Elsevier.

Sanders, W. (2012). Winning Aboriginal votes: Reflections on the 2012 Northern Territory election *Australian Journal of Political Science*, 47(4), pp. 691–702.

Shire of Halls Creek. (2011). *Halls Creek Tourism Plan v2 July 2011 – consultation draft*. Retrieved from: http://av-relay.hcshire.wa.gov.au/InfoRouter/docs/Public/Reports%20and%20Other%20Publications/Halls%20Creek%20Tourism%20Plan%20v2%20July%202011%20-%20Consultation%20Draft.pdf (accessed: 16 November 2012).

Smith, A. (2009). Impacts on Aboriginal spirituality and culture from tourism in the coastal waterways of the Kimberley region, North West Australia. *Journal of Ecotourism*, 8(2), pp. 82–98.

Smith, M. K. and Robinson, M., eds. (2006). *Cultural tourism in a changing world: Politics, participation and (re)presentation*. Clevedon: Channel View.

Tai, H. (2007). Development through conservation: An institutional analysis of Indigenous community-based conservation in Taiwan. *World Development*, 35(7), pp. 1186–1203.

Tourism Northern Territory (2010). *Quick stats, report period: Year ending June 2010*. Retrieved from: http://www.tourismnt.com.au/Portals/3/docs/research/Quick_Stats_YE%20Jun%2010_v2.pdf (accessed: 31 October 2012).

——— (2011). *Quick stats, report period: Year ending June 2011*. Retrieved from: http://www.tourismnt.com.au/Portals/3/docs/research/Quick_Stats_YE%20June%2011.pdf (accessed: 31 October 2012).

Tourism Research Australia (2010). *Indigenous tourism in Australia: Profiling the domestic market*. Canberra: Department of Resources, Energy and Tourism.

——— (2011a). *The economic importance of tourism in Australia's regions*. Canberra: Department of Resources, Energy and Tourism.

——— (2011b). *Snapshots 2011: Indigenous tourism visitors in Australia*. Canberra: Department of Resources, Energy and Tourism.

Tuchman, G. and Fortin, N. (1989). *Edging women out: Victorian novelists, publishers, and social change*. London: Routledge.

Whitford, M. and Ruhanen, L. (2010). Australian Indigenous tourism policy: Practical and sustainable policies? *Journal of Sustainable Tourism*, 18(4), pp. 475–496.

Williams, R. (1974). *On high and popular culture*. Retrieved from: http://www.newrepublic.com/book/review/high-and-popular-culture# (accessed: 31 October 2012).

Zeng, B., Gerritsen, R. and Stoeckl, N. (2010). Contribution of Indigenous culture to tourism development: A case in Central Australia. *International Journal of Culture and Tourism Research*, 3(1), pp. 165–185.

Zeppel, H. (2010). Managing cultural values in sustainable tourism: Conflicts in protected areas. *Tourism and Hospitality Research*, 10(2), pp. 93–104.

PART IV
POVERTY ALLEVIATION AND ECONOMIC DEVELOPMENT

14

Poverty Alleviation and Indigenous Communities in Peninsular Malaysia

Nor'Ain Othman and Norliza Aminudin[1]

Chapter Synopsis

Malaysia covers an area of about 330,803 square kilometres with an estimated population of 29.7 million, the most multi-ethnic and multi-religious country in South East Asia. Among the Malaysian populations, 67% are Bumiputeras (Malays and indigenous people), 26% Chinese, 8% Indians, and 1% other ethnic groups. In the country's effort to become a progressive and high-income nation, various high-impact strategies were adopted. Nonetheless, for a country that has indigenous communities which are considered to live below the poverty line, the needs of these special target groups are also addressed through integrated programmes of the Tenth Malaysia Plan, 2011–2015. The Department of Orang Asli Development (JAKOA) under the Ministry of Rural and Regional Development is responsible for the integrated programme that involves land development and ownership, medical programmes, and education and economic modernisation of the indigenous people towards the betterment of their economy in their rural livelihood. It helps to strengthen their capabilities and literacy and to reduce the incidence of poverty among them. Challenges and issues in implementing an integrated programme and its sustainability in improving the economy of indigenous communities are elaborated in this chapter.

Introduction

Indigenous peoples in Malaysia represent 12% of 28 million approximate population of the country (Wessendorf, 2011). Orang Asli are the indigenous people of Peninsular Malaysia. They consist of the Proto-Malay, Negritos, and Senoi tribes. In every group of the Orang Asli, they appoint a leader whom they call *Batin* or in the Malay language *penghulu*. The Department for the Development of Orang Asli (Jabatan Kemajuan Orang Asli/JAKOA, 2013) is the only government agency that is responsible for the welfare of the Orang Asli. This agency works with a mission

1   The authors would like to thank all those who have helped in completing this chapter, which includes students of HTT7I2 Tourism Destination Analysis. Special appreciation goes to the indigenous communities of the Mah Meri at Carey Island; the Jakun and Semoq Beri of Kampung Mas Orang Asli Settlement; the Semai at Sungai Ruih, Cameron Highlands; and the Bateks at National Park in Pahang. Gratitude also goes to a few individuals who were willing to be interviewed but preferred not to be named.

to develop the socio-economic well-being of the Orang Asli community and to enable them to participate and compete actively in the mainstream economic, social and political development of the country, while at the same time preserving the Orang Asli identity, culture and tradition. This chapter discusses the challenges and issues in implementing an integrated programme and its sustainability in improving the economy of indigenous communities that focus on certain tribes: namely the Mah Meri Cultural Village, Pulau Carey (Carey Island), Selangor; the Batek tribe at National Park, Pahang; and the Semai of Ulu Geroh, Gopeng, Perak. The narrative of this chapter is based on a field-based study which employed a qualitative case study approach with semi-structured interviews, focus group discussions and work with key informants of related agencies. It would be interesting to observe how some of the indigenous tribes embarked on various economic activities from agriculture, forest conservation, fishing and traditional handicraft to tourism (Hinch and Butler, 1996).

The Indigenous Communities in Malaysia

In Malaysia, the three main groups of indigenous people are the *bumiputra* (local-born Malay residing in the country); the Orang Asli (literally meaning 'original people'), aborigines of Peninsular (West) Malaysia; and the *anak negeri* (natives) of East Malaysia, comprising the states of Sabah and Sarawak. The indigenous people of Peninsular Malaysia consist of three major tribes – the Senoi, Proto-Malay, and Negrito – and each of the tribes has six sub-tribes or ethnic groups. The sub-tribes of Senoi are Semai, Temiar, Jahut, Che Wong, Mah Meri and Semoq Beri; Proto-Malay are Temuan, Semelai, Jakun, Kanaw, Kuala and Seletar; and Negrito are Kensiu, Kintak, Jahai, Lanoh, Mendriq and Batek. Each group is located in a different part of Peninsular Malaysia and has its own language and culture. They live a nomadic lifestyle and their activities include fishing, hunting and gathering of forest products. Indigenous peoples of Malaysia are estimated to be about 178,197, of which the largest tribes are the Senoi (representing 54.91%), followed by the Proto-Malays (42.27%), and the smallest group is the Negritos (2.81%). The breakdown of the numbers of indigenous people by ethnic group, location, and estimated population is shown in Table 14.1. There were more males than females, with a distribution of 93,003 males and 85,194 females (see Table 14.2). Table 14.3 on p. 268 shows the breakdown of indigenous people according to ethnic and sub-ethnic group according to location and population.

Table 14.1   Numbers of indigenous people in Peninsular Malaysia by ethnic group

State	Senoi	Proto-Malay	Negrito	Total
Johor	55	13,083	1	13,139
Kedah	19	-	251	270
Kelantan	12,047	29	1,381	13,457
Melaka	28	1,486	1	1,515
Negeri Sembilan	96	10,435	-	10,531
Pahang	29,439	37,142	925	67,506
Perak	50,281	605	2,413	53,299
Selangor	5,073	12,511	3	17,587
Terengganu	818	41	34	893
Sum	**97,856**	**75,332**	**5,009**	**178,197**
Percentage	**54.91**	**42.27**	**2.81**	**100%**

Source: Department of Statistics, Malaysia, 2010.

Table 14.2   Indigenous people in Peninsular Malaysia by gender

State	Male	Female	Sum
Johor	6,702	6,437	13,139
Kedah	155	115	270
Kelantan	7,140	6,317	13,457
Melaka	778	737	1,515
Negeri Sembilan	5,461	5,070	10,531
Pahang	35,323	32,183	67,506
Perak	27,716	25,583	53,299
Selangor	9,254	8,333	17,587
Terengganu	474	419	893
Sum	**93,003**	**85,194**	**178,197**

Source: Department of Statistics, Malaysia, 2010.

In the country's effort to become a progressive and high-income nation, various high-impact strategies were adopted. Nonetheless, for a country that has indigenous communities which are considered to live below the poverty line, the needs of these special target groups are also addressed through integrated programmes (Prime Minister's Office 2013a). This integrated programme involves a land development and ownership program which is a catalyst that would enable the indigenous communities to become land owners and active farmers contributing towards the betterment of their economy in their rural livelihood. It helps to strengthen their capabilities and reduce the incidence of poverty among them.

OCCUPATION

The Orang Asli population has shown a growing trend due to an overall improvement in their quality of life and livelihood. The majority of the Orang Asli live in rural areas and they are engaged in a variety of occupations, such as agriculture or forest resources. The Semai, Temiar, Chewong, Jah Hut, Semelai and Semoq Beri, for example, live close to or within forested areas where they engage in hill rice cultivation, hunting and gathering. On the other hand, the Orang Kuala, Orang Kanaq, Orang Seletar and Mah Meri live close to the coast and are mainly fishermen. The Temuan, Jakun and Semai are involved in permanent agriculture and now manage their own rubber, oil palm or cocoa smallholdings. Less than 1% of the Orang Asli populations are still semi-nomadic, largely from the Negrito group such as Jahai and Batek.

EDUCATION

There have been significant improvements made in the overall enrolment of the Orang Asli in education, entering primary and secondary school, tertiary education and universities with the government's assistance. The JAKOA Annual Report (2012) mentioned that a total of 477 aboriginal students were able to claim their entire university education in Malaysia, where a total of 254 students are new entrants and 96 students have successfully completed their studies in various fields. A total of 11 aboriginal students have also successfully completed courses at bachelor,

Table 14.3   Numbers of indigenous people in Peninsular Malaysia by ethnic and sub-ethnic group

Region	Negrito						Senoi								Melayu Porto				Sum
	Kensiu	Kintak	Lanoh	Jahai	Mendriq	Bateq	Temiar	Semai	Semoq Beri	Che Wong	Jah Nut	Mah Meri	Temuan	Semelai	Jakun	Orang Kanaq	Orang Kuala	Orang Seletar	
Johor	-	-	-	1	-	-	5	20	6	6	16	2	762	38	7,091	123	3,454	1,615	13,139
Kedah	208	30	10	3	-	-	14	5	-	-	-	-	-	-	-	-	-	-	270
Kelantan	-	1	2	530	344	504	11,908	132	1	2	4	-	16	2	10	1	-	-	13,457
Melaka	1	-	-	-	-	-	-	21	-	-	-	-	1,427	-	-	-	-	-	1,515
Negeri Sembilan	-	-	-	-	-	-	24	48	2	1	8	13	7,884	2,464	85	-	2	-	10,531
Pahang	-	-	1	15	3	906	186	18,876	4,421	610	5,328	18	5,220	4,769	27,125	23	3	2	67,506
Perak	28	163	269	1,838	12	3	18,541	31,437	62	19	219	3	225	229	134	1	14	2	53,299
Selangor	-	-	-	-	3	-	356	895	9	8	43	3,762	12,055	222	205	-	28	1	17,587
Terengganu	-	-	-	-	-	34	-	3	811	4	-	-	1	-	40	-	-	-	893
Sum	237	194	382	2,387	362	1,446	31,038	51,437	5,313	651	5,618	3,799	27,590	7,727	34,722	148	3,525	1,620	178,197
Sum Total	5,009						97,856								75,332				

Source: Department of Statistics, Malaysia, 2010.

master and PhD levels in several countries such as Australia, Ireland, Canada, India, Indonesia and Russia in various professional fields. The government is successful in integrating the Orang Asli into mainstream society.

HEALTH

As most Orang Asli live in rural areas, health is of concern, especially diseases afflicting the Orang Asli such as tuberculosis, malaria, leprosy, cholera, typhoid, measles, whooping cough, and malnutrition due to poor quality of life that the Orang Asli experience. The government has provided basic amenities such as piped water, an electricity supply and toilet facilities to interior rural settlements. The government has shown serious efforts in taking various approaches towards advancing the development of the Orang Asli in improving their situation and addressing the need to modernise them. The Department of Orang Asli Development under the Ministry of Rural and Regional Development is responsible for assisting the indigenous people in Peninsular Malaysia.

Government Roles and Programmes to Modernise the Orang Asli

OWNERSHIP OF LAND

Currently, the Orang Asli settlements are located all over Peninsular Malaysia and usually the people are inclined to live among their own tribe. As of 2012, the indigenous people are estimated to number about 178,000 living in about 870 settlements or villages. Most Orang Asli still maintain a close physical, cultural, and spiritual relationship with the environment (Nicholas, 2004). The status of Orang Asli gazette land was given some form of recognition by the government, and it is the responsibility of the state government to accept the Orang Asli's rights to their traditional territories. JAKOA, on the other hand, are involved in the implementation of an Orang Asli settlements area land survey for the preparation of a Multi Plan and Certified Plan (PA) for the purpose of gazetting. In addition, the expanded scope of the project involves land acquisition (LA) of land owned by individuals or the state government for the benefit of the Orang Asli community. This project is in line with the implementation of the Land Ownership and Land Development Policy for the Orang Asli.

THE ROLE OF ORANG ASLI DEVELOPMENT, MINISTRY OF RURAL AND REGIONAL DEVELOPMENT

In Malaysia, the government agency that represents Orang Asli welfare is the Department of Orang Asli Development (Jabatan Kemajuan Orang Asli/JAKOA), under the Ministry of Rural and Regional Development. Formerly known as the Department of Orang Asli Welfare, it was established in 1954. JAKOA is a government department that is quite unique because of the duties and functions of the department, dedicated to bringing progress to the indigenous peoples of the country in aspects of education, economy and culture. JAKOA's vision is to be the 'driving organizational excellence in the aboriginal community to develop on par with the premier community', and its mission is to develop the socio-economic well-being of the Orang Asli community and to enable them to participate and compete actively in the mainstream economic, social and political development of the country, while at the same time preserving the Orang Asli identity and culture. JAKOA's objectives are to:

- increase the income of indigenous peoples and thus remove them from poverty;
- expand the scope of coverage of infrastructure and social amenities to all aboriginal villages;
- empower indigenous communities through comprehensive human capital development;
- improve the health of indigenous peoples to enhance well-being;
- preserve and uphold traditional knowledge and indigenous heritage;
- improve the effectiveness of the practice and culture of an organisation of good governance.

There are a few programmes initiated by JAKOA in order to achieve the agency's mission and objectives. These include, firstly, a *medical programme* intended to help Orang Asli communities improve their health condition. As the Orang Asli live far from clinics and other medical facilities, the agency set up medical posts at settlements with at least one partially prefabricated building containing an examination area, a few patient beds, a medical storage area, a two-way radio, and a living area for a medical assistant. Some posts also have a helicopter landing pad for emergency evacuations. Doctors tour the medical posts every month to treat patients and listen to their problems.

Secondly, an *education programme* aims to improve standards of living by providing new occupational opportunities. In 2012, JAKOA had successfully placed a total of 477 aboriginal students at universities across the country, while 11 people have managed to pursue their studies abroad in various fields.

Thirdly, *economic modernisation*, which is to 'modernise' Orang Asli economies, to shift them from subsistence activities like hunting, gathering and growing crops for their own consumption to activities directed towards market-oriented economies that include selling commodities or labour and buying food and other necessities.

ABORIGINAL PEOPLES DEVELOPMENT STRATEGIC PLAN 2011–2015

The government gives special attention to Orang Asli communities to improve standards of living, generating capacity and capability in line with Malaysia's vision to become a high-income developed country. As such, the JAKOA Annual Report 2012 reported that the Ministry of Rural and Regional Development under JAKOA formulated the Aboriginal Development Strategic Plan 2011 – created specifically to realise the goal of advancing and bringing progress to the aboriginal community in all areas of the field throughout Malaysia. They strengthened education as one of the main agendas of human capital and created more than 500 aboriginal entrepreneurs from 2011 to 2015. The plan also provides guidance, direction and strategies for the development of indigenous peoples for five years (2011–2015) in a comprehensive manner premised on the Master Plan for Rural Development. Table 14.4 illustrates the six cores and strategies contained in the Aboriginal Development Strategic Plan 2011–2015.

Economic Development of the Orang Asli

JAKOA's strategy of increasing household income has led to potential economic activities and economic development projects. Some of the projects are short-term cash crops, farming, commodity rubber and oil palm cultivation and the development of entrepreneurs among the Orang Asli. The related agencies will give assistance to the farmers to implement agricultural

Table 14.4 JAKOA core and strategic plan 2011–2015

Core 1: Human capital development

Strategies:
- Raise awareness of early childhood indigenous education
- Strengthen indigenous students' understanding of the interior in the national language
- Reduce the dropout rate of indigenous students
- Improve and maintain excellence in indigenous students learning
- Produce trained indigenous labour
- Identify empowered indigenous leaders and peoples

Core 2: Move to economic activities and viable industry, competitive and resilient integration

Strategies:
- Expand commercial indigenous farming projects
- Expand cash-crop indigenous projects
- Expand livestock and fisheries projects with other agencies and indigenous cooperative
- Promote high-value economic initiatives
- Increase the capacity of indigenous farmers in agriculture
- Produce viable indigenous entrepreneurs
- Expand business assistance to indigenous entrepreneurs
- Empower indigenous cooperatives
- Create rural economic growth centres
- Create eco-tourism programmes in indigenous villages

Core 3: Extended access infrastructure

Strategies:
- Implement housing assistance programme (PBR)
- Improve road facilities
- Provide rural electrification (BELB)
- Provide/improve rural water supply (BALB)
- Provide basic amenities in indigenous villages

Core 4: Improving life quality of indigenous peoples

Strategies:
- Enhance service delivery to better life quality of indigenous peoples
- Strengthen the quality of life infrastructure in indigenous settlements
- Increase awareness of quality of indigenous lifestyle
- Strengthen and coordinate data and research findings related to the quality of indigenous lifestyle
- Improve the quality of JAKOA hospital services

Core 5: Researching, collecting, preserving and highlighting traditional knowledge and natural heritage

Strategies:
- Research, collect and preserve traditional culture, heritage and indigenous artefacts
- Establish and enforce the protection of traditional culture and heritage of indigenous artefacts
- Document and publish research on indigenous culture, heritage and artefacts
- Cooperate with other agencies to promote traditional heritage and indigenous cultural artefacts
- Strengthen museums as educational centres of indigenous cultural heritage
- Economic empowerment through traditional heritage resources and indigenous cultural artefacts

Core 6: Improvement of service delivery systems and good governance

Strategies:
- Provision of quality information and communication technology (ICT)
- Potential human capital management (multi skills)
- Efficient administration and implementation of high performance

Source: JAKOA Annual Report, 2012.

projects in short-term cash batches and entrepreneurs engaged in small-scale enterprise activity such as retail, culture, knowledge of traditional medicine (herbs) and handicrafts.

MAH MERI TRIBES, CAREY ISLAND, SELANGOR

The Mah Meri tribes, a sub-group of the Senoi, are well known for their craftsmanship – and have received the UNESCO Seal of Excellence on their wood carvings. The Mah Meri is perhaps the most commercialised indigenous community in Peninsular Malaysia. Four generations ago they were known as the sea gypsies, leading a lifestyle that was similar to a few other ethnic groups in this South-East Asia region; nonetheless, now they are settled in an area gazette for them on Carey Island. The development of the Mah Meri Cultural Village started in November 2009 on a 1.85 hectare site that provides facilities and services such as a cultural learning centre, Mah Meri crafts, historical gallery, replica village and flotilla boats, and traditional restaurants. The village is fully equipped with learning facilities used to demonstrate and teach tourists about the skills of dancing and music, mangrove timber sculpturing, palm leaf origami, pandanus leaf weaving and tree bark cloth making. The Mah Meri are proud and happy to showcase their culture and tradition through arts, dance and handicrafts to local and international tourists. The relevant agencies involved in the success of managing this project are the Ministry of Rural and Regional Development, Ministry of Information, Communication and Culture, JAKOA and the Selangor state government.

According to Othman (2007), the organisation involved in marketing collaboration can be from both profit and non-profit organisations; and, in the case of Mah Meri Cultural Village, it involves travel agencies, DiGi (a communications company), the Malaysian Handicraft Centre, the National Museum Department and Tourism Malaysia. The type of tourism partnership model discussed is that the public sector depends on private investors to provide services and to finance the construction of tourism facilities, while private tourism projects require government approval, infrastructure development and support. Cooperation between government agencies and private sectors in tourism is significant in ensuring the projects are running smoothly; to avoid misunderstanding and conflict; to reduce work redundancy; and to avoid duplication of research and development projects.

BATEK TRIBE, NATIONAL PARK, PAHANG

The Batek tribe is in the family of the Negritos, which is the smallest group, and can be said to be leading a semi-nomadic lifestyle. There are 13 settlements of Batek at the National Park, Malaysia's premier park and the largest in the country, covering over 4,343 square kilometres (434,300 hectares) across the three states of Kelantan, Terengganu and Pahang. There has been an increase in tourists visiting Taman Negara, and one of the main attractions is visiting the indigenous settlement. A study was conducted on the visitors' impact on the park and the findings indicated that there was a need to monitor and control the recreational activities such as the canopy walk, cave exploration and aboriginal settlement that are essential for the safety of visitors, privacy and to ensure the quality of visitors' experiences (Othman et al., 2002).

Most of the tourists visiting the settlement were entertained by simple activities such as the traditional way of lighting a fire and trying their hunting weapon by blowing darts using blowpipes. Handicraft items such as bracelets, bangles and hair clips are being sold to the tourists as souvenirs. The younger generations of the Batek tribes are more adventurous towards modernisation, becoming nature guides or boatmen and migrating to urban areas. The tribe has also experienced a decrease in their wild food sources and increased dependence on commercial foods such as rice, sugar, biscuits, tea and coffee which can be obtained from nearby villages. The government tried to encourage the Batek to give up their semi-nomadic existence, perceived by the authorities as primitive, and tried to relocate them to Kuala Atok, on the south bank of the Tembeling River, close to Kuala Tahan. However, there was strong resistance from the chief of the tribe.

JAKUN AND SEMOQ BERI TRIBES, SUNGEI LEMBING, PAHANG

Not many tribes are as open and willing as the Mah Meri in sharing their culture with the rest of the world. A settlement of two indigenous tribes – the Jakun and Semoq Beri located at Sungai Lembing, Pahang – is experiencing visits from local and international tourists as they pass the settlement on their way for picnics, camping and hiking, watching the sunrise and sunset, and photography activities. Sungai Lembing – blessed with the natural beauty of caves, waterfalls and hills – has become a tourist attraction among historians and nature lovers. According to an interview with the chief of the settlement, known as *Tok Batin* (headman), tourism development is not affecting their daily life. They go on with their normal activities, engaging in hill rice cultivation, hunting and gathering of forest products. However, they appreciate the effort of the government in establishing a primary school at the settlement, supporting the cost of education expenses for the community through free stationery, textbooks and school uniforms. The *Tok Batin* is proud to mention to us that a few of the teachers at the school are from his own communities. The existence of the school has at least reduced the difficulty of attaining academic knowledge due to poverty. In terms of health facilities, there has been an improvement in provision and facilities for the Orang Asli. Baer (1999) found that there is sufficient information on Orang Asli health available to enable health personnel to plan and provide better healthcare facilities for the benefit of the Orang Asli. Most of their health problems are easily preventable and curable.

SEMAI TRIBES, ULU GEROH, GOPENG, PERAK

Another interesting project to discuss in this chapter is the local community-based ecotourism and conservation training among the indigenous Semai of Ulu Geroh, Gopeng, Perak. The project demonstrated a volunteer partnership in the community, incorporating the Malaysian Nature Society, Malay Guiding Society, Perak Department of Forestry, Perak Department of Orang Asli Affairs and the Perak State government. It provides a platform for multi-stakeholder involvement and cooperation for ecotourism at Ulu Geroh. As a result, many Semai are trained as nature guides and act as stewards for the rare and endangered *Rafflesia* flower and the Rajah Brooke's Birdwing butterfly. Indirectly, the community manages to increase their knowledge and skills as well as increase their income, contributing towards creating sustainable tourism in Ulu Geroh.

MISCELLANEOUS PROGRAMMES

JAKOA also introduced commercial farm development projects with crop plantations of rubber and oil palm commodities to commercially produce outcomes such as skilled manpower in farming and additional income through dividend payments and wage work. The scope includes the development of a new farm and farm infrastructure construction. The issue of poverty and low socio-economic status among the Orang Asli community is a challenge, so JAKOA implemented the farm community development project. A new farming concept was designed specifically to ensure improved quality of life and well-being of the community. In the development of entrepreneurship among the Orang Asli, the government provides grant aid schemes such as working capital, business premises, business equipment/agriculture/livestock, and rent payment for premises in a strategic business centre location. The agriculture input assistance project is one of the components of the Orang Asli Quality of Living Improvement programme and was begun in 2008. The main objective of this project is to provide assistance for the Orang Asli smallholder farmer/gardener with a horizontal eye relief scope as an input and agricultural equipment to ease the burden due to the increase in material costs in 2008. In 2011, a total of 95 Orang Asli villages were identified, especially in the states of Perak, Pahang and Selangor which are involved in the upgrading of the water supply system. JAKOA also provided housing to the poor and extremely poor Orang Asli community; upgraded the infrastructure at the Orang Asli settlement; and conducted entrepreneur training to improve their products and marketing skills. Some settlements, especially in Cameron Highland and National Park in Pahang, have received help from the government and have been equipped with facilities such as electricity, water supply, roads, multipurpose halls and kindergartens. Some of the indigenous people in Cameron Highland with an entrepreneurial spirit can be seen selling forest products such as wild orchids, bamboo, petai (*Parkia speciosa*), roots, durian, and honey.

Conclusion

In the effort to improve the economy of indigenous communities, various programmes and activities have been planned and implemented by the government through the Tenth Malaysia Plan 2011–2015 and the Aboriginal Peoples Development Strategic Plan 2011–2015. The programmes include education, health, infrastructure, housing, land ownership and increasing skills and income to further improve their standard of living and move them forward towards modernisation. The indigenous students have demonstrated outstanding performance in education through JAKOA scholarships and cooperation from the Majlis Amanah Rakyat (MARA), the Public Service Department (PSD), and the Ministry of Education. It is believed that the indigenous people can be potential leaders of the country. Through the transformation plans, rates of literacy and poverty can be improved among indigenous peoples (Prime Minister's Office of Malaysia, 2013b). Tourism, as the second contributor to the country's economy, can definitely benefit the indigenous people to sustain and showcase their heritage and culture to the local and international tourists. Traditional handicrafts, arts, dance, music, wood sculptures and Orang Asli pastimes have become popular products and services to be marketed to the world. The spirit of entrepreneurship among indigenous communities has shown their ability and skill in business, with the hope of increasing their income and improving their livelihood.

References

Baer, A. (1999). Rainforest Malaria, mosquitoes, people. *Malayan Nature Journal*, 53(4), pp. 299–305.
Department of Statistics, Malaysia (2010). *Profile of the Orang Asli in Peninsular Malaysia*. Kuala Lumpur: Department of Statistics.
Hinch, T. and Butler, R. (1996). Indigenous tourism: A common ground for discussion. In R. Butler and T. Hinch (eds), *Tourism and indigenous peoples*. London: International Thomson Business, pp. 3–19.
Jabatan Kemajuan Orang Asli (JAKOA). (2012). *JAKOA Annual Report 2012*. Kuala Lumpur: Department of Orang Asli Development Publication.

Nicholas, C. (2004). *The Orang Asli and the contest for resources: Indigenous politics, development an identity in Peninsular Malaysia*. Copenhagen: International Work Group for Indigenous Affairs (IWGIA).

Othman, N. (2007). *Tourism alliances and networking in Malaysia*. Selangor: University Publication Center (UPENA) UiTM.

———, Lim L.K., and Anuar, N. (2002). Sustainability analysis: visitors impact on Pahang National Park, Selangor. *Proceeding of the 4th World Research Conference for UPENA*. Selangor: University Publication Center (UPENA) UiTM.

Prime Minister's Office of Malaysia (2013a). *The Tenth Malaysian Plan 2011–2015*. Putrajaya: Prime Minister's Department of Malaysia.

——— (2013b). *Economic Transformation Programme: A Road map for Malaysia*. Putrajaya: Prime Minister's Department of Malaysia.

Wessendorf, K. (2011). *Indigenous peoples in Malaysia*. Copenhagen: International Work Group for Indigenous Affairs (IWGIA).

15

A Composition of Variable Economic Activities: Cases of Three Groups of Indigenous Peoples of South Asia

Azizul Hassan

Chapter Synopsis

This study identifies three groups of indigenous peoples from the southern part of Asia. These are the Chakma of Bangladesh, the Sherpa of Nepal and the Shan of Myanmar. The identification and selection of these groups considered their recent advancements in terms of economic activity and livelihood generation. This study aimed to reach a generalised meaning of indigenous peoples through definitional analysis. However, the central focus was to outline shifting economic activities and explore the factors responsible. This study mainly relied on a literature review and personal observation, followed by closer engagements with the lifestyle of these peoples. The socio-economic backgrounds were segregated according to evidence of participation in both mainstream and conventional economic activities. The result analysis and presentation pursued social narratives. The study highlights that the Chakma of Bangladesh are more 'pragmatic' and backed by government policy frameworks. The Shan of Myanmar are more 'devout' as a result of having an abundance of agricultural resources and the wider influence of their religion. The Sherpa of Nepal are characterised more as a 'traders' due to their interaction with trade, tourism, and wage earning. The study thus concludes that several actors are functional in accelerating the economic advancements of the Chakma, the Shan, and the Sherpa groups of indigenous people.

Introduction

Indigenous populations in recent times have been facing increased challenges in terms of resource allocation and control of access to resources. The declining trends of cultural diversities are obvious. These are occurring faster than ever before, due to globalisation and the rapid acceleration of technology-based applications. The notions of 'traditional' and 'indigenous people' are intertwined, and in many cases barely show any form of distinctive features (Stavenhagen, 2013). Indigenous peoples are inseparable parts of large countries across the world. The notions of 'tribe', 'Aborigine' and 'indigenous' are parallel in that they represent similar meanings and features:

> The terms 'indigenous peoples', 'indigenous ethnic minorities', "tribal groups", and "scheduled tribes" describe social groups with a social and cultural identity distinct from the dominant society that makes them vulnerable to being disadvantaged in the development process. (World Bank, 1991)

Indigenous peoples have long been following conventional lifestyles along with mainstream populations. However, differences between the three identified cases of this study are apparent. The activities that indigenous peoples have adopted over the years are mostly conducive to their local economic structures and settings. Due to the enormous pressures of modernity and the need to survive, considerable parts of these communities, with their pristine socio-cultural settings, appear to be subject to a dubious future. The impacts of changing situations on their lifestyles are becoming more visible with the contributions of diverse actors. These have also become influential through the outcomes of numerous factors, including social, economic and political. It is questionable at present whether indigenous peoples will be able to continue their conventional lifestyles where the world is increasingly being reshaped with the support of technology. The practices and activities of indigenous peoples are constantly shifting from one place to another, and thus embracing different modes of economic activity that can hardly be identified as purely their own. Indigenous peoples have historically been subject mainly to capitalistic influences that justify the pressures on their conventional socio-cultural lifestyle which is under constant threat. On the other hand, mainstream social and economic patterns also become relevant to their economic actions. Indigenous peoples can hardly be separated from the local populations without considering their original lifestyle patterns. The availability of and access to resources needed for the survival of indigenous peoples can hardly be identified as sustainable. In South Asia, they are also the subject of increasing exploitation by the local populations, where incidents of attacks on indigenous people have become more frequent in recent times (Datta, 2012). The fact is that indigenous peoples are an inevitable part of a nation, and who also contribute to the national economy. However, in almost all cases they lag behind in comparison to their local counterparts. This study has identified three indigenous groups in three countries to examine their position in terms of engagement with the national economy and their activities directed towards survival. The three cases are the Chakma of Bangladesh, the Sherpa of Nepal and the Shan of Myanmar. This study aimed to reach a generalised meaning of indigenous peoples through definitional analysis. However, the central focus was to outline the shifting economic activities and to explore the factors responsible for them.

Literature Review

INDIGENOUS PEOPLES: THE DEBATE

Terms like 'indigenous', 'original', 'First Nation', 'Aboriginal', 'tribal', 'Native' or 'ethnic minority' are parallel and represent similar types of peoples. However, in this study the term 'indigenous peoples' is used to better establish the study context. From a general understanding, the gap between Indigenous peoples and the mainstream population is easily identifiable, mainly due to dissimilar physical and cultural traits. From a very basic perspective:

> *On an individual basis, an indigenous person is one who belongs to these indigenous populations through self-identification as indigenous (group consciousness) and is recognized and accepted by these populations as one of its members (acceptance by the group) … this preserves for these communities the sovereign right and power to decide who belongs to them, without external interference. (United Nations, 2013)*

On the other hand, apart from by the United Nations (UN) or the International Labour Organization (ILO), indigenous peoples are characterised from diverse viewpoints. The academic definition of indigenous peoples is still ambiguous, offering no concise form of understanding. Several theoreticians from diverse backgrounds and perspectives have offered definitions. However, there is still a need for an agreed definition of indigenous peoples, as one is not widely available in academia, and thus there is always a demand for this. According to Hughes (2003), the definition of indigenous peoples is ambiguous. In addition, indigenous peoples are normally referred to in the plural to reflect the diversity of peoples within a group as a whole.

These attempts are made to render these terms workable and more convenient. The viewpoints and perspectives used to define indigenous peoples are almost symmetrical. Many researchers and academics have contributed to the notion of indigenous peoples from their own understandings, which have followed the diversities and critical exploration of the relevant situations. The notion of the 'first people' as parallel to 'indigenous people' is developed by Burger (1990), who relates these to the relationship with and ownership of land. Very often, it is believed that there is a close relationship between indigenous peoples and ethnic minorities, while in many cases they are viewed as dichotomous. However, not all ethnic minority groups can be characterised as indigenous peoples. Nomadic groups such as Gypsies are exclusively an ethnic minority, but cannot be classified as an indigenous group of peoples (Moretti, 2012). One of the significant definitions of ethnic minorities which has been offered is:

> *A group numerically inferior to the rest of the population of a state, in a non-dominant position, whose members – being nationals of the state – possess ethnic, religious or linguistic characteristics differing from those of the rest of the population and show, if only implicitly, a sense of solidarity directed towards preserving their culture, traditions, religion or language. (Capotorti, 1979: 568)*

It is thus obvious that the term 'indigenous people' cannot be easily definable and involves complexities, features are common and similar in almost all situations. It is also certain that there are hardly any general characteristics that can be identified as obvious when defining indigenous peoples. However, the form of self-identification with pre-colonial societies, different beliefs, language patterns, less dominant social structures with poorer access to resources, and suppression are a few basic features of indigenous peoples.

As an obvious feature, indigenous peoples are considered to be subject to suppression and discrimination. Cultural processes, political policies and colonisation are responsible for the devaluation or exclusion of indigenous peoples in national demographics (Axelsson and Skold, 2013). For example, it is common practice in South Asia for indigenous peoples not to be offered equality in accessing livelihood-supporting facilities compared with the mainstream local populations (Bhagwati and Panagariya, 2013). In this part of the world, indigenous peoples are also vulnerable to the trafficking of their women, forced child labour, lack of education and the unavailability of basic resources required for a decent standard of living (Tiwari, 2004). The actual number of indigenous peoples across the world is largely unclear as these peoples are scattered widely and divided on the basis of geographical location. However, according to one estimate, 370 million people across the world can be identified as 'indigenous' (International Work Group for Indigenous Affairs/IWGIA, 2013). In terms of minority considerations, the debate becomes more intense with the involvement of linguistic, religious or ethnic minorities (Smith, 1999). However, for a concrete and more precise understanding, use of the term 'indigenous peoples' should cover all these aspects. These peoples consider themselves to be disadvantaged and marginalised from mainstream economic activities. However, the number of indigenous peoples is gradually decreasing with modernisation, industrialisation and the pressures of more economic activities. Land rights are crucial and, in many cases, these peoples' rights to land properties are ignored.

In countries of South Asia like Bangladesh, Myanmar and Nepal, indigenous peoples are typically non-dominant in terms of their participation and control over the state-level economic development decision-making process. The vital indicator is their lesser capacity to include themselves in the decision-making process, whether it be local, national or international. According to Chakma (2001), indigenous peoples are meant to be separated based on different perspectives, ranging from the economic to the socio-political; and this includes racism, discrimination, marginalisation, suppression, imperialism and colonialism as inseparable features. These peoples are marginalised and their representation in decision-making bodies is also much reduced. In order to ensure policy effectiveness and a stronger role played by both national and international agencies, the profiles of indigenous peoples appear to be important for including them in the development policy planning agendas (Blaser et al., 2004; Hassan & Burns, 2014). However, their weaker position is an issue that is viewed as isolating them from common development practices. The importance of indigenous peoples is a fundamental part of policy initiatives, but the extent or degree of their involvement is a considerable factor on which more emphasis should be placed. Across the world, there are many examples of how access to and control over land or forest properties can be ignored or denied for the sake of development planning initiatives (Gilbert, 2006).

Traditionally, indigenous peoples as minorities are differentiated from local populations, leaving very little scope for equal participation. In such circumstances, the crisis of their identity becomes dominant where they are viewed as being disadvantaged. Indigenous peoples are not treated as inevitable elements of national development plans and initiatives. A form of differentiation persists in almost all cases to formulate a common framework for considering their inclusion in development activities (Minde, 2008), as their inclusion in development frameworks requires clear commitments mainly by government, political bodies and all relevant parties.

INDIGENOUS PEOPLES AND THE ROLE OF INTERNATIONAL AGENCIES

The United Nations is playing a crucial role in setting and establishing frameworks for common rights for indigenous peoples. The most essential and useful document as outlined by the UN is the Declaration on the Rights of Indigenous Peoples of 2007. This is important and has established a set of guidelines for countries across the world to establish both working and legislative agendas for these peoples in order to respect their identity and rights on cross-country perspectives. This document also emphasises the need for agreed commitments to value their culture and language while offering them more access to natural resources, health, education and employment. The necessity of including indigenous peoples in ordinary development agendas has become universal following the involvement of the UN, the International Labour Organization (ILO), the

World Bank (WB), and other concerned international agencies. 'Indigenous' as an issue has found its way into the UN at least for the last four decades, whereas ILO engagement is much longer. For decades these agencies have constantly been trying to formulate a common definition of indigenous peoples through debate or expert opinion. Still, an accepted definition of indigenous peoples is yet to be adopted by any of the UN agencies, and this is crucial. In the 'Problem of Discrimination against Indigenous Populations', Jose R. Martinez Cobo, the Special Rapporteur of the Sub-Commission on Prevention of Discrimination and Protection of Minorities, offered the most cited ideas of indigenous peoples. This was defined as:

> Indigenous communities, peoples and nations are those which, having a historical continuity with pre-invasion and pre-colonial societies that developed on their territories, consider themselves distinct from other sectors of the societies now prevailing on those territories, or parts of them. They form at present non-dominant sectors of society and are determined to preserve, develop and transmit to future generations their ancestral territories, and their ethnic identity, as the basis of their continued existence as peoples, in accordance with their own cultural patterns, social institutions and legal system. (United Nations, 2013)

To make the features of indigenous people clearer, additional information was offered:

> This historical continuity may consist of the continuation, for an extended period reaching into the present of one or more of the following factors: Occupation of ancestral lands, or at least of part of them; Common ancestry with the original occupants of these lands; Culture in general, or in specific manifestations (such as religion, living under a tribal system, membership of an Indigenous community, dress, means of livelihood, lifestyle, etc.); Language (whether used as the only language, as mother-tongue, as the habitual means of communication at home or in the family, or as the main, preferred, habitual, general or normal language); Residence on certain parts of the country, or in certain regions of the world. (United Nations, 2013)

According to the International Labour Organization (2013), the Draft Declaration on the Rights of Indigenous Peoples by the Working Group on Indigenous Populations from 1982 was an important move in its search for the definition of indigenous peoples. This organisation adopted two notions, 'tribal peoples' and 'indigenous peoples', in consideration of their country-based contexts. Tribal peoples cannot be viewed as indigenous in certain cases when they live in different places outside their domiciles. The explanations of these concepts are:

> a) tribal peoples in independent countries whose social, cultural and economic conditions distinguish them from other sections of the national community and whose status is regulated wholly or partially by their own customs or traditions or by special laws or regulations;

> b) peoples in independent countries who are regarded as Indigenous on account of their descent from the populations which inhabited the country, or a geographical region to which the country belongs, at the time of conquest or colonization or the establishment of present state boundaries and who irrespective of their legal status, retain some or all of their own social, economic, cultural and political institutions. (ILO, 2013)

For the United Nations, these two terms are synonymous. However, for UN member states, an agreed definition of indigenous peoples was still an unsettled issue until the end of the 15th session in 1997. The statement on the Draft Declaration on the Rights of Indigenous Peoples mentioned that:

> Indigenous peoples have a collective and individual right to maintain and develop their distinct identities and characteristics, including the right to identify themselves as Indigenous and to be recognized as such. (United Nations, 2013)

DEVELOPMENT AND ECONOMIC DEVELOPMENT

Development initiatives for any communities are crucial for their general advancement (Hassan & Forhad, 2013). In certain cases, the process of development can become a form of threat to the existence of these indigenous peoples with regard to their cultural and communal entities. The development process and programmes very often turn into political tools and include the exploitation of natural resources typical of the livelihood of indigenous peoples (Payne, 2005). These practices, in general, lead to the deterioration of communal or socio-economic well-being. Indigenous peoples very often fail to understand and conceptualise the notion of development and its involvement in their traditional lifestyles. Development by itself is abstract and can appear in various forms defined from diverse perspectives and by different individuals. Theoretical ambiguity is common in these peoples' general understanding of development and development agendas. However, development to these people is generally viewed as a form of 'advancement', 'progression' or 'improvement' – that is, a gradual shift away from the existing deteriorating situation (Tribe et al., 2010). However, from a common understanding, it is unlikely that the majority of responses lead to economic development. Resources as well as the capacities and knowledge for capitalising on them are limited, and this requires further in-depth elaboration and critical consideration.

Development is attached to commitment, self-recognition and general empowerment, which highlights that this should be considerate and meaningful and contribute to the fulfilment of socio-cultural goals or approaches. The notion of development should not be viewed as immaculate and inseparable from national policy frameworks, and should involve the traditional views, beliefs or spiritual aspects of the community and society (Sharman and Mistry, 2008). Indigenous peoples are a marginal part of a country's entire population. In many cases, they also lack a proper sense of identity along with diminished interaction with general society and other communities. They are a non-dominant group in society, having poorer access to resources and less capacity to use them. The drive to improve their existing situation is essential and an obvious necessity to enable them to participate in mainstream development policy planning and initiatives (Dale, 2006). The idea of development represents diversity in terms of understanding and conceptualisation. However, from the indigenous peoples' viewpoint, the meaning appears to be contextualised and concrete. According to Raja Devashish Roy – a member of the UN Permanent Forum on Indigenous Issues (UNPFII) and the present chief of the Chakma, Bangladesh:

> Development is best defined contextually, by the community concerned. The 'must haves' are: (a) it is conceived, designed and implemented by the community itself; (b) if it is externally conceived and designed, it must be implemented only with the free, prior and informed consent of the community, and with its substantial participation; (c) it respects the cultural identity and integrity of the community concerned, and the larger ethnic, social, cultural group to which the community belongs; (d) it is respectful of the local ecology and environment; (e) it balances the immediate needs of the current members of the community with the long-term needs of future members of the community. (as cited in Mihlar, 2012: 7)

Economic development is abstract and can hardly be defined through any specific features. However, this kind of development can be outlined through various aspects that relate to social, economic or political characteristics (Nafziger, 2006). There are certain indicators that can define economic development and thus enable one to identify its status, yet still there is a lack of definition of economic development. From a common understanding, economic development can be viewed as the actions taken by communities or policy planners that are sustainable by nature and positively contribute to the process of livelihood and economic status upgrading (Grabowski et al., 2012). Economic development measurement in any particular society can appear in both numerical and analytical formats.

The initiatives for economic development embrace specific areas like human or capital infrastructural development and the sustainable use of available resources (Jerome, 2011). Typically, economic development leads to increased productivity and contributions to the national economy. Economic development as a process contributes to the general well-being of a region with a positive social structure (Long, 2001). This can also make significant contributions to human livelihood through positive impact support. Economic development in developing countries is generating interest for dependency theorists who argue that relatively poverty-stricken countries in the world cannot formulate and initiate development actions in similar manners. A gap always remains between countries that advance the argument that economic development follows a symmetrical progression for every single country. When the discussion moves to economic development, the world is clearly divided between the developed and the developing (Eatwell et al., 1989). Economic development relies on the improvement of typical indicators such as poverty, illiteracy or life expectancy. The acceleration of gross domestic product (GDP) is the most crucial marker that acts as a parameter for economic development (Brezina, 2011). Features of globalisation also influence economic development in many cases. However, for indigenous peoples these influences are not as effective as in other situations.

The notion of 'economic development' is wider and, apparently, does not seem to have any universally accepted meaning. However, there are several interpretations to make this term understandable, usable and accessible to academia and experts. Economic development differs from general development and economic growth in that it is related to the general well-being of the region, area or nation. Economist Michael Todaro (2000) outlined three objectives related to the notion of economic development which show some relevance to indigenous peoples and their general economic conditions. The first point is life-supporting services or products. This indicates the need to enhance accessibility and thus to broaden the delivery of products or services that support life and human existence on earth (basic needs for survival) – i.e. food, health, shelter, protection, education, and clothing.

Economic development is related to providing access to resources to fulfil these needs which should be readily available to individuals and society in general. The second indicator of economic development is increased income. This is particularly associated with access to better living standards which is concerned with increased income, better education, and better and more employment opportunities with more concentration on human or cultural significance. These are essential not only for personal development but also for increasing both narrow individual and wider national interests. The third marker of economic development is lack of restrictions on social and economic choices. There is a demand for the expansion of choices available to both the state and individuals. Allowing people to make decisions is not only crucial for individual purposes but also to address human desolation and unawareness.

Three basic features that are related to economic development are necessary for an overall understanding of this concept. The requirements of human-cultural values, self-confidence and increasing awareness are important to facilitate the practical application of the conceptual understanding to economic development. Measurement of economic development is outlined in the Human Development Index (HDI), which is associated with human resource capacity enhancements (Joshi, 2008). This index is atypical and is the result of efforts initiated by the United Nations Development Programme (UNDP). This is published annually to show the achievements of individual member nations. From another perspective, economic development is related to poverty and steps towards poverty alleviation.

The contributions of Nobel laureate Amartya Sen (1999) are convincing for both the theoretical and practical understanding of economic development. Sen views development as concerned with the increase of capacities and choices of underprivileged peoples. Economic development also indicates free will with respect to political, social or cultural issues. Illiteracy, starvation, persecution, and early mortality are all sources of human suffering, and development allows people to eradicate these conditions. In contrast, other economists like Bhagwati and Panagariya (2013) view economic development as simply eliminating and alleviating unemployment and poverty within an emerging economic context. In general, and in the simplest form, economic development is linked to the improvement of basic human living standards.

INDIGENOUS PEOPLES AND ECONOMIC DEVELOPMENT

Indigenous peoples have initiated separate lifestyles which include their own distinctive ways where influences of external factors are active. From the perspective of resource utilisation, indigenous peoples are capable of achieving a balance between existing demands and possible future needs (Barbier, 2009). It is a strong certainty that these peoples have the ability to direct their traditional and non-traditional livelihoods. By taking responsibility for their own societies through the engagement and utilisation of common economic practices, these peoples have been able to create distinct forms of economic activity from the mainstream societies (Anderson, 1999). The economic systems of indigenous peoples are unlikely to be as large as those at state level. These practices are small scale and mainly managed within a certain area. Very often, the economic practices and processes of indigenous peoples do not represent similarities, and they are mostly diverse in terms of region and circumstances (Elias, 1991).

Indigenous economic activities can easily be separated from national economic agendas in that they are logical, parallel and concerned with national economic settings. Almost all of these indigenous practices are uncommon and related to indigenous lifestyles (Jupp, 2001), yet they are inseparable from the national economy as regards their contributions and outcomes. They are, nevertheless, detrimental and only supposedly support almost all of the active national economic indicators. National-level economic legislation and frameworks are in many cases less responsive and display less sensitivity to indigenous economic practices (Castillo, 2004). Serving the interests of diverse groups and associations is important for helping indigenous economic activities to exist and flourish. Nevertheless, indigenous peoples can fully accord with and execute their practices within changing economic situations. These peoples' existence and survival depend on the activities they perform to generate their livelihoods. These are common where state-level policies do not necessarily always support these actions (Das, 2001).

In South Asia, the indigenous peoples are mainly farmers with unprecedented dependence on *Jhum* cultivation (slash and burn/shifting). In addition, they predominantly rely on hunting, animal rearing, and arts and crafts (Sharma and Shukla, 1992). Control of and access to resources like land and forests are the basis of economic practices of these peoples. They are treated as marginal where modern production and distribution systems are active (Minahan, 2012), and existing rules or systems are not always supportive of them. The trend of displacing indigenous peoples from their ancestral places is quite common and to some extent is not always considered illegal. Habitat displacement results in the loss not only of access to tangible resources but also of heritage and cultural norms (Gupta, 2005). This is one of the reasons why indigenous peoples can rarely be included in the market economy system, as indigenous economic production is inadequate to follow and meet market demands. The produce mainly aims to fulfil internal consumption needs and does not strive for industrial manufacture. Food production largely meets family or community demands, and any surplus supports a barter system (Nwonwu, 2010). On the other hand, although demand for artisans or craftsmen is relatively higher, they tend to serve relatives first and are very unlikely to move beyond the village territory. The inclination towards skill and knowledge sharing outside the community is very rare indeed (McGovern, 2012).

Methodologies

This study is mainly an outcome of the conceptual understanding of identified areas of economic development, indigenous peoples and enterprises in academia. Engagement with respondents from the three different indigenous groups was dominant in terms of data generation and analysis. The cases were purposely selected due to their involvement in both local and mainstream economic activities. However, the study relied on three different approaches while researching the three groups. The researcher spent considerable time with the Chakma of Bangladesh as part of his degree in anthropology, albeit with a decade gap: a first field visit to the Chittagong Hill Tracts of Bangladesh in early 2002, and a second in 2012. This time is significant in terms of offering the opportunity to witness identified facts and patterns of change due to events over a specific period. For the Shan of Myanmar, observations were made with the support of Shan friends living both in and outside Myanmar. On the other hand, data for the Sherpa of Nepal came from personal sources of three Nepali friends who had been living in London for more than a decade. In every case, both online and offline resources were also used, and the most reliable respondent from each group was selected as the key respondent. In today's technology-ruled world, both LinkedIn (a business networking website) and Facebook Messenger were used to contact overseas respondents and gather useful data for the purposes of the research. The data and information were cross-checked with relevant experts and academics in the identified areas to check originality and validity. The study followed social narratives in result presentation and supported the use of digital communication platforms like Facebook Messenger.

The Cases

General and economic development are fundamental demands for indigenous peoples. However, some indigenous groups have made considerably more progress than others, and traditionally they are vulnerable to poverty and discrimination. Three case studies are provided that can be viewed as models for others: the Chakma people of Bangladesh, the Sherpa of Nepal, and the Shan of Myanmar.

THE CHAKMA

The Chakma have experienced development at least at a faster pace than similar indigenous peoples, as evident from the following statement from a Chakma respondent:

> Our present king, Dr Devashish Roy, is our inspiration and is a barrister by profession. He is also
> a member of the United Nations Permanent Forum on Indigenous Issues [UNPFII]. This is very

uncommon, and I really doubt if any king of other indigenous groups of peoples in the entire world can achieve such respect. (R1)[1]

This statement symbolises the huge difference between conventional indigenous peoples and the Chakma. According to Singh (2010), the Chakma (Changma) indigenous peoples mainly live in the Chittagong Hill Tracts of Bangladesh, eastern India, and Myanmar. However, as mentioned, this study focuses particularly on the group within the Bangladesh geographical territory. Chakma have been present in the Chittagong Hill Tracts district of Bangladesh for hundreds of years. Indeed, the Portuguese historian Lavanha mentioned Chakma settlements back in 1550 around the Karnaphuli River. These peoples have a unique culture, traditions, rituals, language, and folklore patterns. Their development appears in diverse forms, and they have advanced in terms of socio-economic status compared to other indigenous peoples:

Before, we had to struggle during the time of illness with our traditional medicinal process. But, the situation is changed in recent decades and we now go to government hospitals where we can visit Chakma physicians. (R2)[2]

Chakma economic development activities appeared following legislative support, with the Bangladesh government allocating a quota system for ethnic minority peoples for admission to higher education intuitions in the country and for securing jobs in the civil service. Most of the Chakma are multilingual, speaking their own languages plus Bangla and English. As an outcome of social interaction, some Chakma are also well conversant with the country's regional languages, which reflects the positive mindset, strong commitment and development tendencies of these peoples. However, areas of the Chittagong Hill Tracts have suffered political unrest for decades due to diverse issues of ownership and control. However, the 1997 peace accord with the government was expected to further these development initiatives. The main factors that helped the Chakma initiate economic development activities concentrate largely on the supportive role of the government. This has resulted in the Chakma's access to mainstream education, and thus the ability to get involved with the national professional system.

In Bangladesh, it has become common in recent years for the Chakma indigenous peoples to be highly educated and occupy important positions in national professional services. Their presence in the United Nations is not merely a representation of themselves, but acts as an example for others to follow.

It is not only important that the Chakma are benefited by government policy initiatives, but their commitments are also crucial for bringing out the maximum advantages from these initiatives. The Bangladesh government is partly acting as facilitator for the economic development activities of the indigenous peoples, with the Chakma as one case. The intention is political, but still these initiatives are offering a base for narrowing the gap between the marginal and the mainstream populations.

THE SHERPA

The Sherpa believe themselves to be developed. This becomes marked when:

The Sherpa are the people living in high mountainous region of Nepal. They are famous all over the world as the mountain climbing people. The main economic activities of Sherpa people are

---

1   R1 was a Bangladesh government official living in Dhaka, the capital city. Contact was made in person while staying in Dhaka in June 2013.

2   R2 served as the key informant and was working as a beauty therapist, based in Chittagong, Bangladesh. This contact was also made in person during the abovementioned time.

tourism and agriculture. The people living near Mt Everest area are hugely benefited by the tourism as Everest region is one of the top tourism destination in Nepal. In the Everest region, many of the Sherpa own tea house, hotel, restaurant, and been involved as tour guides, peak climbing, tour operators, etc. The majority of the Everest climbing records belong to the Sherpa. For the other Sherpa living beyond Everest, the main source of income is still farming in the rural mountain region. The Sherpa, as I can assure you, are far [more] developed than other Indigenous peoples in Nepal. Several factors acted as facilitators but, I must identify two of them: tourism and overseas migration. As many days [as] the Himalaya will exist, the Sherpa will also exist symmetrically.(R3)[3]

According to Fisher (1990), the Sherpa are identified as a sub-group of the Bhotia. These indigenous peoples live in eastern Nepal and around the highlands of the Himalayas. Some of them also live in Darjeeling, India. The Sherpa are close to the Tibetan peoples in relation to language, physical traits and cultural patterns, and they are viewed as friendly and welcoming. Traditionally, these peoples earned their livelihood from trading, where the men used to embark on long-distance trips that lasted for months. However, importantly, the Sherpa act as middlemen between Tibetan and Nepali traders in the lower regions.

Good literacy rates and a traditional ability to interact well with foreigners have enabled the Sherpa to reach relatively higher positions compared to other similar peoples. However, their conventional role as traders can hardly be ignored. The Sherpa came to light when in 1953 Sir Edmund Hillary reached the summit of Mount Everest accompanied by local guide Tenzing Norgay (Shea, 2005). This reflected the Sherpa's abilities as porters, tourist guides, and mountaineers:

I am staying in the United Kingdom and this is an unreachable dream for many of other indigenous peoples in Nepal. We are economically much developed and we can never ignore the roles of trading behind this. But, I must admire the role of overseas Sherpa who are positively contributing [to] the community with their higher earnings. (R4)[4]

The development process among the Sherpa is more consolidated than among others. Tourism, and particularly 'mountain tourism' as a niche, is serving as a catalyst for economic development initiatives. Their roles are also comprehensive, ranging from cooks to guides, and these jobs are the backbone of the Sherpa's economic development. The occupations of these peoples traditionally centred on four identified patterns within the mountain environment: cultivation, animal husbandry (yak derivatives), trading, and mountaineering. Mountain tourism set a solid platform for employment and income generation. This resulted in the rise of property prices and more business opportunities where tourist facilities are multifarious and have reached certain standards.

However, an important shift took place towards building tourism-related infrastructures and increasing overseas immigration. For the last few decades, these indigenous peoples have been involved in a surge in immigration to other developed countries of the world. The United States, the United Kingdom, Australia, and many countries in Europe are favoured places. New York has a considerable number of Sherpa immigrants, and London also accommodates a large number of these peoples who occupy prestigious roles as Ghurkha soldiers in the British Army. Otherwise, most of the Sherpa immigrants overseas are typically engaged in relatively low-paid jobs, but are admired for their natural capacities to work harder and longer.

---

3   R3, a Sherpa based in Nepal, ran a tour-operating firm in Kathmandu. Initial contact was made through LinkedIn.

4   R4 was also a Sherpa and used to live in London. This person was contacted through working capacities in London. However, this person moved to the United States in mid 2013.

THE SHAN

According to Yawnghwe (2010), the Shan are comparatively well-known indigenous peoples in Southeast Asia throughout Myanmar, Thailand and China. The Shan is a large group with five major subdivisions: the Tai Khamti, Tai Neua, Tai Khuen, Tai Lue, and Tai Yai. Of these subgroups, this study focuses on the Tai Yai, who are considered to be the 'Shan Proper' and who mainly live in Myanmar. The Burmese (Myanmar) Shan are believed to have originated in and migrated from China, and started living in Myanmar over 1,000 years ago. The Shan state is divided into northern and southern, with the capital cities being Lashio and Taunggyi respectively. The traditional economic activities of the Shan are agriculture related, which has enabled them to witness economic development, at least to some extent.

These peoples rely on agriculture as their main form of livelihood generation through growing and cultivating crops, and marketing a number of products. However, the role of illicit narcotics such as opium in accelerating their economic development initiatives cannot be ignored. The Shan state is believed to be the largest opium producer in the world (Sargent, 1994). Animal husbandry is another means of livelihood generation. Agricultural works are typically massive and require outsider and migrant workers to support them during the peak harvesting period. Political unrest with the demand for equal opportunities and greater access to resources has lingered over the years. Surplus agricultural production has enabled the people to reach a stable level to oppose national policies that are usually viewed as discriminatory. General political stability is very much in demand for Myanmar, and the Shan are set to continue fighting for equal rights and opportunities. Particular roles for different groups are crucial for accomplishing this aim:

> Yes, we are not fully supported by the Myanmar government and this is particularly important. The need for a better and [more] prosperous community is always a demand for us and we are struggling to reach our goal. (R5)[5]

The natural production and general processing facilities of opium and heroin in this state has had a twofold outcome: economic development and the suppression or displacement of local populations:

> Undoubtedly, the Shan state can become developed only on the basis of rice production. The state can produce unbelievable amounts of rice. Still, the trend of making quick profit and pressures of different gangs has pushed the Shan to engage in illegal production of heroin and opium. This practice leads to rivalry, the import of arms and thus to create unrest and tension in the entire region. But, in a general context, the state is economically developed. (R6)[6]

The role of illegal narcotics production is a fact and agent of economic development for the Shan. However, this is debatable and can hardly be generalised where the ecological settings of this region are suitable for this kind of production. This practice may appear to be profit-oriented, but the limit and extent of its sustainability is always questionable. The Shan are an excellent example of a combination of the typical nature of production capacity, illegal intervention, suppression, and resistance.

---

5   R5 was a Shan living in Singapore. This political activist was forced to leave Myanmar due to his dynamic political engagement with the Shan movement. Initial contact was made through Facebook.

6   R6 was also a Shan trader based in Myanmar. Initial contact was made through R5 during a business stay in Singapore.

Conclusion

Different concepts are used to identify similar groups of peoples across the world. International agencies, and particularly the United Nations (UN), have played an unprecedented role in identifying these peoples (Capotorti, 1979; Chakma, 2001). This study used the term 'indigenous people' as documented in the UN guidelines. While an agreed definition is ambiguous, this study suggests as a general understanding that indigenous peoples generally have a form of self-identity and are viewed as a minority, with their socio-cultural and economic practices distinct from the mainstream population. From a cross-national perspective, the objectives of this study were to observe the involvement of indigenous peoples in economic activities and to analyse the reasons for their economic advancement. The three identified cases were: the Chakma of Bangladesh, the Sherpa of Nepal, and the Shan of Myanmar.

This study also offered a conceptual understanding of indigenous peoples and the economic development of these three identified cases. The cases in this study represent diverse socio-economic structures, particularly from the South Asian background. This is an important part of the world because of its geo-political significance. Also, the number of indigenous peoples in this part of the world is subsistent, with a visible trend of increasing day by day. General improvements and economic development are symmetrical. These are abstract and relate to community development, sustainability, and the increase of capacities and choices for underprivileged peoples (Mihlar, 2012; Sen, 1999). Indigenous peoples are normally marginalised with substantial production competencies or even minimal representation in the national economic agenda (Nwonwu, 2010). Still, the three identified cases of this study represent their clear engagement with the economic development initiatives followed in their own ways.

Issues of human rights violation and discrimination are quite common among the indigenous peoples in this area. The results of this study outline three different active paradigms for the cases. State-level support, the input of tourism and overseas immigration, and the natural capacities for agricultural production are the three main facilitators of economic development for these three separate groups of indigenous peoples. There is an ever-present demand for the acceleration of economic development activities for indigenous peoples. Numerous groups of peoples across the world are engaged in actions and efforts to contribute to and promote these to maintain their basic existence. This is particularly the case when attention is drawn to two notions of indigenous peoples and economic development. The need to encourage economic activities for indigenous peoples thus entails enormous contributions from other communities as well as the entire nation. Discrimination is a fundamental issue to be addressed for bringing equality to societies as well as countries. Poverty eradication and steps towards developing a causative economy are necessary. International agencies, and particularly the UN, are concentrating on development initiatives among these indigenous peoples.

The elimination of legislative and structural barriers is required to divert development initiatives in a certain direction for improving living standards. Also, promoting and supporting the indigenous peoples' generated economic activities requires emphasis to ensure positive contributions. The interests and concerns of indigenous peoples involve factors related to general socio-economic structures. Prioritised aspects of development initiatives, with problem identification and the formulation of guidelines, are also necessities. From diverse contexts, this study thus highlights the perspective analysis and suggests prioritised development initiatives as major areas for consideration. The gross outcomes of the Millennium Development Goals (MDGs) to be achieved by 2015 can hardly be consolidated in terms of development practices among these indigenous peoples. The abilities of each agency aimed at supporting enterprises and promoting economic activities cannot be considered to be similar. A form of deficiency becomes persistent, thus leaving more space for development inventiveness among indigenous peoples. Inability to formulate, suggest and encourage enterprises from indigenous peoples is not uncommon, and the effect of marginalisation also appears to be a key challenge. Discrimination appears in resource allocation and policy implementation. In the case of prolonged discrimination, this can lead to communal unrest and a widened gap between mainstream society and indigenous peoples. The dire possibility of conflict and inequality can also lead to socio-communal disturbances. Patterns of poverty alleviation and economic development can be viewed as practices rather than the demands of circumstances. The development of partnerships and cooperation between communities, societies and states is also essential.

Indigenous peoples across the world can rarely benefit from similar types of development initiatives if their situations and circumstances are dissimilar. Ideologies, knowledge sharing, or thematic concerns demand efficiency and soundness in development planning and implementation. The Chakma of Bangladesh, as outlined by the respondents in this study, enjoy the benefits of the government's supportive initiatives for indigenous peoples through quota allocation. This enabled them to face less competition in securing positions both in educational institutions and in the civil service. The Sherpa of Nepal, even though they are dependent on available resources in the Himalayan Mountain regions, have recently benefited greatly from higher earnings through overseas migration and tourism. Meanwhile, relatively, the Shan of Myanmar are lagging behind the others, with governmental or institutional support followed by political unrest. Still, the abundance of natural resources for agricultural production has enabled them to attain a much anticipated position that is economically sounder. Thus, this study identifies the Chakma of Bangladesh as more 'pragmatic', backed by government policy frameworks; the Shan of Myanmar as more 'devout' and having an abundance of agricultural resources and wider religious influence; and the Sherpa of Nepal as 'traders' due to their interaction with trade, tourism and wage earning.

Economic development in every community should be based on theoretical and practical accuracy, areas in which increased emphasis is required to face and mitigate existing disputes. This study thus concludes that indigenous peoples have the potential to become involved in mainstream economic policy frameworks. Emphasis needs to be concentrated on both legislative and institutional capacity enhancement. Closer interaction with the respondents could possibly bring out better results for this study where a volatile political situation and lack of security acted as barriers for engaging in participative approaches. A better type of research design for a potential study can be crafted through reducing the effects of these identified barriers.

References

Anderson, R. B. (1999). *Economic development among the Aboriginal peoples of Canada: The hope for the future.* North York, ON: Captus.

Axelsson, P. and Skold, P. (2013). Introduction. In P. Axelsson, and P. Skold (eds), *Indigenous peoples and demography: The complex relation between identity and statistics.* New York: Berghahn, p. 1.

Barbier, E, (2009). *Natural resources and economic development.* Cambridge: Cambridge University Press.

Bhagwati, J. and Panagariya, A. (2013). *Why growth matters: How economic growth in India reduced poverty and the lessons for other developing countries.* New York: Perseus.

Blaser, M., Feit, H. A. and McRae, G. (2004). Indigenous peoples and development processes: New terrains of struggles. In M. Blaser, H. A. Feit, and G. McRae (eds), *In the way of development: Indigenous peoples, life projects and globalization.* London: Zed, p. 1.

Brezina, C. (2011). *Understanding the gross domestic product and the gross national product.* New York: Rosen.

Burger, J. (1990). *The Gaia atlas of first peoples.* London: Gaia.

Capotorti, J. (1979). *Study on the rights of persons belonging to ethnic, religious and linguistic minorities*. New York: United Nations, para, 568.

Castillo, B. H. (2004). *Indigenous peoples in isolation in the Peruvian Amazon: Their struggle for survival and freedom*. Copenhagen: International Work Group for Indigenous Affairs (IWGIA).

Chakma, S. (2001). Behind the bamboo curtain: Racism in Asia. In S. Chakma and M. Jensen (eds), *Racism against Indigenous peoples*. Copenhagen: IWGIA, pp. 176–180.

Dale, R. (2006). *Development planning: Concepts and tools for planners, managers and facilitators*. Ghaziabad: Academic Foundation.

Das, J. K. (2001). *Human rights and Indigenous peoples*. New Delhi: New Apcon.

Datta, M. B. (2012) *Understanding security practices in South Asia: Securitization theory and the role of non-state actors*. Oxford: Routledge.

Eatwell, J., Milgate, M. and Newman, P. (1989). *Economic development*. New York: Norton.

Elias, P. D. (1991). *Development of Aboriginal people's communities*. North York, ON: Captus.

Fisher, J. F. (1990). *Sherpas: Reflections on change in Himalayan Nepal*. Berkeley: University of California Press.

Gilbert, J. (2006). *Indigenous peoples' land rights under international law: From victims to actors*. New York: Transnational.

Grabowski, R., Self, S. and Shields, M. P. (2012). *Economic development: A regional, institutional, and historical approach*. New York: Sharpe.

Gupta, A. (2005). *Human rights of Indigenous peoples: Comparative analysis of Indigenous peoples*. New Delhi: Isha.

Hassan, A. & Burns, P. (2014). Tourism Policies of Bangladesh – a contextual analysis. *Tourism Planning & Development*, pp. 1-4. doi: 10.1080/21568316.2013.874366

Hassan, A. & Forhad, A. (2013). The Role of NGOs in the Sustainable Development of Bangladesh. *Present Environment & Sustainable Development*, 7(2), pp. 59-72.

Hughes, L. (2003). *The no-nonsense guide to Indigenous peoples*. Oxford: New Internationalist.

International Labour Organization (ILO). (2013). *Convention No. 169*. Retrieved from: http://www.ilo.org/indigenous/Conventions/no169/lang--en/index.htm (accessed: 1 December 2013).

International Work Group for Indigenous Affairs (IWGIA). (2013). *Who are the Indigenous Peoples?* Retrieved from: http://www.iwgia.org/culture-and-identity/identification-of-indigenous-peoples (accessed: 1 December 2013).

Jerome, A. (2011). *Infrastructure for economic development and poverty reduction in Africa*. Nairobi: United Nations Human Settlement Programmes.

Joshi H. M. (2008). *Human development index, Rajasthan: Spatio-temporal and gender appraisal at Panchayat Somiti/Block Level*. New Delhi: Concept.

Jupp, J. (2001). *The Australian people: An encyclopedia of the nation, its people and their origins*. Cambridge: Cambridge University Press.

Long, C. (1991). *Participation of the poor in development initiatives: Taking their rightful place*. London: Earthscan.

McGovern, S. (2012). *Education, modern development, and Indigenous knowledge: An analysis of academic knowledge production*. New York: Routledge.

Mihlar, F. (2012). *Voices from the margins: Including the perspectives of minorities and Indigenous peoples in the post-2015 debate*. London: Minority Rights Group International.

Minahan, J. (2012). *Ethnic groups of South Asia and the Pacific: An encyclopedia*. New York: ABC-CLIO.

Minde, H. (2008). *Indigenous peoples: Self-determination, knowledge, indigeneity*. Delft: Eburon.

Moretti, M. (2012). *International law and nomadic people*. Milton Keynes: AuthorHouse.

Nafziger, E. W. (2006). *Economic development*. Cambridge: Cambridge University Press.

Nwonwu, F. O. C. (2010). *Indigenous knowledge systems in Igbo traditional agriculture*. Milton Keynes: AuthorHouse.

Payne, A. (2005). *The global politics of unequal development.* Basingstoke: Palgrave Macmillan.

Sargent, I. (1994). *Twilight over Burma: My life as a Shan princess.* Honolulu: University of Hawaii Press.

Sen, A. K. (1999). *Development as freedom.* Oxford: Oxford University Press.

Sharma, N. and Shukla, S. P. (1992). *Geography and development of hill areas: A case study of Arunachal Pradesh.* New Delhi: Mittal.

Sharman, J. C. and Mistry, P. S. (2008). *Considering the consequences: The development implications of initiatives on taxation, anti-money laundering and combating the financing of terrorism.* London: Commonwealth Secretariat.

Shea, T. (2005). *Climbing Mount Everest: Understanding commutative, associative, and distributive properties.* New York: Rosen.

Singh, D. K. (2010). *Stateless in South Asia: The Chakmas between Bangladesh and India.* London: Sage.

Smith, L. T. (1999). *Decolonizing methodologies: Research and Indigenous peoples.* London: Zed.

Stavenhagen, R. (2013). *Peasants, culture and Indigenous peoples: Critical issues.* Berlin: Springer.

Tiwari, J. (2004). *Child abuse and human rights.* New Delhi: Isha.

Todaro, M. P. (*2000*). *Economic development.* Harlow: Pearson.

Tribe, M., Nixson, F. and Sumner, A. (2010). *Economics and development studies.* Oxford: Routledge.

United Nations (UN). (2013) *The concept of Indigenous peoples.* Retrieved from: https://www.google.co.uk/?gws_rd=cr&ei=tEi7UoS9FarnywOWpIHADw#q=%E2%80%98On+an+individual+basis,+an+indigenous+person+is+one+who+belongs+to+these+indigenous+populations+through+self-identification+as+indigenous+(group+consciousness)+and+is+recognized+and+accepted+by+these+populations+as+one+of+its+members+(acceptance+by+the+group) … this+preserves+for+these+communities+the+sovereign+right+and+power+to+decide+who+belongs+to+them,+without+external+interference%E2%80%99+ (accessed: 1 December 2013).

World Bank (WB). (1991). *The operational directive.* Retrieved from: http://www.ifc.org/wps/wcm/connect/835cc50048855270ab94fb6a6515bb18/OD420_IndigenousPeoples.pdf?MOD=AJPERES (accessed: 1 December 2013).

Yawnghwe, C. T. (2010). *The Shan of Burma: Memoirs of a Shan exile.* Singapore City: ISEAS.

16

The Raffia Palm Industry in Nigeria: A Case Study of Annang Society in Akwa Ibom State

Umoh Samuel Uwem and Oyewo Adetola

Chapter Synopsis

This study particularly focuses on the palm industry of Nigeria that in a sense acts as the major manufacturing niche. Palm trees of different species – such as the Raffia (*Raphia hookeri*) and the Oil Palm (*Elaeis guineensis*) – are cultivated for their commercial value and are of immense benefit to the indigenous communities as they play a vital role in the development of rural economies. Agricultural and economic related activities such as Palm wine tapping, Palm oil trading and Raffia weaving within the Raffia industry are major occupations practised in Annang society located in the Palm belt of the south-south region of Nigeria. The popularity of the Raffia Palm made the town of Ikot Ekpene famous, known as 'Raffia City'. This study mainly adopts a qualitative research approach and relies on personal observations and face-to-face interviews with different stakeholders and beneficiaries. The results of this study outline that the Raffia Palm industry is playing a vital role in providing avenues for employment, poverty alleviation, sources of livelihood and the growth of mainstream industries in the rural society as identified, which leads to communal development. Yet, despite the potential of the industry, it thrives only at subsistence level, constrained by customary land ownership, primitive technology, associated health hazards, socio-economic change and poor marketing.

Introduction

Rural communities in south-east Nigeria depend almost entirely on the Raffia Palm for their livelihood. The Raffia Palm grows abundantly in many parts of West Africa, particularly in the swampy and semi-swampy areas of the equatorial rainforest or derived savannah (Ewuim et al., 2011). The Nigerian oil Palm belt covers 24 states, including all nine states of the Niger Delta (Akwa Ibom, Abia, Rivers, Edo, Imo, Ondo, Bayelsa, Cross River, and Delta). The bulk of the trees and their essential parts – such as fronds, leaves, trunk, and roots – are used for several purposes, including

Palm oil, Palm kernel oil, Palm wine, Raffia weaving, Palm kernel cake and other by-products. From the raw materials are processed Raffia Palm wine; bottled Palm wine; Raffia oil: piassava production and utilisation; Raffia production (bamboo and mat products); and Raffia pulp for papermaking (Ndon, 2003). It is an important crop for the farmers in the community, and most households earn their livelihood from it (see Figure 16.1). This provides a source of income to a wide range of market intermediaries and Palm wine tappers in West Africa (Mbuagbaw and Noorduyn, 2012). During the pre-colonial and colonial era in Nigeria, an Annang household was capable of owning as many as 500–1,000 Palms (Edet, 1997: 23).

Figure 16.1   Raffia palm trees

However, the tree is fast becoming depleted due to bush burning, neglect and ageing of the trees, resulting in low yields, industrialisation and urbanisation. To mitigate this loss, the state government is involved in forest preservation and has three reserves in Stubbs Creek Forest Reserve (SCFR) with 310.87km^2 in Eket and Oron local government areas; 5.18km^2 in Odu Itu; and 2.59km^2 in Obot Ndon in the Ikono local government area. However, it must be admitted that despite the enormous potential of the industry, it is still constrained by manual technology, a land tenure system, health hazards, a poor marketing structure, and low investment in large commercial farms, to mention but a few. Against this background, the chapter discusses the economic development of Annang Society.

Research Methods

The study area was the Annang Society of the Akwa Ibom State. The Annang is one of the major ethnic groups of Akwa Ibom, located in the Niger Delta region in the coastal south-southern part of Nigeria and southwestern Cameroon. Presently, it includes eight of the state's 31 local government areas, namely Abak, Essien Udim, Etim Ekpo, Ika, Ikot Ekpene, Obot Akara, Oruk Anam, and Ukanafun. It is bounded by the Ngwa and Ndoki in Abia State to the north, the Isuagbu to the east, and the Adoni of Rivers State to the west (Aniekan, 2002). The research was carried out in two local government areas, namely Ikot Ekpene and Essien Udim. Ikot Ekpene is known as the regional centre of commerce and is referred to as 'the Raffia city' or locally as 'IK'. The study combined a review of secondary materials and primary data. Structured interviews were administered to 15 randomly selected actors involved in the industry, such as Raffia weavers, Palm oil sellers, Raffia merchants and Palm wine tappers. Observations were also made and snapshots taken of different activities within the industry.

Table 16.1   Some terms associated with the Raffia Palm in English and Akwa Ibom

	English term	Term in Akwa Ibom
1	Raffia Palm	*Ukot Eyop*
2	*Trunk*	*Ekpad*
3	Leaves	*Iya/Eyei*
4	Stem fibre	*Nnyang*
5	*Raffia* (leaf fibre)	*Ndam*
6	Raffia leaf blade	*Ekpi*
7	*Piassava* (leaf-sheath fibre)	*Idid*
8	Roofing mats	*Nkanya*
9	Palm wine	*Ukot*
10	Oil	Mmanyanga
11	Palm kernel	*Isip*
12	Palm oil	*Aran*
13	Fibre	*Ikpok*
14	Palm wine	Ukot
15	Bamboo ladder for Palm wine tapping	Ebet Ukot

Source: Fieldwork, 2013.

Economic Activities in Annang

Until recently, the rural areas in Nigeria were synonymous with farming, but recent trends have revealed that non-farm activities are also a source of income in the rural economy for longer or shorter periods at different times of the year; sectors include government, commerce, manufacturing, and services. Nonetheless, farming is dominant in Annang, with the cultivation of crops on small-scale peasant farms usually planted as compounds which produce food crops such as cassava, maize, rice, yam, cocoyam (*ikpong ekpo*), fruits and vegetables used for family consumption, with the surplus sold in the local markets. Cassava is valuable because garri and fufu are derived from it and it is the staple food, while the estate farms specialise in growing cash crops such as rubber, cocoa, and oil Palm. Agriculture is the main occupation of the populace residing in rural areas and remains the main contributor to the gross domestic product/GDP (over 70%) (Makarfi and Dandago, 2013). Non-farm activities include crafts and artisan work (such as local tailoring, bricklaying, carpentry, blacksmithing and furniture making); commercial motor vehicle driving and motorcycle riding, popularly referred to as *Okada*; motorcycle and vehicle mechanics, etc.; coffin making and the mortuary business; trading in agricultural produce; selling other non-agricultural products such as clothing, soap, confectionery and bakery products; and menial jobs like the collection and sale of firewood, hawking of fast food and load carrying in the markets and other public places.

THE RAFFIA PALM INDUSTRY

In Annang, the industry is a variable free market, most of the time a 'one-man business', and has export potential. Unlike other jobs where people gain promotion to senior levels, such jobs do not exist here. The profitability of the vocation is seasonal as production and distribution of goods may change depending on prices, demand/supply factors and the bargaining power of traders/customers. Sales points are in the villages, neighbouring communities and the city; prices of the products are higher in the cities than in the villages, perhaps due to transportation factors. Various activities occur in the Raffia industry such as Raffia weaving, Palm wine trade and Palm oil trade. The Raffia tree is one of the most economically useful plants. The trunk is used for roofing, umbrellas, furniture, fish traps, ladders/poles, building frameworks, mats, baskets, and Palm fruit shifts. The leaves, called 'fronds', are used for baskets, roofing/thatching, and firewood for cooking and for heating houses during cold nights. Piassava is used for fine-textured charcoal, local gunpowder, coarse ropes, and brushes (see Table 16.1). It has also been considered as a potential source of pulp for paper production. There are unsubstantiated claims that the Raffia roots are used in traditional medicine for the treatment and prevention of several diseases such as stomach ailments, abdominal pain, and other associated sicknesses (Mbuagbaw and Nootrduyn, 2012; Akachukwu, 2001; Akpan and Edem, 1996).

RAFFIA WEAVING

Ikot Ekpene has a long history of transforming the Raffia into cloth, shoes, hats, handbags, and mats (see Figure 16.2). Women are mostly involved with the weaving carried out with bamboo sticks and wood. The peak sales period is usually during the months of April, September and December, and at festive periods such as Easter and Christmas when cane baskets are especially used for the packaging of gift hampers as individuals and companies order products. A complete set of Raffia cane furniture ranges in price from (Nigerian Naira) ₦25,000 to 150,000 depending on specification and durability. Experience and dexterity are needed for the work. In Annang there are different types of mat weaving such as:

• Small roofing mat (*Nkanya*). This involves two frames made of split bamboo shafts. The Raffia leaflets are attached one after another to the bamboo frames. The size of the roofing mat may be up to 1m × 2m ($2m^2$).
• Large roofing mat (*Ikpotu*). This is used for local ceilings, thatched roofing and the construction of canoe houses. The large mats may be up to 5m × 7m ($35m^2$). *Ikpotu* is similar to the small mat except that the leaflets used are longer, carry four or five frames instead of two, and are joined together instead of bending a single leaflet.

However, the art of weaving is dying out in locals' pursuit of other lucrative jobs and the craft sometimes has poor aesthetic value as people prefer imported materials.

Figure 16.2   Raffia palm products

PALM SAP AND PALM WINE TAPPING

In Annang, the *Idim ibom* species is reputed to produce the greatest amount of wine (Ndon, 2003). The unfermented milky-white sap contains about 10–12% sugar ferment within two hours as a result of natural microbial flora; the sugar level decreases rapidly as it is converted to alcohol and other products. Brands of Palm wine have nutritional, medical, religious and social uses which have increasingly enhanced the demand for it to be offered at weddings, funerals, and other events and cultural ceremonies. It is known by a variety of names in different countries such as *Matango, Fitchuk*, and *Mbu* in Cameroon; *Doka* and *Akpetesin* in Ghana; *Toddy* in India; *Lambanog* in the Philippines; *panam cullo* in China; and *Emu, akaikai*, and *Ogogoro* in Nigeria (Mbuagbaw and Nootrduyn, 2012; Ndon, 2003).

In Annang, Palm wine tapping is a male-dominated vocation, involving special tapping skills that are often hereditary, although it does require training. This corroborates Mbuagbaw and Noorduyn's (2012) assertion that Palm wine tapping is a common occupation in many Palm-growing regions of the world, mainly non-Islamic countries where alcohol is not prohibited. The skills needed are Palm tree climbing, felling, hole boring, and facilitation of the free flow of Palm wine. In the process of tapping the wine with a chisel-type instrument called an *Onon Ukot* (see Figure 16.3), the tappers cut away the crown part (young inflorescence at the top of the Raffia Palm) and an incision is made at the base of the inflorescence (*usiak iso ukot*, meaning local technique), a technique which does not kill the tree immediately. Tapping duration varies from 23 to 90 days. The wine can be collected thrice a day – in the morning, afternoon and evening – if it is good. The wine tapped in the morning is greater than what is obtained in the evening as the night favours increased sap flow. In the interval between morning and evening, some mild tapping may be done from noon to 1.00pm. During the intervals, the pot suspended on the tree is filled with Palm wine, to be emptied by the tapper. The wine tapped during this period is known as *Ukpe Ukot*. This type of tapping does not involve vigorous tapping as in the morning and evening. *Ukpe Ukot* is only meant for the removal of foam-like mucus (*ato*) formed on the incised base (*iso ukot*). It is believed that without the removal of the foam-like mucus on the young inflorescence at the top of the Raffia Palm (*iso ukot*), the tree would die off. Fire is applied to the tree to increase the sap flow (*mmon ukot*). The application of fire to the tapping panel is known as *ndot ikan uko'*. Fire is heavily applied during the Harmattan period (*akarika*) as it decreases the sap flow of the Palm wine.

Palm wine tapped from swampy areas does not produce quality wine due to the excessive water absorbed by the roots – as a result, the sap is mixed with water and it is not as palatable as that of the 'upland' wine tapped from the lowlands. A full-time tapper is capable of tapping 20 trees a day. The tappers may not necessarily be the owners of the Palm trees as some are tapped for those who own the trees for a monetary or Palm wine reward. At times, 'expert movements made the work look deceptively safe but serious injuries and some deaths have occurred'. It is estimated that the local market sale for Palm wine each day is $9.30 for 3.7 litres, while the average retail price per 60cl bottle of Palm wine at bars, hotels and restaurants is ₦100.

Figure 16.3   A palm wine tapper with a tapping chisel (*Onon Ukot*)

However, Palm wine production and sale is still low due to the demand for imported drinks. Manual technology as described above can cause contamination by bacteria from dirty collection containers and unfiltered water used to increase the quantity, which sometimes leads to outbreaks of diarrhoeal diseases (Bisi-Johnson et al., 2011). The Nigerian Institute for Oil Palm Research (NIFOR, 2013) pointed out that the fermentative ability of the *Zymomonas* species and other microorganisms present in the wine has been a major problem in the bottling of Palm wine and the distribution for consumption in Nigeria. The trade is strenuous and labour intensive, with inherent risks such as falls and accidents which result in severe injuries including mouth tears, fractures, dislocations, amputations, and spinal trauma – all requiring hospital admission with prolonged, expensive medical and rehabilitative care and a risk of death (Mbuagbaw and Okwen, 2006). Palm wine trade is officially unrecognised, and associated with low income and little appeal for youths, especially with the advent of 'white-collar jobs' which has caused rural–urban migration for alternative easier and better-paid jobs.

This is further aggravated by over-reliance on the crude oil economy in the state with the presence of oil-producing companies like Exxon Mobil. To make the occupation more profitable, through the initiative of NIFOR, formations of clusters of 10 tappers have been established, each harvesting 150 litres of Palm wine per day, with a series of local processing plants supplying the bottled product to vendors (see Table 16.2). It was estimated that each tapper's earning would be ₦120,000 ($750 or €570) per month.

Table 16.2   Tapping duration and yield of Palm wine

Tapping Duration (days)	Average Yield (litres)	Total Yield (litres)
46	17.4	799.0
23	8.4	194.0
20	5.6	111.0
31	12.5	38.5
28	16.0	447.0
52	16.2	843.0
48	13.8	662.0
49	15.3	748.0
58	13.7	795.0
50	12.5	625.0
59	13.5	929.0
37	17.4	275.0
31	7.5	231.0
38	8.6	325.0
28	9.9	278.0
89	8.8	247.0
113	8.0	715.0
38	7.0	827.0
78	6.5	246.0
79	7.3	566.0
65	8.2	651.0
52	6.1	398.0
48	6.3	327.0
	7.4	355.0
Total		11,979.0

Source: Nigerian Institute for Oil Palm Research (NIFOR), 2013.

PALM OIL

Palm oil production starts with the trees that are producing fruit, the harvesting of the fruit, and then the processing of the fruit. Production systems are made up of wild groves and planted farms, with the wild groves producing about 80% of the total fruit for processing. Palm oil is extracted from the Palm fruit, a sessile drupe, one-seeded fruit enclosed in a fleshy pulp of variable shape about 20–50mm long. Oil Palm requires nursing before planting into the field. The seedlings have to be raised for 10–15 months before planting, which is a major factor contributing to the high cost of seedlings. The oil Palm tree starts to bear fruit from the third year, and the yield per tree increases progressively with age until it peaks at around 20 years. The yield begins to decline from year 25 to 40 when the economic life of the tree ebbs. It is mainly propagated by seeding through pre-nursery and field nursery practices (Ugochukwu et al., 1999). There are three varieties of oil Palm: Dura, Pisifera, and Tenera (see Table 16.3). The preferred variety among Palm oil farmers is a Tenera hybrid of the Dura (female) and the Pisifera (male). Tenera seedlings are produced by NIFOR and commonly referred to as the extension work seeds (EWS). The fruit of the Tenera variety contains 25% oil, in terms of weight, and the Dura variety 18%, so the same amount of Tenera can yield 30% more oil than the equivalent fruit of the Dura (NIFOR, 2013).

There are 17 characteristics which are used to define and grade Palm oil in order for it to be traded internationally. Dominant among them are the levels of free fatty acids (FFA), dirt, iodine value, and other contaminants (NIFOR, 2013; Foundation for Partnership Initiatives in the Niger Delta/PIND, 2011).

Table 16.3   Characteristics of the three fruit varieties of oil Palm

Dura	Pisifera	Tenera
Thick shell	Shell-less	Thin shell
Thin mesocarp	Mainly monocarp	Thick mesocarp
Viable embryo	Unviable embryo if present seed sterile	Viable embryo
Large kernel	Very small kernel and sometimes no kernel in most fruits	Good size kernel
Contains very small quality of oil	The oil content of the fruit is the highest among the three fruit forms	
Unimproved	Unimproved	Improved

Source: Nigerian Institute for Oil Palm Research (NIFOR), 2013.

There is a huge market for three major oil Palm products, as outlined below.

1. Low-quality technical palm oil (TPO), which is used for direct sale and unprocessed oil. Women play a significant role in the traditional production technique (the use of foot power and the mortar and pestle are common methods) of processing fresh fruit bunches (FFB) which is inefficient, laborious and time consuming, leading to low yields and poor product quality. TPO is the largest of the various product channels; it is the least productive source but is shrinking due to very weak vertical coordination between traditional processors and mini processors. In Nigeria, the volume of oil required in the traditional food market is three times more than the requirement in the industrial market. Palm oil with free fatty acids between 5 and 30% is acceptable in this market due to the various requirements for Nigerian

cuisine. The traditional market is served by small-scale producers of Palm oil which account for more than 70% of local production (650,000 tonnes).

2. Special Palm oil (SPO) is used in the processing industry by large mills and is often refined. SPO always sells at a higher price than TPO and supplies the industrial market, which utilises the high-quality crude and refined Palm oil and fractions (olein and stearin) as raw materials for their products: soap, frying oils for noodles, bakery fats, etc. Although SPO oil has a higher value, there is constant tension between SPO and TPO as the latter is in constant easily accessible demand and is easier to process than SPO. SPO and Palm kernel oil (PKO) can be further refined into refined, bleached, deodorised oil (RBDO) and refined Palm kernel oil respectively.

3. PKO has been growing in demand over the years for the industrial market due to its use in the manufacture of artificial cream fillings, soap, cosmetics and personal care products as well as for emulsifiers in the food processing and pharmaceutical industries and the in production of toiletries, tobacco, alkyd resins, paints and varnishes, cellophane, explosives, polyurethane, etc.

The supply of TPO, SPO, and PKO to the end consumers or end users is carried out through local and foreign sources. The local source is characterised by three main actors, namely Palm oil dealers, secondary processors, and automated processing plant owners. There are also three main groups of end users: 1) household consumers of TPO; 2) commercial users of TPO; and 3) industrial users of SPO, SPO value added products, PKO value added products, and PKO.

Table 16.4   Palm oil products and uses

Food uses	Non-food uses
Cooking oil, shortening, food frying (margarine, bakery fat, frying oil, cocoa butter substitute	Cosmetics and personal care
Bakery fats, confectionery fats, ice cream fats, infant nutrition fats	Oleo chemical (stearine), soap, detergent, biodiesel, lubricants
	Candles, pharmaceuticals, grease, surfactants
	Coatings, paint, lacquers, leather work, biodiesel
	Sludge from palm kernel waste is used for traditional soaps and fertiliser; fuel for mills; briquettes as substitute for fuel
	Palm kernel shells are used as an energy source; mosquito coils; industrial raw materials
	Processing waste – namely empty bunch refuse, fibre, shell, sludge, and mill effluent – constitute about 74–76% of the total mass of the oil products

Source: Foundation for Partnership Initiatives in the Niger Delta, 2011.

PALM OIL PROCESSING AND TECHNOLOGY

Palm oil extraction can be manual or involve the use of mechanical pressing units. The traditional processing method in use by rural Palm oil processors is the mortar and pestle. The manual unit is referred to as 'low production technology', while the mechanised units are referred to as 'intermediate technology' production. Any methods applied invariably influence the yield of oil, its quality, and price. An efficient processing technique increases the quality and quantity of food available for consumption and trade (Ini-mfon et al., 2013). According to Akpan (2008), the processing begins with harvesting the ripe Palm kernel bunch (*Ayom*) growing in clusters and weighing between 20 and 30kg, which are cut down by men with the aid of climbing ropes and machetes. The fruits are gathered by women and children and carried by head portage for processing. The women work communally in groups of two or three using the technique of cooking the Palm fruits in a pot and pounding the cooked fruits in a wooden mortar or mashing them using a vessel that resembles a canoe. About 10–20 bunches of Palm kernels take 48 hours to process to yield approximately 20 litres. Household members are the major source of labour; they are not paid wages for their labour, but in some instances those in the operating mills are commercially engaged, receiving a processing fee. Omoti (2004), in a study of the profitability of Palm oil processing enterprises and determinants of factors that affect the net returns of the Palm oil process, revealed that labour cost was a significant negative determinant of net returns. The finished product is stored in 25 litre kegs, or drums if in larger quantities, and put on planks to prevent the oil from solidifying. The mechanised oil extraction from fruit follows the same basic steps in either case:

1. steam sterilisation of bunches (inactivates lipase enzymes and kills microorganisms that produce free fatty acids, reducing oil quality);
2. stripping fruit from bunches;
3. crushing, digestion, and heating of the fruit;
4. oil extraction from macerated fruit (hydraulic pressing);
5. Palm oil clarification;
6. separating fibre from the endocarp;
7. drying, grading, and cracking of the endocarp;
8. separating the endocarp from the kernel;
9. kernel drying and packing.

The product of step 5 is termed crude Palm oil (CPO), which can be either TPO or SPO. In order to produce the more advanced products (RBDO), it must be refined to remove pigments, free fatty acids, and phospholipids.

SMALL-SCALE PROCESSING EQUIPMENT (SSPE)

The parboiled fruits are pounded and digested, producing a mash from which oil is extracted using a local spindle press (Akpan, 2008). Local fabricators have produced smaller scale processing systems that are easier to manage and are within the reach of some local entrepreneurs (small mill operators) in accordance with NIFOR guidance to fit any budget. These include Palm fruit strippers, sterilisers, clarifiers, nut/fibre separators, digesters, Palm nut crackers, and cutting platforms. The hand-operated hydraulic system, which uses a separate digester (horizontal or vertical type), is very popular and prevalent (Oseni et al., 2002). Other equipment includes a digester, spindle press, axe, spade, shovel, rake, machete, and drums for cooking fruits and classification of oil (Ini-mfon et al., 2013). The oil yield of the hydraulic system is between 70% and 90% depending on the strength of the man operating the hand pump, whose work efficiency diminishes in the latter part of the day due to tiredness (Oseni et al., 2002). These kinds of semi-mechanised, integrated, small-scale processing equipment (SSPE) have been improved considerably since their initial introduction.

Prevalent kinds are the digester, press, and a small engine. They cost about ₦1 million and capture about two-thirds of the available oil (12% for Dura). Efforts have been put in place by the state government for rural farmers to access SSPE and improved motorised harvesters – which has the capacity for harvesting 500–900 fresh fruit bunches (FFB) per day – to replace manual climbing of Palm trees.

INDUSTRIAL-SCALE PROCESSING EQUIPMENT (ISPE)

The medium-scale processors are able to process about 0.5 tonnes of FFB per hour, and the equipment includes a screening machine, boiler, digesters, press, clarifier, and generator. These are able to produce SPO, and employ about 10 personnel to operate. They require a good source of water and can generate a 13–14% yield of oil (equivalent to 50–70% of available oil). The large-scale processors can handle more than 1 tonne of FFB per hour (attached to estates with large mills) and may process up to 60 tonnes of fruit per hour, with yields of 15–18% of oil from the fruit (equivalent to 75% of available oil in the Tenera variety). New models with increasingly high extraction efficiency and requiring less labour input have also been developed by NIFOR. These include the:

* NIFOR large, with throughput capacity of 0.5–1.0 tonnes of fresh fruit bunch/hour (FFB/hr);
* NIFOR medium, with throughput capacity of 0.25–0.5 tonnes FFB/hr;
* NIFOR mini, with throughput capacity of 0.1–0.25 tonnes FFB/hr.

However, the equipment is capital intensive; therefore, it is beyond the reach of the peasant farmers and requires sophisticated infrastructure.

Figure 16.4   Palm oil

Source: Perfect Business Guide, 2014.

Impact of Palm Oil on Wealth and Poverty Alleviation in Annang

The Niger Delta region, which includes Akwa Ibom, is one of the oil Palm producing states in Nigeria that account for 57% of the national oil Palm area. Nigeria is the third largest producer of Palm oil in the world after Indonesia and Malaysia; however, it is a net importer (Udo, 2012). Many communities in the state consider Palm oil production to be a culture rather than a business (Ini-mfon et al., 2013). This is very pertinent as the rural community is poverty-stricken, characterised by a lack of basic infrastructure such as roads, water, sanitation, education, and electricity, which are not readily available in the rural area's communities. The prospects for job creation are high as Palm oil production is a major vocation in the rural communities, involving hundreds of thousands of poor producers and tens of thousands of poor processors. Domestic annual production of Palm oil in Nigeria is currently around 900,000 tonnes (Ini-mfon et al., 2013).

Palm oil has the prospects of providing employment for millions of unskilled and semi-skilled people. The importance of the tree crop lies in its capacity for providing direct employment to about 4 million Nigerian people in the 20 oil Palm growing states in Nigeria, and indirect employment to numerous other people involved in processing and marketing (Ini-mfon et al., 2013). About 25 litres is sold for ₦6,000 ($40).

As an essential food item, about 90% of the Palm oil produced ends up in food products, while the remaining 10% is employed for industrial production because of its many uses (see Table 16.4). Production of Palm oil is more sustainable than other vegetable oils (see Figure 16.4). It consumes considerably less energy in production, needs less land, and generates more oil per hectare than other leading vegetable oils such as rapeseed, Europe's leading oil, or soybean. In a bid to encourage local production of Palm products to satisfy local demand, importation of bulk crude and refined vegetable oil was prohibited in Nigeria in 2001. In response to this ban and the consequent increased demand for local products, there has been some increase in private sector investment in the development of new oil Palm plantations and the expansion of existing ones. Smallholdings and out-grower schemes were also being promoted by the federal and state governments.

Palm oil sales serve as an important income generator for women as gross earnings are reasonable enough to encourage their participation in the business. This is imperative as females occupy a dominant place in socio-economic life but are marginalised. It has been pointed out that women make up a large number of the rural poor, which accounts for 60% of the Nigerian population, and are more vulnerable than men to economic dwindling, deterioration of natural resources, and general neglect in the areas of development efforts (Nwosu and Nwawill, 2010; Ani, 2004). Thus, the business empowers the traders economically, enabling them to pay levies for community projects, and helping them to meet family responsibilities (e.g. payment of children's school fees). Traders (middlemen) seem to benefit more from the Palm oil trade due to inefficiencies resulting from weak value chain coordination. Many of the farmers prefer to sell the fruits because of the tedious processing stages, thus the sale of unprocessed fruits results in a loss to the seller and a great economic gain to the buyer.

It is in recognition of this that the oil Palm cluster was formed in the community to make the business profitable; it comprises oil Palm farmers, nursery operators, oil Palm processors, fabricators of oil Palm machines, and input suppliers. The cluster is registered; has a constitution and properly elected executives; meets regularly; and trains the community extensively in oil Palm farming. Cluster members have been trained in group formation and dynamics, management, conflict resolution, communications, accounting, etc. The nursery operators have successfully raised Palm oil seedlings through NIFOR training and sold them to oil Palm farmers, while the fabricators have produced processing technology that suits the processor's budget. However, it must be admitted that challenges facing the business are affecting its competitiveness and potential for growth, among which are:

- The lack of proper scaling of locally fabricated milling technology adversely affects the extraction rate and volume of Palm oil production.
- There are still problems of low productivity; quality of oil with high fatty acids; emphasis on local use only; and limited transformation and uses of the primary or secondary products for either food or non-food applications.

This might not be unconnected to inefficiency due to the high cost of labour, lack of linking roads for transportation, electricity, water, and inadequate credit facilities (Ukpabi, 2004). This is further aggravated by land and capital issues: land is a fundamental factor of production; and land tenure is still a common phenomenon in rural communities such as Annang, based on the family (inheritance system) and communal system (community property), which can be acquired by an individual, family, community, or government agency either for temporary or permanent use and is sometimes an impediment to agricultural activities. Informal and formal sources of credit are too costly or unavailable. Formal lending is highly collateralised and attracts very high interest rates as the farmers lack collateral. Without the ability to obtain micro-credit loans, they are limited to their producing capacity. These credits could be useful for procuring agricultural input such as fertiliser, seedlings, farm implements, and food processing equipment, which could result in increased productivity and more income to diversify economic activities and optimise gains.

Conclusion

It is clear that the Raffia Palm tree plays a vital role in the growth of rural economies as it provides avenues for poverty alleviation, a source of livelihood, and employment for millions of unskilled and semi-skilled people. Thus it is pertinent to reposition the industry to enhance the productivity, profitability, and sustained growth of the rural economy of Annang to enhance the resilience of the indigenous agricultural households.

References

Akpan, P.B. (2008). *Oil women of Akwa-Ibom State-World Rainforest Movement*. Retrieved from: http://wrm. org.uy/oldsite/countries/Nigeria/Akwa_Ibom_State.html (accessed: 30 December 2013).

Akachukwu, C. O. (2001). Production and utilization of wine palm (Raphia hookeri Mann and Wendland): an important wetland species occasionally visited by honey bees. *Proceedings of Aquatic Science*, pp. 282–297.

Akpan, E. J. and Edem, D. O. (1996). Antimicrobial properties of the mesocarp of the seed of Raphia Hookeri. *Nigeria Journal of Biochemistry and Molecular Biology*, 11, pp. 89–93.

Ani, O. A. (2004). *Women in agricultural and rural development*. Maiduguri: Quilla.

Aniekan, N. (2002). *Annang language: Varieties and proto-forms*. Retrieved from: http://www. annangheritage.org/ (accessed: 30 December 2013).

Bisi-Johnson, M. A., Adejuwon, A. O. and Ajayi, A. O. (2011). Meddling with a cultural heritage: traces of salicylate in adulterated palm wine and health implications. *African Journal of Food Science*, 5, pp. 536–540.

Edet A. U. (1997) *Palm wine among the Ibibio*. Uyo: Concept.

Ewuim, S. C., Akunne, C. E., Anumba, A. and Ataga, H. O. (2011). Insects associated with wine from raffia palm (Raphia Hookeri) in Alor, Nigeria. *Animal Research International*, 8(1), pp. 1328–1336.

Foundation for Partnership Initiatives in the Niger Delta (PIND). (2011). *A report on Palm oil value chain analysis in the Niger Delta*. Retrieved from: http://www.pindfoundation.org/research-and-publications/research/ (accessed: 30 December 2013).

Ini-mfon, V. P., Sunday B. A., Samuel J. U., Daniel, E. J. and Ubong, E. E. (2013). Factors affecting performance of palm oil processors in the South-South Region of Nigeria. *International Journal of Agricultural Economics and Extension*, 1(4), pp. 17–23.

Makarfi, A. M. and Dandago, K. I. (2013). Agricultural resource tapping and utilization for states' economic development in Nigeria: the role of chartered accountants. *Journal of Agricultural Economics and Development*, 2(6), pp. 217–225.

Mbuagbaw, L. and Noorduyn, S. (2012). The palm wine trade: occupational and health hazards. *International Journal of Occupational and Environmental Medicine*, 3(4), pp.157–164.

——— and Okwen, P. M. (2006). Mouth laceration due to fall in wine tappers: a report of 2 cases. *International Journal of Surgeons*, 7(2).

Ndon, B. A. (2003). *The Raphia Palm*. Lagos: Concept.

Nigerian Institute for Oil Palm Research (NIFOR) (2013). *Report 2012*. Retrieved from: http://faostat.fao.org/DesktopDefault.aspx?PageID=339&lang=en&country=159 (accessed: 30 December 2013).

Nwosu, I. E. and Nwawill, O. M. (2010). Assessment of perceived effectiveness of adult educational programme as poverty alleviation strategy among rural women in Njikoka Local Government Area. *Journal of Agriculture Biology Food System*, 1, pp. 57–64.

Omoti, U. (2004). Problems and prospects of oil palm development processing and potentials in Nigeria. *Paper prepared for African Investment and Development Agency Conference on attracting private foreign investment into Nigeria's oil palm industry*. Kuala Lumpur.

Oseni, O. K., Faborode, M. O. and Obafemi, O. O. (2002). Comparative evaluation of the digester-screw press and a hand-operated hydraulic press for palm fruit processing. *Journal of Food Engineering*, 52(3), pp. 249–255.

Perfect Business Guide (2014) *How to start business in Nigeria*. Retrieved from: http://perfectbusinessguide.com/how (accessed: 30 December 2013).

Udo, U. O. (2012). Analysis of Palm oil prices in Ini local government of Akwa Ibom State. Unpublished degree project. Obubra: Cross River University of Technology.

Ugochukwu, O. G., Otegbade, J. O., Ifeonu, P., Okeke, E.U. and Idris, S. A. (1999). *STAN Agricultural Science for Senior Secondary Schools*. Ikeja: Longman Nigeria.

Ukpabi, U. J. (2004). Sustainable post harvest technologies for the major food crop and flesh. *Paper presented at the workshop for Abia State local government agricultural officers, NRCRI*. Umudike, 10–12 May.

17

Arctic Regions of the Republic of Sakha (Yakutia): Problems and Prospects

Elena Totonova

Chapter Synopsis

Analysis of the economy of the Arctic regions revealed that the development of tourism can become a factor of local development. The development of the tourism industry is set to create a positive image of the Arctic, which will make the region attractive not only for tourism but also for investment in other sectors of the economy. The development of local government is the potential development of indigenous territories. The development of institutions in the North (the periphery) contributes to the creation of incentives to work in partnership with indigenous peoples, businesses, and authorities (public private partnership). Currently, tourism is one of the directions of development of the economy of the North, where the local population is not only working in this field, but also continues to engage in traditional farming. As a result, the development of tourism is considered a point of local economic growth and a type of economic diversification.

Introduction

Heterogeneity of economic space influences development of the economy and government policy. Differentiation of the development of regions leads to an increase in poverty and the rise of contradictions. Differentiation of the development of the northern regions depends on resource availability, climatic conditions, distance from the centre, and also the country's economic development.

Currently, the socio-economic development of the regions of Russia depends on the effectiveness of structural reforms in the economy. In the Sakha Republic, as in many northern regions of Russia, there is a need to overcome the direction of economic development that relies on raw materials, which requires the diversification of the regional economy of the country.

The Arctic regions of the Republic of Sakha (Yakutia) are characterised by selective involvement in the exploitation of natural resources, patchy distribution of production, and a disproportioned economy reducing the efficiency of manufacturing. The Arctic areas have a complex scheme of delivery of goods, distinguished by high transportation costs, leading to higher prices in the maintenance of the population. The crisis of traditional sectors of the economy has led to an increase in social problems.

Analysis of the Economic Development of the Arctic Regions of the Republic of Sakha (Yakutia)

The Arctic regions of the Republic of Sakha – which include the territory of the Anabarsky, Bulunsky, Ust-Yansky, Allaikhovsky, and Nizhnekolymsky regions – occupy a coastal part of the Arctic Ocean. The total area is 593.9 square kilometres with 43 settlements. The location of many settlements (population 33,000 people) along the coast is connected with the rich fish stocks and convenient location for transport along the coastal rivers (Lena, Olenek, Yana, Indigirka, Kolyma). Extremely low population density and the sparsity of the population are connected with uncomfortable conditions for human habitation and the distance from the centre of the republic (see Table. 17.1).

Table 17.1   Area and administrative/territorial divisions of the Arctic regions of the Republic of Sakha (Yakutia), as at January 2012

Region	Area (000 sq km)	Population (000s)	Inhabitants (000s)	Administrative divisions			
				Cities	Urban villages	Villages	Rural villages
Allaikhovsky	107,3	2,9	0,03	-	1	5	6
Anabarsky	55,6	3,4	0,06	-	-	3	3
Bulunsky	223,6	9,4	0,04	-	1	8	9
Nizhnekolymsky	87,1	4,6	0,05	-	1	3	12
Ust-Yansky	120,3	7,8	0,06	-	3	7	7
Republic of Sakha (Yakutia)	308,35	955,9	0,31	13	42	364	586

Source: Federal State Statistics Service (Yakutia), 2012a.

When considering the features of the socio-economic development of the Arctic regions, we observe a fairly strong differentiation between regions. That is, the Arctic regions are characterised by selective involvement in the exploitation of natural resources, patchy distribution of production, and the presence of distortions in the economy, reducing the efficiency of manufacturing (see Table 17.2). For example, in the Allaikhovsky and Nizhnekolymsky regions, traditional land use dominates (reindeer herding, fishing); there is no manufacturing (Totonova and Sleptcov, 2013).

Due to the presence of mineral resources, the Ust-Yansky (gold, tin) and Bulunsky and Anabarsky (diamonds) areas have well-developed mining industries. Therefore, the greatest volume of shipped goods and services of own production belongs to industrial areas such as Ust-Yana, Anabar, and Bulunsky. For example, until recently, the Ust-Yana region extracted crucial parts of tin, antimony, and tungsten for the economy and the military-industrial complex of the country.

But, despite the presence of the extractive industry in the Arctic (Anabar, Bulunsky, Ust-Yana), the local population is occupied primarily in traditional nature management. The quality of life of indigenous peoples of the North is greatly influenced by the development of domestic

Table 17.2   The main indicators of the economy of the Arctic regions of the Republic of Sakha (Yakutia), 2012

Regions	Average per capita monthly income (000 Rubles)	Number of unemployed people (000s)	Volume of goods and services of their own production (million Rubles)	Volume of retail trade (million Rubles)	Volume of paid services to the population (million Rubles)	Total completed housing (million Rubles)
Allaikhovsky	19.79	0.11	152.3	255.6	35.2	-
Anabarsky	35.78	0.07	14,073.6	343.6	32.5	1,902
Bulunsky	19.70	0.12	1,684.6	605.1	88.0	306
Nizhnekolymsky	18.26	0.09	281.5	364.0	67.7	431
Ust-Yansky	22.00	0.19	688.9	627.3	119.1	615

Source: Federal State Statistics Service (Yakutia), 2012b.

reindeer breeding and the hunting of wild deer: 70,000 deer, which comprise 35 per cent of the deer population of the republic, are concentrated in five Arctic regions. The highest numbers of reindeer herds are in the lower Kolyma and Bulunsky areas. In the mid-1990s there was a decline in reindeer herding, and only in 2003 did it become possible to stop the process, which was largely due to the moratorium on procurement of the meat of domestic reindeer.

Fishing is the main income-generating industry. Fishing communities of the Arctic provide 73 per cent of the total catch in the republic. For most inhabitants of the Arctic regions it is the only source of livelihood and employment. In 2011 Arctic regions extracted 3,100 tons of fish. There is fragmentation of the fisheries. The main problem is the preservation of fish and the weak material-technical base (Federal State Statistics Service, 2012b).

In the Arctic regions there are few organised hunting units. Under federal law, hunting units are fixed for hunters for a period of 25 years. According to the Hunting Department of the Ministry of Nature Protection of the Republic of Sakha, in Arctic regions there are 68 fixed plots of hunting grounds, which accounts for 16 per cent of all hunting lands of the country, where there is wild deer hunting.

The Bulunsky area (sea port of Tiksi) has a favourable geopolitical position from the point of view of prospects of development of international relations, and trade, of the Northern sea route. The revival of the Northern sea route has had a direct impact on the socio-economic development of the Arctic regions by developing the port of Tiksi and the river port of Green Cape. The port of Cape Verde is located 3 km from the town of Cherskii, centre of the Nizhnekolymsky region.

Basically, the port specialises in the transportation of petroleum products. Supplying the population and institutions of the social sphere in the Arctic with the main types of socially important food products is accomplished through a wholesale company, JSC Yakutopttorg, and individual entrepreneurs.

The annual budget of the republic reserves means reimbursing staple groceries delivery costs to provide social support for the population. Delivery of socially important food products is carried out according to the 'northern territories' and in the framework of the state programme of the Republic of Sakha (Yakutia): *State support of the delivery of goods to the Republic of Sakha (Yakutia)* for 2012–2016. As a result, prices for socially important food products in the Arctic regions of the republic compete with the prices of individual entrepreneurs. Thanks to subsidies allocated from the republic's budget, it is possible to keep in check the sharp growth of the price of bread for the population of the Arctic (Federal State Statistics Service, 2012a).

Thus, as a result of analysis of the economy of the Arctic regions, it is possible to draw a conclusion that the areas having reserves of minerals (see Table 17.2) are the most developed. For example, production of diamonds in the Anabarsky area is budget-forming, but other types of production are not developed. As a result, the area depends on activity of the enterprises of JSC Almazy Anabara and JSC NizhneLenskoye.

Indigenous peoples of the Arctic in severe conditions created a specific culture of traditional industries: northern reindeer breeding, seal hunting, and catching fish. Unique breeds of cattle and horses well adapted for the severe extreme conditions of the North were created. But now the traditional types of management are not competitive, which is caused by high transport costs of production and the absence of modern enterprises specialising in complex processing of raw materials. The crisis state of traditional branches of the economy led to an aggravation of social problems. The majority of the rural population has no work and lives below the poverty line. The unemployment rate exceeds the average across the Russian Federation by 1.5–2 times. Specifics of the fishing farms include the seasonality of fishing (summer season: end June–September, winter season: November–December). It provides only seasonal work.

Therefore, among the main problems which local authorities and the population face are unemployment, and also the state of health of the local population. In these conditions the local population itself looks for a way out of the created situation. Many leave their settlements, come back to historical places of accommodation, and live there with the rough fishing and hunting.

Current trends of development of the economy of the Arctic regions include the strengthening of the role of small businesses. Lately small businesses have proved to be one of the most dynamically developing spheres of the economy, promoting reduction of unemployment and increasing the number of employed people.

According to 2010 data, the number of small businesses in the Arctic regions consists of 149 units. In the structure of small businesses by type of economic activity, the retail trade (Bulunsky, Ust-Yansky), construction (Ust-Yansky), the manufacturing industry (processing of fish in the Allaikhovsky area), agriculture (Nizhnekolymsky, Bulunsky), and other kinds of activity prevail. The average number of employees of small enterprises in the Arctic regions is 720. The greatest number of people employed is observed in the Ust-Yansky (447 people) and Bulunsky (258 people) regions, with the smallest in Anabar (36 people). The highest average monthly nominal added salary of 15,300 Rubles is observed in the Ust-Yansky area, and the lowest in Anabar – 8,200 Rubles. As a whole, for 2008–2011 there has been growth of indicators of activity of small enterprises (see Table 17.3). But the level of development of small business in the Arctic areas considerably lags behind the development of this sector in the central and southern regions of the republic (Totonova, 2014).

Currently, the main areas of service and tourism can be developed with the help of small businesses. These areas include hospitality, travel agencies, the development of crafts, the development of new tourist routes, and the development of public power.

Compared to other tourist areas, the Arctic region has the least number of hotels and similar accommodation facilities. The problem is the lack of funds and lack of investor interest in the construction of hotels. The maximum number of persons staying in hotels is observed in the Bulunsky region, where, in 2012, 1,296 people were accommodated, who on average spent three nights in hotels. Good indicators are the Ust-Yana district (91 persons, 9 nights) and the lower Kolyma region (125 people, 3 nights). Despite some growth in the number of people staying in hotels, these figures are much smaller than in the central regions of the republic. But, in general, for 2009–2012 in the Arctic regions there is a noticeable growth of hotel services.

Table 17.3   Indicators of activity of small enterprises in the Arctic regions of the Republic of Sakha (Yakutia), 2000–2010

	2000	2003	2004	2005	2006	2007	2008	2009	2010	% change 2010 from 2000
Number of small enterprises (units)										
Republic of Sakha (Yakutia)	2,598	2,462	2,575	2,577	2,947	3,295	4,275	4,952	5,012	192.9
Allaikhovsky	8	8	6	8	8	10	9	7	8	100.0
Anabarsky	-	4	2	5	9	9	13	8	9	225.0
Bulunsky	25	23	24	23	32	37	35	39	39	156.0
Nizhnekolymsky	9	1	-	-	12	13	16	21	26	288.9
Ust-Yansky	39	32	41	43	56	57	61	68	67	171.8
Average number of workers										
Republic of Sakha (Yakutia)	16,453	18,970	20,073	22,396	23,762	28,175	37,995	42,464	44,536	270.7
Allaikhovsky	183	157	121	121	123	138	123	118	117	63.9
Anabarsky	-	55	8	14	42	28	44	45	36	65.5
Bulunsky	159	148	211	182	189	209	226	240	258	162.3
Nizhnekolymsky	33	1	-	-	31	19	44	124	162	490.9
Ust-Yansky	389	215	207	287	358	396	446	439	447	114.9
Average monthly nominal added salary of workers (Rubles)										
Republic of Sakha (Yakutia)	2,475.3	5,751.4	6,699.1	7,795.9	9,574.3	12,424.4	14,441.0	16,127.4	18,517.0	748.1
Allaikhovsky	2,733.9	5,345.6	6,097.0	6,190.4	8,026.7	9,630.0	11,068.8	10,960.7	11,967.2	437.7
Anabarsky	-	2,012.4	8,947.9	8,306.5	17,368.3	7,223.2	9,904.2	7,827.2	8,217.6	408.3
Bulunsky	1,102.7	1,749.4	1,390.8	2,345.0	2,691.4	5,020.2	6,475.4	7,723.1	8,784.5	796.6
Nizhnekolymsky	2,950.5	-	-	-	7,768.3	8,888.2	15,793.8	8,857.3	9,282.3	314.6
Ust-Yansky	3,054.3	1,812.0	5,085.0	6,209.7	8,138.9	10,936.7	13,290.1	16,041.3	15,339.8	502.2

Source: Federal State Statistics Service, 2012a.

A feature of the Arctic is its informational isolation – isolation from global and national information systems. The development of information systems in Arctic villages, connecting them with external centres, in addition to solving specific economic and social problems also provides the conditions for overcoming the digital divide. Therefore, development of information systems and technologies is a pressing issue.

Local Self-Government of Indigenous Peoples as a Potential Development Site

The analysis of the economy of the Arctic regions revealed that the development of tourism can become a factor of local development. The development of the tourism industry is set to create a positive image of the Arctic, which will make the region attractive not only for tourism but also for investment in other sectors of the economy.

The development of local government is the potential development of indigenous territories. With the development of the local government comes the creation of new institutional structures affecting the development of the territory.

Arctic regions of the Republic of Sakha (Yakutia) are rural settlements with preserved traditional kinds of households with a relatively high proportion of indigenous people. The main task of local government is to create conditions for economic development and increase entrepreneurial activity and living standards.

But experience of tribal communities, deer farms, municipal farms arising from the collapse of the state farms, and state farm fishing shows that without state aid they will not survive. Their association is made with the help of the commercial association with different forms of ownership. This initiative comes from the very indigenous peoples who support the local authorities. For example, one of the measures for the development of reindeer herding is the formation of state orders for reindeer holding a new land, taking into account the changing forms of economic organisation.

Achievement of objectives aimed at accomplishing these tasks can be done in conditions of political and economic independence of the republic's municipalities. Therefore it is necessary to solve the problem by reducing the level of subsidisation of municipal formations; introducing advanced techniques and technologies to optimise the expenditures of local budgets; improving their legal and regulatory framework; establishing a system of municipal statistics; creating the conditions for the development of the local economy through the use of their own potential; developing small business and the private sector; implementing investment projects; and creating an effective system of training and retraining personnel in local government.

In solving the problems of indigenous peoples, a greater role is played by the interaction of all levels of government and public organisations of indigenous peoples. One of the most influential non-governmental organisations (NGOs) is the Association of Indigenous Peoples of the North, Siberia and Far East of the Russian Federation (RAIPON). For priority setting and the definition of areas of support, agencies of the federal and regional authorities draw on the Association of Indigenous Peoples.

For state support for tribal communities seeking to preserve traditional ways of life, there is a gradual transfer of functions of government. An example of community self-government (economic) is a municipal establishment (*Halanchinsky nasleg*, which is organised as follows:

One productive tribal cooperative community – the nomadic tribal community (*Turvaurgin*), with 13,000 deer (2012) and 10 deer production (industry) forcing teams where 160 people are working now; two Nomadic tribal cooperative communities (*Nutendli*), having 2,500 deer.

Tribal communities and other indigenous organisations have amassed considerable experience in the field of self-government. In recent years, a lot of work has been done for the recognition of the rights of indigenous peoples of the North, but it takes work to design the right legal framework for addressing the challenges. But the social status of these organisations does not allow them to really influence the decision-making question, and they are not always considered adequately. As a result, the Association of Indigenous Peoples of the republic is mainly engaged in the revival and development of the traditions, culture, and language of indigenous peoples.

Thus, indigenous peoples are now experiencing a difficult stage in their development. Despite the critical socio-economic situation (worsening demographics, declining living standards and quality), indigenous peoples have a distinguished stable ethnic identity, sufficient education level, their own ethno-cultural institutions, and some opportunities for self-development.

The main goal for them in modern conditions is to search for new development criteria and an optimal model of their future. That is, their development will depend directly on indigenous peoples' own activity and conscience; state policy in relation to them; their role and place in the national relations system; and their degree of integration (Sulyandziga et al., 2003).

The Republic of Sakha's (Yakutia) Arctic region's area management efficiency depends on the local communities' development in large, medium, and small settlements, and the quality of its human capital – which includes the level of professional qualifications, the ability for continuous learning, and health conditions. Investment projects and institutional arrangements should be adapted to the peculiarities of local communities (land, ethnicity, age, gender, social structure) and the level of entrepreneurial activity (Pilyasov, 2008).

Local community development, training, and education for the municipal and state authority to control the environmental condition should be a priority of state policy in the North. Strengthening the local economy here can be achieved through working with leaders of tribal communities and their training programmes, thereby ensuring economic sustainability. Traditional subsistence needs support in the creation of new companies for fish, raw fur, and mammoth trade processing and souvenir production.

Thus, the development of institutions in the North (the periphery) contributes to the creation of incentives to work in partnership with indigenous peoples, businesses, and authorities (public private partnership).

Indigenous Tourism Development and Adaptation to the Market

Currently, tourism is one of the directions of development of the economy of the North, where the local population is not only working in this field but also continues to engage in traditional farming. As a result, the development of tourism is considered a point of local economic growth and a type of economic diversification.

Although Arctic regions have potential for tourism development, the capacity of local communities is not implemented fully. Therefore, in conditions of insufficient funds for infrastructure development, natural conditions and resources may allow the development of natural types of tourism. Development of environmental, cultural, scientific and extreme tourism, and sport hunting, fishing, and cruises is important for the Arctic region (Totonova and Sleptcov, 2014).

There is a 'mixed strategy' for the development of Yakutian Arctic regions. Tourism development is a 'growing point' in this strategy. According to the theories of local development, an area becomes variegated. The growth pole nears there and the periphery is filled with new economic and social relations. Based on this concept, according to Melnikova (2013), the depressed economy of the North, formed during the Soviet era, may change by diversifying the economy. That includes the organisation of new industries, the development of a new kind of tourism, and natural resources development. The development of North tourism takes into account such specific features as climate, the presence of permafrost, ecology, and surrounding areas. Upon that the optimum load is the maximum level of use that can withstand the natural and cultural components of the territories.

The basis for the development of ecological tourism in the Arctic is a network of protected areas and natural and recreational resources. Eco-tourism in protected areas, according to international standards, implies the involvement of local people in the business of manufacturing souvenir products and providing catering services, guides, agents, and others. Also, eco-tourism is considered to be a self-financing mechanism for protected areas, so the economic component is predominant, but the environmental safety of protected areas is also taken into account. The main function of protected areas is the conservation of natural systems.

Areas of 27 protected Arctic territories (the number of which increases every year) and the presence of 18 important bird areas of international importance contribute to the development of environmental and scientific tourism in the tourist zone. These kinds of tourism do not require a developed tourist infrastructure. In this case the process of self-development of the territory should be concentrated on the following sources: trained staff, investment, governance, advertising, marketing of territory, etc.

The most pertinent areas of ecological tourism development are: arranging tourist routes in protected territories; monitoring the animals in their natural habitat; developing special programmes for protected territories (field research); the creation of ecological trails, etc. Birdwatching, which works on the basis of resource reserves (white and hooded cranes, natatorials), and paleontological tours are significant in the Arctic tourist zone.

The weaknesses of the development of eco-tourism in the Arctic regions are: remoteness from the major tourist centres; seasonality of the climate; difficult access to areas; substandard tourism infrastructure; poor quality of service; lack of trained staff; and lack of marketing research. However, one can highlight the strengths for further development of ecotourism:

- the biological diversity of arctic wildlife;
- unique communities and ecosystems;
- access to the Arctic Ocean (polar cruises);
- a good environmental, social, and political context;
- low population density and large areas of unused land;
- the historical and cultural heritage of indigenous peoples;
- functioning of the national system of protected areas (15 years) and developed tourist routes.

In order to attract tourists, ecological and extreme tourism are combined. Moreover, this activity is also popular among domestic tourists. So, to increase attendance, we use a combination of different types of tourism with a varied programme and the availability of cheap hotels.

The specificity of the Arctic regions is the prevalence of hunting farms where workers, who are the indigenous peoples of the North, are employed in hunting wild reindeer. The sportive and amateur bush meat hunting is developed there.

Fishing and hunting tourism is highly diverse and might include hunting, fishing, the culture of indigenous people, attending sporting events as a spectator, and others. A specific feature of this tourism is obtaining various hunting licences that permit hunting, fishing, and the export of trophies. In addition, there is risk involved, so to ensure the safety of such tours highly skilled instructors and guides are required. Hunting tourism has quite a high cost and can be attributed to the category of elite tourism. Hunting tourism is one of the most promising directions of tourism development. Hunting and fishing are the basis for extreme tours.

Cultural tourism includes all kinds of tourism aimed at cognitive and study objectives. Programmes of such tourism are based on the introduction and study of human cultural and natural heritage. Tourism contributes to the conservation of aboriginal culture and traditional lifestyles. Tourism products of ethnographic tours should be focused on the traditional way of life, folk crafts, ethnic cuisine, and traditions of natural resource use. Ethnographic tours (focused on the study of indigenous cultures) can be based on local history museums, which are available in almost every district centre and in many villages. Ethnographic tourist expeditions can be realised in the route options (visiting indigenous communities). For example, tourists and scientists are attracted to the village of Russkoe Ooste in the Allaikhovsky district, located on Yano-Indigirka lowland, as it represents the unique culture of the Russian old believers (mostly Russian Pomors from Nizhny Novgorod who arrived in Allaihu in the late sixteenth century). Ethnographic tours can be made part of combined tours.

Scientific tourism also has good prospects of development in Arctic regions, where tourists are involved in research on nature and conduct field observations. But purely scientific ecological tourism makes up a relatively small proportion of tourists. This kind of tourism is a source of information about remote and unexplored areas necessary for science, and for proper planning of the development of ecological tourism.

For example, every year in Tiksi about 16 Russian and international expeditions are conducted, which contributes to the development of scientific tourism. Currently, in the area of Tiksi are situated: the Polar Geocosmophysics Observatory of the Institute of Cosmophysics Research and Aeronomy (Siberian branch of the Russian Academy of Sciences); International Seismic Station *Tiksi*; Nature Reserve of federal significance 'Ust-Lensky'; territorial administration of the hydrometeorological service; and the hydrographic organisation in Tiksi (branch of the federal state institution Hydrographic Enterprise (Totonova, 2014).

River and polar cruises refer to a special type of tourism, as it is a labour-intensive, capital-intensive type of tourism. It combines several types of tourism, such as recreational, sports, educational, and others. In the late twentieth century, cruising became the fastest growing sector of the tourism industry. The most popular cruises for foreign tourists are to the North Pole and expeditionary routes across the Arctic Ocean. Despite the high cost of such tours, such journeys are desirable. Cruises in the Arctic attract more volunteers who want to go to extreme climatic conditions, to observe wildlife (polar bears) and rare birds (Birzhakov, 2007).

Thus the optimal state regulation and support of economic development can become a driving force for local development. As the tourism industry consists of a large number of related and supporting sectors it can also contribute to the development of small and medium enterprises. Taking into account that tourism is one of the leading sectors of e-commerce, it is not only about expanding the consumer audience of the North tourist products, but also about the development of infrastructure and communications. As a result the northern tourist industry is adapting to the changing needs of the global travel market. The formation of the network economy is a key indicator of the post-industrialisation of a society.

But with the predominance of the unilateral longitudinal direction of the transportation networks (especially in the North) in terms of seasonality and transport difficulties, large distances lead to the predominance of 'expensive' air transport (found in the North). The worn-out material of the technical base of the transport system (70 per cent) and dependence on seasonal conditions increase the distance from the centre of the republic.

The existing transportation network in the Arctic regions of the republic, with a predominance of meridional direction ('south–north'), was formed as a result of:

- the presence of large northern rivers of the Arctic Ocean basin, which allow one to use 'river-sea' and 'sea-river' vessels;
- the network of federal highways, 'Lena' and 'Kolyma'.

The low accessibility of the northern districts of the country and an underdeveloped road network are factors hindering development of tourism in the area. In recent years, there has been a problem of light aviation (for which there is no alternative in the North) due to an inability to pay and the high cost of maintaining the airports. Financial opportunities of the northern areas cannot solve the problem, so subsidising the development of air transport should be a priority of regional development.

Transportation of tourist groups is possible only by air (helicopter) or waterways. Many of the difficulties in the development of the productive forces are driven by the unreliability of infrastructure and the high cost of transport. Therefore, the expansion of the scope of tourism in Yakutia is directly dependent on developing aviation and river fleets on domestic routes. Proceeding from this, the development of internal and inter-district transport is a burning issue: it would significantly expand the geography of tourist routes, especially in remote areas of the republic, in the future.

Thus, analysis of natural and socio-economic indicators of the Arctic regions of Yakutia provides a basis for selection of two local points of growth for tourism development (Tiksi and Cherskii in the future). According to the experience of tourism development in the Bulun area, development of natural resources for tourism purposes begins with the most 'transport available' seats (nodes). For example, Tiksi is the northern 'gateway' of Yakutia. Therefore, the main features of local centres of tourism are tourist specialisation, its development, and the level of the recreational development of the territory. A common problem of perspective development is often seen from the perspective of tourism. The Nizhnekolymsky district is a supporting local development area of Arctic tourism, which also has a river port, protected areas, and interesting developed routes.

Given the remoteness of the northern territories, the special significance requires the development of information technology, not only for management but also for the economy and social sphere of the North. This is determined by the fact that they allow a reduction in the cost of public services, cut costs, and facilitate the establishment of economic and social communication resources (Lazhentsev, 1996). This gives rise to 'the effect of the new resource', which is available for the northern territory and causes direct participation without intermediaries in regional and world markets. Therefore, the main purpose of regulation under this conceptual position is the development of informatisation of the economy and management of social northern territories.

Conclusion

In the context of a rapidly growing network economy, the process of information dissemination intensifies. Furthermore, market openness and rising levels of education, mobility, and income of the population are factors in the development of the network economy. These factors need to be improved and used in tourism business information technology. Thus, in the creation of the North's competitive tourism services, it is important to diversify the economy (which is heavily dependent on the commodity sector) for the development of the northern regions without considerable industrial potential and for socio-cultural development. The state's task is the creation of a competitive tourism industry. The state should provide the infrastructure necessary for the development and operation of tourism, and the legislative base.

References

Birzhakov, M. B. (2007). *Introduction to tourism*. St Petersburg: Gerda. (In Russian).

Federal State Statistics Service (2012a). *Yearbook of the Republic of Sakha (Yakutia): Article collection 2001–2012*. Yakutsk: Territorial Body of Federal Service of the State Statistics of the Republic Sakha (Yakutia). (In Russian).

————— (2012b). *The economy of districts and towns of Sakha Republic (Yakutia) of 1990, 2000, 2005–2012*. Yakutsk: Territorial Body of Federal Service of the State Statistics of the Republic Sakha (Yakutia). (In Russian).

Lazhentsev, V. N. (1996). *Territorial development: Methodology and experience of regulation*. St Petersburg: Science. (In Russian).

Melnikova, L. V. (2013). Problems of modeling economic space in contemporary literature. *Region: Economics and Sociology*, 2(78), pp. 20–36.

Pilyasov, A. N. (2008). *And the last shall be first: The northern periphery towards the knowledge economy*. Moscow: Librokom. (In Russian).

Sulyandziga, R. V., Kudryashov, D. A. and Sulyandziga, P. V. (2003). *Indigenous peoples of the North, Siberia and Far East of the Russian Federation: Overview of the current situation*. Moscow: RAIPON. (In Russian).

Totonova, E. E. (2014). *Modern features of the spatial development of the Arctic regions of the Republic of Sakha (Yakutia)*, 2(100), pp. 19–23. (In Russian).

————— and Sleptcov, S. S. (2013). Northern tourism opportunities and Northern Development. *Bulletin of the National Academy of Tourism*, 3, pp. 30–33. (In Russian).

18

The Urges of Language Adaptation for Economic Development within the Garos of Bangladesh

Mashrur Imtiaz and Azizul Hassan

Chapter Synopsis

The Garos are an indigenous group of people predominantly residing in parts of India and Bangladesh. These people have their own language called 'Garo' or 'A-chik'. This language is based on solid ground in terms of speaker numbers and a strong sense of feeling. Based on personal observation and focus group discussions, the objective of this chapter was to establish the level of respect among the Garos towards their own language in relation to the demand of socio-economic development standing. It also delineated the capacities of these people to face the influences of globalisation, which has close proximity with Bengali and English language adaptation. Results demonstrate changes in Garos society where there is a form of constructive relationship between language adaptation, livelihood generation practices, and activities focused on economic development. The traditional language pattern has also been changed due to the ongoing pressure of global socio-cultural influences, such that the Garos people are more willing to practise Bengali and English as facilitators of better livelihood and economic development. The study also suggests that these are the peoples who are adapting with Bengali and English as the languages of their imminent socio-economic advancement, along with their engagement with development provisions.

Introduction

Indigenous peoples of a country like Bangladesh are associated with different economic stages, ranging from food gathering to industrial labour. This presents their holistic activities in a relatively non-structurally framed national economy. The engagements of a group of indigenous people are sometimes overlapping and appear as an outcome of language and skills adaptation. It is unlikely there will be any potential for a specific language to remain the single common medium of communication within indigenous groups forever. This becomes the case particularly when the effects of globalisation and digitalisation processes become involved.

Bengali is the national language of Bangladesh and the basic medium of the national educational system. On the other hand, even with its crucial position and the invariable capacities to offer benefits, the English language still creates some sort of panic mainly due to its rarity among the indigenous peoples. However, considering the inevitable attachment of both Bengali and English to employability and various development processes, the importance of adapting them turns into a necessity, to some extent. Also, both of these language adaptations are believed to possess the capacities to be the foremost instrument for economic growth and can act as an indicator of indigenous groups' engagement with the national development agendas. In addition, it is often granted that language adaptation as the general medium of communication can largely help to bring about a positive approach in lifestyles, especially for indigenous peoples who are traditionally left as marginal. The Garos are one of the largest groups of indigenous people residing in parts of India and Bangladesh, and are primarily agro-pastoral. These people have their own language known as 'Garo' or 'A-chik' and have a lifestyle that is centuries old (Minahan, 2012). However, in recent years the Garos people have been taking considerable action to shift their conventional occupations towards wage employment in different sectors covering government, non-government, and technical.

The recent trend of indigenous peoples' adaptation of languages other than their own has become acute. These people appear to be getting familiarised with the language acquisition process and, in most cases, the national language of a certain country and English as the international means of communication are the basic selection. It is reasonable that the role of language adaptation is becoming a useful tool of communication and is playing a supporting part as the means of education together with economic development. The overall development of a community partly depends on the realisation that there is an interrelationship between language, communication, and socio-economic activities. Moreover, the inclination to take it for granted makes it clear that language is an intrinsic part of human life. From an individual perspective, it is difficult to grasp the importance of language as an influential tool of development. Indigenous populations across the world are receiving added emphasis in terms of development initiatives and policy programmes. These peoples are partly or fully subject to the influence of general economic factors. Regarding the Garos indigenous group of people of Bangladesh, it has been stated that:

> Even in outlying areas like Bangladesh, most children of Garo parents still learn the Garo as their first language. Whether they will still be doing so a century from now is by no means certain. (Burling, 2003: 171)

Another statement highlights the reality of language adaptation by the Garos:

> All adult Garos in Bangladesh are able to use Bengali for practical purposes and many are fluent ... the influence of English is more recent, but it now competes with Bengali as a source of borrowings ... too little has been printed in Garo to sustain a richly literate community, and well-educated Garos must rely upon English or Bengali for many literate purposes. (Kar, 2014: 3)

Based on these statements with relatively different contents, the objective of this study was to establish the level of respect among the Garos towards their own language in relation to the demand of socio-economic development standing. It also delineated the capacities of these people to face the influences of globalisation, which has close proximity with Bengali and English language adaptation. The present study relied on personal observation and focus group discussions. This study explored, outlined, and analysed the patterns of language adaptation of the Garos that act as a valid form of progress in their conventional socio-economic livelihood within the Bangladesh geographical area. The Garos were historically primarily agro-pastoral; but, in a world of globalisation, they arguably started rapidly accepting sector-based employment covering both governmental and non-governmental agencies. This trend is clearly parallel to established economic development agendas of that identified locale and is harnessed as a force to meet their basic needs of survival. Perceptibly, many indigenous peoples are conforming to the language acquisition process at a faster pace than ever before in almost every country in the world. Mostly, the national language of the specific country and English as the international medium of communication are the principal choices.

Indigenous Peoples: A Theoretical Rhetoric

Indigenous peoples are very often labelled as 'tribal', 'aboriginal', 'First Nation', and so on. A clear and straightforward definition is difficult. However, in a general sense, these peoples are not necessarily incorporated into the mainstream or national level economy, and the socio-economic structure of these peoples is remarkably different from that of the non-indigenous people of society. Within their ecological surroundings, they simply fit in their little command over technology, while their economy can be said to be narrow. Mehta stated that the notions of tribal and indigenous peoples are synonymous; however, they practise different types of occupations to sustain themselves, live on a marginal economy, and emphasise the specific indigenous patterns which are normally generated through indigenous knowledge sharing. In his words:

> usually considered an economically independent group of people having their own specific economy and thus having a living pattern of labour, division of labour and specialization, gift and ceremonial exchange, trade and barter, credit and value, wealth ... land tenure, and good tangible and intangible economic status. (Mehta, 1994: 5)

The Garos: Demographics and Language Testaments

ETHNICITY

Information about the definite number of Garos in Bangladesh is unclear and contradictory due to the lack of recently available data. On the basis of the data as presented in the literature, a yearly based framework was developed by Muhammed et al. (2011) as shown in Table 18.1.

However, Leung and Meggitt (2012) believe that the number is 100,000 and that it was as much as 120,000 in 1995 (Joshua Project, 2005). Again, Islam (2008: 8) states that: 'No one knows certainly how many Garos live in Bangladesh, (Bal, Ellen: 1999). According to the Census report in 1991, there are 64,280 Garos who live in Bangladesh.' The World Bank (2008) argued that the number of Garos was 68,210 in 1991 and 100,951 in 2001. However, Lewis (2009) opines that the number was 120,000 in 2005. There is a clear contradiction in the presented data regarding the actual number of Garos. The use of the official figure of the Bangladesh government as cited also shows dissimilarity. Thus, to generalise on the grounds of available evidence, no fewer than 100,000 Garos are currently residing in Bangladesh. The Garos display some similarities in their appearance and physique with the Chinese or Tibetan origin Mongoloids (Bhattacharjee, 1992). Very often, they are identified as the 'A-chik', which has a meaning like 'people of the hill', and as the 'Mandi', that is the 'humans' (see Figure 18.1). However, their relationship with the hills still

Table 18.1   The Garos population in Bangladesh: a conceptual debate

Year	Population	Reference
1991	68,210	Census (Bangladesh Bureau of Statistics, 1991)
1993	102,000	Gain, 2005
1997	105,000	Sangma, 2010
1997	100,000	Burling, 1997
2005	120,000	Lewis, 2009
2010	125,000	Joshua Project, 2011
2010	130,000	Drong, 2004

Source: Muhammed et al., 2011.

Figure 18.1   Adult members of the Garos

remains a subject for further research mainly because of the lack of detailed information on their origin. It is apparently believed that these people originated from the Garos Hills and were named after them. However, the reverse opinion is even stronger – that the Garos Hills were named after the Garos people (Nawaz, 2003).

Playfair (1909) identified the Garos as savages with a thirst for blood. However, this claim is not necessarily generalised. The Garos in current times are considered to be educated, modern, and friendly. Updated official data on the actual number of Garos is a dilemma and mostly unavailable. The main habitats of the Garos indigenous people are in the Indian subcontinent, and they are one of the oldest indigenous groups in this region. The majority of the Garos live in northern India, with a considerable number in parts of Bangladesh. However, according to Burling (2003), in

Figure 18.2   Children of the Garos

general most of the Garos people live in the western part of the Meghalaya district of India around the Khasi Hills, and around 10,000 Garos live across the border with Bangladesh on the south side of the Garos Hills. Relatively smaller settlements are found in Bangladesh, with the highest density in districts such as Mymensingh, Netrokona, Jamalpur, Gazipur, Tangail, and Sylhet (Muhammed et al., 2011).

LANGUAGE TESTAMENTS

The name of the Garo language is also a dilemma. Researchers like Islam (2008) suggest that the language's name is *Achchik Katha*, whereas Rahmatullah et al. (2012) believe it is *Mandi khusik*. On the other hand, Burling (2003) termed the language *Garo*. Khaleque (1983) argued that the Garos people are scattered in different areas of Bangladesh with a very poor network of communication where the influence of Bengali and English is strong, and a form of language acquisition can be possible. In this chapter, the Garo language is termed the 'Garos' in order to avoid complexities. In general, the Garo language is spoken by almost 700,000 people residing in north-western India and Bangladesh (Burling, 2003). However, the number was 400,000 in 1978 (Maloney, 1978). This represents an increasing trend of Garo language speakers. Language patterns of the Garos are interesting in terms of features and applications as this language is unwritten and has been transmitted orally over generations (Bose, 1985).

Primarily, it is believed that their language is the outcome of the *Bodo Garos* division of the Tibeto-Burman language family, having similarities to the *Boro Kachari*, *Kok Borok*, and *Dimasa* languages (Brahma, 2012). The language of the Garos follows five main typologies: *Chibok*, *A'tong*, *Abeng*, *Dual*, and *Megam* (Kim et al., 2012). Unlike any other language of indigenous groups of people, the Garo language is constantly facing tremendous pressure and borrows dialects from other languages, mainly Bengali. The basic necessity to fit within a national economic setup to meet recurrent demands is crucial for this language. This process is then followed by globalisation and the expansion of cultural influences of other countries.

In Bangladesh, Bengali as the national and English as the international language are concurrently altering the positions of languages of indigenous groups of people, including the Garos (Rahman, 2006). However, this process is viewed as adaptation by the Garos, not necessarily as forced or habitual. Competencies in both of these languages, Bengali and English, enable them to strengthen their candidacy in the competitive job market and to secure well-respected positions within the mainstream Bengali society. One figure shows that around 600 languages of the indigenous people have nearly reached extinction (Blair, 1990). Still, the Garo language has not reached the stage of extinction, mainly because of the number of speakers.

EDUCATION

As stated by Burling (2003), in Bangladesh most of the Garos children learn the Garo as their first language, and that author predicted that this practice would continue. On the contrary, Kar (2014) argued that this trend would change, but that the moment is uncertain. However, these relatively contradictory assertions have laid the ground for this study. In recent times, the Garos have developed one of the highest literacy rates among all the indigenous groups of people in Bangladesh, and this has reached almost 80 per cent (Joshua Project, 2005). This is quite surprising where, traditionally, these indigenous people were left as marginalised and cut off from almost all socio-economic benefits. The expanded facilities for education among the Garos people are not a recent phenomenon but highlight the long-term involvement of interested groups, mostly the Christian missionaries and the Bangladesh government (Islam, 1986). This type of involvement is sometimes considerable and positive where the Garos people are believed to maintain a distance from the mainstream societal structures in terms of control over access to resources.

Christian missionaries have played unprecedented roles in promoting the adoption and spread of education facilities among the Garos (Wimbish, 1989). The medium of instruction in education is Bengali. Existing and future Garos generations are already able to realise the importance of being educated and thus to bring about positive changes in their lives. This incorporates the adaptation of both the Bengali and English languages. However, more emphasis is placed on English language adaptation. More educated Garos people like to move to cities, with clear ambitions to get better and well-paid jobs, and they often tend to set up their own business enterprises. In addition, the government is undertaking activities that sometimes result in increased well-being for these Garos people (Mackenzie, 2012).

SOCIO-ECONOMIC PRACTICES

The traditional Garos society and economy are poverty-stricken and relatively less advanced. However, these people have emerged with huge prospects backed by their higher literacy rate, educational capacities, and continual support from donor agencies and the Christian missionaries (Karlsson, 2013). The Garos indigenous groups of people are mostly highly productive with increased potential, and are engaged in employment in numerous areas, mainly small-scale business and agricultural related activities. In any case, when they move to towns they take employment in industries such as fashion, beauty parlours, non-governmental organisations (NGOs), and so on.

The economic development activities and practices of the Garos indigenous groups of people take on diverse forms. These practices incorporate both agricultural and non-agricultural aspects. The predominant trend is staying in cities with education- and skill-supported employment adoption (Butler, 2008). However, in the truest sense, this form of employment is heavily supported by language acquisition. The majority of the Garos indigenous people constitute the local labour force of the areas through their active participation. However, this process is declining nowadays in a steady manner. These are the people who critically need the application of development initiatives in every sector of their lives. A form of deterioration in personal economic status among the Garos indigenous people is not a rare phenomenon, particularly in the case of Bangladesh. Among these indigenous people, some are still at the most primitive phase of living (Flatt, 2014). They continue to live in isolated areas and perform native agricultural or non-agricultural work. Most people of this type are still in the food gathering stage in an almost stagnating condition.

Literature Review

LANGUAGE ADAPTATION AND ECONOMIC DEVELOPMENT

Language adoption has somehow managed to become attached to the mainstream economic considerations in the South Asian region, and especially in a country like Bangladesh (James, 1999). Following the process of nation building in this country, there are almost no inter-language conflicts with the local and indigenous groups of people. This was mainly because of the effective role and actions of the government to support and promote indigenous languages. However, the supremacy of Bengali as the national language and English as the international language has always been granted (Marak, 2002). Securing the identity of indigenous peoples is truly important to safeguard their linguistic identity as well as to prove their capacities to become an effective medium of major communicative languages. For this to be achieved, the influence of pragmatic thoughtfulness is required to be applied in the real-life situations of indigenous peoples like the Garos. This helps to create a bridge between the adaptation of languages and economic development practices. The areas of language and development are complex and affected by vast webs of both internal and external factors.

Larsen-Freeman and Cameron (2008) identified this as a further challenge: to recognise complexity and to generate simplistic solutions to problems. Still, there should be an attempt to manage the complexities and in some ways to divert them towards positive or beneficial outcomes. Markee (2002) offered an accepted and well-defined explanation of both language and development, namely that language has the communicative competence and elaborated capacities to accelerate development initiatives. However, a wider concept needs to outline that development ensures welfare, including a common ground of resource sharing with a dispersion of socio-politico-economic power and practices. The existing relationships between language adoption and development can be of different kinds. A useful categorisation is provided by Appleby et al. (2002) that identifies language *in*, *as*, *for*, and *of* development. This categorisation embraces four aspects: first, language *in* development, where languages, with both Bengali and English as examples, are viewed as playing an essential role in the socio-economic development of a specific country. Second, language *as* development, where these two languages are taught 'as an end in itself'. Third, language *for* development, where the languages are used 'as a tool for other domains of development'. Last, language *of* development: 'the discourses that construct the ways in which development happens'.

ADAPTATION OF BENGALI AND ENGLISH FOR ECONOMIC DEVELOPMENT AS A REALITY

Bengali is a national language and is associated with an identified nation of the world. In contrast, English is viewed mainly as the language for development at both individual and national level. Indeed, the race for individual prosperity and economic development at the national level seems to have overtaken issues of class, identity, and fear of cultural invasion from erstwhile dominating languages (Kim et al., 2012).

As the language of development, English is appearing in an influential role in the national and political scenario of indigenous peoples more than Bengali. The increase of English use in the global perspective has become connected with the urge towards a norm of learning in general, and more specifically with employability. On the other hand, Bengali is acknowledged to be the traditional medium of communication within the geographical area of Bangladesh. This has become the urban view rather than the rural, but this is beneficial for achieving a more specific and purified concept of the paired relevance of development and language adaptation. It is believed that since the 1990s, English has emerged as a genuine world language (Crystal, 2004). To analyse the complex relationship of illusion and reality, the need to pursue a congenial balance of language adaptation and development initiatives is pressing.

The UN Millennium Development Goal (MDG) remarked that the relief of poverty is a prime concern of development; but social, national, and cultural developments also ensure gross economic progress (Marshall, 2013). This relates to the demand for language adaptation for indigenous groups of people. Education and language adaptation are the keys to merging these social, national, and cultural aspects for the perfection of economic development. As English is now widely considered a lingua franca or a 'world language', it seems apposite to analyse the relationship between English and development considerations. Coleman (2010), in a British Council commissioned report, has understood this existing relationship using examples from language and development conferences held in different regions of Asia and Africa since 1993. He concludes that language adaptation, and English in particular, plays diverse roles in development, including:

a. increasing individuals' employability;
b. enabling international collaboration and cooperation;
c. providing access to research and information;
d. facilitating the international mobility of students, tourists, workers, and others;
e. facilitating disaster relief and disaster preparedness;
f. acting as an impartial language in contexts of disharmony.

Again, according to Coulmas (2009), language adaptation examines the process by which a speech community is forced to adopt an active role in making its language suitable for changing and functional requirements. Following the present point of view, language adaptation can be the marker of the Garos people's development.

This is becoming the key term for the overall growth of *unprivileged indigenous peoples like the Garos and this is a* well-supported view. Research has also attempted to explore the existence of possible links between language use and the development process and how the languages of indigenous peoples can act upon their economic status (Djité, 2008; Harbert et al., 2009). These conceptualisations can be applied in terms of the economic and other relevant growth of the Garos people in various ways. On the other hand, numerous studies have cross-checked the legitimate roles that language can play for indigenous peoples in development contexts (Hornberger, 2002; Vavrus, 2002). Tembe and Norton (2008) explained that language learning projects in development contexts must be carefully aligned with community needs and ambitions on the grounds of indigenous needs. They discovered the symbolic lure of language adaptation and suggested that indigenous research approaches can be used to adjust the process of education to their own inspirations and ideology.

LANGUAGE ADAPTATION AS AN ISSUE OF 'GAROS' IDENTITY AND THE GAROS ECONOMIC SYSTEMS

Identity is an essential factor for both the individual and the group among indigenous peoples. This is related to exclusiveness or uniqueness and is viewed as a means to position them within complex societal structures. Identity is considered to be a form of pride (Pareek, 1989). Identity is developed through interaction with one's name, body, history, nationality, religion, geographical factors, and so on (Isaacs, 1975). Language is treated as one of the most powerful tools of identity formation of a certain group of people. The development of identity is concerned with two crucial aspects: a sense of a person's belonging and the self-esteem he deserves to have (Isaacs, 1975). The discussion of the identity of the Garos is typically provoked more by politics than by socio-economic aspects. With respect to the Garos, even though they are identified as the 'A-chik' or the 'Mandi', their sense of identity is strong enough to support them over centuries. As argued by Jengcham (1994), most of them prefer not to be called 'Garos', as they believe that this name was developed either by the Europeans or the Bengalis. However, this claim appears to be convincing as there is evidence to support it (Allport, 1954). Playfair (1909) argued that the Garos expect to be identified as the 'Mandi' or as the 'A-chik'. Language adaptation or acquisition is visible among the Garos as these people are mostly believed to be bilingual. They have their own language called the Garos (Burling, 1997). According to Sangma (1998), they are still adopting mainly Bengali and, in certain cases, English as their second and third languages. The main reason for Bengali adoption is to communicate and interact with the local populations, whereas English is used as an advantage to ensure better employability. Other than this, the Garos use their own language within their community.

Dahl (2012) showed that the unique features of marginal areas inhabited by indigenous peoples are characterised as having limited accessibility, and fragility and diversity. Gupta (2006) described the principles of indigenous economic systems by arguing that indigenous peoples have well-developed systems to govern their societies. It was also argued that their traditional and existing economic systems typically ensure sustainable utilisation of resources along with social responsibilities and harmonious relationships through cooperation. There are some constraints that are responsible for the depleted development process of indigenous groups of people. Vaid (2004) remarked on some of these constraints in particular, which are mainly of three types. First, the destruction of forests is crucial, because the forests are not only the source of livelihood for indigenous groups of people, but their existence also demands an elaborate interrelationship between indigenous people, the forest itself, and the ecosystems. The diminishing forest resources are threatening the imminent food security of these people. Second, a lack of awareness is prevalent among indigenous groups of people about various developmental programmes launched by the government of Bangladesh, which can result in exploitation. Last, the protection of indigenous rights and concessions is critical. Indigenous groups of people are given numerous rights and concessions under various statutes of the government, but these people still remain deprived of the benefits arising out of such statutory planning. This is mainly because of their ignorance and the lack of concern of the implementing authorities. Donor agencies are helping with the adaptation of international language.

The International Fund for Agricultural Development (*IFAD*, 2013) proposed some measures to support sustainable development for indigenous groups of people. IFAD had positive experiences following the outcomes of the indigenous development initiatives of these people through the provision of small local development funds managed directly by indigenous communities and common-interest groups. There was also a strengthening of the existing indigenous peoples' organisations and governance systems. In addition, they genuinely included women without gender bias for development projects aiming to reduce poverty. Although indigenous societies are often more egalitarian than mainstream societies, especially in Asia and particularly in Bangladesh, the males tend to be supreme and act as dominators (Dey & Sultana, 2009). Surprisingly, almost all of these restraints can be found among the Garos people, specifically in their economic development processes. Garos society is believed to be matrilineal (Chowdhury, 2007).

THE PARADIGM OF GAROS ECONOMIC DEVELOPMENT

The concept of development is imbued with several meanings and connotations. Smelser (2013) viewed this as the ramification of the entire socio-cultural framework established through economic, ecological, or technical changes within which the process of modernisation usually happens. It was also argued that the concerned authorities determine the process of transformation of a traditional society. Still, these economic and modern changes move together and they conceive language as the medium of communication (Jengcham, 1994). In such situations, language adaptation becomes the main mode of communication. Thus, the adaptation of both Bengali and English gains importance and eventually many possibilities appear with positive impacts (Bal, 2007). Very often, academics interpret development from the perspective of human affairs.

According to Olusoji (2012) development emphasises personal security and the conscious promotion of well-being that persistently enables optimising the realisation of their individual potential. Economic development is stimulated by capital investment and has remained the centre of the modernisation process and mainstream policy thinking (Hassan & Forhad, 2013). Anderson (1999) argued that it is also designed to move societies on a linear path from traditional subsistence agricultural systems to industrialised economies and market production. In 1960, Rostow, while describing the stages of economic development, argued that this leads traditional societies towards economic maturity and mass consumption, where every country would follow the way of prosperity as mapped by developed nations. In this sense, economic development follows a similar pattern along with the modification of contemporary trends which include economic growth, organisational efficiency, establishment of political institutions as well as modern attitudes and behaviour, and advanced aspects related to education, health, and employment generation.

Methodologies

This study mainly relied on personal observation and focus group discussions. The presentation of the results followed the qualitative research methodological approach. These research techniques are useful in terms of generating in-depth information, and they also possess validity in applied linguistic research (Bernard, 2011; Perry, 2011). The study areas covered Garos habitats of Bangladesh in the Mymensingh, Netrokona, and Tangail districts. Engagement of the authors with the Garos groups of indigenous people and the community was interesting. The main author made personal observations during a six-month stay within the Garos community in 2004, while the second author was a team member for the socio-linguistic survey of the Garos as carried out by a Texas-based non-profit educational corporation, the Summer Institute of Linguistics, Inc. (now SIL International), during 2007–2012. During their stay and their interactions with the Garos, a considerable number of focus group discussions (FGDs) were carried out, and of these 10 relevant to the theme of this study were selected. The FGDs that were carried out with the Garos indigenous group of people included four identified types of respondent (general populations, heads of Garos society, Garos migrant workers, and external development practitioners). Closer participation in the Garos livelihood offered the opportunity to learn about their mindset and opinions directly. Such engagement enabled the researchers to make more rapid personal observations and thus to collect, accumulate, justify, and present data covering a decade through a cross-comparison method. The observations, views, and thoughts were cross-checked to construct logical arguments and to explore the development engagement of the Garos. The information as presented in this chapter was carefully selected after considering its validity and reliability.

Findings and Discussion

LANGUAGE ADAPTATION AND ECONOMIC DEVELOPMENT

The Garos are getting acquainted with both the Bengali and English languages, symmetrically. It is no longer a myth that indigenous groups of people can learn and speak languages that do not belong to them. According to one comment:

> Language adaptations by the Garos are simply necessities and the result of broader outlook. The Garos youths are realistic about their future while, the elders are also optimistic in terms of encouraging them to adapt other languages. (FGD, 5)

This statement thus questions the validity of the statement of Burling (2003) where it was claimed that most of the Garos children in Bangladesh are taught the Garos as their first language. It is obvious that the Garo language is primarily taught within the home environment. Again, it was also observed that the Garos are adapting languages like Bengali and English. Contributions of non-government organisations cannot be ignored while discussing the process of language adaptation of the Garos. The Christian missionaries are playing anchor roles for this purpose together with the Bangladesh government agencies (Mackenzie, 2012; Wimbish, 1989). However, the views regarding these missionaries are expressed as:

> If you see, we, the Garos are far more advanced than others. This is mainly because of these missionaries. They have offered us education but, partly wiped our basic identity, language and religion those we belonged to us. (FGD, 1)

The view of the above statement is debatable and simply highlights those organisations responsible for the welfare of the Garos indigenous groups of people. Programmes of these organisations are mostly delivered in both Bengali and English. They seem to have passed a message to members of the Garos about exploring the world through their own eyes.

Strengthening learning capacities in Bengali and English among indigenous girls was another bold initiative. Although the Garos people are dominated by women, the men are not much ignored. In many cases, they even enjoy more freedom to take and implement decisions. Through proper education and English adaptation, the broad picture of equity between females and males is much improved.

Social, local, and voluntary organisations working for them appeared to suggest the Bengali and English languages to the Garos people as valid mediums of communication. The Garos have positioned them as a prominent example of embracing the drift towards economic progression through language adaptation where the Garo language possesses less importance in virtue of its limited capacities to meet increasing demands. The inclusion of the Garos people in the development projects helped them to override the limitation of being single-language users and to become able to adopt more languages. Development cooperatives and other institutions appeared to be working together towards making the Garos more capable of ensuring economic development. In this case, emphasis was placed on language adaptation and education with Bengali and English as the mediums of communication.

ADAPTATION OF BENGALI AND ENGLISH FOR ECONOMIC DEVELOPMENT: AN APPLICATION OF REALITY

Authentic research and training programmes on different schemes can bring out new insights. Modern research and training facilities, in most cases, are conducted in English where, within the Bangladesh geographical area, the language is Bengali. Not only in oral form, but also the written capacities of both Bengali and English are commonly mastered by the Garos people. The writing symbol or the grapholect is a trans-dialectal language formed by a deep commitment to writing. Writing gives a grapholect power that far exceeds any oral dialect (Bizzell, 1992). So, the capacities of written forms of Bengali and English can be treated as a development tool for the Garos people. Over the years, the Garos have experienced a huge import of both Bengali and English words and dialects. It is generally thought that the Garos are very reluctant to apply their knowledge of Bengali and English in practice and reality. As was argued:

> We know the values of Bengali and English language and this is why we are always eager to learn these languages. Knowledge over these languages helps us to enhance our position and opportunities. (FGD, 6)

As Bangladesh is less of a multilingual country than its neighbour India, it is more or less accepted that Bengali and English are the two main dominating languages. Vocational training centres are established in parallel to conventional educational institutions with an aim to make the Garos more capable of facing the growing challenges of employment and livelihood generation. In these establishments, both Bengali and English are taught as mediums of operational languages. The fruitfulness of such involvement became visible as, firstly, indigenous people got the opportunity to work with modern equipment as well as to become familiar with technical terms of Bengali and English that influenced their lives. A local Garos tea stall owner argued:

> I have to sell tea to the local Bengali peoples. If I do not know Bengali, how would I be able to talk to them? (FGD, 9)

On the other hand, a migrant Garos entrepreneur with a clothing and beauty parlour business in the capital city, Dhaka, argued:

> I do not see any offence to adapt Bengali and English. This is helping us in huge ways or our economic development. (FGD, 10)

It is thus evident that the Garos have already started adapting the Bengali and English languages to fit in with the economic development activities. This supports the prediction of Kar (2014) that these people will inevitably begin language adaptation.

THE ISSUE OF 'GAROS' IDENTITY THROUGH LANGUAGE ADAPTATION AND THE GAROS INDIGENOUS ECONOMIC SYSTEMS

It is evident and commonly accepted that the Garos identity is becoming more 'bilingual' than practising only their own language. Language adaptation by the Garos is more or less generalised where the medium of education is Bengali. However, findings of this study revealed that there is very little space for a possible conflict between their own and the adopted languages as these people are aspiring to and focused on their communal well-being:

> We have very strong emotion for our own language that we use while communicating between us. Still, we are adapting Bengali and English to make our economic systems more congenial. (FGD, 9)

The national policy support for indigenous peoples in Bangladesh is favourable for maintaining the identity of the Garos. In cases where a form of suppression or exploitation takes place, these are generated mostly by individuals, whereas the state involvement is virtually none. This study also reveals that the Garos are adapting Bengali and English parallel to their own language and there are very few incidents of language conflict. Evidently, the Garo language is not at the extinct stage despite the strong trend of language adaptation. This thus implies that the Garos have had a stronger sense of their identity and sentiments for their own language preservation for centuries, notwithstanding that is not even written.

Losing ownership and control over the land is becoming a reality for the Garos. Basic reasons for this are the lack of national policy support, political pressure, unfavourable land ownership legislation, and so on (Hassan & Burns, 2014). Traditionally the Garos depended on agriculture and this trend forces them to change occupation or, in most cases, to migrate to cities and towns. Relatively lower educated Garos are adopting occupations like day labourers, while others search for better-paid jobs. Language adaptation like Bengali and English is supporting this endeavour. Outside their villages, the Garos are employed in private and public services, tea gardens, beauty parlours, garments factories, defence services, and so on. However, none of these jobs can offer them betterment without clear speaking and understanding capacities in both Bengali and English. There are some specific measures that can be applied for the betterment of the Garos indigenous groups of people in terms of their economic development. Theoretically, economic development and language adaptation are interrelated (Coleman, 2010). It is also important to relate the national language, Bengali, and the global language, English, as the instruments for the livelihood improvement of the Garos people. Generally, the Garos are able to diversify resource use and production capacities. The opening of external markets promotes specialised production and encourages resource use intensification and exploitation of niche opportunities. The Garos have managed to gain increased concern for their environmental and socio-economic consequences. Following maximum exposure of their own products, the Garos people are using Bengali and English for extended communication. Therefore, various development modalities are connected with these language adaptations. English is mainly considered to be the medium of instruction and development initiatives in developing countries by donor agencies and funding organisations. But one Garos argued that:

> The fact is that most of these funds are used for the proficiency improvements in the recipient country instead of focusing on development works, particularly in the field of education and industrialisation. (FGD, 4)

A general Garos expressed his views:

> *Traditionally we are cultivators and animal hoarders. However, these were subject to seasonality and we are shifting towards self employment. This is as I believe a sign of change of traditional economic practices. (FGD, 8)*

The supreme state of English as the global economy language has meant that English language education is increasingly being promoted in various development approaches. On the other hand, Bengali creates the platform to explore the local and national opportunities.

THE PARADIGM OF GAROS ECONOMIC DEVELOPMENT

In recent decades, increased numbers of Garos people have settled in specific places with reliable sources of livelihood generation. Economic development among the Garos of Bangladesh is mainly appearing in the forms of earning support and employment generation. In the past, their identity and reputation as head hunters and fierce warriors in battle were more dominant than as farmers. Practically, it becomes impossible, to some extent, to create any blockade between them and the typical economic upheavals or slowdowns. Both theoretically and practically, practices for survival by these people and ordinary populations are intertwined and connected to each other. As was argued:

> *We were also identified as head hunters and are believed to raid villages of the enemies and bring the chopped heads as sign of their victory ... but the situation is changed. (FGD, 2)*

In recent times, the majority of these people have become more associated with having both public and private sector employment. They are more capable of competing with local populations in terms of securing jobs and sources of livelihood generation. However, a form of invisible marginalisation is apparently forcing the Garos to face unexpected competition.

The future of these people largely relies upon the NGO-supported education programmes, and these are possibly the best ways for them to articulate their urge for inheritance of land and other resources. These people have less control over the means of making a living and a reduced scope for resource allocation. Again, as one Garos opined:

> *The most worthy ownership of human being is the language because, without exchange of information, the world is more like an empty page. To experience various life aspects and to deal with the alternations of environment and surroundings related complexities, humankind depends on their language. (FGD, 3)*

Almost all types of scientific and technological innovation require the presence of language in order to deliver them to society. As argued by Rostow (1960), traditionalism should move towards economic development with mass consumption. The involvement of developed nations, and funding and donor agencies is also responsible for the ongoing economic development process of the Garos (Marshall, 2013). It was also argued that:

> *We, the Garos, sometimes turn as 'guinea pig' to test different development models and initiatives. However, we must say that their involvements are beneficial for us. (FGD, 7)*

However, almost all of the development practices are transformed into reality though the adaptation of languages like Bengali and English. Theoretically, these verbalisations of concepts and thoughts depend on the adaptation of national and international languages.

Conclusion

This study firstly suggests putting an end to the ambiguity concerning the actual number of Garos living in Bangladesh, and proposes that this should not be less than 100,000. The basic objective of this study was to establish the level of respect of the Garos towards their own language in relation to the demands of socio-economic development standing. It also delineated the capacities of these people to face the influences of globalisation, which has close proximity with Bengali and English language adaptation. Garos men visibly enjoy dominant positions in many cases with respect to decision making, employment, and livelihood generation – even though Garos society is matrilineal. The persistent patterns of employment are accepted by the Garos indigenous groups of people to support their livelihood generation activities and economic development. Still, there is a small number of printed items that can support the Garo language and serve a literate Garos community.

Well-educated Garos mandatorily have to rely on Bengali and English for many purposes, including education and employment. One pertinent fact about indigenous groups of people and language adaptation for economic development is the truth of the general belief that these people are required to position their language as a means of communication in all spheres of life. However, the overall development process depends on linguistic and also on various non-linguistic elements. But this change and growth can only be conveyed through the adaptation of the national and international languages, Bengali and English. More familiarity with Bengali and English can spread indigenous knowledge and intensify economic development activities. Shared indigenous knowledge is mostly a sacred concept which ought to be exposed to the maximum number of recipients.

The experience of using the traditional Garos myths and knowledge in modern developmental and cultural messages has shown that they are extremely effective in publicity if they are interpreted through Bengali and English. As mentioned earlier, this study intended to outline the level of respect of the Garos towards their own language in relation to the demand of socio-economic development standing. While this study suggests that the Garo language is not a derogatory or incompetent language for the execution of development tasks, Bengali and English are more effective in present situations. This study also delineated the capacities of the Garos people to face the influences of globalisation which has close proximity with Bengali and English language adaptation. The chapter added an epilogue that unveils the utterance of exceptional ideas and incidents in Bengali and English; and by exerting these languages with their indigenous customs, the Garos can bring out a holistic pattern of economic development in their society.

Something not to be forgotten to help preserve the identity of the Garos: the aspirations of indigenous peoples, somehow, claim their own individuality and rightful trends in all ways. For the actual development of the Garos people, these facts should not be overlooked with emphasis on Bengali and English. This study demonstrates that Bengali and English language adaptation by the Garos is not threatening the Garos identity. The Garos have been well capable of preserving their language for centuries through oral practices among themselves within the family and community environment.

This study intended to analyse patterns of Bengali and English language adaptation that act as a valid concern in the Garos economic livelihood, and to determine how this language adaptation process can be the foremost concern for the economic development of the Garos indigenous people. Control over languages like Bengali and English is acting as a crucial factor for both general and economic developments. The gravity of Bengali and English should be merged with the following aspects with real consciousness: recognition and respect of all the indigenous rights of the Garos people, including local, collective, and international perspectives; respect for the Garos culture and knowledge procedures; the right to meaningful participation from the national perspective of Bangladesh; and autonomy of action for their own realisation of development along with management of their own affairs where possible.

This study explored, outlined, and analysed the patterns of language adaptation of the Garos that act as a valid form of progress in their conventional socio-economic livelihood within the Bangladesh geographical area. A basic limitation of this study was the lack of available funding that possibly could have expanded the range and diversity of the respondents. This study thus indicates that the Garos are already on the move to adapt with languages like Bengali and English. Based on the findings of this study, a potential area of research could be the exploration of alterations of the Garos identity as imposed by language adaptation and shifting economic development practices.

References

Allport, G. (1954). *The nature of prejudice*. Cambridge, MA: Addison-Wesley.

Anderson, R. B. (1999). *Economic development among the Aboriginal peoples of Canada: The hope for the future*. Ontario: Captus.

Appleby, R., Copley, K., Sithirajvongsa, S. & Pennycook, A. (2002). Language in development constrained: Three contexts. *TESOL Quarterly*, 39(3), pp. 323–346.

Bal, E. (2007). Becoming the Garos of Bangladesh: Policies of exclusion and the ethnicisation of a 'tribal' minority. *South Asia: Journal of South Asian Studies*, 30(3), pp. 439– 455.

Bernard, H. R. (2011). *Research methods in Anthropology: Qualitative and quantitative approaches*. 5th edn. Lanham, MD: AltaMira.

Bhattacharjee, P. N. (1992). *The Garos of Tripura*. Tripura: Directorate of Research, Tribal Welfare Department.

Bizzell, P. (1992). *Academic discourse and critical consciousness*. Pittsburgh: University of Pittsburgh Press.

Blair, F. (1990). *Survey on a shoestring: A manual for small-scale language surveys*. Dallas: Summer Institute of Linguistics.

Bose, J. K. (1985). *Culture change among the Garos*. Kolkata: Institute of Social Research and Applied Anthropology.

Brahma, P. (2012). Phonological variation of lexical items in Bodo and Dimasa – a brief note. *Language in India: Strength for today and bright hope for tomorrow,* 12(1), pp. 478–491.

Burling, R. (1997). *The strong women of Modhupur*. Dhaka: University Press.

——— (2003). Garo. In G. Thurwood & R. J. LaPolla (eds), *Sino-Tibetan Languages*. London: Routledge, pp. 169–192.

Butler, S. J. (2008). *Bangladesh*. London: Lonely Planet.

Chowdhury, K. A. N. (2007). *Residence, gender and power in the Garo society of Bangladesh*. Dhaka: University of Dhaka.

Coleman, H. (2010). *The English language in development*. London: British Council.

Coulmas, F., ed. (2009). *Language adaptation*. Cambridge: Cambridge University Press.

Crystal, D. (2004). *The language revolution*. Cambridge: Polity.

Dahl, J. (2012). *The Indigenous space and marginalized peoples in the United Nations*. New York: Palgrave Macmillan.

Dey, S. & Sultana, S. (2009). The socio-cultural impacts of economic changes to matrilineal Garo society in Bangladesh. *International Journal of Green Economics*, 3(2), pp. 184– 198.

Djité, P. (2008). *The sociolinguistics of development in Africa*. Bristol: Multilingual Matters.

Flatt, J. H. (2014). *In love with Bangladesh-the heart of a missionary*. Bloomington: WestBow.

Gupta, A. (2006). *Human rights of Indigenous peoples: Protecting the rights of Indigenous peoples*. Delhi: Isha.

Harbert, W., McConnell-Ginet, S., Miller, A. & Whitman, J. (eds) (2009). *Language and poverty*. Bristol: Multilingual Matters.

Hassan, A. & Burns, P. (2014). Tourism Policies of Bangladesh – a contextual analysis. *Tourism Planning & Development*, pp. 1-4. doi: 10.1080/21568316.2013.874366

Hassan, A. & Forhad, A. (2013). The Role of NGOs in the Sustainable Development of Bangladesh. *Present Environment & Sustainable Development*, 7(2), pp. 59-72.

Hornberger, N. (2002). Multilingual language policies and the continua of biliteracy: An ecological approach. *Language Policy*, 1, pp. 27–51.

International Fund for Agricultural Development (IFAD). (2013). Indigenous people and sustainable development. Paper presented in the *Twenty-Fifth Anniversary Session of the Governing Council*. Rome: International Fund for Agricultural Development.

Isaacs, H. R. (1975). *Idols of the tribe: Group identity and political change*. New York: Harper & Row.

Islam, M. R. (2008). *The changing Garo adivasi culture of Bangladesh: A case study of marriage rituals*. Unpublished MPhil dissertation. University of Tromsø.

Islam, Z. (1986). *A Garo village in Bangladesh: A Sociological study*. Varansai: Benaras Hindu University.

James, M. W. (1999). Transforming laments: Performativity, and rationalization as linguistic identities. In G. B. Palmer & D. J. Occhi (eds), *Languages of sentiment: Cultural constructions of emotional substrates*. Amsterdam: Benjamins.

Jengcham, S. (1994). *Bangladesher Garo samproday*. Dhaka: Bangla Academy. (In Bengali).

Joshua Project (2005). *The Garos of Bangladesh*. Retrieved from: http://joshuaproject.net/profiles/text/t11826.pdf (accessed: 1 May 2013).

Kar, A. (2014). *The Garo: A language profile*. Retrieved from: http://www.cs.berkeley.edu/~akar/docs/Garo.pdf (accessed: 1 May 2013).

Karlsson, B. G. (2013). *Contested belonging: An Indigenous people's struggle for forest and identity in Sub-Himalayan Bengal*. London: Routledge.

Khaleque, K. (1983). The Garos of Bangladesh: Religion, ritual and worldview. *Southeast Asian Ethnography*, 7, pp. 129–156.

Kim, A., Kim, S., Ahmad, S. & Sangma, M. (2012). *The Garos in Bangladesh: A sociolinguistic survey*. Retrieved from: http://www-01.sil.org/silesr/2012/Garo_2012–007_final.pdf (accessed: 1 May 2013).

Larsen-Freeman, D. & Cameron, L. (2008). *Complex systems and applied linguistics*. Oxford: Oxford University Press.

Leung, M. & Meggitt, B. (2012). *Bangladesh*. Chalfont St Peter: Bradt.

Lewis, M. P. (2009). *Ethnologue: Languages of the world*. Dallas: SIL International.

Mackenzie, A. (2012). *History of the relations of the government with the hill tribes of the north-east frontier of Bengal*. Cambridge: Cambridge University Press.

Maloney, C. (1978). Language and modern civilization in South Asia. In K. Ishwaran, B. Smith & R. Rao (eds), *Contributions to Asian Studies*. Leiden: Brill.

Marak, C. R. (2002). Preface. In C. R. Marak (ed.), *Garo literature*. New Delhi: Sahitya Akademi.

Markee, N. (2002). Language in development. *TESOL Quarterly*, 36(3), pp. 265–274.

Marshall, K. (2013). MDGs meet religion: Past, present and future. In R. Wilkinson & D. Hulme (eds), *Development goals and beyond: Global development after 2015*. London: Routledge.

Mehta, P. C. (1994). *Voluntary organisations and tribal development*. New Delhi: Shiva.

Minahan, J. B. (2012). *Ethnic groups of South Asia and the Pacific: An encyclopedia*. Santa Barbara: ABC-CLIO.

Muhammed, N., Chakma, S., Hossain, M. D., Masum, M. F. H., Hossain, M. M. & Oesten, G. (2011). Case study on the Garo ethnic people of the Sal (*Shorea robusta*) forests in Bangladesh. *International Journal of Social Forestry (IJSF)*, 4(2), pp. 197–211.

Nawaz, A. (2003). The Garo. In S. Sirajul (ed.), *Banglapedia – 2003*. Dhaka: Bangla Academy.

Olusoji, O, A. (2012). Effects of English language on national development. *Greener Journal of Social Sciences*, 2(4), pp. 134–139.

Pareek, U. (1989). Synergic pluralism- psycho-social dimensions of ethnicity of India. *Indian Journal of Social Work*, 1(3), pp. 303–16.

Perry, F. L. (2011). *Research in applied linguistics: Becoming a discerning consumer*. New York: Routledge.

Playfair, M. A. (1909). *The Garos*. Guwahati: Spectrum (reprinted 1998).

Rahman, M. (2006). *The Garos: Struggling to survive in the valley of death*. Dhaka: Empowerment through Law of the Common People.

Rahmatullah, M., Azam, M. N. K., Malek, I., Nasrin, D., Jamal, F., Rahman, M. A., Khatun, Z., Jahan, S., Seraj, S, & Jahan, R. (2012). An ethnomedicinal survey among the Marakh sect of the Garo tribe of Mymensingh District, Bangladesh. *International Journal of PharmTech Research*, 4(1), pp 141–149.

Rostow, W.W. (1960). *The stages of economic growth: A non-communist manifesto*. Cambridge: Cambridge University Press.

Sangma, U. (1998). *Adibashi Barta*. Sunamgonj: Tribal Welfare Association. (In Bengali).

Smelser, N. J. (2013). Toward a genereal theory of social change. In N. J. Smelser (ed.), *Essays in Sociological explanation*. New Orleans: Quid Pro.

Tembe, J. & Norton, B. (2008). Promoting local languages in Ugandan primary schools: The community as stakeholder. *Canadian Modern Language Review*, 65(1), pp. 33–60.

World Bank (WB). (2008). *Bangladesh-Indigenous/Tribal Population and Access to Secondary Schools: Indigenous Peoples Plan (Draft)*. Retrieved from: http://www-wds.worldbank.org/external/default/WDSContentServer/WDSP/IB/2008/04/07/000334955_20080407073927/Rendered/PDF/IPP2800IPP0P101Draft0March026102008.pdf (accessed: 1 May 2013).

Vaid, N. K. (2004). *Who cares for tribal development?* New Delhi: Mittal.

Vavrus, F. (2002). Postcoloniality and English: Exploring language policy and the politics of development in Tanzania. *TESOL Quarterly*, 36, pp. 373–397.

Wimbish, J. (1989). *WordSurv: A program for analyzing language survey wordlists*. Dallas: Summer Institute of Linguistics.

Conclusion

Katia Iankova, Azizul Hassan, and Rachel L'Abee

Coming to the end of this book, we hope that we contributed as much as we were able to the ongoing indigenous studies research. As researchers we do have a moral and ethical obligation as to how we investigate and represent indigenous people. Researchers, mostly non-indigenous, are very often accused by the Natives of 'making their careers on their account and giving nothing in return'. Therefore we do have the ethical obligation to contribute to the wellbeing and prosperity of the communities that we are researching in the most genuine and trustworthy way with the knowledge that we generate. The topic of economic development therefore was carefully chosen as one of the most important for the future of these communities, as economic and financial stability are the platforms of socio-cultural flourishing of a society. This is a topic that the indigenous communities themselves point to as a priority. In this concluding part, without repeating them, we would like to reiterate some important themes emerging from the researchers' contributions to this collection.

In an interconnected globalised reality, indigenous communities cannot stay intact, sheltered from all the tremendous and rapid economic changes that humanity has undergone in the last few decades. Their survival in hyper-technology oriented societal contexts engendered changes that in some cases they embrace or in other cases, resistant to them, they refuse to adapt to. The right of choice and the strategies and reasons behind it are extremely important to understand and can serve as lessons for other indigenous and non-indigenous societies. The connection or purposeful disconnection of the main economic streams, and the ways that indigenous people safeguard against turbulent influences of the market and mainstream economy, are impressive.

In the last decades, movements of land rights claims, cultural recognition, and equal opportunities for participation in political life have been rising. Cases of these are seen and studied in Australia, New Zealand, and Mexico. The success of gaining such recognition is uneven – success stories of such cases are rather rare in the African and South American continents. Nevertheless, from the last decade, indigenous people have become internationally more solidary and united. Numerous international forums and summits mark some cornerstone events – such as the United Nations Indigenous Forum 2012 which celebrated the anniversary of the Permanent Forum of Indigenous Issues established by the Economic and Social Council in 2000. As recent as September 2014, the United Nations Global Coordinating Group organised a conference in New York stressing economic development. Countries such as Canada, Australia, and the USA had already established indigenous peoples' own representative institutions, and developed and implemented national action plans including sections of economic development and political structures. The aim is that other countries follow and, according to their own particularities in political systems, adopt this idea; and adapting it would give more space to indigenous populations within political and economic decision making for future development. The increased involvement of women as leaders of political and economic activities is crucial. Indigenous women have become visibly more active in the business world in the past decade. This is a positive sign of more balanced economies where different leadership styles can make a difference in the indigenous economic system with alternative models and worldviews of development to mitigate negative social and environmental impacts of free market, male-dominated logic.

Traditionally, major economic activities provoke some form of hostility within indigenous communities. Involving indigenous peoples in national policy processes is often a difficult task. Indigenous people are often the subject of major state and private projects developed on their ancestral territories, like dam construction, mining, housing, or deforestation. Their involvement in the decision-making process is crucial for the prosperity of these communities. Indigenous communities need guarantees to respect their rights and a fair share of the economic gains.

The general aim of development, and particularly economic development, should be geared towards meeting the human need for happiness, self-actualisation, and economic prosperity respecting the foundations of sustainable development. A concept that appeared in the late 1980s was claimed by indigenous people as being an intrinsic part of life and behaviour for centuries: living in greater harmony with the environment embedding human activities rather than exploiting it. Today, and already for a few decades, the neoliberal turn overtaking the societies has gone against this philosophy, making it difficult to be achieved. Indigenous nations, living in a highly interdependent reality of the twenty-first century postmodern world, are also facing the challenges to achieve sustainability objectives, be they environmental, economic, or social aspects. Access to, control of, and capacities to use resources have become important issues over the years as demographic pressure and overdevelopment by external economic forces have interests in exploiting indigenous territories and resources. The strategies for dealing with these issues vary from country to country and, in general, the more countries have established a clear and well-designed policy framework, the less corruption and poverty are present – and the easier it is for the indigenous populations to deal with these complex challenges and establish their own models within the existing political and economic parameters. It depends on the capacities of each individual country to provide such policy infrastructure and harmonise efforts between the mainstream society and the indigenous minorities. A good and mutually agreeable relationship is essential for both indigenous peoples and governments to decide on an effective set of policies to improve the economic conditions. Poverty alleviation among indigenous communities is one of the most urgent problems to be resolved; and despite the efforts of political authorities in creating programmes for development and different aid that they receive from international organisations, these problems are still very acute. Still, the basic strength that they render is their ability to become self-reliant, and this remains so in large parts of the Asian and African contexts.

The vulnerability of indigenous communities consists in their 'otherness', in their different lifestyles and cultural expressions compared to the 'Occidentalized' world, which in its own turn is highly fragmented. In fact, indigenous culture is more about *being* than *doing* – being part of the environment rather than owning and exploiting it for the sake of serving one's own purposes. The understanding of economic values and mechanisms from both sides and placing them in a larger societal context is crucial for the successful integration between economic forces. Through diverse activities such as tourism, sports and cultural events, art, or knowledge exchange, indigenous people come into contact with non-indigenous cultures. These activities make indigenous peoples more conscious of the value of their own culture and present it to outsiders – indigenous and non-indigenous visitors. They will also make this space to talk about their social problems and through sharing them they will gain self-reflection and self-awareness as to what they are and what they want to be(come). Integrated economies would contribute to the unique social constructs of their societies. These lead to pride, self-esteem, and cultural and identity affirmation.

Colonialism historically had disastrous impacts on indigenous peoples by annihilating entire populations, assimilating them, and, on many occasions, physically exterminating large masses of indigenous nations. We only need to remember the extinct Beothuk in Newfoundland, Canada, or the Patro communities in Bangladesh which abandoned their motherland. Although the majority of indigenous cultures were traditionally matriarchal and nomadic, the colonial system imposed patriarchal values and a sedentary lifestyle. This caused a shock to indigenous social structures and ways of life; created distortions that left a heavy heritage of identity crisis and replacement of traditional values; and led to the well-known social and health problems derived from it – such as domestic violence, alcoholism, suicide, low self-esteem, loss of identity and active use of mother tongues, obesity, and diabetes in countries like Canada, the USA, and Australia.

Today another danger is present, the new colonialism: a softer version through external economic forces that are causing economic leakages, exhausting natural resources and depriving indigenous peoples of access to their own sources of wealth. While the colonial powers of the past have been identifiable, today's realities are much more complex. Who is to blame for the increasing and massive immigration and inner migratory movements spreading globally, affecting indigenous and non-indigenous populations? How to prevent the increasing hominisation of national cultures caused by the intensification of the use of mass media, intensification of the exchanges, the virtual realities? Today's colonialism is much more complex, and lessons from the past need to be fully understood and applied to the new realties in order to arm the communities with tools to face the post-modern realities. Still, wounds of colonialism have not healed and it has taken decades for indigenous people to release their frustration, their sorrow and pain. It took time to become resurrected and be displayed publicly, to share the pain of the vexation that indigenous people live with, and it will probably take even longer to forgive. But this process, however painful and long it can be, is now crystallising into a more positive outcome of empowerment and self-consciousness of its own strengths and intellectual and social capacities. The proliferation of initiatives on a political and economic level is mushrooming across countries. This book is only following this stream of the renaissance of indigenous people by presenting one of the most important pillars of national stability and prosperity – economic development and opportunity for sustainable growth.

Index